Access Technology for Blind and Low Vision Accessibility

Second Edition

Access Technology for Blind and Low Vision Accessibility

Second Edition

Yue-Ting Siu
and
Ike Presley

With additional material by

Diane Brauner
Chancey Fleet
Jessica McDowell
Joshua A. Miele, Ph.D
Ed Summers

APHPress
American Printing House for the Blind

Printed in the United States of America.

Title: *Access Technology for Blind and Low Vision Accessibility, Second Edition*

Names: Siu, Yue-Ting; Presley, Ike, authors

Description: Louisville, KY: APH Press, American Printing House for the Blind,
[2020] | Includes bibliographical references and index.

Identifiers: ISBN 9781950723041 (epub) | ISBN 9781950723058(mobi) |
ISBN 9781950723034 (pbk. : alk. paper)

www.aph.org

Contents

Foreword

What is it like to live and work with technology in 2019? The question is so broad as to encompass almost every aspect of our daily lives: technology curates our news and social networks, mediates how we read and write, informs where and how we travel, and augments our ability to find, retain, organize and sort through information in search of what's relevant and helpful at any given time. Increasingly, technology frames our creative endeavors: people working in fields as diverse as architecture, musical composition and journalism rely on high-tech tools to capture, refine and share their ideas.

Those of us who are blind and visually impaired need equitable access to technology so that we can independently pursue the full range of our passions, goals, and responsibilities. Often, we need to use tools that were designed to appeal to a user with typical vision; usually, we work, study, and live with people who are sighted. Our divergent access needs mean that we will have to continually discover alternate ways of doing the everyday work of learning and self-expression, from early childhood on. Our success depends on our ability to find the tool for any given task that will best support the way we work (with no or low vision, in combination with our other abilities and preferences); and access to learning materials and a community of support that can help us work effectively and with confidence.

Professionals, parents and others who support people who are blind or visually impaired can facilitate our discovery and exploration of technologies like screen readers, refreshable braille, tactile graphics, and magnification so that, whether we're student or adult learners, we can make informed and satisfying choices about how technology fits into our lives. A tech-aware cane travel instructor [or certified orientation and mobility specialist (COMS)] can introduce a newly blind person to wayfinding tools like GPS and transit maps (and help that person cultivate enough experience to know when not to trust them). A teacher can show a student how to adjust and test out different colors, fonts and text-to-speech voices to find the combination that feels just right. A parent can advocate for homework assignments to be made available in an accessible, electronic format, and be part of the team that supports his child in learning how to independently access the material once it's provided. Ultimately, our use of technology will be independent and a matter of personal choice; but students and people who are newly blind, like all learners, need mentorship and guidance. We need professionals and parents to model a positive, resilient and inquiring approach to technology. We should learn that "Is this accessible?" is a dead-end question; "How can I access this?" works better. We should be encouraged to cultivate our problem-solving and improvisational skills: we need to get comfortable with trouble-shooting, doing research, switching platforms, and trial and error to become resilient users of technology. When an access barrier seems insurmountable, we need to learn to reach out to access technology users we know and those around the world—our community of practice—for guidance. When a document or app is inaccessible, we need the self-advocacy skills to pinpoint the problem, communicate clearly about it, and propose solutions. With a solid working knowledge of assistive and accessible technology and a commitment to helping each individual discover his or her own best workflow, professionals and parents can empower people who are blind or visually impaired to become independent, confident technology users for life.

This book will introduce you to the full spectrum of technologies that support people with low or no vision. You'll learn about nonvisual access through screen readers, tactile graphics, verbal description, sonification, and braille, as well as tools that enhance and adjust images to take best advantage of an individual's usable vision. You'll discover specialized hardware and software such as braille displays and portable magnifiers, but you'll also find that lots of mainstream technologies—from iPads to online collaboration tools—support equity of access. As you engage with technology in your daily life, you'll notice how the specialized and off-the-shelf tools in this book could apply to you: which access method might you use if you were writing a paper, getting GPS directions or designing a presentation with different vision? Hopefully, you'll be motivated to try out the many access features that are available on your own computer and smartphone, and to develop your own community of practice (fellow students, professionals and experienced users of accessible technologies) to keep you engaged and informed as these technologies evolve.

Chancey Fleet
Assistive Technology Coordinator
New York Public Library—Andrew Heiskell
Braille & Talking Book Library

Acknowledgments

This book is the product of a true community effort. To my mentors Frances Mary D'Andrea and Ike Presley, who passed the torch from their first edition and paved the way for this edition; to all the contributing authors and reviewers who filled in the gaps in expertise; and to my current and former students who continue to teach me: thank you. This second edition presents a breadth of content that would not have been possible without these ongoing partnerships.

I also thank the following people who inspired me to just "go for it" with this edition: Craig Meador (for his unapologetic leadership), Cathy Kudlick (for excavating my intended message), and Chancey Fleet (for crystallizing my understanding of equity and information access). Thank you also to my editor Larry Marotta (professional cat herder) who knew just when to push and when to give me space and nurture the authoring process.

Finally, thank you to my dear friends and family who tolerate the dark periods when I disappear into a universe of work. You are my biggest cheerleaders, whose various cheers sustain and remind me of the importance of work-life balance.

Ting

Contributing Authors:
Adrian Amandi
Diane Brauner
Lainey Feingold
Chancey Fleet
Lucy Greco
Jessica McDowell
Joshua A. Miele, Ph.D
Ed Summers
Adam Wilton, Ph.D

Introduction

Although the history of digital technology for blind and visually impaired people is relatively short, an evolution of nomenclature is already warranted based on how digital media have changed the nature of nonvisual and low vision access to information. Many terms that previously represented the "assistive" sector of "specialized" technologies deserve an update; tools for accessing information are now more available in mainstream culture with smaller categories of devices that are exclusively designed for blind and visually impaired people. Tools that were once "assistive" now simply provide universal *access* to information with diverse rather than "specialized" technologies. Updating our terminology implies a broader shift in philosophies about blindness and the role of technology in empowering a low incidence population. These terms also appeal to wider audiences, which makes it easier to connect communities of allies. Best discussed in lively conversations with a mixed company of blind and sighted folks, other implications might range from all the affordances modern technology has to offer, to "dark patterns in accessibility tech" (Fleet, 2019). These conversations will be most fruitful when a range of privilege regarding one's access to information is discussed across socioeconomical, sociocultural, educational, intellectual, and sensory spectrums.

This second edition book, *Access Technology for Blind and Low Vision Accessibility* embraces a nomenclature that shifts the power of information from a privileged to equally entitled community of diverse learners. In this context, the term "learners" includes any student who needs to learn how to use access technology either for personal reasons or to teach others. Any stakeholder (blind or visually impaired technology user, educator, researcher, parent) can learn the foundations of access technology and develop more impactful questions before reaching out to a more experienced colleague. This knowledge is best developed as a collective practice for community benefit rather than kept exclusive among "experts" who inevitably become gatekeepers to professional development. Blind and visually impaired people can also lead and teach sighted colleagues from unique perspectives that could otherwise be difficult to convey by a sighted technology user.

As anticipated, this second edition includes categories of technology and combinations of mainstream and specialized tools that were unavailable when the first edition was published in 2009. In this edition, we also situate a service provider as an accessibility facilitator (Siu & Emerson, 2017) whose primary role is to empower blind and visually impaired learners of all ages (school-age through adult). Our goals are to present tools and concepts for nonvisual and low vision engagement with information, and deliberate technologies on the horizon with educated doses of optimism. We invite other accessibility facilitators on this journey to consider how technology can be leveraged to promote equitable opportunities for leadership and membership within a community while also being aware of how technology can disable any individual at any given time.

HOT TOPICS

Disability. Accessibility. Technology. Community. These terms can evoke a multitude of emotions and reactions, depending on an individual's past experiences and context in which they are used. These words can carry positive or negative connotations, and may even serve as calls to action depending on if the associated implications are perceived as the language of an ally versus helper. These implications can also convey how we perceive the relationship between a minority demographic and its equitable access to information. This is particularly relevant when considering the role of a service provider who works alongside school-aged or adult students who are blind or visually impaired. Understanding the complexity of these words, what they mean, and how they position us, can help a community ensure that blind and visually impaired people have dignified access and equitable engagement with

all activities of self-determined living. While recognizing that service providers can facilitate progress in accessibility practices, it is of utmost importance to understand how we can empower blind and visually impaired learners to advocate with their own voices. A service provider's actions must not occlude a mission of social justice that **every** individual is entitled to self-driven access to information.

Our book embarks from this conceptual foundation and invites the reader to share goals for achieving equitable access and opportunities in education, employment, and personal endeavors for every member of a community. Underlying assumptions can produce ripple effects that impact how needs are assessed and services rendered, and how a service provider perceives his or her own role throughout the course of discovery, trial, and troubleshooting process of a learner. The tools and workflows that are introduced can also significantly impact a learner's independent and timely engagement with information. For these reasons, we will begin with the following discussion of foundational terms and concepts before delving into the content and chapters of the book.

Disability

When utilizing the term "disability," two opposing philosophies dictate how this term is construed. The **medical model,** which focuses on deficits related to an individual's inability to perform in some standard way, is one philosophy that is typically adopted by medical practitioners and used to identify functional limitations in order to qualify an individual for additional services (Triano, 2000). This philosophy adopts an ableist stance that uses normalcy as the criteria for achievement (Hehir, 2002). When practitioners follow a medical model, an individual's needs are inevitably contrasted with those of a nondisabled population's, with solutions that focus on matching a nondisabled ideal. As a result, recommended tools might focus on fixing an individual's "deficits" (for example, tools that synthesize vision when vision is impaired) rather than recommending tools that leverage an individual's strengths (i.e., recommending tools for auditory and/or tactile access when visual access is unavailable).

An opposing philosophy, the **education model,** celebrates an individual's achievements a bit differently. Once so-called deficits are redefined according to individual strengths and diverse learning needs are recognized with recommendations for differentiated instruction. With this mindset, the education model becomes immensely more impactful than a diagnosis and description of limitations from the medical model; solutions are better focused on leveraging an individual's existing or potential abilities to access an environment rather than "fixing" the individual's deficits. Equally important is a commitment to ensure that environments are accessible to a diverse range of individuals, which incidentally engages greater creativity and multiple points of access for everyone in a community. This approach better engages the individual as an active agent in his or her own life and celebrates diversity rather than perpetuating notions of deficit.

Despite well-meaning intentions, the language that has evolved when discussing disability can be riddled with uncertainty. Historically, **person-first language** has been adopted and even evangelized among professionals and academic writing–particularly in the United States (Dunn & Andrews, 2015). This language intends to reduce stigma towards disability by acknowledging the individual as a person rather than stereotyping one's identity with a disability. Examples of person-first language include "individual with a visual impairment" or "a person who is blind." However, in recent years, the disability rights community has challenged the use of person-first language and instead promote an identify-first language in order to establish pride in one's diversity (Bogart, Lund, & Rottenstein, 2018). Proponents of identity-first language prefer references such as "blind individual" or "visually impaired person," claiming disability means valuing disability and empowers a disabled person to choose his or her own identity (Brueggemann, 2013). Identity-first language can quell person-first euphemisms (Jernigan, 2009); combat the stigma of disability that person-first language implies (Gernsbacher, 2017); and more firmly establish true equity among all individuals by recognizing disability as a characteristic similar to ethnicity or gender. Just as ethnicity or gender is encapsulated within one's identity, so is disability. Identity-first language is ultimately a rally-cry against ableist assumptions that perceive disability as a deficit that requires compensatory grammar. For readers who were trained to adhere to person-first language, the shift in language (and perhaps philosophy) can be challenging! A general recommendation is to refer to one's disability as another inherent characteristic; for example, if you would normally describe an individual as Asian (not "person with Asian-ness"), you could similarly refer to an individual as blind (rather than "person with blindness"). If you would normally describe an individual as female (not "person who is female"), you could similarly refer to an individual as visually impaired (rather than "person who is visually impaired"). In deference to academic style but in greater support of being allied with disability rights communities, this book will generally use identity-first language with some uses of person-first language interchangeably.

In addition to how disability can be communicated in medical and educational practices, the language of the law, policies, and related interpretations retain equally charged implications for disability and equity. The Preamble of the United Nations Convention on the Rights of Persons with Disabilities states that "disability results from the interaction between persons with impairments and attitudinal and environmental barriers that hinder their full and effective participation in society on an equal basis with others" (The United Nations, 2006). This proclamation firmly situates the cause of disability in a community's prejudices about disabled people and poorly designed environments that exclude rather than include disabled individuals. In essence, this preamble states that contextual factors rather than a diagnosis are what disable a person. Although this notion might be novel to some, the idea actually has longstanding roots in the laws of our country.

The Americans with Disabilities Act (ADA) (Americans With Disabilities Act, 1990) addresses issues of access in physical spaces such as street corners, building entrances, and multi-floor buildings. As a result, curb cutouts, entryway ramps, and elevators are necessary designs that ensure everyone can maintain mobility throughout physical environments. When anyone is dependent on any of these features in order to access a street or building, he or she becomes disabled only when those access points are unavailable, thereby limiting access to some part of the physical environment. The ADA can also protect digital accessibility and ensure that disabled people have equal rights in online spaces such as websites, software applications, and digital media (Feingold, 2018). In anticipation of this updated interpretation of the law, standards, guidelines, and tools exist to guide the design of digital environments including proper layout and formatting, alternate, or multisensory access to images and video, and compatibility with tools that facilitate alternative access. When individuals depend on technology to access digital environments (similar to needing a wheelchair to navigate physical environments), they become disabled when digital access points are overlooked (similar to a building lacking a ramp or elevator). Inequities of access in the digital environment have just as many or perhaps even more serious implications than the physical environment; as communities around an individual evolve to purely digital environments that were never designed to have an analog (physical) counterpart, inaccessibility of any part of the digital landscape directly limits one's access to information. This becomes a critical issue when considering how information is directly related to power and status within one's community; lack of power results in disenfranchised populations, which implores further discussion about implications of accessibility.

Accessibility

Ed Summers, Senior Manager of Accessibility and Applied Assistive Technology at the SAS Institute, summarizes accessibility as "the absence of barriers" (in conversation, Fall 2016). As aligned with notions of (dis)ability related to attitudinal and environmental barriers, how can practitioners and service providers ensure accessibility for individuals with visual impairments?

In addition to addressing needs that arise from the impact of visual impairment on learning, development, daily living, and employment, technology can be a great mediator in achieving optimal accessibility to environments for education, employment, and entertainment purposes. Having a sensory disability inherently limits one's access to information via one sense. Technology and diversified skills leverage other senses to overcome challenges of a sensory disability. However, poor technology implementation and/or lack of well-developed sensory skills can also limit potential bridges to accessible information. To ensure that technology is successfully implemented, two primary goals must be met: The built environment must be designed with accessibility in mind, and the end user must possess savvy and flexible use of a variety of no-, low-, and high- tech tools.

To address the built environment, an entire community must be called upon for inclusive solutions. Accessibility must be personalized, with the understanding that any member of a community is potentially going to experience some form of sensory loss personally or with a loved one due to age or unforeseen events. Legislation such as ADA might set forth mandates and automated accessibility checker tools might support the ensuing standards, but no approach is more effective than the personal one when evaluating usability and accessibility. Robust infrastructure is important to accommodate evolving user needs, and forward-thinking planning is invaluable to support evolving technology. In other words, architects of built environments, whether physical or digital, must design for both present and future needs. The most effective strategy an architect can adopt is to ensure that spaces are born accessible. That is, from the moment an environment is conceptualized, inclusive access is integrated into the blueprint of the design. When this critical step is overlooked, intervention in the form of remediation is required. Ultimately, remediation decreases productivity and perpetuates an inefficient system that sabotages the overall value of every individual in a community; ensuing outcomes pass along a far greater cost than what would have been incurred if accessibility were part of the initial design.

Technology

Assuming an accessible environment is established, a blind or visually impaired person can simply focus on the skills and tools that are needed access any environment and complete a desired task. In some cases, simple introduction of technology can empower an individual to regain a sense of independence and self-determination that has been lost. In other cases, technology can ensure that independence is not lost to begin with. With these high stakes in mind, what are the implications for practitioners who play key roles in ensuring equitable opportunities for every student?

Make options accessible as soon as possible! This mantra is just as important for adult students as it is for children. Although certain prerequisite skills might be necessary to achieve proficiency in using a particular device, complete mastery of prerequisite skills should not preclude an individual from experimenting with technology and

evaluating options for oneself. Use of alternate senses for accessing information can develop alongside, or even be supported by, the technology in question. Blind and visually impaired people are entitled to as many options and uses of technology as typically sighted peers and colleagues; this entitlement can be overlooked by organizations that limit funding to one device per student and is an area that often requires greater education and advocacy.

Remember that the experts in access technologies are the everyday users. Sighted practitioners can provide a great service by connecting blind and visually impaired students with blind and visually impaired mentors who can bridge connections to greater learning communities. Practitioners can also educate their students about resources for ongoing learning, how to advocate for accessible tools and environments, and facilitate students' engagement in their own disability communities. Practitioners can serve as a critical gateway to prepare savvy consumers and advocates for equity in community membership.

Technologies that were specifically designed for blind and visually impaired people began in the mid-1900s (Cooper, 1950) and became more widely available in the 1970s and '80s (See research on "reading machines for the blind"). At that time, manufacturers, service providers, and users referred to these tools as *assistive* technology because it seemed logical that the tool would assist the individual in accomplishing a task. As tools and mindsets have matured, the term *access* is a ready replacement for *assistive.* The technology simply provides an individual with access to tools and information that are needed to accomplish a task. That term *assistive* has an almost paternalistic implication: that individuals with a disability cannot accomplish educational, employment, and personal tasks on their own, and that help or assistance is needed from well-intentioned members of society through the development and use of assistive technologies. Recall the Preamble of the United Nations Convention on the Rights of Persons with Disabilities as mentioned earlier; the environmental barriers to print and digital information for blind and visually impaired people can be broken down not so much by "assisting" the individual but by ensuring accessible environments and appropriate tools and training are available to ensure a person's equitable access to information. It is the "attitudinal" barriers that result in the greatest restrictions and this is highlighted by the continued use of the term **assistive technology** that implies a blind or visually impaired person is incapable of accomplishing a task without assistance.

At the time of this writing, the distinction between assistive and access technology remains a topic for on-going discussion. The authors advocate for the term **access** while recognizing that **assistive** persists in legal provisions for education and communication technologies. These terms can therefore be construed interchangeably while the law catches up to modern nomenclature.

For children, the Individuals with Disabilities Education Act (IDEA) dictates the accessibility of learning environments and related technology; for individuals of all ages, the ADA guides accessibility of community and workplace environments. Regardless of the environment, a practitioner's role is to ensure that every student has the knowledge and skills to use a range of low and high tech tools for accomplishing any tasks of choice. This requires a commitment to ongoing professional development to maintain skills and develop adequate proficiency to evaluate needs for, and provide appropriate instruction in, access technology. In addition to working on technical and other soft skills, a thoughtful practitioner ultimately nurtures the development of critical thinking skills so that a student is prepared to be in charge of his or her own accessibility.

Community

Just as blind and visually impaired students need their own communities for learning, practitioners must also connect with communities of practice (CoPs) (Wenger, 1998) to support ongoing professional development in access technology (Morash & Siu, 2016; Siu & Morash, 2014). Luckily, CoPs that support technology proficiency are many and varied! Practitioners might include any of the following professionals:

- **Teachers of Blind and Visually Impaired Students (TVIs)** are special education teachers with a specialization to work with students who are blind or visually impaired. Their scope of practice includes technology evaluation and instruction as related to blind and low vision needs as described in the Expanded Core Curriculum (ECC).

- **Access Technology (AT) Specialists** are more generally qualified to know a greater range of technology that meet the needs of individuals with various disabilities. However, an AT specialist does not necessarily have expertise in the differentiated needs of blind and visually impaired individuals unless he or she has had explicit experience or earned an additional certification in visual impairments.

- **Rehabilitation Specialists** work with adults and related therapists who focus on a range of needs for employment and independent living, and often incorporate technology instruction to facilitate one's independence in the community and workplace.

- **Other Service Providers** who might use technology in their work with youths and adults include but are not limited to job coaches, occupational therapists (OT), physical therapists (PT), speech and language pathologists (SLP), and augmentative and alternative communication (AAC) specialists.

- **Instructional Technology (IT) professionals**—Though not in their direct purview, IT professionals in K–12 and higher education, and in various work environments, can be an integral part of setting up and maintaining the infrastructure for technology. They might also offer input in establishing a system for device, software, and file management.

Family members can also be valuable stakeholders since their support and encouragement have tremendous influence on an individual's technology adoption. Friends and mentors who are also visually impaired can be significant partners who can be called upon for more specific psychosocial and device support, and troubleshooting.

Aside from the education or rehabilitation team whose primary focus is on the individual's development of skills and tool use, anyone who is involved with building the physical or digital environment can be engaged to ensure successful outcomes. This segment of the community might include software and hardware developers, website designers, administrators and employers who make purchasing decisions about which technologies will be used, and classroom teachers who create their own materials and manage online learning platforms. In other words, any area in which the individual needs to interact and engage with information is ripe for partnership with community members who can help ensure fair points of access.

It is important to remember that in every partnership, the focus is best placed on the needs and preferences of the end user. Technology is best used to ensure blind and visually impaired individuals are seamlessly integrated within their home, school, and work communities. Isolated or exclusionary uses of technology and access points should be kept at a minimum and avoided as much as possible. Although at the time of this writing a great majority of practitioners in schools and rehabilitation agencies are sighted, the book's ultimate mission is to prepare as many competent blind or visually impaired individuals as possible to equalize disabled people's representation and self-advocacy in schools and the workforce.

HOW TO USE THIS BOOK

This book is written to be a beginning resource about technology for low vision and nonvisual access to information. Possible readers might include but are not limited to: Students in TVI preparation or access technology programs; practitioners who work with blind or visually impaired students of all ages; everyday access technology users who are in a position to train others; IT specialists, administrators, and researchers who want to promote meaningful technologies and accessible designs; and interested families and colleagues. The book is divided into two parts: **Part 1** provides an overview of available and emerging technologies, and **Part 2** provides a guide to evaluation and initial instruction.

Part 1

Part 1 is designed to give the reader a foundation for understanding what technologies are available for visual, tactile, and auditory engagement with different types of information (including physical and digital multimedia). Tools and devices are presented within categories of tasks so that technology is always considered within a context of purposeful and meaningful uses. As aligned with the legal definition of assistive technology, we include a range of no-, low-, and high-tech tools for the reader's consideration. Although some of these tools have overlapping features, maintaining focus on what task needs to be accomplished can help organize a reader's understanding of each type of tool.

Because of the large number of products available, five categories are used to organize how various technologies are presented for the reader:

- Technologies for Accessing Print Media
- Technologies for Accessing Digital Text
- Technologies for Authoring
- Technologies for Producing Alternate Media
- Strategies for Accessing Multimedia and Data

Once technologies are organized into one of these categories, we subdivide each chapter according to three sensory modalities for access: visual, tactile, and auditory, with the understanding that different formats will allow an individual to access information using single- or multi-modal strategies. When reading about the different types of technologies, readers are encouraged to evaluate the fit of tools depending on an individual's needs, preferences including strengths and limitations in using various senses for accessing information, and priorities for what tasks need to be accomplished with more independence. Because technology often requires troubleshooting, readers might also take into consideration the level of technical support various technologies may require. In addition to the practitioner's own troubleshooting abilities, other technical support might be sought from local or online experts, technology manufacturers or vendors, other individuals who use access technology on a daily basis, or other school or workplace staff if working with mainstream technology.

In general, a list of considerations is presented with each sub-category of tools and devices to help determine the best fit for each student. These considerations are the primary reference points when contrasting different options throughout the technology evaluation process. Emerging technologies are mentioned briefly with enough information so that the reader is informed enough to consider the viability of new tools as they become available. Specific brands or device names are used sparingly due to the fleeting nature of technology developments and in order to keep technology considerations focused on the access features an individual

requires. Generalizing one's vocabulary to technology features rather than particular brands also aids the development of search terms that can be used for further research, and collaboration with others who might have a broader knowledge of technology. Both of these practices can result in considerations for a more expansive range of solutions beyond those specifically made for visual impairments.

Tech tips and sidebars are also referenced throughout **Part 1** to accompany the introduction of different types of technologies. Most Tech Tips link readers to pertinent pages on the Paths to Technology website hosted by the Perkins School for the Blind, who has graciously agreed to allow us to provide links in this book to their content. While specific tips may not work for every student, they provide examples of how technology can be introduced or used in instruction. Readers might find inspiration in a tech tip and apply similar concepts to individualize instruction for different students. Tech tips might be presented in whole or simply provide the search terms to locate further reading from an online source. Sidebars are meant to provide a more in-depth explanation of a concept that deviates slightly from the main focus of a chapter's section.

Part 2

Part 2 is designed to provide the reader with a conceptual and practical framework to guide a comprehensive technology evaluation process. This process can be applied to every student regardless of age, diagnosis, or nature of the visual impairment. Each step of the evaluation process will refer the reader to templates and forms in the appendix that can be used to support the data collection and decision-making process. Regardless of a student's age, we encourage all practitioners to evaluate technology needs and options alongside the student; by partnering with the student throughout every step of technology evaluation and instruction, adoption and implementation can become natural extensions of the evaluation and learning process.

Technology options have become **device-agnostic.** This means that many accessibility features and program applications are no longer dependent on a particular type of device such as desktop or laptop computer, tablet, or smartphone, and are increasingly available online or via a downloadable application (app). Modern technology trends include working across multiple devices that allow an individual to begin a task on one device and then finish it on another. Device-agnostic habits shift the focus from a limited number of hardware solutions to how (or if) a particular device fits into an individual's lifestyle or personal preferences. Most individuals, blind and sighted, use a number of different tools and devices for working and playing; the same principle applies to access technology and justifies reasonable investments to support equitable engagement in various tasks. Technology decisions ultimately depend on an individual's current and anticipated workflow.

HAPPY TRAILS!

Finally, remember that the ultimate purpose of access technology is to facilitate one's independent and efficient engagement with information. Access technology is best considered with this question in mind: How can a tool or device optimize this student's experience in a particular situation? As practitioners, our goal is to empower the student to be in charge of his or her own accessibility. It requires flexible uses of no-, low-, and high- tech tools; accessible media; and accessible environments. It requires a mindset for letting the task define how we think about technology and determine the best tool for any personal endeavor related to education, employment, entertainment, or independent living. Technology can be a great mediator for ensuring equity in pursuits in competitive environments as well as for basic community membership.

We encourage the reader to develop a vocabulary for conducting Internet searches that yield additional solutions and perspectives related to access technology. We hope this book opens doors to exciting conversations about empowerment, privacy, and affordances that come with access to information. Keep an open mind when considering accessibility options, find a community to engage with, and have fun when collaborating with community partners!

REFERENCES

Americans With Disabilities Act. , Pub. L. No. 101–336, 104 Stat. 328 § (1990).

Bogart, K. R., Lund, E. M., & Rottenstein, A. (2018). *Disability pride protects self-esteem through the rejection-identification model.* Rehabilitation Psychology, 63(1), 155.

Brueggemann, B. J. (2013). *Disability studies/disability culture. In M. L. Wehmeyer (Ed.),* Oxford handbook of positive psychology and disability (pp. 279–299). *(pp. 279–299). New York, NY: Oxford University Press.*

Cooper, F. S. (1950). *Research on reading machines for the blind. In P. A. Zahl (Ed.),* Blindness; modern approaches to the unseen environment *(pp. 512–543). Oxford, England: Princeton University Press.*

Dunn, D. S., & Andrews, E. E. (2015). *Person-first and identity-first language: Developing psychologists' cultural competence using disability language.* American Psychologist, 70(3), 255.

Feingold, L. (2018). *Protecting digital accessibility ensures equal rights for disabled people. Retrieved October 30, 2019, from ABA Journal website: http://www .abajournal.com/magazine/article/disability _rights_digital_accessibility_feingold*

Fleet, C. (2019). *Dark Patterns in Accessibility Tech. Retrieved October 29, 2019, from Data & Society website: https://listen .datasociety.net/dark-patterns-in -accessibility-tech/*

Gernsbacher, M. A. (2017). *Editorial perspective: The use of person-first language in scholarly writing may accentuate stigma.* Journal of Child Psychology and Psychiatry, 58(7), 859-861.

Hehir, T. (2002). *Eliminating ableism in education.* Harvard Educational Review, 72(1), 1–33.

Jernigan, K. (2009). *The pitfalls of political correctness: Euphemisms excoriated.* Braille Monitor, 52(3). Retrieved from *https://www.nfb.org/sites/www.nfb.org/files /images/nfb/publications/bm/bm09 /bm0903/bm090308.htm*

Morash, V. S., & Siu, Y. (2016). *Social predictors of assistive technology proficiency among teachers of students with visual impairments.* ACM Transactions on Accessible Computing (TACCESS), 9(2), 4.

Siu, Y., & Emerson, R. W. (2017). *Redefining roles of vision professionals in education and rehabilitation.* Journal of Visual Impairment & Blindness.

Siu, Y., & Morash, V. (2014). *Teachers of students with visual impairments and their use of assistive technology: Measuring teachers' proficiency and their identification with a community of practice.* Journal of Visual Impairment & Blindness, 108, 384–398.

The United Nations. (2006). Convention on the Rights of Persons with Disabilities. Treaty Series, 2515, 3.

Triano, S. (2000). *Categorical eligibility for special education: The enshrinement of the medical model in disability policy.* Disability Studies Quarterly, 20(4).

Wenger, E. (1998). *Communities of practice: Learning as a social system.* Systems Thinker, 9(5), 2–3.

Part 1

Overview of Access Technology for Blind and Low Vision Accessibility

CHAPTER 1
Overview of Technology for Blind and Low Vision People

The term "assistive technology" has been used to define a wide variation of tools for individuals with disabilities including visual impairments. The Individuals with Disabilities Education Act (IDEA) states, "The term 'assistive technology device' means any item, piece of equipment, or product system, whether acquired commercially off the shelf, modified, or customized, that is used to increase, maintain, or improve functional capabilities of a child with a disability" (Sec. 602 (1)(A)). As one might imagine, this definition allows a broad interpretation of what constitutes assistive technology and how it can be implemented.

Although IDEA utilizes the term "assistive technology," this book adopts "access technology" for practical and philosophical purposes. "Assistive" will mainly be used in this chapter in reference to legal definitions; "access" will otherwise be used to discuss technologies in ensuing chapters. This evolution in terminology is necessary to update our concepts of how technology facilitates individuals' access to information. The language we use has certain affordances, and can color how educators approach teaching and learning. Access technology ". . . embodies both accessibility and the disability-specific technologies that [blind and visually

impaired individuals] sometimes use" (Lauridsen, E., 2017). This term provides a more positive vantage point for practitioners to situate the role of technology and collaborate with someone whose disability has impacted their information access. By shifting from "assistive" to "access," practitioners can better promote autonomy and agency rather than a permanent state of dependency. As a result, blind and visually impaired individuals can be better prepared to exercise rights of privacy and independent access to information. Understanding how these terms are valuable for legal versus practical and philosophical purposes will guide the reader in adopting the appropriate usage (see **Introduction**).

Although individual needs and preferences dictate how technology is implemented into one's practice, accessibility of the built environment and public information tends to be driven by legal mandates and public awareness. In order to prepare readers to proceed along an approach that can be understood by partners who recognize the law but might lack disability training, this chapter is generally organized according to the IDEA framework. Although IDEA was written to guide services for school-aged students, the principles of education accessibility have equivalent application for adults in workplace and rehabilitation contexts via Section 504 of the Rehabilitation Act of 1973 (Section 504) and the Americans with Disabilities Act (ADA). IDEA is divided into two major sections, with the second section further sub-divided into categories of service:

- **Assistive Technology Devices (Sec. 602 (1)(A))**
- **Assistive Technology Services (Sec. 602 (2))**
- Assessment of user needs (Sec. 602 (2)(A))
- Acquisition and customization of assistive technology (Sec. 602 (2) (B, C))
- Collaboration and professional development to support the student (Sec. 602 (2)(E, F))

Knowledge of the law helps practitioners, families, and students (of all ages) advocate for needed devices and services (See **Appendix A** starting on page 357). IDEA also outlines the responsibilities of educational teams when constructing Individualized Family Service Plans (IFSP) and Individualized Educational Plans (IEPs). Beyond the educational setting, a rehabilitation counselor "represents the state agency in the creation and implementation of the Individualized Plan for Employment (IPE)", previously known as the Individualized Written Rehabilitation Program. The purpose of these plans, whether in school-, community-, or home-based settings, is to outline the services the individual will receive. The Rehabilitation Act Amendments of 1998 (P.L. 105- 220) further mandates that the IPE specify what the agency and individual will do to move the individual toward and into employment.

Content Vocabulary
Individualized Family Service Plan (IFSP)

An **Individualized Family Service Plan** is a family-based, written plan of treatment designed to address the address the unique needs of a family and their child with a disability.

Ultimately, practitioners' missions in determining appropriate technology devices, supports, and services for individuals are most successful when keeping in mind the right of every member of a community to have independent and timely access to information.

Assistive Technology Devices (IDEA Sec. 602 (1)(A))

The legal definition of "assistive technology" is admittedly broad. Generally speaking, the aforementioned definition mandates that any and all tools can be used to facilitate learning and development of a student with a disability. Medical or implanted devices fall under the purview of a physician and therefore are not included within

THE DISABILITY RIGHTS MOVEMENT

Treatment and perceptions of disability have undergone transformation since the 1900s. This has happened largely because people with disabilities have demanded and created those changes. Like other civil rights movements, the disability rights movement has a long history. Examples of activism can be found among various disability groups dating back to the 1800s. Many events, laws, and people have shaped this development. To date, the 1990 Americans with Disabilities Act (ADA) and the subsequent ADA Amendments Act (2008) are the movement's greatest legal achievements. The ADA is a major civil rights law that prohibits discrimination of people with disabilities in many aspects of public life. The disability rights movement continues to work hard for equal rights.

Organizations by and for people with disabilities have existed since the 1800s. However, they exploded in popularity in the 1900s. The League of the Physically Handicapped organized in the 1930s, fighting for employment during the Great Depression. In the 1940s a group of psychiatric patients came together to form We Are Not Alone. They supported patients in the transition from hospital to community. In 1950, several local groups came together and formed the National Association for Retarded Children (NARC). By 1960, NARC had tens of thousands of members, most of whom were parents. They were dedicated to finding alternative forms of care and education for their children. Meanwhile, people with disabilities received assistance through the leadership of various presidents in the 1900s. President Truman formed the National Institute of Mental Health in 1948. Between the years 1960 and 1963, President Kennedy organized several planning committees to treat and research disability.

The U.S. Congress has passed many laws that support disability rights either directly or by recognizing and enforcing civil rights. Civil rights laws such as Brown v. Board of Education and its decision that school segregation is unconstitutional laid the groundwork for recognizing the rights of people with disabilities. Several sections of the 1973 Rehabilitation Act, which specifically address disability discrimination, are especially important to the disability rights movement. Section 501 supports people with disabilities in the federal workplace and in any organization receiving federal tax dollars. Section 503 requires affirmative action, which supports employment and education for members of traditionally disadvantaged minority groups. Section 504 prohibits discrimination against individuals with disabilities in the workplace and in

(Continued)

their programs and activities. Section 508 guarantees equal or comparable access to technological information and data for people with disabilities. The regulations for Section 504 of the Rehabilitation Act of 1973 were written but not implemented. In 1977, the disability rights community was tired of waiting, and demanded that President Carter sign the regulations. Instead, a task force was appointed to review them. Afraid that the review would weaken the protections of the Act, the American Coalition of Citizens with Disabilities (ACCD) insisted they be enacted as written by 5 April 1977, or the coalition would take action. When the date arrived and the regulations remained unsigned, people across the country protested by sitting-in at federal offices of Health, Education, and Welfare (the agency responsible for the review). In San Francisco, the sit-in at the Federal Building lasted until April 28, when the regulations were finally signed, unchanged. This was, according to organizer Kitty Cone, the first time that "disability really was looked at as an issue of civil rights rather than an issue of charity and rehabilitation at best, pity at worst."

The 1975 Education of All Handicapped Children Act guaranteed children with disabilities the right to public school education. These laws have occurred largely due to the concerted efforts of disability activists protesting for their rights and working with federal government. In all, the United States Congress passed more than 50 pieces of legislation between the 1960s and the passage of the ADA in 1990 . . . .

. . . [I]n 1990, protesters gathered on the steps of the United States Capitol building. They were anxiously awaiting the passage of the ADA, which had stalled due to issues around transportation. Public transit companies fought against the strict regulations for accessibility, and their lobbying efforts slowed the entire process. In response, a group of individuals with disabilities headed for the Capitol. They tossed aside their wheelchairs, walkers, and crutches and ascended the steps. This event has since become known as the "Capitol Crawl." By dragging themselves up the stairs, these protesters expressed their daily struggles due to physical barriers. In so doing, they highlighted the need for accessibility. Iconic images of this event spread across the country. The Americans with Disabilities Act ultimately passed in July of 1990 and was signed by President George H.W. Bush. The ADA and other civil rights legislation have transformed opportunities for people with disabilities. However, over 25 years later, there is still much work to be done.

Perri Meldon (https://www.nps.gov/articles/disabilityhistoryrightsmovement.htm)

a school's responsibility for assistive technology (Sec. 602 (1)(B), "IDEA '04 Assistive Technology Definition Revision," n.d.). More specifically, assistive technology includes no-tech tools such as braille, large print, bold ink pens, optical devices (magnifiers and telescopes), and low-tech battery-operated or single function tools such as talking calculators. Assistive technology also includes high-tech tools that often have multiple functions, require higher voltage power, and are available as hardware (physical devices) or software (program applications). These tools can be specialized for people with disabilities, or can also include mainstream technologies that were designed for nondisabled use, but allow customization to meet a range of individual accessibility needs or preferences. Customization of technologies can be carried out by adjusting built-in features for multi-modal (enhanced visual, auditory, or tactile) access, or by enhancing the device for alternative access with peripheral hardware or additional software. The breadth of options requires that anyone working with or using technology must have a practical toolkit that includes a range of low- and high-tech options that are flexible enough to meet an individual's unique needs. Because each type of assistive technology has pros and cons, even after comparing the features of different devices, the ultimate decision of what tools to include in one's toolkit is based on personal practice and experience.

Content Vocabulary
Assistive Technology

Assistive technology refers to items designed specifically to improve the functional capabilities of individuals with a visual impairment or other disabilities. The term includes everything from screen magnifiers for low-vision computer users to braille.

Because technology changes so quickly, it is difficult if not impossible to maintain proficiency and knowledge of every available device or software. Rather, it is more reasonable for practitioners to understand practical concepts for technology evaluation and implementation, maintain a general breadth of knowledge and understand what types of options are available, possess the specific vocabulary to identify the various features of technologies that showcase these options, and utilize resources to obtain more comprehensive knowledge as needed. For these reasons, For these reasons, recall that Part One of of the book presents the overarching types and features of technology related to common tasks that require a student to engage with information. Each chapter presents vocabulary that can be utilized as search terms to aid the reader in finding the most current technology options in that area of information access. Sidebars are embedded throughout each chapter to elaborate upon the main content and identify specific relevant technologies.

In order to achieve successful technology adoption, an education or rehabilitation team must understand an individual's needs as warranted by the most efficient use of sensory learning channels. Specialists and service providers must also exercise respect for an individual's personal choice by presenting an adequate number of options to the individual. Once technology features are matched to an individual, his of her activities should justify the product decision and implementation plan. Additional considerations must be made for constraints imposed by various tasks, the available media, the existing infrastructure to support technology use, and spending budget. By discussing various technologies along a more conceptual approach grounded in pedagogy and by avoiding the identification of specific brands as much as possible, recommendations for access technology can remain focused on meeting individuals' needs and be flexible enough to update tools as needs change.

The critical need for practitioners to engage with a community of practice that supports technology cannot be underscored enough! Whether such a community exists in a face-to-face or virtual space is less relevant than exercising regular habits of engagement with colleagues who can develop and sustain one another's technology proficiency (Morash & Siu, 2016). Together, practitioners can maintain a more sustainable body of knowledge even as the available tools in both the digital and physical worlds quickly evolve.

Provision of Assistive Technology Services (IDEA Sec. 602 (2))

The second part of IDEA defines assistive technology service as "any service that directly assists a child with a disability in the selection, acquisition, or use of an assistive technology device" (Sec. 602 (2)). Although the legal mandate is broad, specific information is available to support services for individuals who are visually impaired. The remainder of this chapter will introduce the three major areas of assistive technology services: assessment, selection, and customization. It will also include basic information on collaboration and providing technical assistance.

> **Teaching Tip 1.1**
> **How this Book Is Structured**
>
> Readers can refer to **Part One** of this book for an introduction to a variety of tools for consideration, and to **Part Two** for more specific guidance in carrying out a thorough technology evaluation.

Assessment of User Needs (IDEA Sec. 602 (2)(A))

In order to make effective assistive technology recommendations and evaluate tools with a discerning eye, it is important that service providers first carry out a holistic assessment of an individual's needs. These needs can span across a number of areas including sensory access requirements as related to one's disabilities, the tasks that an individual must accomplish, and the nature of information that an individual must access. Capturing user needs in each of these areas can determine how effectively an individual is currently performing the tasks of daily living, learning, and working. Assessments are typically carried out with the purpose of evaluating the current system and identifying how best to meet an individual's needs.

In the field of visual impairments, the words "assessment" and "evaluation" are often used interchangeably. In fact, the language used in IDEA refers to the process of capturing user needs in terms of *assessment* rather than evaluation. Regarding assistive technology services, a combination of formal and/or informal measures can assess an individual's needs for technology. From a more holistic perspective, "evaluation" more aptly describes the process of observation and determination of how one's workflow compares to a sighted peer's. (See **Appendix A.**)

Blind or visually impaired individuals are a unique demographic that require special considerations for how their visual impairment impacts learning, how they access information (through visual, auditory, or tactile means), and how they maintain independent and primary access to information as much as possible. For those in the K–12 education system, a multifaceted approach is necessary to capture all of the dimensions of a student's needs, and is critical in de-

signing an educational plan that supports access to an expanded core curricula. For individuals in rehabilitative or employment contexts, an equally holistic approach is necessary to align the individual's personal preferences and habits with the existing infrastructures that support daily living and employment.

Content Vocabulary
Core Curriculum/Expanded Core Curriculum

The **core curriculum** refers to the general education requirements expected to be learned by every student in a classroom. It may include specialized instruction for students with disabilities. The **Expanded Core Curriculum** is a set of concepts and skills outside of the academic curriculum that are impacted by vision impairment. These areas of development are typically learned incidentally, but blind and low vision students require direct instruction.

In the school system, an **Individualized Education Plan (IEP)** drives instructional planning and service delivery (Karger, 2004). The IEP is reviewed annually to ensure that a student's current needs are adequately captured while a differentiated system of supports is identified that will mediate the impact of visual impairment on learning. Although an IEP must consider future implications of a student's disability on learning, including transition planning, it is important that the IEP also focuses on meeting current needs. A student's toolkit will and should be updated as needs change. For individuals moving toward employment, an **Individualized Plan for Employment (IPE)** (previously known as the Individualized Written Rehabilitation Program) outlines the services the person will receive from adult rehabilitation agencies. Ideally, either the IEP or IPE are developed after comprehensive assessment(s) from various related service providers (if a student) or rehabilitation counselors (if an adult). These assessments aim to identify how an individual's disability impacts his or her ability to access to information. Next, the assessment data is used to make recommendations for meeting the individual's accessibility needs and for justifying a practitioner's services.

Content Vocabulary
Individualized Education Plan (IEP)

An **Individualized Education Plan** (IEP) is a written plan with educational goals based on a professional assessment of a student's particular strengths and learning needs.

Individualized Plan for Employment (IPE)

An **Individualized Plan for Employment** (IPE) is a written proposal detailing an individual's vocational goals, and the training needed to realize those aspirations. Specific funding sources to underwrite the necessary training are sometimes included in the plan.

Without comprehensive assessments of user, content, and tool attributes, technology implementation will be shortsighted and difficult to sustain. This section will summarize optimal assessments that should inform an ideal assistive technology plan.

Clinical low vision examination. Individuals with usable vision will benefit from a clinical low vision exam. This exam determines how visual abilities can be enhanced for various tasks by using optical and non-optical devices such as monoculars, magnifiers, video magnifiers, and tinted lenses (Corn & Erin, 2010). A low vision specialist, who is authorized to prescribe optical devices, conducts this exam in a low vision clinic. Often, the optical devices identified with this exam become part of the individual's toolkit along with a range of other high- and low-tech tools.

Data from the initial low vision exam will contribute information on the user's visual strengths and needs. When individuals experience changes in vision or accessibility needs (such as, but not limited to, changes in educational media or tasks to access information), the low vision exam and other assessments that are described below should be repeated to accurately reflect the user's current needs. Although students may often be referred for a low vision exam in addition to other assessments, the low vision exam is often the primary functional assessment tool for adults outside of the school setting.

Functional vision assessment (FVA). The FVA is a key component of a comprehensive evaluation process that determines a student's eligibility for educational vision services. It must be conducted by a certified or credentialed teacher of blind and visually impaired students (TVI) (Sacks and Zatta, 2016; Holbrook, McCarthy, Kamei-Hannan, 2017; The Bill of Rights for All Children with Visual Impairment, 2019). Using a variety of formal and informal measures for data collection and evaluation, the FVA must cover all aspects of functional vision regardless of diagnosis (Sacks and Zatta, 2016; Holbrook, McCarthy, Kamei-Hannan, 2017). An FVA is carried out to determine the need for and extent of educational vision services. After a student is deemed eligible for educational vision services, it is imperative that the student receives an updated FVA every three years as part of a comprehensive triennial evaluation *or* whenever a student's needs change (as a result of changes to a student's vision or learning environment).

The FVA provides functional implications that complement clinical findings from a medical eye exam. Because the FVA documents a student's visual functioning for the purpose of access to education, its results can serve as justification for educational vision services from a certified TVI (Holbrook et. al, 2017). However, because the purpose and scope of assessment differs among specialists, a TVI is not qualified to make medical diagnoses based on the functional findings of an FVA. Similarly, a medical professional cannot determine educational vision services based on findings from a clinical evaluation.

> **Content Vocabulary**
> **Medical Eye Exam**
>
> A **medical eye exam** is an assessment used to diagnosis eye-related disorders. It is more comprehensive than a routine eye exam, which only tests for common problems like nearsightedness, farsightedness, or astigmatism.

Recall that adults receiving rehabilitation services typically receive a clinical low vision exam instead of an FVA. Once students graduate from educational to adult rehabilitative services, as adults, they need to provide evaluators with valuable information regarding their functional use of vision. Therefore it is important that students maintain good documentation of their previous FVAs and can competently discuss their own functional vision prior to graduation from the educational system.

Learning media assessment (LMA). While the FVA details a student's functional vision, a learning media assessment (LMA) documents how a student *best* accesses information. The LMA is another essential component of a comprehensive evaluation process; it identifies the primary, secondary, and possibly tertiary sensory learning channels including use of visual, auditory, or tactile senses. An

LMA considers a student's efficiency of access, preferred senses for comprehension and manipulation of various media, and use of different senses for different tasks (Holbrook et. al, 2017). These considerations are especially important when conducting an LMA because determining a student's primary and secondary sensory learning channels cannot be based solely on the student's diagnosed visual impairment or medical condition. Determination of a student's sensory learning channels is an educational decision that must be made by the educational team including input from the parent or guardian and student. While the process considers input from the medical community and the parent or guardian, these determinations cannot be prescribed by a medical practitioner or any single person. Like the FVA, the LMA is best conducted under the guidance of a TVI, requires a variety of formal and informal measures, and evaluates all aspects of learning media regardless of an individual's diagnosis.

Although the LMA is an evaluation process that is typically conducted with school-aged students, it is equally important that assessments of adult technology users include information on the primary and secondary (and tertiary if relevant) sensory channels for accessing information given that technology recommendations are most effective when selected to match an individual's unique sensory learning channels.

Expanded Core Curriculum evaluation. The expanded core curriculum

(ECC) refers to skills outside of the academic curriculum that are impacted by vision impairment. These areas of development are typically learned incidentally, however students who are visually impaired require direct instruction to develop missed concepts. These areas include compensatory skills, orientation and mobility, social skills, independent living skills, recreation and leisure, career education, use of assistive technology, sensory efficiency skills, and self-determination (Hatlen 1996, National Agenda 2nd ed.). Evaluating a student's needs as related to the ECC helps prioritize and justify a TVI's instruction in areas that might not directly support learning standards as defined by the academic core curriculum. However, these needs warrant as much importance as academic areas due to positive correlations with future independent living and competitive employment.

Technology evaluation. A technology evaluation is best accomplished with close collaboration among a specialist who is certified to assess needs related to a visual impairment, the individual in question (regardless of age), and other related service providers who are knowledgeable about available resources, performance expectations, and technology infrastructure. In the school environment, a qualified and certified TVI can adequately evaluate technology needs for a student who only has needs related to nonvisual or low vision learning. For students with multiple disabilities and needs that include other cognitive or motor considerations, collaborative assessment with an assistive technology specialist and service providers who support those related areas can ensure that the full range of technology options are considered. Adults who are receiving evaluation from a rehabilitation agency can benefit from working with a specialist who is trained in assessing technology specific to nonvisual or low vision needs (see **Appendix 1.1, What Is CATIS?**, p. 34).

Based on the aforementioned assessments (clinical low vision, functional vision, learning media, and expanded core curriculum), and with additional trials and considerations of all possible technology options, a technology evaluation compiles all the data and contrasts how different tools can be employed to carry out various tasks that align with the individual's priorities. The technology evaluation must justify recommendations for tools and practices that would facilitate an individual's engagement with information. An effective technology evaluation addresses the following eight quality indicators. Each is important to the development and implementation of effective technology services (QIAT, 2005).

- **Consideration of AT Needs**
- **Assessment of AT Needs**
- **AT in the IEP, IPE**
- **AT Implementation**
- **Evaluation of Effectiveness of AT**
- **AT in Transition**
- **Administrative Support for AT**
- **AT Professional Development**

These quality indicators will be further discussed in **Part Two** of this book as part of a larger presentation regarding effective technology evaluation and services. Keep in mind that in the case of a school-aged student, a TVI would include several assessment components as part of a comprehensive evaluation process (See **Figure 1.1 A Comprehensive Evaluation Process in the IEP for the K-12 student**). A holistic evaluation process can support recommendations when technology needs have been identified throughout all areas of assessment. For school-aged students with multiple disabilities and additional technology needs, a school team with external evaluation support, or adults receiving rehabilitation services, a technology evaluation might be a standalone report that is submitted in addition to a separate evaluation of other needs. **Figure 1.2, A Comprehensive Evaluation Process in the IPE for an Adult Receiving Services from a Department of Rehabilitation,** summarizes what a comprehensive evaluation process might include for an adult who receives rehabilitation services.

Acquisition and Customization of Assistive Technology (Sec. 602 (2)(B, C))

As part of providing assistive technology services, IDEA mandates that an educational agency (such as a school district or county office of education) is obligated to acquire any devices or applications a student requires. The educational agency is also charged with ensuring maintenance and

Figure 1.1:
A Comprehensive Evaluation Process for Educational Vision Services in the IEP for the K-12 Student

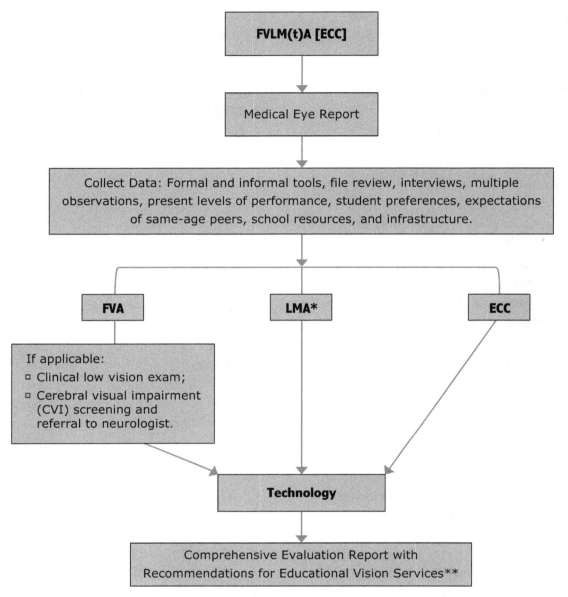

* = Braille should be considered for all students with a visual impairment [regardless of a diagnosis of oculomotor or neurologically-based visual impairment] unless otherwise determined by the IEP team

** = A separate evaluation process by a certified orientation and mobility specialist (COMS) would be required to determine recommendations related to orientation and mobility services and technology

OVERVIEW OF TECHNOLOGY FOR BLIND AND LOW VISION PEOPLE

Figure 1.2:
Components of an Evaluation Process to Support Development of an IPE for an Adult Receiving Services from a Department of Rehabilitation

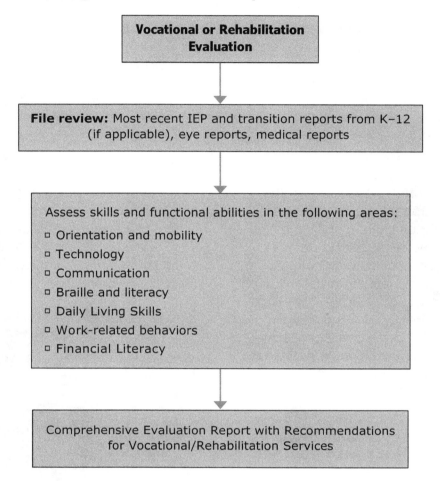

Vocational or Rehabilitation Evaluation

↓

File review: Most recent IEP and transition reports from K–12 (if applicable), eye reports, medical reports

↓

Assess skills and functional abilities in the following areas:

- Orientation and mobility
- Technology
- Communication
- Braille and literacy
- Daily Living Skills
- Work-related behaviors
- Financial Literacy

↓

Comprehensive Evaluation Report with Recommendations for Vocational/Rehabilitation Services

customization for any technology a student is using. Low incidence funding is designated to help educational agencies meet the costs of visually impaired students' devices, and can also be used to purchase either specialized or mainstream technology that is designated for a visually impaired student's use. Because some devices, particularly specialized equipment, can sometimes be very expensive, educational agencies might prefer to borrow a device before purchasing it. Access technology is generally available in two forms:

- **Specialized assistive technology.** Specialized devices are tools built specifically for individuals with a particular disability. When meeting the needs of people with visual impairments, these technologies are intended for low vision or nonvisual access. Examples of devices in this category include refreshable braille displays, video magnifiers, and screen reading applications. Because visual impairment is a low incidence disability, there is less demand for these specialized products. As a result, the market is small, has minimal competition to encourage developers to reduce prices, and has a limited profit margin to recover a company's research and development costs. Expertise in using specialized assistive technology is also more limited due to the fewer numbers of people who use these devices. Despite their relatively higher prices and limited technical support, specialized assistive technology can still be more user-friendly because the devices or applications are specifically designed for the visually impaired user. Features for low vision or nonvisual access are integral to the device, and workarounds focus more on accessing media formatted for mainstream accessibility rather than workarounds for the device itself.

▫ **Mainstream technology (customized for individualized use).** Unlike specialized assistive technology, mainstream technology is designed for use by the typical user who does not have any sensory disabilities. However, mainstream technologies can be customized as needed to meet a range of access needs. Examples of mainstream technologies that are often utilized as access technology include Microsoft® Windows or Apple® laptops and desktops, Web-based computing devices such as Google Chromebooks™, touchscreen tablets such as iPads® or iPods, and smartphones. Because mainstream technologies are primarily used by the

general public, this larger demand ensures that these devices are more competitively priced and technical support is more readily available. Although this category of technology is not specifically designed for low vision or nonvisual use, mainstream devices and applications can sometimes be more flexibly deployed than some single-function specialized technologies. This is possible because features for low vision or nonvisual access are usually add-ons or optional settings that can be turned on or off at the discretion of the user. By extension, workarounds tend to focus on the device or application and its compatibility with peripheral devices or access features.

Content Vocabulary
Low Incidence Funds

Low-incidence funds are resources used to supplement other funding when purchasing materials or equipment for individuals with disabilities that occur in a small percentage of the general population, including hearing and vision impairments and deafblindness.

Specific recommendations for specialized versus mainstream technology will vary based on an individual's needs and preferences. However, as awareness of digital accessibility increases, and as the accessibility of mainstream platforms comes under the purview of the Americans with Disabilities Act (ADA), individuals with visual impairments will likely continue to experience improved access to a greater number of options.

Communities of Practice for Assistive Technology Collaboration and Access to Resources ((Sec. 602 (2)(D, E, F))

In addition to defining assistive technology for students with disabilities, IDEA clearly states that assistive technology service must be coordinated with other services or interventions (Sec. 602 (2)(D)), training or technical assistance must be provided to the child and/or the child's family (Sec. 602 (2)(E)), and training or technical assistance must be provided to the practitioners who are substantially involved with "major life functions" of the child (Sec. 602 (2)(F)). With so many options available for assistive technology, it is easy to feel overwhelmed by the sheer breadth of tools that require coordination, training, and/or technical assistance. Given the time investment needed to master a high-tech device and the financial resources required to acquire devices for use, even the most tech-savvy individual might struggle with the daunting tasks of learning and maintaining a literal or figurative database of available tools. For these reasons, it is important that collaboration with other service providers extends beyond the evaluation process. Ongoing collaboration can be helpful in device acquisition, customization, and implementation into practice. In fact, practitioners' engagement with a pro-technology community can even help practitioners achieve greater levels of technology proficiency (Morash & Siu, 2016; Siu & Morash, 2014).

What might this community of practice look like? Among the many iterations of professional learning communities, Etienne Wenger's community of practice (CoP) framework (Wenger, 1998) is well-suited for professionals in the visual impairment field because of the multi-tiered social structures they must navigate in order to adopt, adapt, and implement assistive technology. In order for a CoP to function as a form of professional development, the following dimensions must be present:

- *Domain of interest.* CoP members invest in a shared collection of knowledge, goals, and purpose, which informs their actions.

- *Community.* CoP members interact by sharing ideas, posing questions, and responding to others' issues.

- *Practice.* CoP members share a "toolkit" of tools, information, anecdotes, and resources. The community nurtures this body of knowledge, and leverages it to inform the domain of interest.

Ultimately, technology proficiency is best gained through experience and persistent professional development. Experiential learning allows instructors to problem-solve technology challenges within the context of a user's experience, and understand how to match the affordances and constraints of a situation with an appropriate recommendation. However, the experiential learning of instructors who teach technology will often be constrained to the needs of the particular learners they serve. To overcome these limitations, practitioners will benefit from engagement with a wider community in order to access a greater range of experiences and expertise. By doing so, practitioners can expand their design thinking regarding how to implement technology with a wider variety of learners beyond those they have personal experience with. Until practitioners develop their own proficient user experiences with various access technologies, they can be limited in their ability to provide tips for nuanced use and more complex problem solving. Just as important is having practitioners match individuals with visually-impaired peers who can provide ongoing mentorship, guidance, and support on a deeper level.

Finally, a CoP bridges an outstanding gap in ongoing professional development for many service providers who work with individuals who are blind or visually impaired. The majority of TVIs are itinerant and therefore teach in isolation, which is a longstanding challenge in itinerant teaching models (Correa-Torres & Howell, 2004; Olmstead, 1995; Swenson, 1995; Yarger & Luckner, 1999). This factor is one among several reported factors—lack of funding, resources, time, and insufficient pre-service training are others—that contribute to the underuse of technology among TVIs (Abner & Lahm, 2002; Edwards & Lewis, 1998; Kapperman, Sticken, & Heinze, 2002). Teaching in isolation ultimately results in a dispersed practice with limited access to on-demand training materials, resources, and technical assistance. Because technology proficiency develops via experiential learning, the

technology proficiency of many TVIs may be dependent on the user experiences they engage with, whether directly or via a community of practice. Without persistent and ongoing professional development, technology knowledge gained in pre-service training can expire quickly. When practitioners have a close connection with a pro-technology CoP, it is easier for them to maintain a general body of knowledge regarding technology and seek more information as needed, rather than feeling overwhelmed by trying to achieve deep knowledge about the entire breadth of technologies (Morash & Siu, 2016).

ROLE OF PRACTITIONERS IN SUPPORTING ACCESS TECHNOLOGY

This book is written for practitioners and stakeholders in supporting access technology for individuals with visual impairments. Readers might include teachers of the visually impaired, assistive technology specialists, classroom teachers, resource specialists, rehabilitation counselors, vision rehabilitation therapists, access technology developers or researchers, and parents, guardians, or other family members. Regardless of his or her professional qualifications, the responsibility of anyone who works with access technology is to empower an individual's access to information. In other words, we are accessibility facilitators (Siu and Emerson, 2017). While sighted facilitators might use access technology on a daily basis, the ultimate experts in access technology for nonvisual or low vision access will always be those individuals who are blind or visually impaired who are also proficient and savvy with a variety of mainstream and specialized technologies. If you are a sighted facilitator, no amount of practice and research can replace the aptitude that can only be acquired by personally depending on access technology and having to navigate accessibility challenges in everyday tasks.

The role of a good instructor, whether sighted or visually impaired, is to provide an unbiased introduction to available technology options. With these options, the instructor can guide the individual in understanding how various tools might or might not fit the task at hand, and to develop the critical thinking skills required to select appropriate tools for various purposes based on the efficiency that the tool provides when completing the desired task. Whenever technical support is needed, it is best for both instructors and individuals to explore solutions together. The ultimate goal is to enable the individual to become independent in troubleshooting for him- or herself.

For readers who might feel less equipped to learn about and teach with technology, fear not! Most learners only need facilitators to open the door to a world of options and then connect them with visually-impaired mentors. Your responsibility as a practitioner is to keep your vocabulary and general knowledge of technology current. You must also know how to seek and locate information about unfamiliar technology as needed by your students or clients.

Setting Up the Environment for Assistive Technology (Sec. 602 (3))

Part One of this textbook presents an overview of technologies used for carrying out various tasks and accessing different types of information and media formats. As the reader reviews the tools that are presented in **Part One,** he or she should consider the specific information environment an individual might engage in using the tools described. Are individuals working with paper media? Digital media? Environmental information? Whatever the format, tools should be employed to achieve optimal and efficient access that is on par with sighted peers.

Before decisions about tools can be made, though, it is important to take a step back and help define an individual's workflow. A **workflow** refers to the infrastructure that is implemented for materials dissemination, engagement, and exchange. Regardless of the multitude of paper materials that still perpetuate school and work environments, a digital workflow is often the most ideal for people who are blind or visually impaired. Digital media must be accessible in order to allow for flexible access by using a variety of assistive and access technologies according to the will of the consumer. In other words, accessible digital media and environments place accessibility into the hands of the individual, who is then empowered to select tools that satisfy both the requirements of a particular task or his or her personal preferences. A workflow easily accommodates multisensory access to information by allowing a visually impaired individual to switch among visual, auditory, and tactile access at any given time. A digital workflow can also facilitate more equitable collaboration between sighted and visually impaired colleagues without additional intervention, as long as the media are accessible. Files that are stored on cloud-based file-hosting services such as Google Drive™ or Dropbox™ are particularly effective in facilitating digital workflows for timely access to information across multiple devices.

Ideally, when learning and workplace environments are universally designed, the ". . . design and delivery of products and services are usable by people with the widest possible range of functional capabilities, which include products and services that are directly accessible (without requiring assistive technologies) and products and services that are made usable with assistive technologies" (Section 3 of the Assistive Technology Act of 1998, as amended, 29 U.S.C. 3002.). In order to advocate for accessible environments, establishing partnerships with technology purchasers, developers, technologists, and content creators can be a powerful strategy to gain momentous support from the larger community. Anyone who designs, authors, and disseminates information can be recruited to ensure widespread accessibility of all media. As practitioners (or accessibility facilitators), we are often

called upon to nurture relationships with community partners to help ensure accessible environments for the individuals we support.

CONCLUSION

Access technology captures the definition of "assistive" as referred to in IDEA (Individuals with Disabilities Education Act) and the definition of "access" as referred to the ADA (Americans with Disabilities Act). However, while this textbook promotes the term "access technology" from a philosophical standpoint, the laws remain tied to the term "assistive technology." Until the laws are revised with new terminology, "access" and "assistive" should both remain used in practice. The definition for devices and tools provided in both Acts is broad and allows for many pieces of hardware and software, which can benefit blind or visually impaired individuals' access to information. A secondary definition in IDEA covers assistive technology services, a concept which is often overlooked, and may be as important or more important than the actual device or tool itself. These assistive technology services include assessment, evaluation, user instruction, and training, along with training and professional development for service providers. There are many pieces of hardware and software applications that can be used to provide information access for people who are blind or have low vision. It is unrealistic to expect that service providers who are not end users will automatically know how to operate and provide instruction for all these accessibility tools. Therefore, it is imperative that AT assessment and evaluation include recommendations that provide opportunities for services providers to acquire the professional development training and skills necessary to deliver meaningful instruction and training to the individuals they serve.

REFERENCES

Abner, G., & Lahm, E. (2002). Implementation of assistive technology with students who are visually impaired: Teachers' readiness. Journal of Visual Impairment & Blindness, 96(02), 98–105.

Correa-Torres, S., & Howell, J. (2004). Facing the challenges of itinerant teaching: Perspectives and suggestions from the field. Journal of Visual Impairment & Blindness, 98, 420–433.

Edwards, B. J., & Lewis, S. (1998). The use of technology in programs for students with visual impairments in Florida. Journal of Visual Impairment & Blindness, 92(5), 302–12.

Holbrook, M. C., Kamei-Hannan, C., & McCarthy, T. (Eds.). (2017). Foundations of Education, 3rd Edition: Volume II: Instructional Strategies for Teaching Children and Youths with Visual Impairments (3rd ed., Vol. 2). New York, NY: American Foundation for the Blind Press.

IDEA '04 Assistive Technology Definition Revision. (n.d.). Retrieved July 31, 2019, from American Speech-Language-Hearing Association website: https://www.asha.org/Advocacy/federal/idea/04-law-assist-tech/

Kapperman, G., Sticken, J., & Heinze, T. (2002). Survey of the use of assistive technology by Illinois students who are visually impaired. Journal of Visual Impairment & Blindness, 96, 106–108.

Morash, V. S., & Siu, Y. (2016). Social predictors of assistive technology proficiency among teachers of students with visual impairments. ACM Transactions on Accessible Computing (TACCESS), 9(2), 4.

Olmstead, J. E. (1995). Itinerant personnel: A survey of caseloads and working conditions. Journal of Visual Impairment & Blindness, 89(6), 546–48.

Sacks, S. Z., & Zatta, M. C. (Eds.). (2017). Keys to Educational Success: Teaching Students with Visual Impairments and Multiple Disabilities. New York, NY: AFB Press.

Siu, Y., & Emerson, R. W. (2017). Redefining roles of vision professionals in education and rehabilitation. Journal of Visual Impairment & Blindness.

Siu, Y., & Morash, V. (2014). Teachers of students with visual impairments and their use of assistive technology: Measuring teachers' proficiency and their identification with a community of practice. Journal of Visual Impairment & Blindness, 108, 384–398.

Swenson, A. M. (1995). Itinerant teaching: an insider's view. RE: View, 27(3), 113–16.

Wenger, E. (1998). Communities of practice: Learning as a social system. Systems Thinker, 9(5), 2–3.

Yarger, C. C., & Luckner, J. L. (1999). Itinerant teaching: The inside story. American Annals of the Deaf, 144(4), 309–314.

Sidebar 1.2:

WHAT IS CATIS?

In 2016, the Academy for Certification of Vision Rehabilitation & Educational Professionals (ACVREP), launched a new certification for assistive technology instructional specialists serving individuals who are blind or visually impaired (Certified Assistive Technology Instructional Specialist for People with Visual Impairments, or CATIS). This can be a stand-alone certification or one added to a professional certification in the blindness field such as Certified Orientation & Mobility Specialist (COMS), Certified Vision Rehabilitation Therapist (CVRT), Certified Low Vision Therapist (CVLT), Certified Rehabilitation Counselor, or credentialed teacher of students with visual impairment (TVI). Individuals with CATIS certification are experts on technologies designed to meet the needs of people who are blind or visually impaired.

The CATIS certification also helps to distinguish such expertise from assistive technology specialists who have more general knowledge of technologies to meet a range of diverse needs, but likely have limited specific knowledge about visual impairments. The technology needs of school-age visually impaired students can be adequately met by a well-trained TVI, whose credential should prepare him or her to evaluate and instruct on technology to support needs related to visual impairment. Although it is recommended that a CATIS-certified service provider be a primary member of a technology evaluation for an adult receiving rehabilitation or vocational services, it is not necessary for school-based IEP teams, where the expertise is provided by a TVI in collaboration with an AT specialist as needed (i.e. to brainstorm recommendations or for students with needs in addition to visual impairment).

CHAPTER 2
Technologies for Accessing Print Media

One of the tasks that continues to be critical for youths and adults with visual impairments is negotiating independent access to printed information. Although much of this information is becoming increasingly available in digital or electronic format, there remains a good deal of information that may only be available in a hard copy printed format. This includes but is not limited to printed text (books, magazines, pamphlets, signs, label, and handwritten materials) and a variety of images (diagrams, graphs, charts, maps, mathematical equations, photographs, and bar/QR codes). With the use of low- and high-tech tools, blind or low vision readers can now access a great deal of this information more independently than was previously possible.

Content Vocabulary
Low Tech/High Tech

Low tech refers to tools that function without power or complex electronic components such as a handheld magnifier, flashlight, or white cane. **High tech** refers to devices with digital or electronic components that require power and maintenance.

This chapter will provide basic information about the tools and workflows that can be used to read printed text and images. Tools for accessing printed text and images are categorized by how they allow the individual to access information, either through the senses of vision, touch, or hearing, or through a combination of those senses. While some people prefer to read using one sense (visual, tactile, or auditory), others might prefer an approach that integrates several senses. Some high-tech tools can facilitate multimodal access by allowing the user to read visually or tactilely while having the text spoken simultaneously. Low-tech tools can be more dependable but limit the reader to using just one sense. For readers who have more than one sensory channel available for reading, the multimodal approach can be very effective for accessing printed text with on-demand options for multi-sensory access. Different aspects of scanning and Optical Character Recognition (OCR) workflows will be addressed within each sensory access category according to their relevance to each sensory access mode.

Content Vocabulary
Optical Character Recognition (OCR)

Optical character recognition refers to software that scans printed or digital text and converts it into a computer-readable format.

Given the range of options that exists for readers who are visually impaired as well as the unique needs and abilities of these readers, selecting tools with the appropriate features involves careful consideration of what works best for that individual to accomplish a specific task in a specific environment. The importance of identifying the task to be completed cannot be overemphasized when selecting tools for accessing information in general.

Reading tasks can be divided into two large categories: continuous text reading and spot reading. The amount of material to be read can greatly determine which tool the user will select and the access method they choose: visual, tactile, auditory, or a combination. To be successful in education, employment, and life in general, a blind or low vision reader will need a varied toolbox along with the knowledge and skills to use these tools with the greatest efficiency for any given task. Some of the tools discussed in this chapter allow information to be accessed as it remains in print form, while other tools convert printed information into an electronic or digital format. **Chapter 3** will provide additional information on accessing text in digital formats.

Content Vocabulary
Continuous Text Reading/Spot Reading

Continuous text reading describes longer periods of sustained reading for work or pleasure. Low vision readers can be susceptible to visual fatigue and therefore benefit from using tactile and/or auditory tools with prolonged reading tasks. **Spot reading** refers to short, intermittent tasks such as reading a label, menu, or sign. Low vision readers can more likely manage these tasks visually using visual aids; if preferred, these tasks can also be managed with tactile or auditory tools.

VISUAL ACCESS TO PRINT INFORMATION

- **Nonoptical Devices**
- Large Print
- Reading Stands
- Acetate Overlays and Typoscopes
- Lighting and contrast considerations
- **Optical Devices**
- Principles of Optical Devices
- Magnifiers
- Monoculars and Telescopes
- **Video Magnification Systems**
- Considerations
- Standalone Devices
- Peripheral Devices

- Magnification Apps
- **Scanning and OCR Workflows**
- Scanning Tools and Apps
- Optical Character Recognition (OCR) Apps

In general, individuals with low vision can see or read printed text and images with tools that allow the user to control magnification, lighting, contrast, and spacing (Allen, Kirkpatrick & Henry, 2016). Technologies that maximize functional vision and assist people in accessing printed information can be grouped into the following broad categories:

- Nonoptical devices
- Optical devices
- Video magnification systems
- Scanning and OCR workflows

At times, these categories overlap. For instance, video magnifiers are both optical *and* video magnification devices. Although these devices could be categorized either way, they have their own unique characteristics and so are presented in a separate category in this chapter.

NONOPTICAL DEVICES

Devices and equipment that do not use lenses to magnify an image nor change the material being viewed are often referred to as **nonoptical devices.** (Foundations of Low Vision, pg. 928) Printed text and images can be **visually enhanced** to cast a larger or better-defined image on the retina

without magnifying the image. This can be accomplished by any of the following:

- Enlarging the material on a photocopier
- Producing hard copy large print with word processing software and a printer
- Bringing the material closer to the eye
- Placing the material on a reading stand
- Changing the hue and contrast between text and background using colored acetate overlays or tinted lenses
- Using a typoscope to reduce visual complexity
- Illuminating the material using task lighting (desk lamps, floor lamps, etc.)

Large Print Texts

Commercially-produced large print materials and books are printed in a minimum of 16 pt type, or more commonly in either 18 pt or 24 point print (Rubin, Feely, Perera, Ekstrom & Williamson, 2006; Large Print Materials. (n.d.). Retrieved August 27, 2017, from https://www.loc.gov/nls/resources/general-resources-on-disabilities/large-print-materials). Although these sizes are most often used for large print textbooks, commercially produced large-print books for leisure reading are usually printed in 14- to 16-point type. Large print materials can be printed or bound in standard or larger page formats.

Advantages

- Higher quality text and images than from enlarging with a photocopier

- Commercial binding makes books more durable for reuse by other students

- Large-print textbooks are sometimes available from commercial vendors

- Leisure reading material available in some libraries, bookstores, and directly from publishers, and in traditional book sizes

Disadvantages

- Expensive

- Large-print textbooks are often too large to fit elementary classroom desks

- When set in large print, a single-volume book may require multiple large-print volumes

- Limited selection of readily and commercially-available books

Another option for providing large print materials is producing them in-house. If the information is available in an electronic format (digitally from the publisher, created digitally, or scanned and converted from a print copy), it can easily be reproduced in large print using a word processor. Once the original printed text is rendered as a digital file, the file can then be printed in the reader's desired font and point size on standard letter-sized (8 ½ × 11-inch) paper. (See **Chapter 5** for additional information about producing materials in alternative formats. Always seek the advice of a legal expert whenever reproducing copyrighted materials.)

Advantages of In-House Production

- Less expensive than commercially-produced large print

- Can be printed on letter-sized paper for storing in binders, notebooks, and folders

- Easier for reader to manage standard-sized paper

- Easily produced in any font and point size

- Minimal training of staff needed to produce customized large print

- Equipment needed for scanning and word processing is generally readily available

Disadvantages of In-House Production

- Extra time required to scan and edit documents and texts

- Images and graphical information may not scan well

- Considerations when reproducing copyrighted work

Reading/Book Stands

Reading or bookstands are available in portable, tabletop, and floor-standing models. These tools allow the user to control the viewing angle of the printed material. The often-overlooked advantage of these flexible and low-cost tools is the ergonomic factor that allows the user to maintain better posture and decrease fatigue by placing materials at a comfortable viewing angle and height. Placing materials on a reading or book-stand helps raise materials so that they

COPYRIGHT AND ACCESSIBILITY—A LIBRARIAN'S PERSPECTIVE

Many educational institutions, [such as], Ohio State, share the mission of advancing and encouraging the spread of knowledge. At times, however, the exclusive rights of copyright owners can impede this mission by conflicting with the important objective of making works accessible to all, particularly to individuals with disabilities. Even with the emergence of new technologies that facilitate instantaneous copying and dissemination of materials, owner control over reproduction and distribution of works has continued to create an obstacle to the growth of works in formats accessible to individuals with print, hearing, or other disabilities . . .

The Chafee Amendment and Performance of Literary Works under §110

One important provision in copyright law that promotes accessibility to copyrighted works is the Chafee Amendment. The Chafee Amendment (17 U.S.C. § 121) permits an authorized entity to reproduce or distribute copies of previously published nondramatic literary works if the copies are reproduced or distributed in specialized formats exclusively for use by blind or other persons with disabilities.

Authorized entities include nonprofit organizations or governmental agencies "whose primary mission is to provide specialized services relating to training, education, or adaptive reading or information access needs of blind or other persons with disabilities." The vagueness surrounding the definition of "authorized entity" has contributed to confusion and reluctance to rely on the protections set forth in the Chafee Amendment . . .

Current & Proposed Exemptions under the Digital Millennium Copyright Act (DMCA)

Section 1201 of the Digital Millennium Copyright Act (DMCA) prohibits any individual from circumventing technological protections measures placed on a work. For example, you cannot decrypt DVDs protected by Content Scrambling System (CSS). The law, however, provides exemptions to this anti-circumvention rule . . .

(Continued)

Sidebar 2.1 (Continued)

The Important Role of Fair Use

. . . In *Authors Guild, Inc. v. HathiTrust*, HathiTrust created a shared digital repository of collection materials from academic and research member institutions, allowing full access to patrons with qualifying disabilities. The district court held this activity was permissible under the Chafee Amendment, stating that educational institutions "have a primary mission to reproduce and distribute their collections to print-disabled individuals . . . [making] each library a potential 'authorized entity' under the Chafee Amendment." The court held, however, that HathiTrust was not precluded from relying on the defense of fair use in the event that they were not authorized entities or did not otherwise fall within the permissible categories of the Chafee Amendment. On appeal, the Second Circuit held that providing full digital access to print-disabled patrons was protected under fair use.

International Considerations: Adoption of the Marrakesh Treaty

U.S. copyright law may also be influenced by international agreements. One international treaty directed to making works more accessible is the Marrakesh Treaty to Facilitate Access to Published Works by Visually Impaired Persons and Persons with Print Disabilities ("The Marrakesh Treaty"). The Marrakesh Treaty is an international treaty administered by the World Intellectual Property Organization (WIPO) which would obligate signatory countries to create mandatory limitations and exception to their copyright laws pertaining to "the right of reproduction, the right of distribution, and the right of making available to the public . . . to facilitate the availability of works in accessible format copies" for the benefit of people with print disabilities. The treaty would also permit exchange of accessible works across borders by authorized entities serving the blind, visually impaired and otherwise print disabled. Finally, the Treaty provides that contracting parties take appropriate measures to ensure that any anti-circumvention restrictions do not prevent the blind, visually impaired, or print disabled from enjoying any of the exceptions provided for in the Treaty . . .

Maria Scheid, Rights Management Specialist at the Copyright Resources Center, The Ohio State University Libraries; excerpted from https://library.osu.edu/site /copyright/2015/08/28/copyright-and-accessibility/

are positioned closer to the eyes and frees up the user's hands to manipulate an optical device or writing instrument while reading. Most readers with low vision can benefit from any type of reading stands.

Figure 2.1:
Tabletop Reading/Bookstand

Desktop stands are able to hold larger books and materials. Although these are available commercially, they can usually be easily be made by a high-school woodworking class or volunteers.

A copyholder is another useful non-optical tool that is similar to a reading- or bookstand. Sometimes referred to as a document holder or recipe stand, these commercially-available tools are used to hold documents and other materials that one might need to read while simultaneously entering text into a computer or referencing notes during a task. Models that are clamped to a computer monitor offer little advantage for a low vision reader due to their inability to bring the reading material closer to the eyes for improved viewing. On the other hand, models that clamp onto the edge of a desk, table, or shelf,

Figure 2.2:
Floor-Standing Reading/Bookstand

A floor-standing reading/bookstand allows the user to have the reading material at his or her optimum viewing distance and height.

that also feature a fully articulated arm can be of great value—the reader can place materials on the copy holder, and adjust the flexible arm to acquire the preferred viewing height, angle, and distance.

Stands of many varieties are found commercially in office or kitchen supply stores, or from vendors who specialize in products for visually impaired consumers. Customized stands can also be designed and then 3D printed, or even constructed from materials found at hardware stores. Designs for customized stands can be found online in several community forums.

Acetate Overlays and Typoscopes

Some individuals with low vision find that placing light-colored sheets of acetate over printed materials can reduce glare, and well as improve contrast and visibility. For example, a transparent yellow acetate sheet used in this way will increase the contrast between black print and a white background, or reduce glare from a white background on glossy paper. Contrast and glare can greatly impact reading ease and ability for any individual whose visual impairment includes functional implications for lighting conditions (Holbrook, Kamei-Hannan, & McCarthy, 2017). Acetate sheets are sold in office supply stores for use with overhead projectors or as report covers. They can also be purchased in theatrical lighting stores, where the sheets are called "gels" and are available in many colors.

Typoscopes are nonoptical devices made from a flat piece of plastic, thin cardboard, or sturdy paper. The typo-scope is designed to obscure part of the reading material and provide a small cut out window for viewing. This tool has two basic purposes: it reduces visual clutter by covering part of the text and images on a page, and its window provides a guide for visual tracking while reading. This is a free or low-cost, low-tech tool that low vision readers might find useful.

Figure 2.3: Typoscope

Typoscopes can be purchased commercially or handmade. These non-optical devices reduce visual clutter while reading.

Lighting and Contrast

Lighting is a critical factor in enhancing visibility. Many individuals with low vision benefit greatly from additional or reduced lighting when performing various reading tasks. Because lighting can also impact visual contrast, lighting adjustments can improve visual access for individuals who have light or contrast sensitivities. Lighting, either natural or artificial, is critical to efficient visual functioning.

Natural lighting in an indoor environment can have advantages and disadvantages for reading and other tasks. While natural light entering through windows can provide illumination of reading materials, it can also result in shadows cast upon or glare reflecting off of various surfaces. This is an important consideration when selecting a seating location in a classroom or work environment. If the individual with low vision is seated facing the windows, he or she may experience an earlier than expected onset of visual fatigue because of the intensity of the natural light. In contrast, sitting with one's back to the windows will most likely result in shadows being cast upon the reading material or work surface, making text harder to see. Individuals usually prefer to sit in a position in which the light comes from a direction opposite their dominant hand in order to avoid shadows that might be cast by their hand, arm, or shoulder. The intensity of natural lighting can be controlled to some degree by the use of window shades, blinds, or curtains. Though the availability of these controls will vary greatly in educational, employment, and personal environments, it is necessary to understand their benefit and take advantage of them when possible or whenever no better lighting option exists.

Artificial lighting is available in the form of overhead or room lighting and task lighting. Indoor environments are illuminated via incandescent, fluorescent, halogen, or LED (light-emitting diode) fixtures as either direct (from overhead) or indirect (reflected) light. Individuals with low vision will often have personal preferences for which type of bulb and placement works best for them, so it is not feasible to say which type is the best for all cases. However, there are a few considerations to keep in mind. In general, indirect lighting causes less glare than direct lighting, but may not be bright enough for efficient functioning. Classrooms and work environments often use fluorescent tube lighting for its economic benefits. Unfortunately, these fluorescent fixtures can cause glare and reflections, particularly when working with devices that have a display screen like a computer or video magnifier. Options to reduce glare include a dis-

play screen filter, anti-glare screen overlay, or paracube lens which directs light straight down as opposed to being dispersed at all angles. While these modifications may not eliminate glare, they will reduce it in many cases and are therefore worth investigating.

One additional aspect of artificial lighting is the color or temperature of the light. In general it is recommended to use lighting with a lower temperature or Kelvin rating. Filters and overlays are also becoming less necessary with newer screen displays that offer built-in options to adjust the brightness and temperature of the display.

Task lighting—either incandescent, fluorescent, halogen, or LED light produced from lamps—can be helpful when viewing printed text and images. In addition, the ability to adjust the intensity and directionality of lighting with filters and dimmer controls can be beneficial for low vision access; recall that some readers function better with additional lighting while others with eye conditions associated with photophobia need to decrease the amount of light to reduce eye strain and fatigue (Corn & Erin, 2010).

Content Vocabulary
Photophobia

Photophobia is a heightened sensitivity to light that can cause discomfort. It is a symptom related to an ocular or neurological condition.

Lighting should be a major consideration when undertaking new construction or major building renovations. A request for a modification to control natural and artificial lighting could be a reasonable accommodation under the Americans with Disabilities Act and Section 504 of the Rehabilitation Act of 1973.

Flashlights are another useful low-tech tool in the classroom or work environment. Handheld and head-mounted types are available, with multi-light LED models offering the widest functionality. Many smartphones and other mobile devices also offer a flashlight feature. The output of flashlights is often measured in lumens. The higher the lumens, the brighter the light. Many models will offer several levels of brightness depending on how many of the LEDs are receiving electricity from the batteries. LED flashlights are readily available and quite affordable, ranging in price from a few dollars up to approximately $100 at the time of writing, depending on features such as rechargeable batteries, levels of illumination, and strobe or flashing mode. Some even have an emergency-signaling mode. Orientation and mobility (O&M) instructors will often recommend a flashlight for night travel, but this is not the only task that can benefit from this type of illumination. Here are a few examples that will hopefully inspire service providers and low vision individuals to consider what other tasks could be accomplished more efficiently using a flashlight.

- **Pen light for locating a keyhole**
- **Flashlight for reading a thermostat or restaurant menu**
- **Head-mounted light for hobbies, crafts, or completing household repairs in which both hands are needed to hold tools**

Figure 2.4:
Handheld Flashlight

Figure 2.5:
Head-Mounted Flashlight

Helpful items such as sun visors, black felt-tipped markers, and bold-line paper are considered nonoptical assistive technology (AT) as well. Nonoptical devices can be very valuable when used alone or in combination with optical and electronic devices by allowing the user greater control of the viewing and lighting environments and visual stimuli. If appropriate for certain eye conditions, tinted lenses (such as sunglasses) can also help adjust for contrast, lighting, and glare, and are available in a wide variety of styles and colors. A prescription from a clinical low vision evaluation will recommend the appropriate color for reading and other activities. In addition, tinted lenses are beneficial for other visual tasks, particularly those performed outdoors (Jose, 1983; Quillman & Goodrich, 2004; Wilkinson, 1996, 2000; and Zimmerman, 1996).

Although it is not always possible to control one's lighting conditions, it is important that individuals of all ages with low vision understand how lighting affects their ability to read and maintain independence and safety in various situations. They will need to be able to evaluate the intensity of lighting in various environments and determine if additional or reduced lighting will improve their efficiency in performing tasks. Service providers should encourage individuals with low vision to get in the habit of exploring and trying various lighting options and tools in order to learn the strengths, weaknesses, and best uses of each resource and grow in comfortability in trying new technology in the future.

OPTICAL DEVICES

Optical devices, both manual and electronic, comprise a wide variety of tools designed to help people with low vision read print, view small objects, and access information at a distance. Devices that use lenses to magnify or enlarge the image of the material being viewed are called **optical devices.** A low vision professional must prescribe optical devices based on the results of a clinical low vision evaluation. (Refer to Chapter 1 for more information.) A clinical low vision evaluation is critical in helping the user select an optical device that best meets his or her needs. Too often, individuals with low vision try out a few magnifiers at a store or evaluate a selection of magnifiers in a catalog, and then simply select the device with the greatest magnification. While high magnification may be believed to be best, it may not be the most efficient feature for the user depending on the task to be completed. To choose wisely, users must understand the basic principle that as magnification increases, field of view (the amount of information that is visible) decreases. While one may appreciate the finer detail that can be seen with greater magnification, a decreased field of view also means that the user may only be able to see one or two letters at a time, or one small area of a picture before having to pan the magnifier back and forth. Panning can reduce reading speed and flow, or cause a reader to lose one's orientation on a page. A good clinical low vision evaluation will help the user find the best balance between magnification and field of view. Diane Brauner gives deeper insights into the issue of magnification in **Tech Tip 2.1: Bigger Is Not Always Better.**

Tech Tip 2.1: Bigger Is Not Always Better

Diane Brauner, Perkins Paths to Technology

Understanding Magnification

Students who have functional vision should certainly use their vision and—when appropriate—low vision tools. For educational tasks, some students with low vision may use vision as their primary learning medium—with or without magnification. Countless students successfully take full advantage of a variety of magnification tools and low vision devices; with these tools, vision is their primary learning medium. Other students are most successful with braille and/or auditory (screen readers) as their primary learning medium. Many of these braille and/or auditory students may use their vision to supplement the braille or auditory especially for tasks such as viewing an image or a math problem. Keep in mind, different tools are used to accomplish different tasks!

Just because a student CAN use his vision, does not mean he SHOULD rely on his vision for every educational task every day. Often students are observed who are leaning over—mere inches—from their tablet, computer or printed paper. For a quick glance at the materials, this may be fine. However, asking the student to maintain that posture all day or to complete an assignment will cause physical issues related to the posture. The solution may be as simple as using an articulating stand to position the materials at the desired height and location. Another option might be using larger font size, magnification device, or magnification software. Eye fatigue and related headaches/migraines are common occurrences for students with low vision. However, careful consideration should be made as to how much magnification is appropriate for different educational tasks.

Bigger Is Better—Right?

Tablets and computers all have built-in large print and magnification features as well as additional magnification apps and software applications. For this discussion and activity, we will use an iPad; however, the same concepts apply to any device.

When schools began adopting the iPad, TVIs were over-the-moon with the simplicity of iOS for young students and the built-in accessibility features. Students could choose their preferred low vision features and settings, to make their educational materials instantly accessible.

While some students use large print font and then choose to pinch out to view an image or specific item, other students may successfully use magnification (Zoom) all the time. The native Zoom app on the iPad can currently be magnified 1–15x. Like all good things, moderation is the key!

Zoom Activity

Why not Zoom to the max? To fully understand the issues, try the following activities.

Note: These activities are beneficial for classroom teachers, family members and even administrators; and, these activities can be used in conjunction with an IEP meeting or as a teacher in-service at the beginning of the year activity.

Home Screen Zoom Activity

- Enable Zoom (Settings > General > Accessibility > Zoom > toggle Zoom on)
- Make sure that Zoom Full Screen is selected.
- On the Home screen of the iPad, Zoom until only one icon fits on the screen. (Three-finger double tap—holding on the second tap—and scroll up.)
- Find a specific app that is in the middle or bottom of the screen (Scroll around the screen by dragging three fingers.)

Was that an easy or challenging activity? Were you lost on the screen? How efficient were you in finding the desired app?

Reading Zoom Activity

This activity requires a document or article. If using the activity with educators/family members, choose a document that is a recent or upcoming homework assignment. The document can be a Pages document or can be an Internet article; the only requirement is that the document is at least one paragraph. Ideally, use a document that has multiple choice questions at the end. If sharing this activity with a group, use a document camera to display the iPad's screen so that everyone can see.

- Open the document/article and Zoom to full amount.
- Ask the group to read the document aloud as you scroll across the characters/words. Be sure to scroll through several sentences (so that you have to navigate from the end of the line back to the beginning of the next line). It is okay to become a little seasick!
- Ask the group what they just read. (It is often challenging to comprehend content when scrolling and trying to put pieces together to make a word!)

Assignment Zoom Activity

Now try completing an assignment—answering questions—with Zoom enable to the max. (For demonstration purposes, questions can be answered verbally.) If possible, use an assignment from your student's classroom or use the questions from the worksheet in the previous **Reading Zoom Activity.**

- Open the document and Zoom full screen.
- If the document has already been read in the activity above, scroll to the bottom to access the questions.

(Continued)

Tech Tip: (Continued)

- Scroll through the first question and the multiple-choice answers.

- Can you easily scroll back to the content to seek an answer?

- Answer the questions. If this is a group activity, ask the group to choose the correct answer.

Summary

Using low vision tools are definitely beneficial for many students with low vision. However, if a student has to scroll across the screen in order to read, then another learning medium should be investigated. Scrolling is not optimal for reading longer passages in a timely manner. Often smart students can slide by in K–12 with low vision devices and/or scrolling but these same students struggle significantly in keeping up with the quantity of reading required in college and in future careers. Having to magnify materials to such an extent that requires scrolling is a strong indicator that a screen reader should be used.

Another indicator is if a student is unable to read at the same rate as his peers. Also, does your student read printed books for pleasure? If not, why not? If a student is a slow visual reader or is scrolling to read, a screen reader will significantly increase the student's reading speed. According to research, students reading large print are 1.5–2 times slower readers than their peers. The "Do You Read Fast Enough to Be Successful?" *Forbes*

article (https://www.forbes.com/sites/brettnelson/2012/06/04/do-you-read-fast-enough-to-be-successful/#6fbb0574462e) states an increase in reading rates of average students with vision:

- Third-grade students = 150 words per minute (wpm)

- Eighth-grade students = 250 wpm

- Average college student = 450 wpm

- Average "high level exec" = 575 wpm

- Average college professor = 675 wpm

- Speed readers = 1,500 wpm

- World speed reading champion = 4,700

What does that mean? On average, undergraduate classes typically require at least 3 hours per week study time per credit or 9 hours per week per 3-credit course. (Much of that study time includes reading; however, "reading" is not broken out separately.) If a student with low vision averages 1.5–2x longer, that would mean at least 13.5–18 hours per week per 3-credit class. In high school, the research states an average of 1–3.5 hours a night on homework; that translates into 1.5–7 hours a night for a low vision student to complete the same assignments!

Does your low vision student complete all of his assignments? What if you could flip things and make your low vision student the fastest reader in his class and cut homework time in half — compared to the time his peers spend on homework? A low vision student who efficiently uses a screen reader is able to read faster than his peers. Talk to any successful professional who is visually impaired and ask what tools make him successful. The guaranteed answer is strong tech skills and a fast screen reader.

Note: Screen reader skills—including fast speeds—should be mastered early; ideally before high school and at the very least, before college begins. Tech skills and speed should not be introduced freshman year of college. The same time frame holds true for students who are currently successful with low vision tools but who have progressive eye conditions.

Principles of Optical Devices

Because of the many complex factors related to optical devices, and because optical devices must be matched to an individual's functional vision and activity needs, they need to be prescribed by a low vision specialist who conducts a thorough clinical low vision examination. However, before the evaluation, providers can help individuals with low vision become familiar with the various kinds of devices available so that they are better prepared for the provider's visit. Even if a practitioner only has a limited selection of optical devices on hand, it is still beneficial for the student to try several different optical devices and then experiment with each. Individuals who have had some basic exposure to various types of optical devices and how they work are better prepared to work with a low vision specialist.

Two important aspects of using low vision devices can be practiced with the individual before his or her clinical low vision evaluation: determining the appropriate distance between the magnifier and the material being viewed (in order to bring the text into focus), and determining the distance between the users themselves and the magnifier. Practicing the skill of adjusting the distance between the magnifier and the viewing material to get the image into focus is important for the successful use of an optical device. Developing this skill will help the individual and the low vision specialist more quickly determine which type of magnifier might be best for completing various tasks.

There are three other principles related to the use of optical devices that are important to understand when selecting appropriate devices for people with low vision.

- **When magnification is increased, the field of view is decreased.**
- **Increased magnification generally requires increased illumination.**
- **Training is required for the most effective use of these devices.**

Field of View

The laws of physics dictate that when an image is magnified, the portion of that image that can be viewed at any one time is decreased. In other words, as the image gets bigger, the amount that can be seen gets smaller. The area that can be viewed through a magnifier at any one time is referred to as the device's **field of view.**

Many individuals will at first choose near and distance optical devices that provide the highest possible levels of magnification. As they begin to use a device, however, they may become aware of the decreased field of view, and then learn to select devices that provide an adequate level of magnification while at the same time offering the greatest field of view. They may also learn to select devices of different powers of magnification for different tasks. Understanding this factor can be very helpful for users and low vision specialists in determining the most appropriate optical devices for various viewing tasks (Corn and Erin, Chapters 7 & 14, 2010).

Lighting

Viewing images or objects under increased magnification generally requires additional lighting. Lighting is a critical factor when using many of the available types of magnifiers, because shadows can be cast by magnifier stands, the user's hands, or even the user's head and body. Distance viewing devices may not work well in dimly-lit environments or when viewing poorly-lit targets. Providing additional lighting and controlling the available light, as explained earlier, are options that can improve the effectiveness of optical devices. (Dister & Greer, 2004; Flom, 2004; Quillman & Goodrich, 2004; Watson & Berg, 1983; Wilkinson, 2002; Zimmerman, 1996).

Training

It is important to realize that effective use of optical devices requires training and practice. An instructor should not assume that because a device has been prescribed, the individual will automatically know how to use it well—or at all. Service providers and family members may not understand why devices sit unused in a drawer, backpack, or desk, when the individual is simply unable to make good use of them. Direct instruction from a fellow low vision reader or certified professional in education or rehabilitation vision services can ensure opportunities for practice in how to use the device to spot, focus, scan, track, and shift gaze until the individual can do these things independently and automatically. Supportive access environments and gaining a student or client's buy-in regarding the value of an optical device are important as well, as many low vision readers may feel self-conscious or uncomfortable when first using prescribed devices. Introductory training should begin with materials or objects of high interest to the learner so that he or she develops a natural understanding of how the optical device enhances functional vision. The individual will be more motivated to learn to use the device to view something that is of high interest and importance. Therefore, make these lessons fun and interesting!

Most optical devices can be classified as devices used for either near vision or distance vision tasks. Eyeglasses and contact lenses are the most widely used optical devices and should be prescribed by an ophthalmologist or an optometrist. Other types of optical devices include **magnifiers** for viewing objects at near (within a range of 16 inches) and telescopes or monoculars for distance viewing (ranges that exceed 16 inches). Video magnifiers, which use cameras and a display screen to capture and project a magnified image, are often classified as optical devices as well. Since video magnifiers are also electronic devices that can be standalone or peripheral devices that comprise a larger computing system, they are described in a later section in this chapter.

Magnifiers

Magnifiers use lenses to increase the size of the image entering the eye. They are available in various sizes, shapes, and powers of magnification, and may or may not have built-in lighting. Many individuals find handheld and stand magnifiers beneficial for near vision tasks such as spot reading. These no-tech tools are the ultimate back-up devices because there is a slim chance of device failure; unless there is a built-in light that requires a battery, there is no need to charge a magnifier, and little maintenance is required besides keeping the tool clean and intact. **Handheld** magnifiers provide a great deal of portability and flexibility, but require some coordination and strength to use. The user must be able to hold

and maintain the device at the appropriate distance from the reading material while moving across a page to read the desired text or view an image. **Stand** magnifiers sit over the material to be viewed and do not need to be held, thus providing a fixed distance between the lens and the reading material. They can be very useful to those with limited motor control and coordination. Pairing magnifiers with nonoptical tools such as additional lighting and a reading stand can improve the user's efficiency and decrease fatigue; however, magnifiers in general can become fatiguing for long periods of continuous text reading. Depending on the low vision reader's personal preferences, magnifiers are likely a better choice for shorter reading tasks or as a backup device for when a high-tech tool fails.

Telescopes

Devices that enhance distance vision include binocular and monocular telescopes. These devices can either be handheld or mounted in eyeglasses frames. Binocular and monocular telescopes are available in various sizes and powers of magnification. Although most have a fixed power of magnification, some can zoom in and out, allowing the user to change the level of magnification. Most telescopes can also be focused to view objects from different distances. Improvements in the field of optics have provided many options for spectacle and head-mounted telescopic systems. Some telescopes clip onto the user's eyeglasses while others are mounted

Figure 2.6:
Sample Handheld Magnifiers

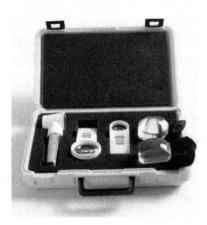

Although handheld magnifiers are portable, a user must be able to hold them at the appropriate distance from a printed page.

Figure 2.7:
A Stand Magnifier

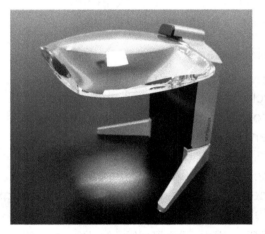

Example of a desktop stand magnifier. Credit: Jamie Maffit, Department of Blindness and Low Vision Studies at Salus University

directly into a carrier lens. This type of system is often referred to as a bioptic telescopic system, and can be used by some individuals in many U.S. states to qualify for a driver's license as a low vision driver. Some telescopes can be fitted with *reading caps*, which when added to the end of a telescope, convert it into a telemicroscope to allow the user to view reading materials at 16 to 18 inches. This is a viable tool for some individuals with low vision who need to read music for practice or performance.

Video Magnification Systems

Video magnification systems make use of a camera to show a magnified image on a display screen such as a computer monitor, mobile device, or television. Although video magnifiers are sometimes classified as optical devices, this class of tools functions very differently from other optical devices such as magnifiers, monoculars, and telescopes, in several significant ways that make them a more efficient tool for completing many continuous text reading tasks. Recall that optical devices are more often preferred for spot reading tasks; many users prefer video magnifiers for continuous reading and spot reading tasks.

Basic differences between optical devices and video magnifiers are as follows:

▫ Magnification range and power: While most traditional magnifiers have fixed powers such as 3X, 5X, or 8X, most video magnifiers allow a higher degree and wider range of magnification from approximately 0X—60X.

▫ Contrast and color filters: Some readers find it easier to read text with reverse contrast (polarity) such as light-colored text printed on a dark background, while others prefer a color filter that customizes text and background colors; for example, presenting yellow text on a black background. Most video magnification systems offer contrast and color filter options while most optical devices do not.

- Functioning in a wider variety of lighting conditions: Most video magnifiers are equipped with a light source and do not require external illumination, as opposed to traditional magnifiers.

- Ergonomics: The short focal length of traditional magnifiers requires many users to either bend over to achieve the appropriate working distance or to hold the material and the magnifier themselves. While these issues can be mitigated using one of the reading stands discussed above, some readers experience physical fatigue more quickly when using these optical devices. A video magnifier allows the reader to select a magnification power that accommodates any preferred working distance, thus allowing the reader to sit in any number of ergonomically correct and comfortable positions. The ease of adjusting magnification power for different working distances is especially helpful for continuous reading tasks.

- Integrated OCR: Optical devices limit an individual to only visual access. Some video magnifiers offer options for on-demand auditory access with integrated OCR that scans and reads the text as it is magnified.

Video magnification systems provide readers with a tool that enlarges reading material sufficiently for them to both maintain a natural posture and to view the materials at a comfortable distance. Video magnifiers were traditionally referred to as closed-circuit television systems (CCTVs), a designation that can lead video magnifiers to be confused with the video monitors used in many security systems. In recent years, video magnification systems have also phased out the need to connect to a television display in lieu of other display options. For these reasons, the authors recommend the term *video magnifier* rather than CCTV.

A video magnification system uses a camera to capture an image of the viewing material and then displays it on a screen such as a tablet or computer monitor. The image can be enlarged by adjusting the magnification settings on the camera, the display screen, or the application that renders the image on the display screen. There are many varieties of video magnification systems, ranging from large desktop models to portable ones that can be carried in a backpack or purse. Desktop models might offer an X-Y table to assist in moving the viewing media back and forth to view all aspects of the enlarged image. The amount of scanning necessary depends on the field of view and how much of the enlarged image can be seen at one time on the display screen.

Video magnifiers are also available as standalone devices, or systems that include a computing device (such as a

THE X-Y TABLE

The X-Y table solves the problem of how to smoothly and efficiently move reading material under the camera of an electronic/video magnifier with a fixed camera. The X-Y table is a flat rectangular tray that is mounted on moveable tracks and placed underneath the camera on a surface. With the reading material placed on the X-Y table, the table can be moved in a smooth and steady motion in four directions: right, left, up, and down. This movement eliminates the need to move the reading material.

Effectively controlling the X-Y table key to the successful use of a desktop video magnifier. Beginning users often have difficulty moving the table and reading material together while moving them from right to left to scan across lines of text. This results in wavy movements that appear to move in two directions on the screen, which can cause some users to experience motion sickness. Others find it difficult to locate the beginning and end of lines of text, or accidentally read the wrong column or row. Efficient use of the X-Y table is a motor skill that can be acquired through guided practice. Two features of X-Y tables allow the user to adjust and control its movement: the **friction brake and margin stops.**

Friction Brake

A *friction brake* controls the amount of force that the user must exert to move the X-Y table. With practice, fine-tuning the friction brake allows the user to move the reading material horizontally while maintaining a line parallel to the bottom or top of the monitor, thus easing the motion sickness reported by some users. The proper adjustment of the friction brake prevents unwanted vertical movement, while at the same time allowing easy movement from one line to the next when needed. Some manufacturers have replaced a friction brake by increasing the rolling resistance of the X-Y table; users with less coordination may still want to look for models with the friction brake.

Margin Stops

Margin stops are another feature of some X-Y tables that help improve the user's efficiency when reading documents with multiple columns. The margin stops control the boundaries or limits of the left and right movement of the X-Y table, so that the reader does not unintentionally move from one column of text into another column of text. Properly adjusting the margin stops improves reading efficiency because the reader does not have to visually determine the boundaries of the column being read or waste time viewing text out of order in the next or preceding columns. At first, users may not realize the benefit of this feature. Monitoring by the service provider and noting the amount of time the user spends locating the end of the line of text currently being read and the beginning of the next line of text may be necessary. Providing the user with this information, demonstration of how to use the margin stops, and guided practice will help them realize the benefit of taking the extra step to set the margin stops before beginning to read longer passages.

Motorized X-Y Tables

Individuals with additional motor disabilities may face additional challenges before achieving proficient use of the X-Y table necessary for efficient continuous text reading. Guided practice using the X-Y table can greatly benefit all users, but depending on available motor skills, some individuals may do better with a motorized or automatic X-Y table where the tray moves automatically at a preset speed. The user can set the rate of movement to match a comfortable reading speed and set the margins to align with the text. Motorized tables are expensive and not widely available, but for some users with limited motor abilities, this feature can make a huge difference in their ability to use a desktop video magnifier successfully.

Some models of desktop video magnifiers no longer have the friction brake and margin stop features. Readers who do not use their video magnifier for extended continuous text reading may not miss these features, but for those who do, these two features can greatly increase reading efficiency and comfort.

computer or tablet) connected to a peripheral camera, or a computing device with applications that offer video magnification features. Regardless of the variations, all video magnifiers have a camera and some type of display screen in common.

Video magnifiers are extremely important tools for individuals who have low vision because they provide the user access to a wide variety of types of materials including small objects; printed or handwritten text; and images such as photographs, drawings, diagrams, graphs, and maps. Video magnifiers can also be used to help individuals see their own handwriting more clearly when filling out forms or worksheets, or even when sketching. Video magnifiers are particularly valuable pieces of equipment for school systems and agencies when a digital copy is not readily available, print and paper media is preferred, or when information is presented at a distance, such as notes on the board.

CONSIDERATIONS

Magnification and resolution

Most video magnifiers offer a wide range of magnification and resolution settings. Magnification refers to the degree of enlargement, while resolution refers to the clarity of details in the enlarged image. Note that when viewing materials on either the low or high end of the magnification range, there will be limitations. A video magnifier that has 5X as its lowest magnification level will limit the amount of information that can be displayed at one time. This can be inefficient when the user needs to obtain an overall perspective on items such as maps, graphs, drawings, or diagrams. On the other hand, the highest magnification settings may not be adequate for other tasks such as viewing the electrical connections on a circuit board or information presented at a distance. The capability of a video magnifier to refocus as the image is magnified depends on the robustness of the camera resolution and zoom capabilities; cameras with an optical zoom typically produce better quality images.

Display size

The size of the display screen is also an important consideration when matching a device to an individual's needs. Although a larger monitor will allow more information to be displayed at one time and at any given magnification level,

remember that bigger is not always better. Smaller-statured individuals such as young children or petite adults may have difficulty seeing to the edges of a large monitor. Conversely, the smaller displays that portable units offer may not be adequate for users who require higher levels of magnification that significantly reduce the field of view. Video magnifiers with monitors mounted on flexible or adjustable arms, or video magnification systems with a peripheral camera that allows the display screen to be positioned in a separate location, can offer the most placement options for ideal viewing (see the later section on **Flex-Arm Camera Models**).

Field of view

One of the more difficult aspects of using a video magnifier is shifting the camera's field of view from one part of the item to the next, since the magnified image shows only a small portion of the material at one time. Unlike some desktop models, portable and handheld models do not have an X-Y table to help move the viewing material back and forth, and instead require the user to move the camera across the text. The user will also need to have enough table or desk space to move the reading material underneath the camera.

Selecting a video magnifier

Given the number of considerations necessary, it is essential to involve the end user when selecting a video magnifier or designing a video magnification system. The level of magnification, resolution and zoom capability, and how the magnifier fits into an individual's workflow must be appropriate for the individual to complete desired tasks. Determining what tasks need to be accomplished with magnification, when an individual requires desktop access to information presented at a distance, and also what future work-flows are anticipated will help deter-mine the best fit for each user.

Numerous developments and ad-vances in the production of cameras, viewing applications, and computing tablets have resulted in a variety of video magnifiers and video magnifica-tion systems that can be divided into several broad categories.

- **Standalone devices: Desktop and handheld video magnifiers**

- **Peripheral devices: Flex-arm camera models, document cam-eras**

- **Magnification apps that enable a mainstream device to function as a video magnifier**

Video magnifiers offer a variety of useful features beyond their basic function of displaying a magnified image. The spe-cific features vary depending on the type of video magnifier. Deciding which fea-tures an individual needs requires care-ful consideration of the tasks he or she needs to accomplish. For example, individuals who need to read information at a distance, such as on a chalkboard or whiteboard in a classroom or viewing a presentation in a business meeting, will need a magnifier with distance viewing capabilities and portability. Some indi-viduals might prefer a standalone video

magnifier while others might prefer to use their personal computing device as part of a magnification system. Under-standing the following features will assist the individual and the service provider in selecting a model that will best meet the individual's needs.

- Continuous zoom magnification with autofocus or fixed-focus—Autofocus is helpful when reading information at a distance or on curved surfaces. Fixed-focus is preferred when the viewing material needs to stay in fo-cus while other elements are placed under the camera (such as when placing a hand under the camera to fill out a form).

- Reverse contrast (polarity) and color filter options—Brightness and con-trast often need adjustment when using these features. Adjustments can improve reading efficiency and increase the time before the onset of visual fatigue.

- Reading guide options: Line guide, text masking or highlighting—These features control the amount of text visible on the screen at any one time and are beneficial to read-ers who have difficulty with visually tracking the same line of text from left to right.

- X-Y table (See **Sidebar 2.2: The X-Y Table**)

- Freeze-frame mode that allows the item being viewed to be removed from the camera while maintaining the image on the display screen

- Near, intermediate, and distance viewing (dependent on the camera capability)

- Optical Character Recognition and Audio Supported Reading (text-to-speech)—These options provide an audio output of the text through synthesized speech. Some units highlight each word in reverse polarity as it is spoken, providing the user both auditory and visual access simultaneously.

- Live image mode—In this mode the user sees a magnified image of anything placed under the camera. This is what one would expect from a traditional video magnifier. This is a useful mode for examining objects and graphical images, as well as for some short reading tasks, but not as useful for continuous text reading without an additional X-Y table.

- Picture image mode—The image captured by the camera can be viewed by using the cursor keys of a computer keyboard or the control keys on a stand-alone system, allowing the user to access both text and graphical information. Using these types of controls to navigate a page of text and graphics eliminates the need for, and the manipulation of, an X-Y table. Careful consideration must be given to the navigation options for this feature if the user intends to use it for continuous text reading. If navigation can be controlled only by continuously pressing the computer's arrow keys, then this will not be a very efficient tool for reading long passages; if the system offers a scrolling or panning option, then it can be effective for some users.

The following sections detail the features that distinguish each category.

Figure 2.8:
Video Magnifier Viewing Features

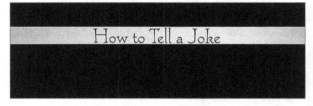

Reverse Polarity: A section of text with white font and a black background

Example of a color filter: A section of text with yellow font and a blue background

Line Guide and Text Highlighting: Photo of a page of text from a book, with a black line that underlines one line of text and a transparent yellow bar that highlights the one line of text

Text Masking: A section of text is shown with everything covered in black except for one line text (it is the on-screen equivalent of a typoscope)

Standalone Video Magnifiers

Based on the advantages and disadvantages of standalone video magnifiers, an individual might choose to have one video magnification system for the workplace or classroom and another one for the home. The decision to have more than one system depends on the tasks and contextual challenges specific to each environment. For example, many students who are reluctant to use a standalone video magnifier in public (and may choose a video magnification system as part of a mainstream computing device such as laptop or tablet as an alternative) might actually prefer a standalone device for use in the privacy of their home.

For individuals who use a computer for school or work, it is recommended that a standalone video magnifier be connected to the computer's monitor or display, allowing the computer and the video magnifier to share the same monitor. The user then controls what he or she sees on the monitor screen: the image from the computer, the image from the video magnifier, or, in some models, one of the images on the top half and the other image on the bottom half of a split screen. It is important to note that the image from the computer will not be enlarged; the user will need to use a screen magnification program on the computer to enlarge its display. (See **Chapter 3** for information on screen magnification software.)

Desktop models

Desktop video magnifiers were the first electronic magnification systems to appear on the market in the early 1970s. They are still in production and offer the best solution for continuous text reading of long passages. These standalone models typically have a fixed or mounted camera, an X-Y table on which to place the viewing material, and a display monitor.

Advantages

- Offer the widest range of magnification and features
- Easiest to use for reading and writing
- Best for continuous text reading

Disadvantages

- Expensive
- Large size and weight
- Lack of portability

While most of the controls are simple and straightforward, specific training in the proper use of these tools will greatly increase the user's efficiency.

Monitor placement is a key concern
when setting up a desktop video magnifier. Ergonomics and a comfortable
reading position for continuous text
reading are important considerations.
An in-line viewing arrangement with the
monitor directly over the reading material provides the best ergonomics for
most users. A general guideline is to
place the monitor at a height such that
the individual's eye-level is approximately one-third of the way from the
top of the display. Setting up an ergonomic in-line system for a small child
can be particularly challenging since
the monitor cannot be set too high, and
therefore will need to be close to the
X-Y table, which can make it difficult for
the child to write under the video magnifier. This situation may require the
use of an adjustable table, the height of
which can be varied for each individual

user and for the task the individual is
completing. The effect of physical
factors and ergonomics on the comfortable use of video magnifiers and other
technology tools—and therefore the
user's success in using them—cannot
be overemphasized.

Portable Video Magnifiers

Portable video magnifiers are available
in two distinct configurations. The first
type relies on a handheld camera about
the size of a computer mouse that the
user rolls or slides over the material to
be magnified, which then displays the

Figure 2.9:
An Ergonomically Poor Video
Magnifier Setup

*This is not an ergonomically-appropriate
setup. Notice that the student's gaze
is below the middle of the monitor, and
that she must keep her neck bent in
order to read the screen's contents.*

**Figure 2.10:
An Ergonomically Ideal Video Magnifier Setup**

This setup is ergonomically-appropriate. Unlike the setup in Figure 2.8, this video magnifier is adjusted so that the student's neck is held in a comfortable position and his gaze is slightly above the middle of the monitor.

image on a small monitor or a separate display screen such as a television. The second type of portable video magnifier was referred to as electronic pocket models in this book's first edition. In electronic pocket models, both the camera and display screen are built into the unit that the user moves over the material to be magnified. These systems are available in several screen sizes, classified as small (3–4 inches), medium (5 inches), or large (7 inches). Some models, particularly the larger ones, offer a foldout stand that allows the user to keep the magnifier at the appropriate distance from the material being viewed. Many of the medium and smaller units provide a foldout handle for either one-handed or two-handed use. Most models in this category offer similar features to those found on the desktop and flex-arm camera models discussed above, such

as polarity and choice of text and background colors.

Advantages

- Portability
- Lightweight
- Excellent for spot reading and short reading tasks
- Many can be connected to larger external monitors, laptops, or tablets

Disadvantages

- Physical manipulation of the device (especially true for models that use a "mouse-like" external camera.)
- Potentially causes more rapid onset of fatigue when used for continuous text reading
- Smaller magnification range
- Most models do not offer continuous zoom magnification; they may only have settings for 3x, 5x, or 8x, but nothing in between

The biggest disadvantage of these types of video magnifiers for text reading is the challenge of moving the camera accurately and efficiently over the reading material. The user must move the camera from left to right over the text without allowing the camera to shift above or below the line of text. To understand how difficult this is, picture a computer user placing the cursor directly under the first word in a line of text and then moving the mouse from left to right, keeping the cursor under each word without moving it up or down. It does not take more than one attempt to experience how difficult this task can be. Therefore, devices in this category of video magnifiers are less useful for continuous text reading and more useful for spot reading.

One additional type of portable video magnifier is a system that is head-mounted. These systems require the user to wear a device similar to a pair of eyeglasses. Most models offer near and distance viewing. A small camera is mounted into the glasses or attached to the side; it either displays visual information on a display screen or provides access to printed information via text-to-speech (see below for additional information). These tools can be very useful for some individuals while others will find the appearance or weight of a wearable device unacceptable. Models in this category have come and gone over the years but continue to reappear with new features that make them desirable for some users.

Peripheral Cameras

Commercially available peripheral cameras can be used as part of a video magnification system. A system with a detached camera as a peripheral device has unique advantages and disadvantages from standalone video magnifiers.

Advantages

- Technical support readily available from anyone familiar with the mainstream device; no specialized knowledge about assistive technology is needed

- Often lower costs due to competitive mainstream markets and larger consumer pool

- Different components can be swapped in/out as technology improves

- Mainstream devices are the same as used by typically sighted peers; can be more easily adopted and used by individuals who are self-conscious about appearing different

- A free-standing camera can be placed in a location separate from the low vision viewer and easily moved for optimal positioning with viewing materials—Most cameras offer both near and distant viewing while some also have an intermediate viewing option useful for grooming or hobbies.

- A free-standing camera can be folded when not in use and placed in a case for protection when transporting it to other locations.

- Less expensive than standalone video magnifiers

Disadvantages

- Range and quality of magnification might not be as robust as a standalone video magnifier

- Requires maintenance and manipulation of several components to function as a video magnifier; more technical expertise might be needed to operate efficiently with additional cables or components that must be charged. More steps required with initial setup.

- Requires connection to a computing device with a magnification app

Disdvantages continued

and any desired video magnification features

▫ Lack of X-Y table for continuous text reading (separate X-Y tables are available from some vendors)

▫ Some peripheral devices do not include a display screen

▫ A camera lens must be repositioned when switching viewing modes: near, intermediate, distance.

▫ Time is required to set up the system for use, and then additional time required to pack up system for transport.

Flex-arm and Portable Cameras

The flex-arm camera is a lightweight camera that is mounted on an arm, stand, or tripod that can be rotated or adjusted to view materials at various distances. The camera can be used independently from the display and connects to the display via Bluetooth®, Wi-Fi®, or a cable. The display can be a television or computer monitor, laptop, tablet, smartphone, or any computing device with a screen. There are three basic configurations in this category:

▫ One—A variation on the standalone desktop video magnifier where the camera is mounted on a short arm that is connected to the top or the side of the monitor of the video magnifier.

▫ Two—A camera or smart lens that is mounted on a stand or tripod with a flexible or rotating head. A camera can take and store pictures internally while the smart lens has no storage capacity, but both devices can zoom in or out, and must be connected to a display to view enlarged images. The camera connects to a display via Bluetooth, Wi-Fi, or a cable.

▫ Three—A back-facing camera on a smartphone or touchscreen tablet that is handheld, mounted on a stand or tripod, or placed on a stand that is set up to point the camera at printed media. The enlarged media are displayed on the smartphone or tablet screen; viewing preferences can be adjusted with built-in magnification features or add-on magnification apps.

Configuration One describes a different camera setup available for a standalone desktop video magnifier. **Configurations Two and Three** require the camera be connected to a computing device with a screen display to view the enlarged media. Many users find configuration three to be a good tool for spot reading out in the community, such as reading menus at a restaurant, particularly in combination with the flashlight feature provided by the device. However, just as with the portable models discussed earlier, the coordination required to efficiently manipulate the camera decreases its value as a tool for reading continuous text or longer passages. In order to function as part of a video magnification system, each of these camera configurations must connect to a computing device with built-in or add-on apps or features for magnification and reading. Magnification apps and built-in features will be discussed later in this chapter.

Document Cameras

Document cameras are traditionally used in mainstream K–12 and higher education classrooms to project an image of worksheets or demonstration materials onto a screen at the front of the room. With recent innovations including wireless connectivity between the document camera and a display screen, using a document camera as part of a video magnification system is becoming more popular. Document cameras can easily capture print media at a near or somewhat far distance. Instead of projecting images onto a screen at the front of the room, they can be connected to an individual's tablet, laptop, or computer for desktop viewing. This is appealing for users who want to feel less conspicuous when using specialized equipment in public, such as in the classroom or on the go. As with flex-arm and portable cameras, the ability to use a document camera as a video magnifier depends on the quality of the camera lens and the available features of the display application. A document camera is sometimes preferred because it can utilize an individual's existing personal computing device as a display screen and makes the user feel less conspicuous when using specialized equipment. Because document cameras were developed for mainstream consumers and general education classrooms, the price points are extremely competitive and often thousands of dollars less than standalone video magnifiers.

Some individuals might still prefer a dedicated video magnifier for the home or primary office location but have a document camera system in the classroom or when working on the go.

Figure 2.11: Document Cameras as Video Magnifiers

Document cameras can be used as part of a portable video magnification system with laptops (top) or tablets (bottom).

The primary setup when using a document camera as part of a video magnification system consists of three parts:

▫ A display screen such as a mobile touchscreen tablet, laptop, desktop monitor, or television

▫ A peripheral camera such as a document camera, webcam, or smart lens

▫ Software that feeds the image from the lens to the display screen; some software is downloadable for free and can be compatible with multiple camera inputs.

Magnification Applications (Apps)

Magnification apps have a combination of desirable features: they have a zoom feature that allows the user to enlarge an image captured by a camera, but they also have the functionality of a portable video magnifier in that they are usable from a smartphone, tablet, desktop, or laptop computer. In order to use one of these devices as part of a video magnification system, it must have either built-in or add-on apps that allow the user to access low vision settings such as zoom adjustment, polarity and color filters, reading guides, freeze-frame or live image mode, OCR, and TTS. Most devices have basic built-in accessibility features that allow an individual to enlarge an image onscreen or reverse its contrast for easier viewing. However, these built-in features can be insufficient for the low vision reader. Fortunately, he or she can find more robust video magnifiers in a variety of downloadable apps available online. These apps are designed to display images from any peripheral camera and include a range of low vision reading tools.

Scanning and OCR Workflows

As technology progresses, the line between print and digital information becomes more blurred. Most hard-copy printed media can be easily converted into a digital format using some type of camera that scans the printed document into a digital format. A camera on a video magnifier, smartphone or tablet, computer, or scanner can be used to capture the print media. Then, by using a scanning app, it can render a high-quality digital version. Once in digital format, images can be magnified on-screen. At this point, by using a process known as Optical Character Recognition (OCR), the text can be further manipulated and converted into readable and customizable formats. One such customizable format is "text-to-speech" (TTS), wherein the text is voiced using synthesized speech. In addition, the text can also be adjusted to a reader's preferred font, color, and text/background contrast scheme. Unfortunately, OCR does not always render text with 100 percent accuracy, so there may be discrepancies between the original text and what is read aloud. Typically, OCR is more prone to producing errors when the printed text is irregularly formatted or includes differently designed sidebar items or tables. OCR renders text most accurately when the printed text is displayed in standard black and white paragraph form with no additional design features (semantic content) such as text boxes or non-traditional text placement. When a standalone video magnifier integrates OCR and text-to-speech with the device, it is sometimes referred to as a "scan and read" feature. Video magnifiers with OCR and text-to-speech capabilities offer additional features that other video magnifiers do not such as the following:

- Reformatted text mode—In this mode the image created by the camera is processed by the OCR software. Then, the text can be displayed on the monitor in the user's preferred font and point size, as well as their preferred text and background colors. Based on the user's preferences, the text can also be displayed as a single line of text moving from right to left across the screen, similar to the "crawl" or "ticker" text often seen along the bottom of the screen in a television news broadcast. Another display option is similar to the word wrap feature commonly seen in word processors. Word wrap ensures that if a word is too long to fit on the end of one line of text, the word processor will automatically move it to the following line. This feature eliminates the need for the user to pan or move the image right and left. Alternatively, the reader can also select settings that will allow the text to vertically move along the screen at the desired speed, similar to how digital teleprompters present lines to actors or performers. While continuous text reading in this mode is very efficient, it is unable to display any of the graphical information on the page. A successful reader must learn to use commands to alternate between the text view and the "picture image mode" in order to view the graphical information.

- Audio Supported Reading (ASR) mode—This mode provides the visual features of the reformatted text mode above but adds the benefits of text-to-speech (TTS). The user will see the text displayed in their preferred font, point size, and color combination, while also hearing each word spoken via synthesized speech. As each word is spoken, it is highlighted on the screen in reverse polarity (that is, light on dark, or dark on light), or in the user's preferred color combination. This process of combining speech with highlighted text is known as Audio Supported Reading (ASR) (Jackson & Hendricks, 2014). This combination of OCR and TTS can also be used to render print media accessible for auditory access or for tactile access with a braille display (More information in **Chapter 3**).

Scan and read technologies are becoming abundantly available for free across mainstream and specialized technologies. Many hardware and software that handle digital text offer built-in "scan and read" features. Some features allow the reader to scan an entire page. Other features convert only the text that is highlighted or visible on the monitor or screen when a command is issued to scan and read the text. The reader might then be required to reposition the page or keep highlighting sections of text in order to read and hear the remainder of the text on the page. Some readers will find this requirement inconsequential, while others might find it frustrating and prefer a different type of tool for continuous reading (see section **Auditory Access to Print Information**).

As new and updated versions of video magnifiers become available, it is imperative that both low vision readers and service providers keep abreast of these advances. This will help them work with clinical low vision therapists to ensure that individuals can continue to benefit from the latest improvements.

Individuals wishing to access printed information visually have a wide variety of optical, nonoptical, and electronic tools available from which to choose. A combination of these tools will likely yield the best results. Thanks to recent innovations, individuals can have a "toolbox" full of tools and resources for obtaining information efficiently and independently in order to achieve their educational, employment, and personal goals. To ensure success, it is imperative that individuals receive appropriate training in the use of these tools and develop their own knowledge about which tools are best for short or spot reading tasks, lengthy continuous text reading tasks, or distance viewing tasks. Selecting and using the appropriate tool for the job is key. Assessing an individual's needs and abilities is the critical determinant in identifying the appropriate tool.

TACTILE ACCESS TO PRINT INFORMATION

Individuals who choose to access information through their sense of touch have also seen a dramatic improvement in tools and technology. Some of these individuals might find that one sensory modality—for example, tactile—is best for certain tasks while auditory might be better for other tasks. Those who primarily use tactile access but have some remaining vision may at times find one of the visual access tools discussed

above to be useful in very specific situations. Over time and in certain environments these preferences may change. For those who wish to access printed information through touch, braille is equivalent to printed text and tactile media can be equivalent to printed images. Tools for producing tactile formats are more specifically discussed in **Chapter 5,** while this chapter will focus on the user experience when accessing printed text and images tactilely.

Braille

Braille is an essential tool for acquiring and maintaining literacy for many individuals who are blind or visually impaired. It provides direct, immediate, and reliable access to information for individuals who use their tactile sense as their primary way to obtain information, and for those whose visual abilities may not sustain visual reading efficiently or for extended periods without fatigue. The direct access to information provided by braille cannot be replaced by auditory access. Hard-copy or paper braille provides information to visually impaired readers in a way that is equivalent to how print information is provided to sighted readers. Knowledge of braille is the cornerstone of literacy, educational achievement, and successful employment for many students and adults.

In addition to the content of the text, braille provides information about the following:

▫ **Spelling of words and terms.** It is essential for readers to repeatedly see or feel the letters to correctly spell words and develop the tactile equivalent of "sight words." Having information in braille exposes the reader to spelling nuances and is the most effective way for a braille reader to develop an appreciation for etymology.

- **Structure and format of printed information.** Information about how text can be organized with headings, subheadings, and paragraphs is not always easily conveyed in an auditory format unless the text is formatted for accessibility with a screen reader. Understanding the relationship of these elements adds significantly to the reader's comprehension of the text. In addition, it is important to understand how written text is organized in order to effectively write documents for business or the classroom.

In order to independently access printed text and images tactilely, a reader needs to interpret the print media and access a re-created version in a tactile format. A blind or low vision individual has several options for tactile access to print media:

- Scan and use OCR to digitize the printed text and prepare for embossing a paper braille copy

- Scan and use OCR to digitize the printed text. Onscreen text that is readable with a screen reader tool can be read on a refreshable braille display.

- Use artificial intelligence to interpret visual media and render in a tactile format (further discussed in Chapter 6).

- Use sighted assistance (either in-person or remote) to interpret the visual information; then choose from a selection of manual and high-tech tools to document the information in a reader's preferred format—hard copy or digital. (More information about authoring tools in **Chapter 4.**)

Just as there are high-quality print materials and competent print reading instructors, there remains a parallel need for high-quality braille and tactile media and tools, as well as competent braille instruction so that blind and visually impaired individuals can maximize their educational, employment, and personal potential.

Technology that can digitize printed media with options for auditory or enhanced visual access does not eliminate the need for braille. Rather, it provides braille readers more immediate access to printed information through embossed (hard copy) braille or a refreshable braille display. While only a small percentage of printed materials is available in hard copy braille, a number of other tools are available that greatly improve the efficiency of hard copy and digital braille production. These options are covered in detail in **Chapter 5.**

Tactile Graphics and 3D Models

In addition to rendering printed text in braille for tactile access, printed images can also be reproduced in a tactile format for tactile access (see **Chapter 5, Technologies for Producing Alternate Formats**). Similar to low- and high-resolution printed images, tactile graphics and 3D models can also be presented in low- or high-resolution for haptic exploration. Although many printed images are not necessary for text comprehension since they simply serve to create visual interest, images that are important to understanding the text can often be conveyed with a thoughtful verbal description (Morash et. al, 2015). In addition, concepts that require spatial understanding are better conveyed in a tactile format.

When accessing tactile media, tactile resolution is dependent on the materials used for producing the media. Different materials will convey a line or corner with more or less precision and crispness. In addition to the time available to create tactile media, the need for durability and replication of certain tactile graphics and 3D models will also influence which methods and materials are chosen to create tactile media. Methods could be hand crafted, machine rendered, or tooled on paper, plastic, acrylic plates, or other materials. The individual who prefers to access print materials in a tactile format can best recommend which materials are optimal for different tactile representations.

Just as visual clutter can make it more difficult for an individual to access information, tactile clutter on a graphic or model can also cloud relevant information. Tactile labels are often used to translate what the various tactile elements represent. Often, these labels are symbols that are explained on a legend, written in braille, or assigned an audio tag that speaks when activated. Because tactile labels on a tactile graphic or model can produce so much tactile clutter that it renders the media incomprehensible, audio labels can help keep the media easy to explore and understand, while still conveying the necessary information. (More details about audio-tactile graphics and models are found in **Chapter 6.**)

Individuals who use tactile media have varying levels of tactile acuity (ability to distinguish tactile details) and preferences. Depending on the materials that are used to create a tactile graphic or 3D model, the details that are included or omitted, and how information is conveyed in the tactile media, tactile media can be just as effective for conveying information as visual print media. Although a good tactile graphic or 3D model might convey only the most important information from the original graphic and not necessarily every visual element contained in the original, it should still enable tactile exploration and perceptual understanding of a spatial concept.

Individuals' use of tactile media improves with repeated exposure and practice. Initial tactile media experiences should be guided so that a nonvisual learner develops optimal strategies for interpreting information in the tactile format (Morash et. al, 2014). These strategies include:

- Use of both hands and multiple fingers for more efficient orientation and exploration
- Use of both hands and multiple fingers for improved comprehension of spatial relationships
- Use of a tactile landmark that serves as an anchor for haptic exploration

After initial instruction in how to explore a tactile graphic, tactile proficiency develops from building a repertoire of experiences with various media.

In certain subjects, individuals work with a combination of printed text along with printed maps or scientific notations. Although any of the methods mentioned above are useful for creating custom-made media, ready-made tactile media are also available from a variety of sources. (See tactile media repositories such as www.btactile.com)

Tactile Tools

Other tactile tools include raised-line measuring tools (rulers, protractors, calipers, and compasses) and tactile kits that support access to a curriculum. Although some tools are readily available (from American Printing House for the Blind and other suppliers), accessible tools sometimes require custom design and construction in order to best fit a user's needs. (See **Chapter 5** for producing materials in alternate formats.) Remember to encourage individuals to use multiple fingers and both hands when exploring tactile media and using tactile tools. It takes direct instruction, practice, and possibly even occupa-

tional therapy (OT) to develop effective dexterity skills for using tactile tools proficiently.

> **Content Vocabulary**
> **Occupational Therapy (OT)**
>
> **Occupational therapy** is the use of assessment and intervention to help individuals develop the necessary skills and strategies to participate in everyday activities.

Tactile Math Tools

Mathematical concepts and calculations can often be difficult to access in a nonvisual format because the media are presented in non-linear designs. Although sometimes necessary to convey spatial layouts for math learning, setting up math problems on a braillewriter can be time consuming and cumbersome. Several other tools—for example the abacus, the Cubarithm, and the Braille Basic Math Kit—allow students to use their tactile sense in the comprehension and application of mathematical concepts. (For more information on tools for mathematics, see Osterhaus, 2008.)

The abacus is an old and valued instrument for computing calculations in many European and Asian cultures. The Cranmer Abacus, designed for use by people who are blind, is available in several versions. The device consists of beads mounted on rods. The rods are then divided by a plastic bar that separates four beads on the bottom from one bead on the top of each row. The user slides the beads from the bottom up to the bar to indicate numerals 1 through 4. The bead on the top can be moved down to represent the numeral 5. The four basic functions of addition, subtraction, multiplication, and division can be performed using this tool. It is a portable device and requires no batteries, a fact that many individuals find very convenient. It is also available in a model with larger beads for people who might have difficulty manipulating smaller ones.

The major benefit of the abacus over other tools such as a talking calculator is that the abacus is a more effective tool to teach mathematical facts. Because of these characteristics, many states allow the use of an abacus as an accommodation when students are taking state-mandated assessments. (Check with your own state department of education for guidance regarding allowable test accommodations.) With the abacus, mathematical problems such as long division calculations are easier for people to compute.

The Cubarithm (Gissoni, 2005) is another time-tested tool that can be used to teach the layout of arithmetic problems to learners who are blind or visually impaired. Weighted cubes embossed with braille characters are placed on a work board divided into sections. These cubes can easily be removed to allow the user to make corrections when necessary. Cubes are placed in the appropriate locations to perform arithmetic calculations. The cubes are relatively small, however, and require a certain level of fine motor ability for their use.

Figure 2.13:
The Cubarithm

Figure 2.12:
The Cranmer Abacus

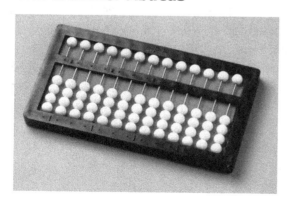

Math Window ® Braille Basic Math Kit is a similar concept to the Cubarithm, except that, instead of weighted cubes, magnetic tiles are used. They are placed on a board divided into raised, open squares. Each tile has both braille and print text identifying them as numbers, letters, symbols of operation, and so on. These tiles can be arranged to display a math problem along with steps for completion. Additional tiles set are available for use in geometry, algebra, calculus, and trigonometry.

It is important to note that tools such as the Cubarithm and Math Window are tactile representations of visual layouts. Blind students must also learn how mathematical information can be represented spatially for full understanding of mathematical concepts.

Learning to access graphical information is extremely important for academic and employment success. The ability to understand and present information in the form of sketches, photographs, diagrams, maps, plans, charts, graphs, or other non-textual, two-dimensional formats is defined as *graphicacy.* Developing the tactile and cognitive skills to understand graphical information cannot be accomplished overnight, however. Therefore, it is essential that teachers of the visually impaired begin working with students to develop these skills at a very early age. The skills needed to develop good graphicacy for both tactile and visual learners require the learner to acquire understanding of basic concepts, and then build subsequent layers of skills upon this foundation in order to gather the salient information in a map or diagram. For instance, it is unrealistic to expect a high school student in an American history class to understand a map depicting the expansion of the United States if he or she has not had several experiences working with simple to complex maps in the past. It is wise to begin teaching graphicacy early, using a strategy that gradually adds and increases the complexity of the graphical information.

AUDITORY ACCESS TO PRINT INFORMATION

Literacy is developed and facilitated through tactile and visual access to printed information. However, at times, auditory access may be more desirable. For example: prior to students entering the room, an instructor writes a homework assignment on the board to read pages 211–225. In this instance, the most efficient way to access this information might be to simply ask a peer if there are any assignments written on the board. The peer can respond by reading the information out loud so that the information can quickly be documented in the learner's preferred format. This example also demonstrates how auditory access might be used for immediate access to information but the information may be reviewed using tactile or visual access.

Other printed information can be more independently accessed with tools that translate visual media into auditory information. Produced in the form of synthesized speech, scanning/OCR workflows and visual interpreter apps are integral to accessing print privately and immediately for shorter tasks or for saving print in a digital format for longer reading tasks. Many methods and tools that support auditory access to print are now available, including but not limited to the following:

- Scanning and OCR workflows
- Text and image identification using human visual interpreters (in real life or with an app)
- Text and image recognition using artificial intelligence
- Talking devices such as calculators, thermometers, scales, measuring instruments, and lab equipment
- Talking apps such as calculators, dictionaries, rulers, protractors, accelerometers, and compasses
- Talking global positioning system (GPS) devices and apps

Deciding when to use auditory access depends on the task and the user's individual preferences. Task duration, reading speed differences across content and sensory channels, and environmental conditions are the most common determining factors. Some individuals find that auditory access is a useful strategy for completing lengthy reading assignments because it can require less time than reading the same information in print or braille alone

Tech Tip

See Paths to Technology post titled "Five reasons why your students should learn to read at a rate of 600 words per minute."

https://www.perkinselearning.org/technology/blog/five-reasons-why-your-students-should-learn-read-rate-600-words-minute

For pleasure reading, some readers might prefer a recorded human voice rather than synthesized speech, or choose braille or large print to enjoy the linguistic nuances of the written word. Text-based subjects such as the humanities and social sciences are very conducive to auditory access. Image- and graphics-oriented subjects, especially those with scientific notations, can be more complex to access auditorily. These subjects require more formatting considerations for auditory access and are better accessed through tactile and visual formats (See **Chapter 6, Translation Considerations for STEAM**).

Tools that allow auditory access to print information are an essential part of the well-stocked toolbox of successful students and employees. However, exclusive reliance on these tools is typically not recommended; print or braille experiences remain critical for individuals with developing literacy skills or for those needing to produce quality written communications.

Auditory access should not be confused with audio supported reading (ASR). ASR involves reading along in print or braille with what is being read aloud. When using the combination of auditory access with braille or print, the reader can obtain the literacy information mentioned in the previous paragraph while at the same time access the information faster than he or she would be able to with print or braille alone. This method of accessing information is not necessarily more efficient for all individuals, but many will find it very beneficial in bridging different sensory modalities. For example, readers who typically read visually but are learning braille often benefit from ASR to ensure ongoing access to information as tactile reading skills develop. The technologies discussed in the following section introduce tools that assist in the process of auditory access and ASR. The potential benefit of these tools and approaches to accessing print information should be explored for all blind and visually-impaired individuals as secondary to visual or tactile access, and especially for those who are shifting from visual to tactile skills as their primary form of access. Incidentally, English Language Learners can also benefit from this added auditory support.

Readers and Visual Interpretation

One of the most widely used methods to access printed media is requesting another person read text aloud or describe an image. This method sacrifices privacy in engaging with information but can provide more immediate access to information. These methods can be no-tech or high-tech depending on whether additional technology is used to mediate the interaction between the blind or visually-impaired individual and the human visual interpreter (use of artificial intelligence will be covered in a separate section). In this section, the term "reader" will be used to refer to a person who reads text as directed by a blind or visually-impaired individual. However, the larger concept of a visual interpreter is inclu-

sive of a reader. When another person assists in describing printed media, the description is unavoidably subjective; the information a blind or visually-impaired individual receives is an interpretation of the printed media as perceived by another. Even if a reader is simply asked to read text, inflection and tone can change how the listener considers that text. The following section will explore the tools and relevant considerations for using readers and visual interpreters for auditory access to information.

Readers

Working with a human reader may not usually be thought of as technology use, but assistive or access technology, as defined in **Chapter 1,** is considered the use of any methodology or device or equipment in support of the performance of a task. This accommodation is allowed on standardized assessments as well.

Readers can be used successfully for tasks in the areas of education and employment, as well as the activities of daily living. However, like other means of access, relying on a live reader to provide real time information has advantages and disadvantages. The keys to working successfully and efficiently with a reader are making sure of the following:

- The reader is well trained in reading only what is printed and as directed by the blind or visually-impaired student or adult.

- The listener is organized and focused, and knows how to direct the reader courteously and efficiently.

Knowing how to work with a reader efficiently can be extremely important for both education and employment, especially when dealing with time-sensitive tasks and high-stakes issues of assessment and promotion exams. This is not a skill that develops incidentally; it requires instruction and practice to be successful. For example, an individual can direct a reader to identify the major headings in a long document first, then drill down to identify the subheadings before reading the desired text. Without training, an individual might instead allow a reader to read straight through the same document from beginning to end and simply wait to hear the desired content. The first strategy provides an overview of topics and allows the blind or low vision individual to prioritize which sections to read first. This is particularly helpful when reviewing a reading passage to answer comprehension questions or when perusing a restaurant menu.

When using a reader, listeners will likely need to take mental or physical notes. Note-taking can be done via braille or print notations or by making an audio recording (see **Chapter 4, Technologies for Authoring Written Work**). Some individuals might choose to record the reader for later review. Others may ask the reader to record their reading separately and then provide that recording to the blind or visually-impaired individual. For an effective recording to be produced, the reader needs to know how to capture high quality audio, how to organize the task according to the listener's preference, and how to share the audio file in a workflow that is most accessible for the recipient. (For additional information on using readers, see Hollbrook, D'Andera, & Wormsley, 2017; Leibs, 1999; Whittle, 1995; Cheadle & Elliot, 1995; Castellano, 2004; Castellano, 2016.)

Remote Visual Interpreter Services

When print media is inaccessible and the blind or visually-impaired individual desires access that is independent and private from immediate company, visual interpreter services can offer preferred tools. These tools require a system that includes a camera that can capture a photo or video, and a device that can send or share the data. Although some systems support a wearable option such as a camera mounted on a pair of glasses, many individuals prefer a smartphone rather than a wearable accessory for better discretion and ease of use. During or after a photo or video capture, the data is sent through a service that connects the blind or low vision individual with one or several people who review the photo or video and reply back with a description. These replies can be in the form of text or audio, and can be immediate or require a few minutes or hours, and can even be from people all around the world!

A number of free and premium apps provide a range of visual interpretation. Most individuals will have several tools on hand and choose to use different ones depending on the task and nature of information. Several factors can determine which tool is selected:

- Immediacy and complexity of the needed information (for example, locating a storefront or airplane gate, finding desired items in a store, understanding the layout of a complicated intersection, completing a timed task)

- Multiple interpretations are desired (for example, weighing subjective interpretations of artwork, clothing, or body language)

- Content-specific expertise is needed (for example, description of architectural details, anatomical distinctions, or scientific notations)

- Duration of the interpretation task (for example, following a long task such as an inaccessible how-to video, versus a short task such as identification of a button on an appliance.)

Sidebar 2.3: **Comparison of Visual Interpretation Apps** presents a thorough list of tips and considerations when using visual interpreter apps. As with all access technology, it is important to introduce students to a variety of options and provide them with enough instruction so they can be informed consumers. First and foremost, it is strongly recommended that these services are used with caution with students under the age of 18; students must be aware that shared photos and videos are being interpreted by strangers who may or may not have

completed background security checks (this is a particular concern with services that connect users with volunteer describers). Users must also be aware of what can be within the scope of a camera and use discretion to avoid sending private or inappropriate images in the background. This is especially important when asking for a description of toiletries containers in the bathroom and other areas where there might be mirrors or other means of exposing personal and private information. Finally, users must be aware of how their data is shared during live sessions and how/if their confidentiality is maintained if the data is saved in a company's database, even if for training purposes. Each company's privacy and confidentiality policies warrant research and consideration. Questions to ask might include:

- Are my data (photos, videos, location, interpreter sessions) stored in a company database? If so, is this data secure?

- If my data are used for training purposes, how will my confidentiality be maintained?

- How are describers trained to maintain my confidentiality?

Text Recognition and Computer Vision Systems

The advent of commercially-available recordings in the late 1970s and early 1980s led to audio formats for Talking Books, and these evolved into superior-quality recordings of commercially-available printed books.

Sidebar 2.3

COMPARISON OF VISUAL INTERPRETATION APPS

Adapted with permission from the National Federation of the Blind. By Chancey Fleet (2017). *Need Vision on Demand? There's an App for That.* Braille Monitor, 60 (7). For the full article, see https://nfb.org/images/nfb /publications/bm/bm17/bm1707/bm170702.htm

If you're a blind person with a smartphone or tablet, you can use it to get visual information on demand. This genre of service is relatively new and can go by many names: you might hear it called remote visual assistance or crowdsourced vision. Personally, I prefer the phrase "visual interpretation" because it precisely names the process of turning visual information into something more useful and because the concept of an interpreter is familiar to people in many walks of life.

Working with a remote visual interpreter can be liberating: you decide what your interpreter can see, when the interaction begins and ends, and whether you need a second (or third, or tenth) opinion. A virtual interpreter can't touch anything in your environment, so you can't be tempted to abandon a task that is "too visual" to someone else's hands. Remote visual interpretation can be an empowering option when you'd rather limit the extent of your interactions with the public, avoid turning friends and colleagues into de facto describers, or when no one around you is available to give you the information you need.

A variety of apps provide remote visual interpretation. Although they vary in price, functionality, and whose eyes are on the other end of the connection, there are some things you'll want to consider when you use any of them.

TapTapSee (free for Android and iOS)

How it works: snap a picture or upload one from your camera roll, and a combination of machine vision and crowdsourced Web workers will send you a quick description. Typically, your answer arrives within 20 seconds and is short enough to fit on a fortune cookie.

When it shines: for the simple things. TapTapSee is great at identifying products and describing photos in brief. I use it on a daily basis to sort

(Continued)

ACCESS TECHNOLOGY FOR BLIND AND LOW VISION ACCESSIBILITY

Sidebar 2.3 (Continued)

and label mystery items in my home and office, get real-time feedback about the photos I'm taking, and double-check that my pen has ink and my handwriting is legible. TapTapSee descriptions are text-based messages that can be read with magnification, speech, or braille.

BeSpecular (free for iOS and Android)

How it works: take one or more pictures, or upload them from your camera roll. Type or record a question, and listen for text and audio replies to come rolling in from sighted volunteers over the course of 20 minutes or so.

When it shines: for rich detail, diverse opinions, and a nuanced understanding of what different people notice when they look at an image. I use BeSpecular to ask for detailed descriptions of clothing and jewelry, ideas about what to wear with what, guidance in picking the "best" photo from a set, and impressions of photos and objects that are important to me. Once I've heard five or six different takes on the same image and question, I can find the patterns of consensus and divergence among the responses and arrive at my own informed understanding of the image. BeSpecular finds a happy medium between the brevity of Tap-TapSee and the live connection used by other apps. There's something special about BeSpecular's format of long-form questions and answers. Outside the rhythm of a live conversation, BeSpecular answers almost feel like postcards from a sighted correspondent passing briefly through your life. They're often full of detail, personality, and emotions like surprise and humor. Once, while delayed on a train at Union Station in Washington, D.C., I asked BeSpecular to relieve my boredom by describing the scene outside my window. One respondent sent me an audio reply that explained, in a tone that was equal parts delighted and chagrined, that I had unfortunately sent her the most boring view she had ever seen. It was one train car, an empty John Deere forklift, and a cloudy sky.

BeMyEyes (free, iOS, with Android reportedly coming soon)

How it works: connect to a sighted volunteer who speaks your language and have a conversation about what they see through the lens of your camera.

When it shines: for exploring, sorting, and troubleshooting. Every time I arrive at a new hotel, I check in with BeMyEyes to take the decaf coffee pods out of play, sort the identical little bottles in the bathroom, and learn the thermostat and media controls. I also use it to find out which food trucks are parked on the streets near my office, decipher mystery messages on computer screens, and grab what I need from my local bodega. Since BeMyEyes is powered by volunteers, I try to make the interaction upbeat and fun and let the person I'm working with decide whether they'd like to bow out of a long task after a certain amount of time. There are just over a half a million sighted volunteers and about 35,000 blind users currently registered with the service, so you can call as often as you like without fear of bothering the same person over and over. The system will always connect you to someone for whom it is a reasonable hour, so Americans calling late at night or early in the morning will be connected to wide-awake people in Europe and Australia. Since the volunteer base is so large, you're likely to get through to someone quickly even when lots of other blind users are connecting.

Aira (iOS and Android, $89 per month and up, available 7 AM—1 AM Eastern)

How to pronounce it: it's a hard *I*, so pronounce it as "Ira."

How it works: use your phone's camera or a Google Glass wearable camera to connect with a live agent. Agents can access the view from your camera, your location on Google Maps, the Internet at large, and your "Dashboard," which contains any additional information you'd like placed there.

When it shines: for tasks that are long, context-dependent, or complex. An Aira agent can start from any address, use Google Street view to find a nearby restaurant, glance at online photos to clue you in to whether it's upscale or casual, suggest and explain the best walking directions to get there, read the daily specials when you arrive, and show you where to sign and tip on the check when you're ready to leave. Agents have watched and described completely silent YouTube videos with me so that I could learn origami models, counted heads in my local NFB chapter meeting, described 20 minutes of nothing but socks until

(Continued)

I found the perfect sock souvenir, read online guitar tabs for me so I could write them down in my own notation, helped me pick out nail polish, and taken spectacular photos through my camera for my personal and professional social media accounts. Aira agents are great at reading handwriting, diagrams, and product manuals that seem to have as many pictures and icons as words. When I can't read something with OCR, Aira can almost always help.

Aira agents are paid, trained professionals. Most of them are unflappable, effective describers who are up for any challenge. Since you pay for their time, you should feel comfortable about asking for what you need, being assertive about the type of descriptive language that works for you, and calling whenever the need arises.

Like any new technology, remote visual interpretation solves old problems and creates new ones. To use it well, we need to understand what it requires in terms of power, data, planning, and effective communication. We must employ it with sensitivity to our own privacy and to the legitimate concerns that people sharing space with us may have about cameras. Just as each of us makes different decisions about when and how to use a screen reader, the descriptive track of a movie, or a sighted assistant in daily life, each of us will have our own ideas and preferences about how visual interpreters fit into our lives. Blind and sighted people working together are just beginning to discover how to use language, software, and hardware in ways that employ visual interpretation to our best advantage. Collectively, we still have a lot to learn. The journey is long, but the view is phenomenal.

Talking Books were first recorded on vinyl records, then cassettes, then flash drives, and finally on digital audio files such as MP3s. The National Library Service for the Blind and Physically Handicapped (NLS), part of the Library of Congress, has been the primary supplier of Talking Books. A variety of mainstream vendors and companies that serve disabled individuals also offer audiobooks, which have high- quality, recorded human voices. **Chapter 3** will discuss tools for accessing these texts in digital formats while the remainder of this chapter will focus on accessing printed information that is not commercially available in a digital format.

Scan and Read Tools

Historically referred to as "reading machines" (Cooper, 1950), scan and read tools support auditory access to printed text. Inventor Ray Kurzweil developed the first reading machine in the last quarter of the twentieth century. Early reading machines were quite large, very expensive, and required many electronic circuit boards and microprocessors. They were limited in their accuracy because of the difficulty in interpreting text in the wide variety of fonts found in printed materials. Nowadays, scanning and OCR workflows (as discussed earlier in the chapter) have replaced reading machines but consist of the same four main components as the initial technology.

- An optical scanner that captures a picture of printed text and saves the text as an image
- OCR software that analyzes and recognizes the image as characters and words
- TTS software that determines the prosody and works in tandem with a speech card to convert the text into synthesized speech
- A speech synthesizer that allows the user to adjust the volume, reading rate, and pitch for reading aloud

The accuracy, customization options, and price of each component can determine which specific products are selected as part of a scan and read system. Similar to standalone video magnifiers, most standalone reading machines have given way to scanning and OCR apps that are integrated within the functionality of an all-encompassing app or computing device. An increasingly popular scan and read system involves the use of a smartphone or mobile touchscreen tablet. Similar to how these tools can be co-opted as a portable video magnifier with features for screen magnification, a smartphone or mobile touchscreen tablet can be part of a robust scan and read system with the help of an installed OCR app. The smartphone or tablet's camera operates as the optical scanner, an OCR app captures the image, and the device uses built-in or add-on TTS and synthesized voices to read the text. This can be challenging for a low vision or nonvisual reader due to the visual nature of the task; the camera must be positioned well enough over the print media so that the text can be scanned, and the device must be held steadily so a clear image is captured. Scanning apps that offer an auto-capture feature require the page edges to be visible; otherwise the user must keep the device steady while activating the capture button. A few strategies and tools can be introduced to facilitate independence in the scan and read process:

- On a flat table, place the smartphone/tablet camera-side down on the print media. Slowly raise the smartphone/tablet away from the print media, keeping the device screen parallel to the table. Use a scanning app with an auto-capture feature so that the image is captured as soon as the app recognizes the page edges. The biggest

COMMON FEATURES IN A SCANNING APP

Batch Scanning

With batch scanning, the user can scan and store multiple pages before the OCR process, rather than processing the pages one at a time. Once all pages are scanned—which usually takes less than a few seconds per page—the document can be exported as a whole for OCR. When the OCR process is complete, the user can access the information at his or her convenience.

Auto Capture

This feature is very convenient for maintaining a firm grip on the mobile device while moving it slowly away from the page. Because the app will automatically capture the document image when the page edges are detected, there is no need adjust or remove a grip from the device to "click" the capture button.

Handling different document types

Scanning apps that allow the user to adjust capture settings depending on the document being scanned can help scan a document and save it with the most true-to-life quality. The document setting must be set before scanning. The most common document settings are: Color document, black and white document, color photo, and grayscale photo.

Flash

Similar to taking a photo, some scanning apps will allow a user to manually turn the flash on or off, or set the flash to automatic so that additional lighting is provided when the camera detects low lighting. Although a flash can be useful for reducing shadows on a document, flash can also cause glare or distorted color on the document. The best lighting conditions for scanning are when there is ambient lighting all around the document. Overhead or spot lighting can cause significant shadows on a document.

Editing a scan

More sophisticated scanning apps can automatically enhance a document image after scanning to remove shadows, adjust for distortion from curved pages, or fix the geometry of a page. Some apps might instead offer a feature for enhancing an image that must be activated by the user. Full-featured enhancement options are similar to a camera app such as adjusting brightness, exposure, and contrast.

Integrated OCR

Premium scanning apps often have integrated OCR so that after a document is scanned, text can be immediately extracted and copied/pasted into a word processor for editing or reading with text-to-speech. As with all OCR tools, the quality of the extracted text depends on the simplicity of how the original text is formatted and if there are additional semantic layouts such as text boxes.

Export options

Most scanning apps (free or premium) allow a user to open the scanned document in a different app (such as an app to annotate the scanned document) or upload and save the document. The save locations can be on the local storage of the computing device (hard drive) or in the cloud. If a user prefers to upload scanned documents to the cloud, the scanning app settings require attention in advance so that the user is signed into the desired cloud account.

---

challenge with this technique is that glare or shadows from overhead lighting can make it difficult for the camera to capture a clean image.

- Use a stand to hold the smartphone/tablet and a document holder to stabilize the print media while moving it into position within the camera's view. The stand and print media can be positioned vertically or horizontally on a table depending on the user's preference. This option is beneficial when needing to manage multiple pages or to support a user with motor coordination challenges that make it difficult to stabilize the device and capture a clear image. Commercially-available and 3D printed stands are available from a number of vendors and 3D printing file repositories.

As mentioned earlier in the chapter, a camera-mounted pair of eyeglasses can also be connected to a device as part of a scan and read system. In this scenario, the user points to text and the camera integrates computer vision and artificial intelligence to recognize it. The audio then plays through an earpiece or from the connected device. This wearable alternative can keep a user's hands free, although often at the expense of wearing the unfashionable device. This technology also remains extremely expensive, can be unreliable,

Figure 2.14:
Scan and Read Setups with a Smartphone or Tablet

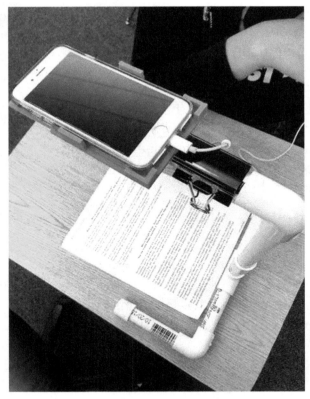

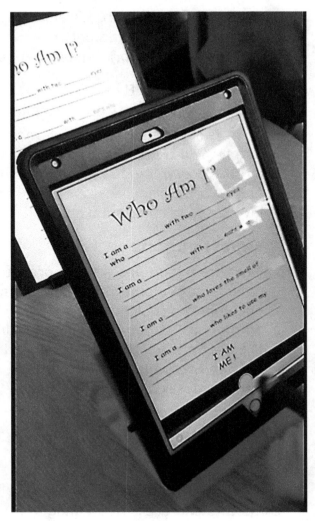

Top: *A 3D-printed frame holds a smartphone that is mounted on a stand made from PVC pipe. A page of text is placed on the table and is centered under the frame.*
Bottom: *A mobile touchscreen tablet propped on a low 3D-printed stand that does not block the camera. A page of text is propped on a document holder that is slanted at the same angle as the tablet and placed about one foot behind the device.*
Right: *A mobile touchscreen tablet secured in a commercially available stand. A reading stand is positioned about a foot behind the tablet and holds a packet of text.*

and most importantly, undesirable for many low vision or nonvisual readers.

Artificial intelligence

Newer developments in artificial intelligence integrate the four components of a scan and read system into one tool. Usually in the form of an app, a tool that integrates scanning, OCR, TTS, and synthesized speech can be very powerful. With computer vision and artificial intelligence, a user can simply point the camera at a sample of text or a simple image and get immediate information about the print media. No human interaction is needed to access this information. Although the privacy and use of one's data can be dubious when employing artificial intelligence (Is the data saved or shared? How will the data be used again?), it does allow the blind or visually-impaired individual more independent access to print media. The quality of the auditory information can vary depending on the tool, but artificial intelligence will continue to improve as technology becomes increasingly sophisticated.

Talking Devices and Apps

A variety of devices and apps with audio output are available to assist blind and low vision individuals with tasks that typically rely on visual indicators. These are colloquially referred to as "talking" devices or apps, and provide auditory indicators for information that are usually displayed visually. This category of tools can be very helpful in science labs where equipment is traditionally designed with visual indicators and print displays. Talking measuring devices

(such as scales and thermometers) and home security and entertainment systems are some common examples that can facilitate a person's access in learning, working, and home environments. Some talking devices only convey information auditorily while other talking devices use speech input as well as auditory output for a fully audio experience. Some talking devices are commercially available—others can be adapted with accessible indicators using an electronic prototyping platform (such as Arduino®) that enables users to combine accessible hardware and software to make interactive objects.

With more prevalent use of smartphones and tablets, talking devices are increasingly available as talking apps. These include talking dictionaries, talking calculators, and talking tactile graphics. The usability of talking apps is 100 percent dependent on whether the app was designed with accessibility for the nonvisual user in mind; if not, the app might convey auditory information but remain wholly inoperable by a blind individual. Some tactile tools (such as the ones described earlier in the chapter) are also available as a talking app, including rulers, calipers, protractors, compasses, and even levelers. Individuals are encouraged to scope the market for new tools that are constantly developing, and to consider teaching students how to prototype their own tools with accessible indicators.

More information about talking tools will be presented in **Chapter 3, Technologies for Accessing Digital Text.**

Multisensory Access

Many multisensory tools are available to assist blind and low vision individuals with accessing printed information. Individuals who wish to access text visually can manipulate their visual access on-screen (change font size, style, color; use text masking or highlighting) or use audio supported reading tools. A reader might also choose to reproduce the information in hard-copy braille; read on a refreshable braille display; or read with text-to-speech or a screen reader. Once tools are organized by their access method, they can be further subdivided according to the task to be completed, whether short or long.

> **Content Vocabulary**
> **Text-to-Speech (TTS)**
>
> **Text-to-Speech** is software that reads text using a synthesized voice applied within a screenreader; as part of an app for reading, document management, or scanning; or as a standalone feature that works across a variety of programs. This can be through the use of a computer screen reader or an application on a smartphone.

Although most of the tools can be categorized by the primary sense used to access information, continued technology developments cross those lines in several ways. When information is converted from print to accessible digital formats, access options become significantly more flexible and customizable. Workflows that support these conversions can better support multi-sensory access that empowers a blind or low vision individual to exercise personal choice in how to access information. Choice leads to empowerment and increased proficiency in accessing information, which benefits the individual's education, employment, and personal life.

REFERENCES

AccessIT: The National Center on Accessible Information Technology in Education. (n.d.). What is audio description? http://www.washington.edu/accessit/articles?1079

Allan, J., Kirkpatrick, A., & Henry, S. L. (Eds.). (2016). Accessibility Requirements for People with Low Vision. Retrieved August 27, 2017, from https://w3c.github.io/low-vision-a11y-tf/requirements.html

Castellano, C. (2004). Using Readers. Future Reflections, *23(3).*

Castellano, C. (2016). Using Readers—The Human Variety. Future Reflections, *35(1).*

Cheadle, B. & Elliott, P. (1995). Of Readers, Drivers, and Responsibility, The Braille Monitor, *38(3).*

Cooper, F. S. (1950). Research on reading machines for the blind. In P. A. Zahl (Ed.), Blindness; modern approaches to the unseen environment (pp. 512–543). Oxford, England: Princeton University Press.

Corn, A. L., & Erin, J. N. (Eds.). (2010). Foundations of low vision: Clinical and functional perspectives, second edition (2nd ed.). New York: AFB Press.

Dister, R & Greer, R. (2004) Basic Optics and Low Vision Devices. In A. H. Lueck (Ed.) Functional Vision: A Practitioner's Guide to Evaluation and Intervention (pp. 61–88) New York, AFB Press.

Edman, Polly. (1992). Tactile Graphics. New York, AFB Press.

Evans, C. (1997) Changing Channels. http://www.tsbvi.edu/Education /audioassisted.htm

Evans, C. Audio-Assisted Reading Access for Students with Print Disabilities. http:// www.rit.edu/~easi/itd/itdv5n12/article5 .htm. ITD Journal.

Flom, R. (2004) Visual Functions as Components of Functional Vision. In A. H. Lueck (Ed.) Functional Vision: A Practitioner's Guide to Evaluation and Intervention (pp. 25–60) New York, AFB Press.

Gissoni, F. (2005). Instructions for the Cubarithm Slate. Lexington, KY: American Printing House for the Blind, Fred's Head Companion, http://fredsheadcompanion .blogspot.com/2005/11/instructions-for -cubarithm-slate.html.

Greer, R. (2004). Evaluation Methods and Functional Implications: Children and Adults with Visual Impairments. In A. H. Lueck (Ed.) Functional Vision: A Practitioner's Guide to Evaluation and Intervention (pp. 177–256) New York, AFB Press.

Hollbrook, M. C., D'Andreea, F. M., Wormsley, D. P. (2017) Literacy Skills. In C. Hollbrook, T. McCarthy, & C. Kannei-Hannan (Eds.), Foundations of education: History and Theory of Teaching Children and Youths with Visual Impairments (pp. 420–421). New York, AFB Press.

Jose, R.T. (1983) Treatment Options. In R.T. Jose (Ed.), Understanding Low Vision (pp. 211–250). New York, AFB Press.

Leibs, A. (1999). How to Find and Manage Readers. A Field Guide for the Sight-Impaired Reader, Westport, Greenwood Press.

Morash, V.S., Connell Pensky, A., Tseng, S.T.W., & Miele, J. (2014). Effects of using multiple hands and fingers on haptic performance in individuals who are blind. Perception, 43, 569–588.

Morash, V. S., Siu, Y. T., Miele, J. A., Hasty, L., & Landau, S. (2015). Guiding novice web workers in making image descriptions using templates. ACM Transactions on Accessible Computing (TACCESS), 7(4), 12.

Osterhaus, S. A. (2008). Teaching Math to Visually Impaired Students. Texas School for the Blind and Visually Impaired. www .tsbvi.edu/math.

Quillman, R.D. & Goodrich, G. (2004). Interventions for Adults with Visual Impairments. In A.H. Lueck (Ed.), Functional Vision: A Practitioner's Guide to Evaluation and Intervention. (pp. 423–475). New York, AFB Press.

Rubin, G. S., Feely, M., Perera, S., Ekstrom, K., & Williamson, E. (2006). The effect of font and line width on reading speed in people with mild to moderate vision loss. Ophthalmic & Physiological Optics, 26(6), 545–554. doi:10.1111/ j.1475-1313.2006.00409.x

Simons, B. & Lapolice, D. (2000) Working Effectively with a Low Vision Clinic. In F.M. D'Andrea & C. Farrenkopf (Eds.) Looking to

Learn: promoting literacy for students with low vision *(pp. 84–116). New York, AFB Press.*

Watson, G. & Berg. R. (1983) New Training Techniques. *In R.T. Jose (Ed.),* Understanding Low Vision *(pp. 317–362). New York, AFB Press.*

Web Accessibility for All. (n.d.[a]). How to Create Descriptive Text for Graphs, Charts & other Diagrams. Madison: Center on Education and Work, University of Wisconsin-Madison. www.cew.wisc.edu /accessibility/tutorials/descriptionTutorial .htm.

Web Accessibility for All. (n.d. [b]). Tutorial for creating accessible PowerPoint presentations. Madison: Center on Education and Work, University of Wisconsin-Madison. www.cew.wisc.edu/accessibility/tutorials /pptmain.htm.

Whittle, J. (1995). On How to Use Readers More Effectively. *The Braille Monitor,* 38(12).

Wilkinson, M. (2000) Low Vision Devices: An Overview. *In F.M. D'Andrea & C. Farren-kopf (Eds.)* Looking to Learn: promoting literacy for students with low vision *(pp. 117–136). New York, AFB Press.*

Wilkinson, M.E. (2010). Clinical Low Vision Services. *In* Foundations of low vision: Clinical and functional perspectives, second edition *(2nd ed., pp. 238–283). New York, NY: AFB Press.*

Zimmermann, G. J., Zebehazy, K. T., & Moon, M. L. (2010). Optics and low visions devices. *In* Foundations of low vision: Clinical and functional perspectives, second edition *(2nd ed., pp. 192–237). New York, NY: AFB Press.*

CHAPTER 3
Technologies for Accessing Digital Text

In the twenty-first century, accessing digital text is embedded in many aspects of daily life. Most people encounter digital text with or without intention for a variety of purposes, including casual or informal study of content on a smartphone, tablet, or computer; daily living tasks such as making decisions using transportation timetables or restaurant menus; casual or informal research on the Internet; casual or formal communications such as text messaging or email; or incidental or dedicated study of posted information such as in museums or other community spaces. Whether it is on social media platforms or workplace stations, digital text is everywhere. Near distance reading might include digital texts such as email, documents, electronic handouts, e-books, webpages, or social media messages. In contrast, digital text presented at a distance might be presented using a variety of display systems such as a projector, interactive whiteboards or television-like monitors, or a variety of electronic displays in stores, fast-food outlets, public buildings, and public transportation.

Sidebar 3.1

UBIQUITY OF DIGITAL TEXT

Contributed by: Lainey Feingold, Disability rights lawyer and author

Digital text is everywhere we look and becoming more prevalent as technology and digital media permeate many of our daily tasks. These interactions can be quite personal, ranging from low to high priority needs. With advocacy to increase awareness in ensuring these platforms are accessible for individuals who are visually impaired, these text formats can ensure the inclusion and independence of everyone in a community.

As you go through your day, think of all the places where a consumer, citizen, patient, youth, or adult, might rely on digital text. Here are some things you might encounter:

- **Talking ATMs**: In 1999, the very first Talking ATM was installed in the United States. That ATM ensured that blind people could bank independently by providing audio output through a private

(Continued)

headphone jack, ATM screens that could be navigated with tactile keys, and a confidential way for a blind person to enter information. Since that first installation, thousands of Talking ATMs have been installed across the country and, increasingly, around the world. Look for a headphone jack next time you visit an ATM. If the ATM has been properly designed and maintained, plugging in a standard headphone should enable a visually impaired user to perform all transactions.

- **Point of Sale (POS) devices**: We take them for granted, but checkout devices often offer a lot of information that may not be available to a blind person. Can a blind person independently enter his or her PIN, or are the number keys on a flat surface? What about color contrast of screen text for people with low vision? Or screen information about available transactions, confidential medical information, or purchased items? Most POS devices in the United States do not have audible output; blind consumers must seek assistance from staff to know what is on the screen, and what options are available.

- **Talking prescription containers**: When blind people receive standard prescription containers with standard print labels, they are deprived of critical safety and health information. There are several solutions on the market, some involving synthesized speech, others providing a simple human recording. All major pharmacies now offer some form of talking label.

- **Web-based health insurance and financial information**: Checking bank balances and finding doctors are just two of the many things that more and more people do online. Health and financial information are examples of text that needs to be read privately. That is one of the reasons that accessibility is so important. Adhering to international standards and involving disabled people in Web and mobile development are two ways to ensure that Web content is usable by everyone, including people with visual impairments.

- **Kiosks:** Kiosks are becoming more ubiquitous in the built-environment, and are another technology where accessible text matters. Restaurants are replacing servers with tablet computers for ordering and payment—mini-kiosks popping up everywhere. Medical facilities replace receptionists with kiosks for registering—sometimes patients must even provide confidential medical information via kiosks. New York City installs kiosks with links to city services, including 9-1-1 emergency services. Blind advocates and people with visual impairments must remain vigilant to ensure that these technologies offer accessibility to all users.

- **Pedestrian Crossing Signals**: The simple words "Walk / Don't Walk" or the pictograph of a red hand or walking character both provide critical information about pedestrian safety. Is it time to cross the street? How much time is left? The digital text or digital images on a crossing signal must be available to people who cannot see. Accessible pedestrian signals offer that information in both audible and tactile ways.

- **Voting**: Digital text appears in two environments that impact the ability of visually impaired people to exercise their constitutional right to vote independently: voting machines and websites containing voting information. Voting machines must be designed with accessibility in mind for blind people to be able to vote. This means audible output that is private and confidential, and a secure input mechanism that allows confidential voting. Before a voter goes to the polls, digital text on government websites provides critical information to allow informed voting choices. Those websites must be accessible. And increasingly, absentee voting is moving online—another area where accessible digital content is important.

- **Advocacy matters.** The advocacy of disabled people, their organizations, and their lawyers has been critical to introducing and maintaining accessible text in these environments and others. Access to information is a civil right, and many laws in both the United States and around the world protect those rights. But without advocacy, laws often don't get enforced, or enforcement is spotty. The blind community relies on many different advocacy strategies to keep digital text accessible. The most common advocacy? Individuals asking for what they need and staying focused until those needs are met. Other times, disability-based organizations advocate for the access blind people need.

Calling a lawyer is a last resort, but has proven very effective in protecting and advancing the civil rights of people with visual impairments. Lawsuits and administrative complaints are important strategies that need to be preserved. Structured Negotiation is another strategy that lawyers for blind people have used to advance access to text-based information. Structured Negotiation is a problem-solving approach to legal issues that avoids lawsuits, focusing instead on solutions and building relationships. *Structured Negotiation, A Winning Alternative to Lawsuits* (Feingold, 2016) is a book that tells many stories of blind community advocacy for access to technology and information.

In addition to accessing media that contain digital text, the basic use and navigation of many devices also requires access to the text labels within programs and menus, and for overall operation and maintenance of the device. This chapter will provide an overview of how individuals with visual impairments might encounter all of these forms of digital text and the technologies that can be employed to read using visual, tactile, or auditory sensory channels. It is important to keep in mind that most individuals will use a combination of senses and tools for reading; the mode of access will depend on the nature of the task and content to be read (See Chapter 4 in Foundations of Education, Holbrook et. al, 2017 for more information on the Learning Media Assessment). The following section discusses how the availability of digital text can present both advantages and disadvantages for low vision and nonvisual accessibility.

CHARACTERISTICS OF A DIGITAL WORKFLOW

While traditional printed materials remain invaluable in certain situations, it is also inevitable that digital media have become more prevalent as computing has become ubiquitous (Alexander, 2006; Siu, 2016). This chapter integrates discussion of digital media within a larger framework of how these materials can be disseminated and accessed in a digital workflow that includes cloud computing. A digital workflow refers to an efficient electronic system for accessing, processing, sharing, and storing work.

Cloud computing is defined as ". . . a model for enabling ubiquitous, convenient, on-demand network access to a shared pool of . . . resources . . . that can be rapidly released with minimal management effort or service provider interaction" (Mell & Grance, 2011). For the purposes of this textbook, cloud computing is considered a system of saving information online that can be accessed, uploaded, or downloaded using any number of devices. This method of computing facilitates a workflow that allows for instantaneous saving and retrieval of information that syncs across devices and sources of information.

**Content Vocabulary
Digital Workflow**

Digital workflow refers to an efficient electronic system for accessing, processing, sharing, and storing work.

Advantages

For individuals who benefit from using multiple senses to read (for example, reading visually or tactilely while listening to text read aloud, or switching access modes at will), digital media can provide great flexibility, portability, and efficiency in multimodal access to information. Flexible use of tools is important to allow an individual to work across different devices, such as beginning a document on a school or office computer, continuing work while commuting by using a smartphone or laptop, and then completing the document on a home computer. Tools

Sidebar 3.2

CLOUD COMPUTING PLATFORMS

Cloud computing platforms are online file repositories that allow users to upload, save, retrieve, and share data files on a network of remote servers

The virtual hard drive is an online (cloud) storage location that acts as a server and saves data files that would otherwise be saved on a physical hard drive. When saving information to the cloud, the data is retrievable using any device that connects to the Internet and the cloud computing platform. This allows for easy file transfer between devices and individuals without a portable hard drive or flash drive or having to meet face-to-face to hand off physical files. Given a reliable Internet connection, cloud computing can effectively facilitate working on-the-go and between devices. Because the files are stored online, retrieval on any device allows a user to access the most current version of a file as long as the previous version was saved online. This process of saving online and allowing any number of devices to access the most current version is referred to as "syncing" across devices. Cloud computing can alleviate challenges in organizing or keeping track of physical hard drives and paper filing systems, allows information to be searched, and allows collaborators to work from the same document at the same time or otherwise access updated versions of files as they are saved to the cloud. This last feature can be particularly useful for group work with collaborating team members who do not share a physical location, such as in the case of itinerant teachers of the visually impaired or tech trainers who have only sporadic face-to-face meetings with service-delivery teams.

In collaboration with students, cloud computing allows teachers to save documents online for students to retrieve, complete, and then submit to a shared online location for the teacher to grade. This process, otherwise known as a digital workflow, can help students manage, organize, and complete their work using the access technology of their choice while working directly with the classroom teacher. The work can also be accessed as soon as it is saved in the cloud. In a classroom context, if the digital materials are saved in an accessible format, a classroom teacher can work more directly with the blind or low vision student with decreasing intervention from an alternate media specialist (such as a braille transcriber) or TVI. If some remediation of

(Continued)

the instructional material is necessary to address braille translation, formatting for a RBD, or rendering the digital text into a computer-readable format, the alternate media specialist can readily access the material as soon as it is saved online, and then post it for the student to retrieve and access with the access technology of his or her choice. This type of workflow can significantly increase the amount of the TVI's direct service time because services can be more focused on instruction in the Expanded Core Curriculum rather than preparation and delivery of instructional materials. The digital workflow also engages students to be in charge of their own accessibility; they can gain more timely and independent access to instructional materials using the access technology of their choice as soon as they are saved to the cloud.

In a postsecondary or employment context, saving work in the cloud not only allows a blind or low vision individual immediate and independent access to digital materials, but also facilitates collaboration with colleagues who do not need to know braille. Assuming professors or co-workers are saving files in an accessible format, a low vision or blind student or employee can maintain his or her own flexibility to access materials using visual, auditory, and/or tactile strategies.

Several options exist that range from free (usually with limited storage) to subscription or fee-for-service products. Considerations when choosing a cloud computing platform include the following:

- **User experiences with:**
  - Assistive technology such as screen readers for auditory or tactile access, or a color contrast scheme for visual access
  - Menu options that match needed features for work
  - Ease of file saving, organization, and retrieval from personal computing devices via word processing programs, Internet browsers, or applications
  - Personal preferences in interface
- **Fit with school's or workplace's existing infrastructure; considerations for cloud computing platforms that are already in use by collaborators. Particularly with students, it is easier to adapt to the same cloud-computing platform as the classroom teachers' when possible to leverage features for folder and file sharing with minimal effort required from teachers.**

- Cost. Most cloud platforms provide a limited amount of space for saving and storing files for free. Platforms vary widely across what is provided before incurring a cost. Costs are usually on a monthly or yearly subscription basis.

- Security and privacy of data stored in the cloud. For individuals working with sensitive information, it is important to read the "fine print" when signing up for an account with a cloud-computing platform. Ownership and confidentiality of information stored online can vary and be held accountable in certain legal situations.

Here are examples of some of the more popular cloud-computing platforms at the time of publication:

- **Dropbox**
- **Google Drive**
- **Box**
- **Microsoft OneDrive**
- **Apple iCloud**

can be selected based on the reader's preference given the task, reading environment, and purpose. Digital media also allow an individual to access information in different formats including visual, auditory, and tactile. The individual has the flexibility to choose his or her preferred method of sensory access depending on the task and his or her personal comfort at that moment. Particularly for individuals who are blind or have low vision, digital media empowers readers to utilize their tool of choice at any given point in time and have maximum independence and flexibility to change their method of access in an instant. For example, a blind individual might use auditory access to read text messages and Web articles, but then switch to a more private refreshable braille display (RBD) in order to read work memos and email. In summary, availability of accessible digital content allows any reader to work across a multitude of devices and utilize any number of technology features for multisensory access.

Disadvantages

Successful implementation of such a system is completely dependent on the infrastructure established to support cloud computing as well as the user's opportunities for training on how to use these tools. To start, end users must have the appropriate technology needed to access digital content, including devices to support the reading task, and Internet connectivity to exchange information in a digital workflow or an equivalent system for information exchange. They must also have a good working knowledge of how to efficiently select, use, and switch among these tools as needed. However, having the appropriate technology and training in its use does not necessarily ensure information accessibility. The content itself must also be formatted for accessibility and multimodal access. As of 2017, the Web Content Accessibility Guidelines (WCAG) state that accessible online content must meet the following four principles **POUR** (Allan, Kirkpatrick & Henry, 2016). For the purposes of our discussion in this chapter, consider how these principles could change to apply to a variety of digital media.

- **Perceivable**. An individual must be able to use their preferred sensory channel to access the information as mediated through any number of digital platforms and tools. In other words, the information must be accessible using vision, tactile, or auditory senses. For example, an image file such as an inaccessible PDF (a picture of text versus an accessible PDF with computer-readable text) or a screenshot of text (an image file) would not be perceivable by someone using auditory access such as a screen reader or tactile access such as an RBD. It would only be readable using visual means. A website with shaded text on a dark background would also not be perceivable by someone with low vision because this tonal combination provides very low contrast.

- **Operable**. An individual must also be able to operate the controls using his or her preferred tool for visual, auditory, or tactile access. One quick way to check a tool's operability is by computing without using a mouse: exploring all elements such as menus, buttons, lists, and form fields using only keyboard commands. If any elements can be accessed only with a mouse, the tool is not fully operable. The content itself must also be formatted so that the user can access an overview of the content with similar ease visually, auditorially, or tactilely. For example, a lengthy article is typically formatted with visual headers and subheaders to organize the content and to allow a reader to skim an overview of topics before navigating to a selected passage. In the same way, a body of text must be formatted to allow for equitable navigation of these headings when using auditory or tactile access. Predictable text formatting and consistent menu placement within programs also helps low vision users quickly find information visually.

- **Understandable**. An individual must be able to understand the content and how the information is laid out. For example, menus, sidebars, and Web content should follow a logical reading order regardless of the user's access modality. Hyperlinks on a website should also be self-described so that it is clear what action will be taken when the link is clicked or activated.

SELF-DESCRIBED VERSUS NON-SELF-DESCRIBED HYPERLINKS

When screen reader users navigate content that contains hyperlinks (links to a website or other content), the screen reader might read the link differently depending on how it is formatted. This can have a significant impact on the user experience in accessing information using auditory or tactile sensory channels. Efficient access and navigation of content is critical for individuals with visual impairments due to the inability to visually survey a large body of information and gain an overview of the content without listening to or reading (via braille) every word. Think of how lengthy some Web addresses can be, with some URLs containing a seemingly random string of letters and numbers. Now, think of how cumbersome it might be to have to listen to every letter, number, and symbol read aloud by a screen reader! Self-described links help address that usability problem by having the screen reader read the text that describes what the link is rather than the characters that comprise the Web address. When clicked, the text will still act as a hyperlink, and will send the user to the appropriate webpage. However, the auditory or tactile sensory access channels are no longer bombarded by a long string of nonsensical verbiage. In order for hyperlinks to appear as sensible text, the text as it should appear must be specified, and then the full Web address inserted in a different field. It is recommended practice to also describe what the user should expect when clicking the link (https://webaim.org/techniques/hypertext/#screen_readers).

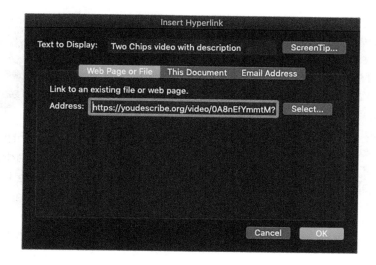

(Continued)

ACCESS TECHNOLOGY FOR BLIND AND LOW VISION ACCESSIBILITY

Sidebar 3.3 (Continued)

For example, rather than describing the link as "Click here," it is better to describe the link as "Play the video." Usually this is done by entering the text that should be displayed, highlighting it, then right-clicking or activating the options menu, then selecting "Insert hyperlink." A pop-up box usually appears with several text boxes for the text to be displayed and the URL.

Here are some examples of self-described versus non-self-described hyperlinks. Try reading each example out loud to experience the difference in effort and time needed to listen to each item in full.

- Self-described: Check out the video "My Job Outside of YouTube:" Non self-described: https://youtu.be/pKt54lA0yys

- Self-described: Plan Toys Braille Alphabet: Non self-described: https://www.amazon.com/Plan-Toys-Braille-Alphabet-A-Z/dp/B00I3VWSIA/ref=sr_1_7?ie=UTF8&qid=1500446021&sr=8-7&

- Self-described: Handout on iOS Overview: Non self-described: https://docs.google.com/presentation/d/1EX4davgVE3zvRRNvVVhJdSgm-3nEJmE6sSfcwL9wqaY/edit?usp=sharing

- **Robust**. An individual must be able to access the content using any number of devices, including mainstream and assistive tools. In this context, *robust* refers to the dependability of the content to display on different devices, platforms, Web browsers, and software versions. This guideline recognizes the flexible use of digital media and strives to ensure that individuals can access information across different devices and platforms depending on their needs. For example, an article posted online should be equally readable on a tablet or laptop computer using any Web browser with any mainstream or assistive technology device.

> **Content Vocabulary**
> **Web Content Accessibility Guidelines (WCAG)**
>
> The **Web Content Accessibility Guidelines** (WCAG) are standards developed by the World Wide Web Consortium to guide the creation of accessible online content.

As technology continues to evolve, the ways in which readers access digital content have become increasingly varied and flexible. No longer are individuals with visual impairments confined to costly and specialized "assistive" technologies. Many mainstream devices have increasingly well-integrated features to support tactile, auditory, or enhanced visual access. Interaction with digital content is now possible with combinations of mainstream and specialized technologies depending on user preference.

Both computing and accessing digital information have become more fluid as technology has become more portable: for example, mobile handheld devices such as smartphones, which have long surpassed their original intended function of making phone calls. Many smartphones and tablets rival the average computer in computing power, similar to how laptop and desktop computers are differentiated more by logistics rather than capability. Some school and work environments might even provide students and employees with laptops or tablets instead of desktops. Because of the myriad combination of devices, peripheral devices, and related software applications available on each platform, discussions throughout the book will adopt a device-agnostic approach, with specific brands named only as examples.

When considering different devices (hardware) and program applications (apps or software), compatibility with a student's personal computing device is of utmost importance. More specifically, compatibility is dependent on the operating system (OS) of a computing device. At the time of this writing, there are generally four different types of operating systems (OS):

- **Apple**
- **Windows**
- **Android**
- **Browser-based**
- **(Another operating system, Linux, is not typically used with K-12 students)**

In order to identify an appropriate array of devices and apps for consideration, a service provider and end user must understand how each OS differs and how to identify the OS of any type of personal computing device. Without this foundational knowledge, it will be impossible to introduce, evaluate, and recommend the appropriate tools to a student.

The chapter will present specific tools and accessibility features available through each mode of sensory access regardless of the computing device the tool is used in conjunction with, rather than discussing specific brands of hardware or software. By providing an overview of reading tools organized by features and settings, an individual can use these terms as search terms when researching accessibility solutions and selecting tools for a task. For specific tutorials on transitioning to a digital workflow, review the many posts that result from searching "Digital Transitions" on Perkins's *Paths to Technology* website at https://www.perkinselearning.org /technology.

Technologies for Visual Access to Digital Text

- **Visual Settings**
- **Screen Magnification**
- **Text-to-Speech (TTS)**

Readers who want to visually read digital text have a variety of tools from which to choose. Before discussing the various categories of tools, the following considerations are presented for the reader to keep in mind when contrasting different options.

- **Screen size and resolution for displaying information.** Recall from **Chapter 2** that screen size depends on how the needed level of magnification impacts the resulting visual field. Considerations for screen size and resolution in this chapter differ slightly because individuals are ideally more engaged in a digital workflow and reading digital text on the screen of a computing device rather than from the monitor of a video magnifier. Personal preferences for scrolling and panning across text versus re-sizing text to fit on a screen are more easily managed via software and the user's choice of a reading app or screen magnification tool. Higher resolution is a desired specification to maintain clarity as onscreen content is magnified. Choosing the screen size of a personal computing device becomes more of a preference and logistical consideration related to the size of the computing device that the individual is willing (and able) to carry. Remember that bigger is not always better. (Recall **Chapter 2 Tech**

Tip: 2.1 *Bigger is Not Always Better*)

- **Physical set up and positioning of the display.** Depending on each individual's ergonomic needs, the display screen of a personal computing device might be attached to a keyboard (such as with a mobile tablet in a case with an embedded keyboard, or a laptop) or completely detached and easily re-positioned separately from a keyboard (such as with a desktop computer or mobile tablet in a case with detached keyboard). When contrasting which setup might work best, there are two factors to consider:

- What is the working distance of the user? Readers who prefer a closer working distance can benefit from a detached keyboard that allows a display screen to be positioned on a stand. The display screen could be a computer monitor or tablet that is raised and positioned for different viewing angles. This consideration is particularly important when reading on a tablet—many tablet cases with an attached keyboard require placement directly on a table, which forces a reader to lean down towards the smaller screen size with a slouched back and craned neck. Alternatively, if a display screen with attached keyboard is elevated to accommodate a more optimal viewing position, it places the keyboard in an equally terrible ergonomic position that forces acute arm, elbow, and wrist angles. For students who do not need a close viewing distance because they can enlarge the material onscreen sufficiently, a display screen can be positioned far enough away to accommodate healthier ergonomics when using an attached keyboard. The only consideration might be to ensure the display screen has an adjustable viewing angle to accommodate height differences between a user and tabletop.

- What tasks and content will the user engage with on the display? When accessing digital content visually on a screen, whether or not a keyboard is attached to the screen can be irrelevant if the user does not need to use the keyboard while viewing the content. If this is the case more often than not, such as using a display to watch videos, for screen sharing, or as part of a video magnification system, then a case that allows the screen to be rotated or flipped to tuck an attached keyboard away can be very useful. When used purely as a viewing device rather than a tool for authoring (which requires use of the keyboard while viewing materials), it is less important if the display can be separated from the keyboard because the two components will not be used together.

▫ **Accessibility of user interfaces and content navigation.** Some program applications (apps) utilize on-screen playback controls such as play, stop, rewind, and fast-forward. If the reader has sufficient vision to operate these controls, then no further consideration is needed. However, if the reader does not have sufficient vision to operate these media controls, the individual must instead choose tools with interfaces that are accessible with a screen reader via keyboard commands and auditory or tactile access. Consider

if the student needs visual, and/or auditory, and/or tactile access to the content and device and apps. When digital media designers follow the **POUR principles** for universal design of user interfaces and all digital content, these considerations become a null point—universal design ensures that anyone can fully engage with information regardless of need and preference.

▫ **Extent of enhancements needed for varied sensory access.** Some computing devices and apps have built-in features for adjusting visual and auditory settings that adequately meet the needs of some low vision readers. These features include built-in adjustments for font style, point size, screen zoom, and text-to-speech. However, if a low vision reader requires further visual or auditory enhancements, then specialized or dedicated tools might be required as add-on features. For example, a standard touchscreen tablet might allow limited zooming to magnify screen content, but the user might still need even more. In that case, an additional magnification app or peripheral camera lens set up for use as a video magnifier would be required. When additional apps or tools are needed, a technology assessment can help determine which tools are compatible with the reader's primary device.

▫ **Flexibility and robustness to switch between modes of sensory access.** This consideration is particularly important for individuals who benefit from multimodal (using multiple senses) access to information. For a low vision reader, vision might be the most efficient way to read short passages or navigate between programs or menus. However, this same reader might switch to auditory reading for longer passages or for reading for pleasure. This low vision reader might also be developing tactile skills for reading in braille and using one sense for **reading to learn,** while learning how to use a different sense to read for pleasure. Readers might also need to annotate text while reading, or bookmark progress for when they switch to another tool in another location. The optimal technology provides these options in as few devices or apps as possible so the reader does not have to learn to use or carry multiple devices.

Visual Settings

When exploring potential technology for visual access, one of the first features to investigate is the ability to adjust the visual settings available for the hardware device and any of the software or apps. Most desktop and mobile computers, software programs, apps, or browser extensions offer a variety of options to adjust visual settings. This section will discuss the following commonly used settings: Operating System Display Properties, Cursor Display Settings, Font and Point Size, Contrast, Text Highlighting and Masking, and Page Zoom.

Adjusting all the visual setting and display properties of devices and software discussed below while employing an ergonomically friendly display screen might be sufficient for some low vision reading tasks. If these adjustments do not allow the reader to comfortably and

efficiently access the digital information regardless of the display options, exploration of other types of access technology will need to be considered. Auditory options are strongly recommended for longer periods of sustained reading if visual fatigue is a factor, or as an intermediary support if the reader is transitioning from visual to tactile reading skills. Recall that a learning media assessment will best determine what tools and strategies are most appropriate for various tasks depending on each individual's strengths and preferences.

The majority of the settings discussed below are truly device-agnostic; that is, most of these features are not limited to one particular type of computer. Variations of most settings can be found across different operating systems, mobile devices, and software applications intended for either mainstream and specialized technologies. More advanced settings might be available by purchasing a specialized program. Differences between built-in and add-on features often vary by the sophistication of customization, which in most cases will affect cost.

Operating System Display Properties. Most devices have display settings allowing the user to adjust the font and point size of menu items, text labels, buttons, icons, and dialog boxes. Each element can be adjusted individually.

Cursor Display Settings. For people with low vision, it can be frustrating to locate the insertion cursor or mouse pointer (also known as the display cursor) on the screen. For these users, it is helpful to either enlarge or enhance them. While some word processing apps allow the user to increase the width of the insertion cursor while working in the app, cursor customizations made to a device's operating systems will apply to all apps. Most devices have some built-in options for cursor adjustment; however usability depends on how much adjustment the individual actually needs. Also, most operating systems will allow the user to select a larger pointer if desired, but for some users, this option is not always helpful. While larger pointers can be easier to see, they can also make it more difficult to click a target precisely. Users might also want to change the pointer color, add a locator such as a circle that surrounds the pointer on the screen, or use a keyboard command to activate pointer movement.

Dedicated cursor- or pointer-enhancing software provides two desirable features for low vision users: a selection of larger cursors or pointers of different shapes, and the option to select a cursor color that provides optimal contrast against the background. Optional cursor modifications include flashing or blinking, color changes or movement within the pointer (for example, a clock's hands may move), pointer trails displayed when the pointer is moved, and concentric circles targeting the pointer when a keyboard command is used (for example, pressing the control key). When installed, these features are available as adjustments to the computer's operating system so that the changes apply to all programs. Other

cursor-enhancing software can be purchased or found as freeware.

Tech Tip

For more information, see Paths to Technology post "Large Mouse Pointer for Low Vision."

https://www.perkinselearning.org/technology/blog/large-mouse-pointer-low-vision

Font Styles and Point Size. Font styles and point sizes are commonly adjusted in a device or program's display properties. While some users may prefer very large type sizes, greatly increasing text size will result in visual clutter if words and lines begin to overlap. This is particularly apparent in some smartphones and tablets. If a reader

Figure 3.1
Differences Among Sans Serif Fonts

Tom was on his way to see Jill.
She came to the door.
(Arial)

Tom was on his way to see Jill.
She came to the door.
(APHont)

Tom was on his way to see Jill.
She came to the door.
(Tahoma)

Tom was on his way to see Jill.
She came to the door.
(Verdana)

All fonts are displayed in the same point size in this figure. Note how different font styles can appear larger or smaller, with different word or character spacing.

requires a point size that results in overlap, he or she can maintain the smaller point size setting but use screen magnification software instead (see section below on screen magnifiers) to make the entire visual presentation larger. Some individuals might benefit from larger point sizes because the text appears less crowded on the screen. The use of sans serif fonts (discussed in **Chapter 2**) on hard copy large print is also appropriate for digital text and can help reduce visual clutter. Always involve the individual in determining preferred font styles—different fonts styles can have different character and word spacing (also known as"kerning") that will affect the appearance of the text.

Contrast. Individuals who are sensitive to bright light may prefer reverse contrast for reading (for example, a yellow font on a dark blue or black background). Contrast can also be adjusted in the display properties of some devices, but possible color or contrast themes will vary across devices and apps. When individuals need to access text in which specific colors are key in understanding the text, they can use a shortcut key command to switch between custom contrast and standard color settings.

Text Highlighting and Masking. Individuals who have difficulty visually tracking words or lines on a screen can benefit from visual markers that highlight text as it is read, or visual environments with reduced clutter. Some e-reader programs allow a reader to customize how text is highlighted on the screen as it is read aloud; for example, he or she can disable the auditory option and read the text visually as it is highlighted. Highlighting speed is adjusted by changing the auditory reading speed. On-screen text may be highlighted by sentence, line, or word. Text masking settings adjust how many lines of text are displayed on the screen at a time, settings that help reduce visual clutter and help to compensate for visual field loss that can make it difficult to recognize all parts of a page. Masking can be combined with text highlighting so that words within a visible line are highlighted while reading.

Although text highlighting accompanies most text-to-speech tools by default, text masking is seldom available as a built-in setting. Instead, masking is more often available in dedicated reading applications. Many companies offer their applications for a variety of platforms including on an operating system (such as MacBook® or PC), as a downloadable app (for Android™ or Apple mobile tablets), or as browser extensions (such as on a Chromebook or Google Chrome™). See **Text-to-Speech** below for more information.

Content Vocabulary
Audio-Supported Reading (ASR)

Audio-Supported Reading (ASR) is a strategy that allows readers to listen to the spoken version of a text while assessing the material in braille or displayed on a screen.

Page Zoom. Most operating platforms also have an option to quickly zoom in or zoom out of a page view. This feature is often controlled by the keyboard shortcut Command+ or Command- (on a MacBook) or Control+ or Control- (on a PC or Chromebooks). Page Zoom has some limitations, however. Many times, as a page is enlarged, much of the page's content may disappear from the screen since content does not resize to fit the screen as it enlarges. This limitation requires the reader to use mouse or keyboard commands to navigate all information in the screen. In cases in which a reader enlarges a page, but it becomes too large to fit on the screen, and the software app does not provide keyboard commands for navigation, it is preferable to use screen magnification software with keyboard commands for panning and scrolling instead.

Screen Magnification

Screen magnification software magnifies or enlarges *everything* that is displayed on a screen, not just those elements specified in the display properties settings. Screen magnifiers adjust how much of the screen is enlarged and viewable at any one time, a feature often called **view mode** or **zoom window.** One possible viewing option is to use the entire screen display for the magnified image, while others display the magnified image on only part of the screen. When the full-screen setting is used, the reader can adjust the panning and scrolling features to change how the magnified portion of the screen follows the cursor as the reader moves

through text. Another option is for the reader to set a magnification or zoom window that can be moved around the screen, a process similar to using a handheld magnifier. This setting enlarges only one portion of the screen at a time, allowing the reader to preview an overview of the screen content and then indicate which portion is magnified. This setting is especially useful when working with maps. For example, the user can first view the entire map, and locate gross features such as bodies of water and major land formations. Next, the user can switch to lens mode and explore smaller map features such as text labels and map symbols. While low vision readers should be introduced to the various viewing settings, they should still learn to access their preferred viewing mode by using keyboard commands to switch between different modes. The type of tasks or reading material often influences how a reader uses a screen magnifier.

It is important to remember that as the level of magnification increases, the **field of view**—the amount of the original text or image that can be seen at any one time—decreases. This decreased field of view will require users to use panning, scrolling, and organized search patterns efficiently to make the most of this tool. This characteristic can lead to confusion when first using screen magnifiers. While users can see and read the content that appears on the screen, they might remain uncertain about the magnified content's location in relationship to the unmagnified portion of the screen. A feature found in some magnifiers provides a keyboard command that switches between magnified and unmagnified views. A shaded rectangle appears on the unmagnified screen that represents the part of the text or image shown in the magnified view. This feature helps the user stay oriented to the unmagnified display while viewing the magnified image.

Tech Tip

See Paths to Technology post "Getting Started with Screen Magnification."

https://www.perkinselearning.org/technology/posts/getting-started-screen-magnification

Screen magnification tools are available in various forms and at a range of price points. Most operating systems offer a free built-in screen magnification feature (for example, Windows Magnifier, Apple Zoom). Other free or at-cost screen magnification tools are also available; lower cost options range around $100 at the time of writing. Mid-priced commercial programs ($300–400) can offer additional features (for example, improved resolution at higher magnification levels, cursor enhancements, contrast and line masking settings, and navigation options) that lower-priced or free options do not. Another feature of several mid-priced programs is audio output, which provides text-to-speech as well as menus and dialog boxes similar to those found on a screen reader. Some screen magnification programs can be

used in conjunction with a screen reader. While free or low-cost screen magnifiers may suffice for beginners, as the user's skills and needs become more sophisticated, a more full-featured magnifier can provide more robust use. It is best to trial different tools and contrast user experiences to determine the best fit for each user.

Users and service providers need to weigh desired features, cost, and compatibility against their computing platforms when deciding which tools to use. Sometimes, the initial selection of a built-in screen magnifier can determine which computing device to purchase; other times, it can be more user-friendly to choose a computing device with a preferred built-in screen magnifier rather than purchasing an additional screen magnification program that may need ongoing updates and compatibility considerations with new operating system updates. Some users may find that combining one of these free or low-cost screen magnifiers with a document camera and viewing app can adequately meet their needs. More often, the user will already have a personal computing device and need to explore the options that are compatible with that device.

It must be noted that selecting a screen magnification system should never be based only on a user's diagnosed visual impairment. Instead, the selection must be made following a comprehensive assessment that focuses primarily on which features allow the user to accomplish desired tasks.

Tech Tip

See Paths to Technology post "Screen Reader for Low Vision Students."

https://www.perkinselearning.org/technology/blog/screen-reader-low-vision-students

Choosing a screen magnifier depends on an individual's functional vision, taking into consideration how much magnification is needed as well as the user's preference of devices he or she will use with screen magnification. Tools might also be selected after comparing the usability of settings available in a built-in magnification system against the need for the more advanced settings that a specialized screen magnification program can offer. Ultimately, a user's reading tasks and personal preferences should determine which tools are chosen to achieve the optimal efficiency in carrying out the task.

Text-to-Speech (TTS)

Although text-to-speech (TTS) describes a category of tools that generate auditory output of text, it warrants a mention here because of the visual support and options available with auditory access. When paired with visual reading, TTS can help individuals with low vision or other print disabilities such as dyslexia improve reading fluency. For low vision readers who use screen magnification software to enlarge on-screen text, a smaller portion of the text can be shown at once—this requires additional time for the individual to scroll through the entire text. Being able to see only a portion of a larger text can have an adverse effect on visual reading speed for some students and affect measurement of reading abilities. However, if TTS software is used in conjunction with screen magnification software, settings can be adjusted so that the screen view follows the text as it is highlighted and spoken aloud. This multimodal approach can improve reading fluency by pacing the reading speed.

However, it is important to set the speech rate to match the reader's individual reading pace to facilitate thorough comprehension. Many individuals with low vision often re-read words and sentences because they are not certain that they identified the text correctly. Media controls can vary between TTS tools as to how easily a reader can play/pause while reading. This feature is an important consideration when contrasting TTS tools. Using TTS for ASR can eliminate inefficient reading behavior because the spoken text immediately confirms or corrects the user's visual perception.

See section **Technologies for Auditory Access to Digital Text** for more information about TTS and ASR.

Content Vocabulary
Text-to-Speech (TTS)

Text-to-speech is software that reads printed or electronic text using synthesized speech.

ACCESS TECHNOLOGY FOR BLIND AND LOW VISION ACCESSIBILITY

TECHNOLOGIES FOR TACTILE ACCESS TO DIGITAL TEXT

- **Refreshable Braille Displays for Input or Output with a Computing Device**
- **Refreshable Braille Displays with Note-Taking Capabilities**
- **Operating System Braille Notetakers**

Digital information can be accessed tactilely with a refreshable braille display (RBD). Commercially available RBDs use a mechanical system of pins that raise and lower to display different dot combinations that represent the dots of a braille cell. At the time of this publication, alternative (non-mechanical) systems remain in research environments with prototypes that are unavailable commercially. Although Unified English Braille consists of six dots, some RBDs offer eight dot configurations—the extra dots can be used for a number of different functions such as computer braille or marking the location of the computer cursor. Commercially-available RBDs display a single line of braille, ranging from 12–80 characters. The braille refreshes to match the cursor movement through text. This can impact how a user engages with digital texts; reading one line at a time can make it difficult to understand how text is laid out—spatial formatting—and can be challenging to gain an immediate overview of a document. At the time of this publication, multi-line or full-page braille displays are emerging technologies that require ongoing research and development before reaching commercial use. Navigation features are available on RBDs that allow the user to move forward and backward through text by character, word, line, paragraph, or heading.

With an RBD, braille readers can access and read digital text on demand without needing to emboss the content on hard copy braille paper or require text to be in a braille-ready file. RBDs can be an essential tool for tactile access when working in a digital workflow because these devices facilitate more immediate, independent, and mobile access to text. Recall from earlier in this chapter and **Chapter 1** the benefits and challenges of a digital workflow: success depends on the formatting of the media and proficiency of the individual to use various tools for accessing information. The reading media must be in a computer-readable format with formatting that ensures efficient navigation of all document elements such as headings, subheadings, lists, tables, and forms. Most importantly, individuals must have adequate training to use more than one sense to access information. The digital workflow is most successful in supporting multimodal access to information for readers who are multi-sensory learners. Accessible digital media empowers an individual to independently, quickly, and easily switch among various sensory access modes. The use of digital text also allows a reader to quickly conduct searches for key words to locate specific phrases or words in text. In comparison, embossed paper braille limits a reader to using only tactile reading strategies, is typically unavailable on-demand, and requires a reader to scan the entire text in order to locate something specific.

However! Despite all the advantages of accessing reading materials in the digital workflow with an RBD, recall the major disadvantage that at the time of this writing, RBDs display only one line of braille at a time with options for the number of characters that can be displayed on one line. Information regarding text layout and paragraph formatting (indenting and justification), are difficult to convey digitally when only one line at a time is visible. Readers who need to learn how to indent paragraphs, create formatted lists, set margins, and otherwise format text will benefit from using a full-page of braille rather than reading braille one line at a time. At the time of this writing, full-page RBDs remain technologies that are on the horizon—readers who need braille displayed on a full page will likely benefit from embossed hard copy (paper) braille in the meantime. For early literacy learners, it remains important to provide reading materials in hard copy (embossed) format while simultaneously introducing an RBD in order to teach students how to understand and interact with formatting information while introducing foundation skills with the RBD (for example, exploring how braille feels on a RBD). Using an RBD is valuable for braille learners because a larger quantity of print media is available electronically

Figure 3.2:
A reader's hands move quickly over a refreshable braille display

and can increase access to braille. An RBD can provide beginning braille readers with more opportunities to practice emerging braille reading skills.

Tech Tip

See Paths to Technology post "Benefits of a Refreshable Braille Display with Emerging Readers."

https://www.perkinselearning.org/technology/blog/benefits-using-braille-display-emerging-readers

At the time of this writing, there are three types of refreshable braille displays (RBDs):

- RBDs for Input or Output with a Computing Device
- RBDs with Note-Taking Capabilities
- Operating System (OS) braille notetakers

Refreshable Braille Displays for Input or Output with a Computing Device

RBDs in this category are peripheral devices that are only operational with a computer. There is no computing brain in a peripheral RBD, similar to how a peripheral QWERTY keyboard works only when plugged into a computer and can connect to any computer with the appropriate port. RBDs connect to a computing device wirelessly via Bluetooth or with a micro-USB cable, and are capable of working with a smartphone, desktop or laptop computer, or touchscreen tablet (See Diane Brauner's YouTube channel for many examples of connecting an RBD to an iPad—similar setups are possible with an iPod, making early learning experiences with this setup very affordable). Interacting with a computer using an RBD requires the computer to have screen reading software installed. A screen reader is needed to translate digital text into its equivalent braille code, and provides a software driver that pairs the computer to the RBD for rendering text in braille while speaking the content via synthesized speech. Text that is read aloud is represented in braille on the RBD. (For a more detailed discussion of screen reading software, see the following section on auditory access.)

RBDs for input or output with a computing device are available in mobile and desktop options. Mobile RBDs generally display fewer characters in one line than desktop RBDs. Cost is proportional to the size (length) of the display, ranging from approximately $900 for 12 cells to $8,000 for 80 cells at the time of writing.

Refreshable Braille Displays (RBDs) with Note-Taking Capabilities

RBDs with note-taking capabilities, sometimes referred to as "smart" RBDs, offer some functionality when disconnected from a computing device but lack a built-in operating system (OS). RBDs in this category are more robust than the previous category of peripheral RBDs; when disconnected from a computing device, an RBD with note-taking capabilities allows a user to take notes on the go, manage files, read books that have been downloaded to the device, and can offer built-in apps such as a calendar and clock. Although this category of RBDs allows a user to work when disconnected from a computing device, these devices do not have a built-in operating system and require connection to a computing device to access the internet.

Operating System (OS) braille notetakers

RBDs are also found on portable electronic notetakers that have a built-in OS (in the first edition of this book, these devices were called accessible PDAs [personal digital assistants]). Sometimes, administrators who approve funding may question the high cost of a tool that is referred to as a "note-taking device." Therefore, it is imperative that evaluators, service providers, and users explain the variety of tasks these apps accomplish, the productivity tools available on these devices, and how a braille notetaker can best fit a user's needs. It can be helpful to provide a parallel reference as a "braille computer" to help people outside the blindness field better understand the value of this category of technology. When used as a standalone device, braille notetakers are all-in-one portable computing devices that, as of September 2019, run a full version of an Android or Windows OS. As a result, braille notetakers have computing capabilities for reading and writing digital files including word processing, emailing, Internet browsing, accessing online libraries, address book, calendar, calculator, digital recorder, time keeping functions (stopwatch, count-down timer), optional GPS on some models, and even listening to music. Because braille notetakers are an all-in-one computing device, these devices can offer more seamless braille translation than a basic RBD that depends on compatibility with a computer's screen reading software and operating system. On the other hand, because braille notetakers are highly specialized devices with less available developer resources than mainstream devices, the embedded operating system can often lag behind those of mainstream computers. Remember that although a braille notetaker can function as a computer, it does not replace instruction and use of a traditional computer. Understanding how to use a traditional (desktop or laptop) computer remains important for success at work or school and can be supported by putting a braille notetaker into "display only"

mode to use as a simple RBD when connected to a mainstream computing device.

While most modern notetakers offer RBD, input options vary; models may have a six-key braille keyboard, QWERTY keyboard, or hybrid braille and QWERTY keyboard. At the time of this writing, some notetakers using an Android OS also provide a virtual (on-screen touch) keyboard in addition to a physical keyboard option. The keyboard option is a personal choice that depends on a user's preference for writing in braille as well as the tasks that need to be accomplished. For example, some individuals prefer to engage in coding (also known as programming) tasks on a traditional computer with a QWERTY keyboard and RBD. Other users who prefer to enter code on a notetaker might prefer a hybrid keyboard for braille input while still needing the functions keys that are found on a QWERTY keyboard (for example, see the QBraille XL from HIMS, Inc.). Remember that braille notetakers can function as a basic RBD when placed in display mode and connected to a mainstream computing device—this is a convenient option when engaging with information on a computer while still having options to review content in braille, with or without auditory support through a computer's screen reader. For instance, sometimes an instructor might ask the student to turn off auditory support to focus on braille instruction while working within a computer interface. This option supports computer and braille literacy, while also providing the power as needed for editing text or programming code.

As with most high stakes technology purchases, the individual who ultimately uses the device must be involved in the demo, trial, and decision-making process. The following are various features of RBDs for consideration in the evaluation and selection process.

Considerations When Choosing a Refreshable Braille Display or Electronic Braille Notetaker

- **Display size.** The size of an RBD affects its portability and cost. Larger displays are more expensive and heavier to transport. Typically, larger displays (more than 20–40 cells) are reserved for desktop use. Larger displays show more text at one time and might be preferred for extended reading because the user will need to scroll less. However, larger displays can also be more tiring and ergonomically unfriendly due to more extreme wrist angles the farther the user moves the hands move from midline. Some activities and tasks, particularly computer or website coding are easier using an 80 character RBD.

- **Refresh rate.** The rate at which the pins refresh as the user navigates through the text varies among RBD models. Advanced braille readers may prefer a faster refresh rate as slower rates can extend reading time.

- **Availability and placement of navigation buttons.** When using a single-line RBD, the user activates controls to navigate the reading media. Depending upon their place-

ment, these navigation buttons might be activated by thumb or finger. If a reader is accustomed to using a thumb or specific finger when using an RBD, he or she likely already has strong preferences in how he or she wants to navigate content. This preference should inform selection.

- **Tactile resolution.** *Resolution* refers to how the braille "feels" to the user and how readable it is. Embossed braille on paper tends to have a "softer" feel overall, but the sharpness of the dots will vary depending on the type of embosser that is used. Resolution may differ among RBDs. Some pins may feel harder or softer than others, while others may seem smaller or larger. Pins are typically made of plastic or metal, while emerging technologies merely emulate the feeling of pins through magnetic interactions or heat. User preference is the main determinant, and resolution preference can be affected by tactile sensitivity, fine motor control, and tactile fatigue related to longer reading tasks.

- **Pin noise.** Similar to how the sound of a turn signal might affect an individual's car-buying decision (Yes, really!), some readers might prefer a particular RBD because of the sounds the pins produce as they refresh. Although this may seem like a minor detail, different types of pin noise can actually be irritating for some readers, so be sure to try a demonstration unit first before purchasing one.

- **Compatibility with needed braille codes.** Some braille displays work better with specific braille codes than others. Word-based text displays works very well with Unified English Braille,, while symbolic math content that is converted into a math code such as Nemeth might sometimes display with errors. While most RBDs support multiple braille codes in contracted and uncontracted formats, if the user has a preferred braille code, it is always wise to check its compatibility with a device before purchasing it. The user should also reassess code compatibility with subsequent software updates.

- **Compatibility with cloud computing platforms.** Because of cloud computing and the collaborative Web-based workflow it affords, a potential electronic notetaker should be assessed to see how well it functions in the required environ-ments. For example, some models easily integrate with Google Drive while others may require additional steps to perform the same functions. A major drawback of some notetakers is their lack of compatibility with the formatting semantics of documents, such as an inability to recognize document headers. If a notetaker cannot recognize formatting semantics, a reader cannot preview the headings and subsections of a document, making long documents very time-consuming to read. Because of the limitations of some notetakers when working in the cloud or accessing document semantics, some users may prefer a peripheral RBD that is connected to a computing device instead.

Sidebar 3.4

SUMMARY OF BRAILLE CODES

Braille is a code (not a language) for tactile reading. Different combinations of dots can represent a letter, group of letters, or whole words. One braille cell is comprised of six dots, arranged in two columns of three dots. The dots are labeled from 1 to 6, beginning with the top left dot and moving down.

When reading braille on a refreshable braille display, the accuracy of how and if the braille is displayed depends on compatibility between devices and compatibility with how the media is formatted. Certain brands of refreshable braille displays (RBD) also may or may not be compatible with the computing device that has the word processing program. For example, if a student is using an RBD with an Apple iPad, it is best to check that the iPad is compatible with the braille display before purchasing a braille display (See Apple website for compatible refreshable braille displays). Compatibility can also depend on the braille translation software used to convert the digital text to braille and the braille code

(Continued)

that is used. Each braille code determines whether or not the media is accessible with an RBD. It is important to check potential device options against what braille codes need to be read. Several braille codes are used to represent various types of text (AFB Press http://www.afb.org/section .aspx?SectionID=164&TopicID=487&DocumentID=5845&rewrite=0):

- **Alphabetic Braille**, also known as Grade One, or uncontracted braille. One braille cell represents one letter.

- **Literary Braille**, also known as Grade Two, or contracted braille. In contracted braille, one braille cell can represent a combination of letters or a whole word. A braille cell that represents more than one letter is known as a contraction. Most published texts and public signage that are available in braille are embossed using Literary Braille.

- **Unified English Braille (UEB).** Implemented in 2016, UEB was developed to consolidate several existing braille codes into one code for English-speaking countries. This code was developed in part to more easily reflect how the English language has evolved to include unique (mostly colloquial) spellings of modern day names and slang words. UEB can be utilized to support both literary and scientific/math notation in braille.

- **Nemeth**. Designed by its inventor, Dr. Abraham Nemeth, the Nemeth braille code has been used since 1952 for encoding mathematical and scientific notation. Although UEB was developed to represent both literary and numerical text, some regions within the United States of America have not adopted UEB for math and have chosen instead to maintain Nemeth.

- **Computer Braille (ASCII)**. Computer braille is specifically used to represent computer notation including technical and logical symbols. It is similar to Alphabetic Braille in that one cell represents one letter or notation. Eight dots can also be used to represent where the cursor is underneath the text on a refreshable braille display. There are no contractions when reading computer braille.

- **Music Braille**. A system entirely different from any of the above braille codes is utilized to represent printed music. The only similarity is the use of the same 6 dots to represent a braille cell.

- **Foreign Languages**. Braille can also represent foreign languages but can vary in dot size and number (for example, Japanese braille differs in the size and number of dots in a braille cell). Contractions might or might not be used in different languages.

- **Connection methods.** Notetakers can vary in what connection methods are offered. For example, options might include: Bluetooth, USB, WiFi, or ethernet. Depending on an individual's workflow, preferences, and connectivity options, this is another notable feature when comparing options.

TECHNOLOGIES FOR AUDITORY ACCESS TO DIGITAL TEXT

- **Audio-Supported Reading (ASR)**
- **Text-to-Speech (TTS)**
- **Screen Readers**

Many low vision or nonvisual readers benefit from dual media that allow use of multiple sensory learning channels. Although listening to text read aloud is a common concurrent or alternate means of accessing digital text, the following considerations are important to consider to ensure success in reading auditorily.

- **Training listening skills.** Individuals must develop auditory comprehension skills as early as possible. Readers must attune to listening for information in order to ensure comprehension. Listening speed has a significant impact on auditory access is for an individual. Beginning auditory readers might read thirty words per minute, while proficient auditory readers can read several hundred words per minute. Reading speed greatly impacts a person's efficiency in completing reading tasks and

should be an instructional priority for all blind or low vision individuals.

Tech Tip

See Paths to Technology post "Five Reasons Why Your Students Should Learn to Read at a Rate of 600 Words Per Minute."

https://www.perkinselearning.org/technology/blog/five-reasons-why-your-students-should-learn-read-rate-600-words-minute

Auditory readers should also attune to 'earcons'—designated sounds, which convey meaning, such as the pinging of an incoming email or the tone heard when an app is opened.

Tech Tip

See Paths to Technology post "iCons and Earcons: Critical but Often Overlooked Tech Skills."

https://www.perkinselearning.org/technology/blog/icons-and-earcons-critical-often-overlooked-tech-skills

The book *Learning to Listen/Listening to Learn* (Barclay, 2012) provides excellent information on how to develop listening skills.

- **Check auditory processing abilities.** Some individuals have neuropathies or concomitant diagnoses that affect auditory processing. These individuals will require differentiated assessment and diagnostic teaching to determine the extent to which receiving auditory information is helpful (Holbrook, Kamei-Hannan,

McCarthy, 2017). Difficulties with auditory processing affect how individuals are trained to use auditory skills for reading.

- **Consider the reading environment.** Auditory access may be preferred when a reader reads faster auditorily than visually or tactilely. It may also be preferred during mobile access, when it is faster to listen to information rather than set up screen magnification or connect a braille display, or for global review of text before using visual or tactile access to edit it. When paired with an earphone, auditory access can maintain privacy. When an earphone is unavailable, the reader should be aware that anyone close by will also hear what he or she is reading. This is an important consideration in the classroom during "silent sustained reading" periods or in public spaces when reading confidential information.

Audio-Supported Reading (ASR)

Individuals with visual impairments can benefit from ASR (Jackson, 2012) in order to confirm or guide what is read visually or tactilely. Low vision readers might switch from visual to auditory access in order to avoid visual fatigue, or to confirm what is displayed on a screen if their vision is inconsistent. Pairing visual and auditory access can help low vision readers who struggle to identify each individual letter in a word, supporting their attention to the shape and size of the word which can be used along with contextual clues to identify the word more quickly and thus enhance reading efficiency. ASR can also help any reader, with or without visual

impairments, improve reading fluency, and develop a joy for reading that is independent from reading proficiency.

Tactile readers can benefit in a similar way to develop braille fluency. Emerging braille readers often benefit from hearing text read aloud to confirm what is felt under their fingers, and also to enjoy the experience of reading braille while developing tactile reading proficiency. Integrating braille and auditory feedback can help improve overall fluency and develop smooth hand mechanics while reading braille. Finally, and possibly most importantly, ASR can be very helpful when scaffolding readers' development of secondary or tertiary sensory learning channels other than their primary or preferred mode of access. This can be critical for developing sensory efficiency skills. Many individuals with visual impairment prefer one sensory channel for some tasks but a different channel for others. Some individuals might have developed only one sense to access information, even though this sense may or may not be the most efficient. This can be particularly true for low vision individuals who have not learned sensory efficiency skills or have a progressive vision impairment that is continues to change how they need to access information. In either case, whether an individual has a stable eye condition, progressive vision impairment, or sudden vision loss (adventitious visual impairment), digital media can provide opportunities for instantaneous multimodal access. A thoughtful Learning Media Assessment (LMA) can inform how individuals utilize which sense for which tasks.

Individuals who need to improve auditory reading skills can benefit from using audio-visual or audio-tactile access to see or feel the words they hear. When learning how to listen, the reader can associate what is heard with the visual or tactile display of text. Practicing with ASR will improve multi-modal sensory efficiency.

Tech Tip

See Paths to Technology post "Getting Started with Audio-Supported Reading."

https://www.perkinselearning.org/technology/posts/getting-started-audio-supported-reading

Text-to-Speech (TTS)

As mentioned earlier in this chapter, TTS facilitates ASR for visual readers. TTS tools are ideal for having text read aloud on-demand to supplement visual or tactile access to text. TTS tools that are not screen readers typically require vision; the interface for selecting the text to be read aloud and starting and stopping the speech are usually accessible only to users who have enough vision to use a mouse (if on a computer) or finger/stylus (on a touchscreen). These interfaces are not compatible with nonvisual interactions unless the developer has made the extra effort to do so. TTS differs from more robust screen reading technologies because it reads only the selected text within a document and does not necessarily read continuously. TTS also does not allow auditory access to a computer's operating sys-

tem, menus, buttons, or dialog boxes. (One exception: Recall that some screen magnification applications offer TTS with enhanced auditory support for reading text and menu items aloud.) TTS can read only onscreen text that is formatted as text; it cannot read text that appears as an image. Often what appears to be coded as text in a program or website is actually just an image file depicting text of text, so it will not be spoken by TTS, a screen reading program with auditory output, or a screen reader. When text is captured as an image file, it must be converted into "readable text" using OCR before it can be read aloud digitally (discussed in **Chapter 2**).

Screen Readers

Screen readers function very differently from TTS technologies and can meet different sensory learning needs. Recall that TTS requires enough vision to select the text to be read, as well as to operate playback controls without keyboard commands. TTS tools are also limited to reading onscreen text and cannot be used to read text in menus, toolbars, pop-up boxes, or application labels. For anyone who cannot use a mouse, finger, or stylus to operate a computer, screen readers provide equitable and independent navigation of digital content and of the computing device.

Screen reading software converts and reads text via a speech synthesizer. Screen readers can voice all of the text displayed including menu options, toolbars, dialog boxes, form fields, media controls, and buttons.

Unlike TTS tools, screen reading tools provide access to all of the information on the screen, not just the body of text, allowing users to interact with accessible applications such as word processors, spreadsheets, e-mail readers, and Web-based programs.

Typically, screen readers are used to provide nonvisual access to information and nonvisual control of computers. However, individuals with low vision can also benefit from screen reading tools in addition to TTS depending on the task, the environmental context, or both.

Sidebar 3.5

HOW A LOW VISION STUDENT USES TEXT-TO-SPEECH AND SCREEN READING TOOLS IN A DIGITAL WORKFLOW: "PASTA GUY", STUDENT BLOGGER ON PATHS TO TECHNOLOGY

"Pasta Guy" is a fifth grader who attends general education classes at his local public school. Pasta Guy is diagnosed with septo-optic dysplasia, which is a congenital syndrome that results in abnormal development of several brain structures. In Pasta Guy's case, his diagnoses include bilateral optic nerve hypoplasia (underdeveloped optic nerve) and under-development of the pituitary gland. Thus, Pasta Guy has low vision and requires assistive technology tools that address contrast (including color and line spacing), magnification, and auditory access. He requires lighting accommodations and has difficulty seeing in very low light or high glare situations. He experiences visual fatigue after about 15 minutes of visual tasks, so it is important he use auditory strategies well before reaching the point of fatigue. Due to efforts required for visual tracking and scanning, he utilizes enhanced visual strategies such as word or line highlighting while reading. Auditory clues also help Pasta Guy with orientation during travel and sports and leisure activities.

Pasta Guy uses a fluid combination of visual and auditory strategies to engage with reading activities. He requires reading tools that allow him to quickly switch between and utilize enhanced visual and auditory settings. Being able to do so assumes that he is provided with digital text materials that are either in an accessible format, or can be rendered accessible with optical character recognition (OCR). He most typically uses vision to read menus, navigate websites and learning programs, and orient to the layout of assessment materials. However, for in-depth reading tasks including documents, books, and assessment content, he switches to auditory strategies to lessen the visual strain and avoid fatigue. If he merely wants to read a short passage, Pasta Guy usually highlights the desired text and uses a keyboard command or gesture to have the passage read aloud (uses text-to-speech). For continuous reading or when he is in uncontrolled lighting situations that render it difficult to use the visual playback controls, Pasta Guy uses an accessibility shortcut to turn on the screen reader and use features for continuous reading and play/pause control without needing to manipulate a mouse and cursor. This is particularly helpful when he is reading in the park (glare!), in a darkened classroom, or simply tired at the end of a day.

Pasta Guy also uses a combination of visual, auditory, and tactile strategies in the authoring process. He has well-developed keyboarding skills that allow him to touch-type without looking at the keyboard. As he writes, he periodically uses text-to-speech to review paragraphs auditorily to catch misspellings and errors that he might have missed visually. Depending on the length of his writing assignment or if he needs to review a large amount of notes for a quiz, Pasta Guy might also turn on a screen reader for continuous reading and mouseless navigation of a larger quantity of text. Because of the flexibility in multimodal access when using digital text, Pasta Guy completes most of his work on a personal computing device so that he can review his own work independently, efficiently, and with minimal visual strain. He limits handwriting work.

Saving all of his work online also allows him to work across a variety of devices including a laptop during school, touchscreen tablet for reading outside and on the go, a desktop shared with other family members, and computers in the school computer lab and library. At times when his laptop is out for repair or low on battery, he can also utilize a classroom computing device as a back-up. Pasta Guy also receives and submits all of his work that is in digital format directly with his classroom teachers. Much of his direct service time with his Teacher of the Visually Impaired (TVI) is spent honing proficiency in using his technology skills for various classroom tasks, learning how to troubleshoot and advocate for his own accessibility needs, and otherwise work on areas of the Expanded Core Curriculum (ECC).

Tech Tip

See Paths to Technology post "Preparing a Low Vision Student to Use a Screen Reader."

https://www.perkinselearning.org/technology/blog/preparing-low-vision-student-use-screen-reader

Information from an LMA will best inform instructors how to show an individual how and when to use either tool. See "Getting Started with Technology" on the Perkins *Paths to Technology* website for tips on introducing screen readers on mobile Apple (iOS), Mac operating system (OS), and Chromebooks (https://www.perkinselearning.org/technology/getting-started).

Mouseless computing. For nonvisual users, screen-reading technology allows auditory access to a computer, software, and onscreen elements such as dialog boxes, menus, controls, and buttons. Accessible programs also include nonvisual media playback controls. Keyboard commands are essential in controlling how a screen reader interacts with onscreen content. Because nonvisual computing does not involve a mouse, fully accessible technologies are said to allow "mouseless computing." As a result, navigating a program or website using keyboard commands instead of a mouse is only an effective strategy for performing a rough accessibility check.

Speech synthesizers. Speech synthesizers generate spoken text from digital. There are both hardware and software speech synthesizers available, but most screen readers come with a built-in software synthesizer. If the user does not like this synthesizer, alternative ones can be downloaded. These synthesizers speak with a computer-generated, sometimes robotic sounding voice, the quality of which varies widely. A limited selection of voices is available with all built-in screen-reading tools. Better quality voices are available for purchase and can be selected based on user preference. Readers typically develop preferences for certain voices, and will benefit from training listening skills to read at the most efficient reading speed.

Braille support. Screen readers vary in how well they support braille. While more established screen readers (for example, JAWS®, NVDA) render braille reliably when used with an RBD, screen readers newer at the time of writing such as ChromeVox™ could benefit from improved braille support. This consideration is significant when choosing an operating system and personal computing device.

Usability. Many mainstream computers have some built in screen reading capability. Features that affect the usability of the built-in screen reader can vary and may sometimes require installing an alternative screen reader program. There are commercial and free alternatives, the choice of which depends on their compatibility with the computer. Note that some devices require sighted assistance to launch a

TECHNOLOGY FOR FREE: FREEWARE/SHAREWARE AND OPEN SOURCE SOFTWARE

Mainstream and assistive technology software is increasingly available for free, or at very low cost, either as a downloadable app or a browser-based tool that can be used online with an internet browser. Examples of freeware include mainstream productivity programs like Google Docs/Slides/Sheets, accessible digital talking book readers such as Bookshare's WebReader, the large collection of apps available on mobile Apple or Android touchscreen tablets, and the increasing array of extensions available on Google Chrome. Shareware, on the other hand, is software that can be acquired for free for an evaluation period. If the user is satisfied with the product and wishes to continue to use it, he or she is obligated on the "honor system" to submit a fee to the developer to help sustain the further development of the product. Even costly feature-rich screen reading technology has a shareware counterpart that offers comparable features and usability. The screen reader NVDA (NonVisual Desktop Access), sometimes referred to as NV Access, is a unique example because it is open source in addition to being shareware. This means the program is available as a free download but the code for how the program is written is also posted publically for people to use and further adapt NVDA for specific needs. This creates a large user community around NVDA and allows for the program to be customizable for creative uses. NV Access asks organizations and individuals to partner with them in continuing the development of the program by making a donation at their website: https://www.nvaccess .org/support/.

Freeware and shareware can be useful in several ways:

- To try out (demo) a type of tool before purchasing a similar item

- To practice tool basics and develop proficiency before purchasing a more feature-rich equivalent

- To access assistive technology when on a budget

- To utilize as a backup when an individual's primary assistive technology is unavailable

- To use as another tool in an individual's toolbox of assistive technology

(Continued)

Sidebar 3.6 (Continued)

Examples of freeware with an equivalent at-cost tool include but are not limited to:

- NVDA screen reader and JAWS screen reader.
- Scanning apps with OCR such as Google Docs or CamScanner and the KNFB Reader app
- Read and Write Google Chrome Extension and Kurzweil program
- iBooks and VoiceDream Reader app

Individuals should always be cautious about downloading programs from the Internet, so it is a good idea to thoroughly research a product among user communities before downloading to ensure it is legitimate. It is recommended that you talk with your IT specialist and discuss how you can download and evaluate freeware and shareware programs in a way that will minimize the risk to computers and networks. Your first request may meet with a negative response, but polite insistence in the value and cost savings can eventually lead to acceptance. In some settings, it may require consultation with a higher authority in the organization to realize the benefit of cost savings and compliance with legal obligations to provide accessibility. Selecting which freeware to add to an individual's toolbox will depend on user needs and preferences and the available features offered on the free versus at-cost versions of the technology.

screen reader; other devices (such as Apple products) are accessible out-of-the-box and enable nonvisual device setup. Some newer screen readers at the time of writing are designed for Web navigation (for example, NVDA and ChromeVox) while more established screen readers (for example, JAWS and Navigator) have excellent software navigation with updated capabilities for Web applications. Built-in screen readers operate best on devices that are designed with accessibility in mind. Screen readers range in price from free downloads up to about $1,000 at the time of writing. Choosing a screen reader depends on its compatibility with the computer as well as its ability to interface a range of programs and Web-based applications. One open-source screen reader, Non Visual Desktop Access (NVDA), offers an open-source license and ensures source codes are available to support user's abilities to tailor the tool to individual needs

NVDA also offers an option for users to download the tool to a USB-drive so that it can later be installed on any PC operating system. This is a useful option for commuting or traveling, as it allows the use of any computer that is compatible with NVDA, should a personal computing device be unavailable (such as when using a shared computer at a public library). Most proficient screen reader users employ more than one type of screen reader and switch between tools based on the nature of the task, the type of content, and the device used. (See **Table 3.1** for a summary of different screen reading options available across a variety of computing platforms.)

It is important to remember that screen readers have more robust features than TTS tools. However, it can be overwhelming to learn all the required keyboard commands while simultaneously developing the necessary listening skills. When teaching an individual how to use a screen reader, focus on the immediate task, and teach only the features and keyboard commands or gestures needed to complete the task at hand.

Tech Tip

See Paths to Technology post "Teaching VoiceOver Gestures."

https://www.perkinselearning.org/technology/blog/teaching-voiceover-gestures-1-finger-tricks-and-tips

Screen reading instruction is most successful when the student uses the features being taught right away within an activity. Provide an early introduction to the technology before the user actually needs it to complete a task in a high-stakes situation.

File Formats of Digital Reading Media

- **TXT**
- **RTF**
- **DOC/DOCX**
- **PDF**
- **ePub**
- **DAISY**

Because accessibility and usability of digital text depends on the format of the media itself, additional information regarding file formats is necessary to aid in understanding how readers might access this type of reading material (See **Sidebar 3.7, Resources for Document Accessibility.**) Specific technologies and tools for producing digital text as alternate media will be discussed in more detail in **Chapter 5;** the following section will provide an overview of how various file formats affect readers' usability of digital text.

Tech Tip

See Paths to Technology post "Common File Types for Visual Impairments and Print Disabilities."

https://www.perkinselearning.org/technology/blog/common-file-types-vision-impairment-and-print-disabilities

Table 3.1
Screen Reader Options Across Computing Platforms

Computing Platform	Screen Reader	Cost as of 2017	Notes
PC	Narrator	Free (built-in)	Improving functionality with each operating system update. Best when installing/updating drivers but otherwise considered by most as a backup screen reader when JAWS and NVDA are unavailable. No add-ons or scripts available to enhance accessibility of mainstream programs.
PC	NVDA	Free (downloaded on computer or USB drive)	Best for navigating web-based content. Uses similar keyboard commands as JAWS. Can be downloaded onto a USB drive to use on public/shared computers. The default synthesized voice can be unappealing for some users but higher quality voices are available for download. Vibrant open source community with many options for add-ons or scripts to enhance accessibility of mainstream programs.
PC	JAWS	$900–$1,100	Excellent for navigating installed programs on the computer and when used with NVDA, is a comprehensive tool for navigating web-based content. There

(continued)

Table 3.1 (Continued)

Computing Platform	Screen Reader	Cost as of 2017	Notes
			is a cost to update JAWS to maintain compatibility with operating system updates. School age students can get a free copy of JAWS through APH quota funds.
Mac OS (desktop/laptop) and iOS (mobile)	VoiceOver	Free (built-in)	Robust for navigating computer programs and web content. Can be controlled using keyboard commands or gestures.
Chromebook	ChromeVox	Free (built-in)	Improving functionality with each operating system update, however Chromebooks offer inconsistent braille support that limits comprehensive usability of the screen reader.

TXT

Digital files in TXT format are often referred to as "plain text" files because the text is shown without formatting. All word processors can read .txt files across all operating systems. While TXT renders the text computer-readable (and able to display on an RBD), it unfortunately does not allow formatting such as different fonts, heading styles, paragraph justification, or nested lists. Without formatting, users are unable to preview text using a table of contents or to skim sections of text via headings using tactile (with an RBD) or auditory (with a screen reader) strategies. The lack of text formatting affects the accessibility of TXT files for auditory and tactile access because it limits equitable and efficient navigation of the content. Although most text documents can be exported as plain text files, TXT files strip all formatting conventions from the resulting document.

RTF (Rich Text File)

RTF files are similar to TXT files in that both are simple and readable, but RTF files are capable of basic formatting

Sidebar 3.7

RESOURCES FOR DOCUMENT ACCESSIBILITY

Documents created in Microsoft Word, Google Docs, and Pages have options for formatting the text for visual and auditory navigation. The main features to focus on are:

- **Use of heading styles (format headers and subheaders of a document following an outline structure)**
- **Formatted lists**
- **Formatted tables**
- **Tags (for PDFs)**

When exporting the document as a PDF or copying or pasting as Web content, the formatting may or may not transfer accordingly. If exporting text from one format to another, or from one platform to another, it is always a good idea to check for accessibility in the final version. Use automated accessibility checkers with caution; these tools do not always catch accessibility issues, or misidentify accessibility failures. The best check is to turn on a screen reader and try to navigate the headings and sections of a document using keyboard commands only. Ensure image accessibility within documents by using alt text to describe images.

Many resources and tutorials are available to support document accessibility:
- **YouTube videos**
- **WebAIM**
- **National Center on Disability and Access to Education**
- **Various university websites that address accessibility, such as:**
  - Berkeley Resource Center for Online Education (BRCOE)
  - San Jose State University
  - Washington University
- **Microsoft Office**
- **Google Docs**
- **Apple Pages**
- **Adobe PDF**

including font, paragraph, and nested lists. RTF files can also embed images, but do produce documents with styled headings that can generate a table of contents to preview the text. Similar to TXT files, RTF files do not provide equitable and efficient navigation of content.

DOC/DOCX

Files in DOC or DOCX format also contain computer-readable text, but they also support more sophisticated options for styled headings and formatting paragraphs, lists, tables, and images. Accessibility of this file format is entirely dependent on whether files are formatted for accessibility. If an author does not employ any heading styles or list, table, or form formatting, DOC or DOCX files are no more accessible than a plain text file. Documents created using Microsoft® Word and Google Docs™ are examples of this file format.

PDF (Portable Document Format)

The PDF format was developed by Adobe® in the 1990s to make documents with text and image formatting compatible with any operating system—so long as the user has downloaded the free Acrobat Reader® software, knows how to open a PDF in a Web browser, or has a compatible application that can open PDFs. This format is typically used for read-only documents or forms that preserve the layout of the source page. Unfortunately, PDFs are notorious for concerns regarding accessibility with screen readers and TTS tools. PDFs can be saved as an image (with non-computer readable—and therefore inaccessible—text), or as a text-PDF that is readable but requires the creator to provide tags that allow equitable navigation. Users who need tactile or auditory access to PDFs will have variable success, depending on whether the author used tags to identify heading structures and list formats. If the PDF is not tagged and accessible, readers who need tactile or auditory access can convert it into a readable DOC format. This can be accomplished with OCR tools that recognize and convert the text into a word processing program. However, recall from **Chapter 2** that OCR as part of a scan and read system works best with bodies of text with simple formatting and layouts such as tables and sidebars. Visual access to PDFs is more easily accomplished because their content can be enlarged using page zoom or a screen magnification tool. Many applications are available for editing or annotating a PDF; while these annotation tools are limited to visual access, they can be quite powerful for a low vision individual who can use a keyboard or stylus to annotate an enlarged digital copy of a form or worksheet.

ePub

One of the technical electronic book standards, ePub is the technical standard published by the International Digital Publishing Forum [http://idpf.org]. Sometimes referred to as a Digital Talking Book (see following section titled **Digital Talking Books**), it is currently the eBook format compatible with the greatest number of eBook reading tools, including both specialized and mainstream technologies.

At the time of writing, the EPUB 3.2 file format is the industry-adopted standard for eBooks (2019) and supports both literary text and math accessibility. (See **Chapter 6** for more information on technologies for accessing math content.) This file format has the most rigorous criteria, but also best supports how text can be laid out and formatted for enhanced visual, tactile, and auditory access. With optimal formatting of text, paragraph, lists, and table structures within a document, a screen reader can access how content is laid out in an ePub and gain a broad overview of the document similar to how visual readers can quickly see headings, subheadings, nested lists, and information organized in tables. Recalling that RBDs display text exactly how it is read by a screen reader, an optimally formatted document such as an ePub facilitates equitable navigation and usability of a text regardless of visual, tactile, or auditory access. As a result, blind or low vision readers are assured digital reading experiences that are the most comparable to readers without visual impairments.

DAISY

The DAISY (Digital Accessible Information SYstem) (Kearney, 2011; www.daisy.org) file format is a precursor to the ePub format, but unlike ePub (which was designed for mainstream publications), DAISY books were specifically designed for people with print disabilities. Although ePubs replace the need for DAISY books, there remain a number of digital audiobook players that utilize this file format. In particular, the National Library Service (NLS) remains a major supplier of digital talking books that use the DAISY format for playback on commercial or NLS-specific devices. Similar to ePub, DAISY files adhere to a technical standard for digital audiobooks, periodicals, and computerized text. By doing so, DAISY files are also considered Digital Talking Books that enable equitable tactile or auditory navigation and facilitate a reading experience that is similar to that of sighted readers. The following section will provide more information on digital talking books.

Digital Talking Books (DTBs)

Thus far, this chapter has discussed the various technologies a blind or low vision reader might use to access digital text in general. The following section provides further information on accessing digital text in the form of a comprehensive eBook. Understanding the accessibility and usability of different file formats, as mentioned earlier, can help a service provider understand how best to ensure reading media are made available to a blind or low vision reader, and what tools must be available to access different file types. While an eBook can be disseminated in any of the aforementioned file formats, DTBs are currently the gold standard in providing an accessible text that most closely parallels a typically sighted reader's reading experience. Understanding how digital text can be available as a complete book and compatible with various eReaders can help determine the optimal digital workflow and choice of preferred reading tool.

Starting with the exception, DTBs from the NLS are provided on memory storage cards, devices that are similar to flash drives. The NLS digital audio-book players access audio recordings that are kept on these memory storage cards, which are housed in a plastic cartridge about the size of a traditional cassette tape. (See www.loc.gov/nls for additional details.) These devices are typically preferred by people who prefer single-function, easy-to-use book players. Because the audio files are formatted as a DTB, the content can be previewed with an auditory table of contents, allowing the reader to navigate the content auditorily.

DTBs are otherwise different from audiobooks because they offer text for visual access and can be read aloud by a number of different screen readers, software applications, and hardware devices. Audiobooks feature text that has been read aloud by a person that has been recorded and saved as an audio file only. DTBs are essentially the digital equivalent of a print book with chapter headings for easy navigation both visually and auditorily. They aim to deliver an on-screen experience parallel to paper formats. DTBs are downloadable files that can be read on a variety of applications.

Most DTBs use the ePub or DAISY file formats, which adhere to technical standards that allow any reader to navigate the digital text by chapter, section, or page. These files provide an overview of the book in a table of contents and the ability to easily search for key words or phrases, and, depending on the reading application, they allow a reader to highlight and take notes (annotate) while reading. Because DTBs contain readable text, they allow for auditory access with TTS or screen reader tools and can be displayed on an RBD for tactile access. Visual options vary across reading applications, but typically include adjustment of font style, size, contrast, highlighting, and masking tools.

Considerations When Selecting an eReader Tool

◦ Readers who are overwhelmed by too many features can be more successful with a standalone device with a simple interface. This is a dedicated device that reads DTBs, audiobooks saved in .mp3 format, and basic digital text files such as those discussed earlier in the chapter. These reading devices include playback buttons allowing the reader to navigate content.

◦ Readers who engage in a digital workflow with other digital media besides DTBs would benefit by reading books on the program or app that they also use to carry out reading, writing, note-taking, and research tasks. Selection of the best application for this depends on its compatibility with the computer as well as the file format of the reading material.

◦ Some eReader applications read only ePub or DAISY files, while others are compatible with many file formats. These applications may include the options to sync with cloud-based file hosting storage systems such as Dropbox, Google Drive, or Microsoft® OneDrive®, allowing books to be both saved to and retrieved from an online account.

○ Readers with print disabilities have privileged access to digital talking book libraries such as Bookshare® and the National Library Service. Some eReaders allow a reader to download and open books directly from these libraries, while other tools require first downloading the book to a saved location or drive (either cloud-based or a physical hard drive), and then opening it from the saved location.

In all, reading applications are constantly evolving, and selecting the appropriate tool will ultimately depend on the reader's preferences and needs regarding learning media and the use of sensory channels. The "Reading Tools" section on Bookshare's website is a good starting point for learning about currently recommended tools that support DTBs (https://www.bookshare .org/cms/help-center/reading-tools).

Digital text on the Web, in mobile apps, and STEAM (Science, Technology, Engineering, Arts, Mathematics) media

The ability to use technology independently to access online resources is critical to freedom of inquiry—the goals should be age-appropriate self-expression and independent access to information. Service providers can work with students on strategies for getting around the mobile and desktop Web to find important information. This includes books and research for homework, but it also includes finding local

businesses, getting directions, and using email and social media in appropriate ways.

Access to digital text is also needed for using applications on a mobile device and accessing numerical formats. (See **Chapter 5** for more detailed information about authoring in numerical forms.) Similar to the formats already discussed in the chapter, text on the Web and STEAM content can be accessible if formatted correctly. Web content must follow the *POUR* principles and use paragraph and heading styles, formatted lists and tables, alt text, and self-described hyperlinks similar to a well-formatted word processed document. Text, menus, and buttons must also be programmed for accessibility to deliver a positive user experience for an individual who uses a screen reader. Because STEAM content can require math and scientific notations, these media need to be written in an accessible file format instead of being presented as screenshots.

Software programs have been developed that not only help users learn mathematical concepts, but also provide tools that can be used to complete math problems and other numerical tasks. Modern spreadsheet programs allow users to manipulate and produce rows and columns of numerical information that can be displayed on the screen or printed on paper in various fonts and point sizes. Math and equation editor software can be used to complete complicated math assignments and many interactive STEAM curricula are now offered online or as an app. Some of these programs can be accessed using screen magnification software, screen-reading software, and refreshable braille displays, but many are not accessible. The accessibility of these types of programs needs to be evaluated before recommending for a blind or low vision student—ideally, product accessibility should be vetted before purchasing it or implemented in an educational or workplace environment.

CONCLUSION

As discussed throughout the chapter, there are many considerations when using technology to access digital text. The reading media must be adequately formatted, and tools must be compatible with various formats and accessible within a reader's access technology. In addition, users must acquire enough technology proficiency to employ a flexible toolkit that can access digital texts in different ways based on the context and tasks. To successfully use this media format, it is important to know both the advantages and limitations of digital text. In most instances, the advantages for readers are worth every effort to negotiate these limitations.

Accessible digital text gives readers with visual impairments the power of choice in deciding how to access information. This includes the range of tools that can be leveraged for multimodal access to information. The ability to choose which sense to employ at any given time—visual, tactile, or auditory—

is the greatest advantage digital text has over paper formats. The freeing nature of being able to access digital text immediately, anywhere, and on-the-go is also unparalleled when compared to paper formats. Individuals who are visually impaired are empowered to access information without a mediator and at will. These advantages are best leveraged when part of a digital workflow. Finally, the technologies and strategies covered in this chapter should serve to debunk every myth that technology is killing braille and literacy for individuals with visual impairments. Rather, technology has the opposite effect of promoting literacy and braille more than ever before by increasing the availability of information in both hard copy as well as electronic or digital braille.

REFERENCES

Jackson, R. M. (2012). Audio-supported reading for students who are blind or visually impaired. Wakefield, MA: National Center on Accessible Instructional Materials.

Alexander, B. (2006). Web 2.0: A new wave of innovation for teaching and learning? Educause Review, 41(2), 32.

Allan, J., Kirkpatrick, A., & Henry, S. L. (Eds.). (2016). Accessibility Requirements for People with Low Vision. Retrieved August 27, 2017, from https://w3c.github.io /low-vision-a11y-tf/requirements.html

Barclay, L.A. (2012). Learning to Listen/ Listening to Learn. New York, NY: AFB Press.

Gill, K., Mao, A., Powell, A. M., & Sheidow, T. (2013). *Digital reader vs print media: the role of digital technology in reading accuracy in age-related macular degeneration.* Eye, 27(5), 639–643. doi:10.1038/eye.2013.14

International Digital Publishing Forum: The Trade and Standards Organization for the Digital Publishing Industry. (n.d.). Retrieved August 27, 2017, from http://idpf.org/

Kearney, G. (2011). *DAISY: What Is it and Why Use it?* Braille Monitor, 54(2). Retrieved August 27, 2017.

Koenig, A. J., & Holbrook, C. M. (Eds.). (2017). Foundations of Education: History and Theory of Teaching Children and Youths with Visual Impairments *(3rd ed., Vol. 2).* New York, NY: AFB Press.

Mell, P., & Grance, T. (2011). *The NIST definition of cloud computing.* National Institute of Standards and Technology. Retrieved from http://faculty.winthrop.edu/domanm/csci411/Handouts/NIST.pdf

Siu, Y. (2016). *Designing for all Learners with Technology.* Educational Designer, 3(9). Retrieved from http://www.educationaldesigner.org/ed/volume3/issue9/article34/index.htm

CHAPTER 4
Technologies for Authoring

Advancements in technology have led to the development of tools that allow individuals to efficiently produce written communications for personal and professional use and create documents that can be shared easily with peers, family members, teachers, and employers. Prior to the invention of typewriters and word processors, the physical process of creating written documents and communicating through writing en masse was a challenge for most writers—particularly for those individuals who are blind or visually impaired. Modern writing tools make the task less tedious while greatly increasing the efficiency of the writer. This chapter will describe various technologies that can be used to author written work.

The production of written documents can be broken down into two phases: the act of organizing information and communicating thoughts in a written format, and the process of revising and editing the written work for publication. Together, these activities comprise the act of authoring. Reliable technologies now exist that provide youths and adults with tools to assist in the physical or electronic production of written communication. These range from low-tech writing tools for short, simple writing tasks to advanced tools for producing longer, more complex written documents. Numerous tools have also been developed to assist the writer with the various aspects of authoring including organizing and outlining of the content, editing and reviewing drafts, and finally dissemination with peers, instructors, or colleagues.

There are many factors involved in the authoring process that beg consideration. Proficiency in authoring is inescapably tied to reading, especially when one considers the need to review, edit, and read what has been written. Fortunately, from a financial standpoint, many of the tools used for reading printed and electronic or digital information (discussed in **Chapters 2 and 3**) can also be used for authoring written documents and materials, thus decreasing, but not eliminating, the number of single-purpose tools which must be purchased that comprise a well-stocked toolbox for people who are blind or have low vision. Organizing and investigating the tools designed for writing and authoring can be accomplished by using a similar strategy to that for reading described in **Chapter 2**.

The first step in authoring involves determining the scope or size of the task to be completed, as well as what features of the available tools might assist the individual in completing the task. Is the writing for personal use or for sharing information with others? Personal writing activities include short tasks—jotting down a phone number, composing an email, copying the page numbers for a reading assignment from the board, making a grocery list, or writing appointments on a calendar—to longer, more involved tasks such as taking notes in a class or meeting, or keeping a journal or diary. Authoring tasks that are intended to disseminate information to others might include creating thank-you notes, text messages, emails, letters, term papers, business reports, or online posts on social media and various websites. Blind and low vision individuals will benefit from tools that offer flexible and efficient task completion. The second step of the strategy considers which media the individual is authoring and which sensory channel he or she will use for the given task. Will the writer accomplish the task exclusively as a tactile, visual, or auditory activity, or through some combination of these senses? These two main considerations will help determine the technologies needed to complete a majority of authoring tasks.

AUTHORING FOR DIGITAL ACCESS

- **Hardware**
  - Keyboards
- **Software**
  - Word Processing Applications
  - Word Prediction
  - Online Workspaces
  - Publishing Digital Content

Low-tech authoring tools for individuals who are blind or have low vision are adequate for short, simple tasks, but for longer and more complex writing tasks, more efficient options are needed. The ideal tool for many individuals is dependent on a robust personal computing device—or set of devices—that allow for efficient production and revision of large quantities of information. Although different individuals might choose different tools at various points in a workflow, the mediation of written work with a computing device ensures for easy collaboration with blind and typically sighted peers, instructors, and colleagues.

The technologies presented in this section are available in a device-agnostic format; all hardware and software options can be paired with any type of computer including mobile touchscreen tablets, smartphones (considered one variant of a mobile touchscreen tablet), desktop or laptop computers, and electronic notetakers. Different users will have vastly different preferences when adopting a personal computing device! These decisions are as personal as choosing a political affiliation; service providers who are asked for input in this adoption process need to make recommendations based on the best fit of a device for an individual given their preferences, the workflow they engage in, and the tasks that need to be accomplished. The key consideration when choosing tools for authoring in a virtual environment is compatibility with the operating system rather than the device itself. Other considerations when choosing personal computing devices to support one's tasks include the following:

- **Length of task to be completed**
- **Portability for mobile work versus durability/sustainability for stationary work?**
- **Battery life when fully charged?**
- **Screen and keyboard size?**
- **Usability of built-in accessibility features versus need to purchase additional specialized tools?**
- **Cost of add-on accessibility tools if required**
- **Compatibility with existing work/ cloud ecosystem**
- **Compatibility and ease of syncing with other devices in one's toolbox**
- **Integration into one's lifestyle**

Note that most individuals effectively use more than one computing device: this characteristic is true for almost anyone, blind or sighted, who engages with digital information.

Hardware

Using a touchscreen device for authoring can be very effective for short, mobile writing tasks that are easily accomplished with either dictation or an on-screen keyboard (e.g., text messaging, social media posts, and short e-mails). Be aware that QWERTY on-screen keyboards require a "hunt-and-peck" strategy to input text, which can be quite visually fatiguing if a user has low vision, and tedious if using a screen reader. For braille users, an on-screen keyboard for 6-key braille entry can be a better option for nonvisual on-screen input. For lengthier tasks, connecting a Bluetooth braille or QWERTY keyboard to a touchscreen device can facilitate greater accuracy and efficiency when using a touchscreen device. Using a keyboard in conjunction with a refreshable braille display (RBD) will support tactile output with or without audio whenever a screen reader or TTS tool is activated.

Keyboards

Regardless of preferences for visual, tactile, or auditory access, individuals who want to make the best use of high-tech tools for authoring need to develop proficient keyboarding skills to enter and manipulate digital text. With or without the aid of a word prediction program, keyboarding is an important skill for all users, and particularly for those who are blind or blind or have low vision. It is most critical because keyboard input allows the creation of and engagement with digital text, which ultimately allows for multimodal accessibility. If additional disabilities are present that require support from other access technologies, further consultation with an occupational therapist, alternative augmentative communication (AAC) specialist, assistive technology specialist, or another professional experienced in using technology with people who have additional disabilities will be very helpful. Many alternative input and output devices exist that can facilitate the authoring process for individuals with multiple disabilities.

For authors who are still developing keyboarding skills, stick-on large print labels can be affixed to a standard QWERTY keyboard. While these relatively inexpensive stickers may seem like a good idea, this adaptation is only appropriate for individuals who cannot touch-type due to physical or neurological issues. Similarly, braille labels are available for a QWERTY keyboard, but should be removed as soon as basic keyboard orientation is understood or kept only in case of a user who can not touch-type. Otherwise, these labels can be counterproductive and interfere with an individual's ability to learn how to type by touch. Keyboard labels are best reserved for orientation to certain keys or to locate keys that are difficult to reach without looking.

Adapted keyboards with high contrast or colorful layouts or with larger keys are also available. Again, unless a user has other additional disabilities to consider, these adaptations will not help a typical user who only has a visual impairment learn how to touch-type. However, several options **are** available for the individual who is capable of touch-typing.

- **Bluetooth keyboards (QWERTY or six-key braille).** Bluetooth keyboards are essential for enhancing productivity on a touchscreen device. Recall that onscreen keyboards require a visual or auditory hunt-and-peck strategy; a connected Bluetooth keyboard is an excellent workaround for more efficient input. An external keyboard that connects to a computer can also improve the ergonomics of a workstation. For example, while the keyboard on a mobile touchscreen tablet case is excellent for ensuring access to a keyboard at all times, working with a peripheral Bluetooth keyboard can allow the tablet to be positioned at a height and distance independently from the keyboard.

- **Onscreen braille input.** Some touchscreen devices will offer a virtual keyboard (with no physical keys) on the screen of the touchscreen device. This method requires a one-time calibration that requires the user to rest his or her fingers on the screen, before the moving the fingers simultaneously for six-key braille input. Some errors can occur if the finger placement doesn't align with the calibrated position, or if some of the keystrokes are not perfectly synced with the corresponding fingers hitting the screen at the same moment.

Keyboarding Considerations

One of the most important aspects of learning good keyboarding skills requires the learner to receive immediate feedback about accuracy of his or her keystrokes. Once the learner has received instruction about the location of the primary orientation keys (the home row), practice is needed to develop the neural motor skills (muscle memory) for touch-typing. This is where keyboarding apps can provide the consistent daily practice that an instructor cannot. A great number of keyboarding apps are available that provide such feedback; however accessibility is often the determining factor regarding which apps are usable by a nonvisual or low vision learner. Often, the letters that a student is prompted to type are in fonts that are too small, have poor contrast,

and are unreadable by a screen reader. The text input from a student's keystrokes can also be hard to read visually or by a screen reader. Plain interfaces without extra graphics for visual interest tend to have the best chance for success (see Talking Typer from APH).

If an accessible and interesting keyboarding app is unavailable, a student can also practice keyboarding using a word processing app with a screen reader. This setup can effectively give the student the visual, auditory, or tactile feedback that is desired. The speech output from a screen reader can hone auditory skills as a second sensory modality for learners with low vision in addition to providing options to adjust font size, style, and contrast as needed. **Sidebar 4.1, Ideas for Differentiating Keyboarding Instruction for Students with Visual Impairments** provides additional food for thought when supporting the development of keyboarding skills.

Sidebar 4.1

IDEAS FOR DIFFERENTIATING KEYBOARDING INSTRUCTION FOR STUDENTS WITH VISUAL IMPAIRMENTS

- When dictating a word for a student to type, tag each letter with "left" or "right." Encourage the student to search the corresponding side of the keyboard for each letter and press the key with the matching hand.

- Use a word processing app with a screen reader

- Identify common words or phrases that will provide incidental opportunities for practicing touch typing throughout the day—what

(Continued)

might the student be required to type every day in the course of their work? Examples: First name, last name, computer or email login, password associated with the most used login

- Practice typing common letter combinations to build muscle memory. Examples: *-ing, the, and*

- Prioritize learning the keys that correspond to keyboard shortcuts or screen reader commands

- Practice writing sentences with the common letter combinations. Focus on capitalizing the first letter of each sentence and include correct punctuation at the end of the sentence. To build muscle memory, write the same sentence ten times or until it is correct three times in a row.

Tech Tip

For more ideas, see Paths to Technology post "Where Do I Start When Teaching My Visually Impaired Student to Type?"

https://www.perkinselearning.org/technology/blog/starting-scratch-where-do-i-start-when-teaching-my-visually-impaired-student-type

Well-considered strategies to develop touch-typing can prepare the student for the next stage: authoring longer and more complex writing tasks using word processing apps.

Software

Using a personal computing device as an authoring tool is ultimately dependent upon the availability of software applications.

Word Processing Applications

A word processing program that allows users to create, save, edit, and print documents is essential to authoring productivity, and its effectiveness is dependent on the proficiency of a user's keyboarding skills. For users who need nonvisual accessibility, a word processing program must be used that works well with a preferred screen reader. For users who need low vision accessibility, other settings within both the program and computing device will help. **Sidebar 4.2 Word Processor Settings for Low Vision Access,** describes settings within a word processor that can be adjusted to optimize low vision accessibility. However, the operation-related elements of the program, such as ribbons, menus, icons, and dialog boxes, typically cannot be enlarged and will require additional screen magnification software to enhance the low vision user experience.

WORD PROCESSOR SETTING FOR LOW VISION ACCESS

Adjusting the settings in a word-processing app by setting a user's preferred font style and point size can be sufficient to make the document accessible for many individuals. (For users who prefer to access a document using a screen reader, many tutorials are available online for recommended keyboard shortcuts that will allow the reader to navigate an accessible document using Headings and access images with alternate text ("alt text"). Most word processing programs offer some options for how text is displayed on the screen similar to the ones listed below. In most versions of Microsoft Word, the following steps can be used to adjust the visual settings:

- Select the **View tab.**

- Select the **Draft or Print Layout view** according to user preference

- Select the **Zoom** option to see Zoom settings.

- Select **Page Width.** This expands the view of the page to the full width of the screen, thus enlarging the text as much as possible while keeping all the text in view at one time.

- **Choose a preferred Zoom percentage.**

- Click Ctrl+D to open the **font dialog box**

- Choose the user's preferred font style, and point size. (Sans serif fonts are recommended)

- Click the **Advanced tab** at the top of the dialog box and experiment with the **Spacing** settings. Expanded pacing slightly increases the space between individual letters (also known as kerning), which can be beneficial to some users and not beneficial to others.

  - Example: This sentence is with Normal spacing.

  - Example: This sentence is with Expanded spacing set at 1 point.

- Choose Okay.

- The user should be recommended to revert font settings selected in step 6 before printing or disseminating the final copy.

Word-processing programs and apps offer great value because of the vast array of editing and formatting features they provide. These programs allow for features that are important to the revision process such as inserting, deleting, copying, and pasting text, as well as integrated spell-checking and auto-correction of common typos. Dictionary and thesaurus features are also often built in, which allow users to access these resources quickly using external reference tools. Writers can use these tools to assist in proofreading and to produce more professional documents. In addition, the formatting features of word processors allow users to create documents that have a more refined appearance for visual readers while also ensuring accessibility for readers who need auditory or tactile access. Accessible word-processing apps have greatly increased the efficiency and effectiveness with which people with visual impairments can produce high quality written communications. Screen magnification software, text-to-speech, and more advanced word processors have provided authors with low vision increasingly sophisticated ways to confirm text as it is being typed as well as to proofread efficiently.

Word Prediction

Word prediction programs or apps work in conjunction with word processors. Prediction software was originally developed for individuals with motor impairments who experience difficulty operating a standard keyboard and are unable to use touch-typing. These users might be able to type with only one or two fingers, use an alternative keyboard, or employ some type of switch to make their selection. When a user types or selects a letter, the word prediction software displays a list of words that start with that letter. The user can scroll through the list or hover the mouse pointer over a word and the program will speak that word. If this is the desired word, pressing the spacebar enters the text into the word processor, inserts a space, and displays another list of words that might logically follow the selected word. If the desired word is not listed, the user types the second letter of the word, prompting the word prediction program to display a new list of words starting with these first two letters. The user reads or navigates the list to the desired word that is then chosen by pressing the spacebar. These word prediction apps are similar to the auto-complete feature commonly found in messaging and emailing apps on smartphones and tablets. Reducing the number of physical keystrokes can significantly improve the writing performance for those with motor impairments, and can also be beneficial to some authors with a visual impairment.

The power of word prediction technology was quickly realized by service providers working with people who have difficulties with spelling and writing because of various print disabilities. If the author knows the initial letter of a word, the predictor provides a list of words staring with that letter. The program's ability to speak the word aloud helps the user select the desired word even if he or she cannot spell it or read it. This is a helpful way to scaffold fluency in the writing process, especially for students whose visual impairment limited early literacy experiences and, as a result, they have not learned "sight" words. However, word prediction apps should not be allowed to interfere with an author's creative process; students must be encouraged to conceptualize their intended sentence first. This way, they will be finding the words included in their intended sentence rather than merely using computer-suggested words to construct a random sentence.

Most word prediction programs allow the user to select the font and point size of the words displayed in the list. This feature and the program's ability to speak the words aloud make this an accessible tool for some individuals with low vision who have difficulty with spelling or a motor impairment that limits their keyboarding skills. For nonvisual authors, compatibility of a word prediction tool with the preferred screen reader will be an important consideration.

Online Workspaces

With cloud computing becoming as common as working offline, collaborative authoring such as working on a group project is also taking place online as much as—or perhaps even more than—in physical spaces. Popular online workspaces can be offered for free, with the Google suite of products (Google Classroom, Google Docs™, Google Slides™, Google Sheets™, etc.) leading the field at the time of this writing. With many schools and organizations "going Google," work efficiency in these environments is a critical skill. Cloud storage platforms (e.g. Dropbox, Box) are also beginning to offer more collaborative work features. Usability, compatibility with an individual's existing workflow, and accessibility are the main considerations when choosing to adopt one platform over another. In cases in which an employer has already adopted a specific platform, an individual must then adapt to that environment by reconfiguring needed access tools.

Regardless of the platform, it is important to recognize that online workspaces are not always easily usable if accessible—and sometimes not at all accessible. This is especially true for workspaces with online editors, media controls, forms, and comment boxes. These interfaces often have authoring areas that are visually apparent but unreadable with a screen reader. When encountering such an authoring environment, alternative tools can be warranted if accessibility issues are impossible to resolve otherwise.

Even when the tools are ostensibly accessible, authoring in online workspaces often requires advanced knowledge and stamina! For the beginner user, introductory tasks can be challenging if the user does not have a thorough understanding of the virtual space. Low vision access can be disorienting if button or menu locations are unknown; for example, an individual who is zoomed in on a particular text element can get lost and lose track of where he or she is within a page of text. It will be important that individuals who need magnification are savvy with toggling different zoom options (full page versus a magnification window) and proficient with adjusting font sizes for working versus publishing (for example, using a large font size to author but resizing to a standard size before dissemination). Assuming the online workspace is accessible, nonvisual access will also require proficiency and flexibility in using screen reader tools as needed. Troubleshooting often requires using more than one screen reader. For users who require mouseless computing, such as navigating content with a screen reader or braille display, it is especially important to understand how the virtual environment is organized in order to anticipate how a screen reader and braille display will encounter information. Explicit instruction that orients the user to the environment should not be overlooked. For example, a screenshot of an online workspace can be printed for visual exploration or adapted into a tactile graphic for tactile exploration. (See AT Specialist Neal McKenzie's workflow for creating a tactile graphic of GSlides in the webcast *TechTalk #3: Swell and Pages for Tactile Diagrams*, https://youtu.be/qGc2ML6t1rI.)

Finally, overall accessibility of collaboration features in a workspace begs consideration. The challenge of being asked to work in an inaccessible environment can exhaust even the savviest screen reader user. As a service provider, it is important to evaluate the accessibility of programs, workspaces, mixed media, and collaboration tools before starting any initial instruction. The tasks that an individual needs to accomplish will determine the ultimate course of instruction for learning the necessary access technology tools.

Publishing Digital Content

In the digital realm, authoring extends far beyond simply writing a report for school or work. Authorship can include the production and dissemination of multimedia such as digital books, audio tracks, or videos. When exploring tools for digital multimedia authoring, consider the following:

- **Usability with keyboard (mouseless) navigation, critical consideration for nonvisual accessibility**

- **Contrast of overall user interface, including visibility of fonts, buttons, menu items, alerts—critical for low vision accessibility**

- **Support for alt text, closed captions, and audio descriptions as needed—it is important that authoring practices result in accessible products for sustainable use**

It is important to remember that with the appropriate tools, anyone can create and disseminate accessible digital multimediacontent to describe visual information that would be missed otherrwise.as iBooks Author, iMovie®, and GarageBand® are leading examples of accessible multimedia authoring platforms; other current products such as Final Cut Pro® and DJ Pro® also deserve recognition for ensuring their platforms are accessible to blind and low vision authors.

**Content Vocabulary
Audio Description**

An audio description is narration added to visual content to describe visual information that would be missed otherwise. The narration supplements the regular audio track with information about scene changes, characters' actions, and on-screen text.

Web authoring is another popular area of authoring and publishing. Websites, blogs, zines, discussion boards, and social media offer many options for disseminating written and multimedia information. When writing and revising for the Web, proficiency in navigating each online environment is essential. Like any sighted author, blind and low vision authors should also implement digital multimedia accessibility practices and know how to navigate tools for formatting paragraph styles, lists and tables, and for adding alt text, captions, and audio descriptions as needed. Anyone authoring for Web design will also need to develop a deeper understanding of file formats, markup languages, and accessible programming to ensure Web content meets W3C standards (World Wide Web Consortium, https://www.w3.org). Service providers supporting an individual with Web authoring will likely need to understand how to orient an individual to the authoring environment for low vision or nonvisual access, how to convert written drafts into plain text or other compatible file formats as needed (depending on the authoring environment), and ensure the author has visual or tactile tools for drafting, editing, and revising. Especially when working with markup or coding languages, sole use of auditory tools is unlikely to be sufficient.

Coding is a digital literacy skill that involves translating directions into a programming language that can direct a computer to complete a desired task. It comprises a variety of languages that are needed for designing programs, Web applications, and websites. Depending on personal preferences, either a code editor application or integrated development environment (IDE) can be used to author code; however, some programmers might prefer the more robust features available in an IDE whereas others might prefer the simpler interface of a code editor application. Code editor applications are more likely to be accessible to a blind programmer due to the ability to enter lines of pure text without having to navigate the extraneous formatting features of an IDE. Note that although most code editors can be operated with keyboard commands, not all editors or even versions of the same editor are necessarily accessible. While **Sidebar 4.3, Accessible IDEs,** discusses a few code editor and IDE options that **are** accessible with a screen reader, in general coding accessibility is actually

ACCESSIBLE IDES

Contributing author: Chancey Fleet

Quorum

One programming language (Quorum) was developed to be easier to learn, and garnered moderate interest when the developers released an IDE that was designed for screenreader accessibility. While Quorum might have offered an easier learning curve to develop coding skills, it is not a language that has been as widely adopted in school curricula.

P5JS

P5JS is another programming language that is referred to as a shape out language and designed to be friendly to beginners. It lets you create images, sounds and animations. Most people think of it as a visual language but in actuality it is a spatial language. The web-based code editor is accessible with screen readers, and includes textual description of the output on the screen. With practice, a user can create original designs in the code editor and then output to an embosser for tactile graphics production.

Arduino

Arduino is a line of very small, very affordable computers that can be programmed to do any number of tasks such as home automation, robotics, and measurement. The IDE is accessible with screen readers after making a simple modification to one's operating system via installation of a Java access bridge. Using non-visual techniques, it is easy to connect the Arduino to a variety of sensors and outputs. Arduino can even be used to make customized accessible tools like light sensors and levelers. Despite the enormous potential of Arduino to empower blind makers, it's easy to get discouraged without the right support because so much of the learning content online is rife with undescribed images and videos. The Blind Arduino project offers a vibrant community of practice that gives blind makers a solid foundation using textual description of boards, explanations of how to set up the integrated development environment to be accessible, and describing some fun, approachable starter projects.

dependent on the accessibility of the code editor rather than the coding language itself.

With the increasing prevalence of online authoring activities, coding is becoming integrated in many educational curricula. Unfortunately, many coding curricula use inaccessible visual programming languages rather than text-based programming languages. To further complicate matters, most curricula are packaged as inaccessible visual interfaces, which then require service providers to understand coding well enough to determine how to adapt instruction for accessibility. Interestingly, programming was originally taught using text-based languages that presented no accessibility issues given an accessible code editor. It has only been with the development of visual programming languages and apps that have rendered coding and computer programming tutorials inaccessible. Several coding tools have since been developed to aid nonvisual and low vision learning in this area, with improving awareness and strategies for teaching nonvisual coding. (Explore: Swift Playgrounds with tactile graphics from the San Francisco Lighthouse for the Blind and 3D printed files from @neal_AT; CodeJumper from APH; CodeQuest.) Note that these nonvisual workarounds would not be needed if products were vetted for accessibility **before** purchasing. When purchasers such as school district make decisions about products without considering accessibility, the resulting inequity is passed down to disabled individuals within the community and becomes a serious liability in many ways. Because coding skills are tied to preparation for many employment opportunities in our digital world, it is imperative that blind and low vision students are not excluded from these education initiatives.

Although sophisticated Web design and coding are beyond the scope of this book (and possibly beyond what a typical service provider would be responsible for), it nonetheless **is** important to know how to ensure accessible instruction in these areas and support the learning objectives that are determined by a content specialist. With proficient use of access tools and accessible instructional materials, individuals can otherwise be referred to content experts who can better teach the technical skills needed for Web design and coding.

CONSIDERATIONS FOR AUTHORING MATH AND SCIENTIFIC NOTATIONS

The low-tech tools and some of the high-tech tools that are discussed in this chapter can be used when engaging in subjects related to Science, Technology, Engineering, Arts, and Math (STEAM) subjects. In addition, there are several considerations needed to ensure students have a firm grasp of mathematical concepts and graphical representations for meaning making.

Authoring with math and scientific notations for screen reader accessibility also requires different tools. These methods are relevant to any individual who prefers to review math and scientific notations auditorily (using a screen reader or sonification) or tactilely (using a RBD). Although a screen reader is necessary for nonvisual and tactile access (recall that a screen reader drives what is displayed on a RBD), it is also a helpful tool for low vision authors who want to review their work auditorily rather than visually. This section will focus on the tools specific to authoring while Chapter 6 will present more information about producing accessible multimedia formats for community consumption. For comprehensive information on math tools and teaching math, please refer to *Foundations of Education, 3rd edition, Volume II, Chapter 15, Mathematics.*

Many math concepts are based on spatial concepts. Blind learners should first become familiar with these concepts using tactile materials and then apply this knowledge to digital math materials. Recall that the abacus is probably one of the oldest forms of making calculations and continues to be an essential low-tech tool for nonvisual computations. The abacus can be used for a wide range of calculations from simple arithmetic to complex long division. Students might use an abacus to draft a math problem first, and then use a braille writer or digital system to document and revise it.

**Content Vocabulary
Abacus**

The Abacus is a calculation tool made up of rods with moveable beads. Those designed for blind computation feature pieces of soft fabric or rubber behind the beads to keep them from sliding inadvertently.

In many paperless twenty-first century classrooms and workplaces, students and employees create and disseminate work with digital charts and graphs. It is critical that individuals with blind or low vision can create digital charts and graphs, share them graphs with others, and glean information from them.

Tech Tip

See Paths to Technology post "Charts and Graphs Skills Review."

https://www.perkinselearning.org/technology/blog/charts-and-graphs-skills-review

At the time of this writing, developers are working to resolve accessibility issues for data visualizations through sonification, or using sounds to convey information. Keep in mind that the state of accessibility of software and hardware is frequently subject to rapid, unexpected changes, so providers must always test accessibility for themselves and prepare their students to do likewise.

Just as digital text must be systematically entered to ensure that it will be accurately read by synthesized speech, math and scientific data must also be input using proper formatting. Stand-alone equation editors (for example, MathType™, Scientific Notebook®) and embedded word processing features (for example, Equation Editor in Microsoft Word, EquatIO® in Google Docs) can support keyboard entry of mathematical and scientific symbols. When output is in a file format such as LaTeX or MathML, a screen reader can follow a logical reading order as when instructed by the math code. These technologies allow an individual to draft, review, and revise math and scientific notations independently.

VISUAL AUTHORING TOOLS

- **Low Tech**
  - Pens and Paper
  - Authoring with a Video Magnifier
- **High Tech**
  - Smart Pens and Smart Tablets
  - Digital Pens/Pencils
  - Stylus

There are several options for supporting a visual authoring workflow. Several of these methods combine high- and low-tech tools, so while a low vision individual might use one tool for visual input, he or she might use a different tool for reviewing their work tactilely or auditorily using any of the methods described in **Chapters 2 and 3.** When considering these options, it is important to first identify an individual's

workflow before selecting potential tools that fit within the workflow. As with all technology, the user should sample a variety of options in order to determine preferences and then select the most appropriate tools for various tasks.

Low Tech
Pens and Paper

The use of low-tech writing tools will likely depend on personal preferences. Despite the increasing likelihood that most of the tasks discussed in this section can be completed digitally, several instances are particularly well-suited for including low-tech authoring tools in a low vision author's toolkit.

- Development of foundational writing skills
- Jotting a quick note, or annotating paper media such as a form or worksheet
- Providing a signature such as on a bill or service authorization
- Creative endeavors such as sketching
- High tech tools are unavailable or not preferred

Low-tech writing tools are often used for short writing tasks, both for personal use and for sharing information with others. Regardless of someone's sensory access preferences or abilities, basic handwriting remains an essential skill for almost every individual. References to the visual shape of letters are prevalent in everyday life, for example when directing a driver to take a "U-turn," describing a building as

"L-shaped," or explaining a circular diagram as an "O". The most effective tools enable individuals to produce writing that is legible to both themselves and others. This is particularly important when taking notes for later study.

Mainstream tools like pens (for example, Pilot FriXion® erasable gel pens in 1.0, .7, and .5MM) and pencils (Castell® 9000 graphite pencils 8B) are commercially available and offer variations in the line thickness, color, and permanence. For most school-aged students, erasable options are very attractive, although note that some erasable inks (such as the Pilot FriXion) disappear in heated conditions such as a hot car! Bolder markers or pens offer better visibility but poor resolution: in order for letters written by wide-tip writing implements to be distinct, they must be written in a larger size, making it difficult to write in standard size legibly or draw small details.

Equally important to the quality of line produced is the contrast provided by the paper background. Pastel colored papers (ivory, yellow, green, etc.) can be useful to some individuals who are sensitive to glare. In addition, paper with bold, wide, or raised lines can help facilitate the low tech writing experience. Similar options exist for graph paper with bold or raised lines, with a range of graph lines and sizes readily available (see options from the APH store or free downloads from the Internet).

As individuals assume more responsibilities, there might be occasions such as authorizing services or paying a bill that requires an individual to provide a signature. Although signature guides are often available as giveaway items or in living aids stores, the quickest method is simply to fold then unfold the paper at the signature line. The resulting fold provides sufficient support to indicate where a signature is needed.

Authoring With a Video Magnifier

Although not as popular among school-aged students, some low vision individuals might choose to complete a writing task with the aid of a video magnifier (See **Chapter 2** for more details about video magnification systems). This method requires the individual to place the authoring media under the camera of a magnification device and then write or draw while looking at the display screen. Successful writing (or crafting or detailed tasks such as soldering) with this method requires practice to develop the hand-eye coordination and tracking needed to look at a location that is separate from where the hand is operating. Although this method requires a video magnification system, it also allows an individual to use standard-size print media and author written information, write annotations, or sketch a diagram independently. Without a video magnifier, engagement with the same media might require the assistance of a scribe (See this chapter's section, **Aural Authoring Tools**).

High Tech

High-tech technologies for low vision authoring include a combination of a low-tech strategies and high-tech tools. If an individual has adequate handwriting and hand annotation skills, and prefers to review his or her work using low vision strategies, these tools can be very helpful. High-tech tools are helpful for annotating digital media such as graphic organizers, diagrams, maps, and worksheets. The following types of tools are available in this category.

Smart Pens and Smart Tablets

Smart pens as described in this section reference strategies for authoring handwritten media and images that can be saved in multimedia formats for visual or auditory access. The Livescribe™ smartpen is a popular example of this type of tool (and is also co-opted for use with audio-tactile graphics. See U.S. Talking Tactile map from Touchgraphics, Inc., available from APH.) An individual can use this kind of talking pen to write notes and draw charts or diagrams on special paper that contains an embedded grid pattern. Embedded in the pen's tip is a tiny camera that tracks the pen's location on the paper by using the grid pattern. This pen allows for two "smart" features: it can simultaneously record an audio tag and write a note or draw a diagram. This is very useful tool when it is difficult to write quickly enough to record all of the important information being spoken. Afterwards, the user can simply touch the pen to a location on their paper notes and the recorded audio tied to the specific moment when the note was written will play back. It is important to note that the recording quality can be poor because the micro-

phone is located inside the pen, which will most likely be some distance away from the speaker. The microphone also picks up ambient noises in the room that may mask or distort the intended speaker's voice. Although the Livescribe™ pen requires charging, the specialized paper does not.

Another "smart" feature is the ability to capture and digitize an individual's handwriting when using a smart pen or using a stylus on a "smart" writing surface. Although touchscreen mobile devices offer some apps that support handwriting OCR, there are also commercially available smart tablets that are designed for digital handwritten note-taking and drawing. Wacom® and reMarkable AS are two such mainstream products that offers a smart tablet (also known as a digital notepad) that digitizes stylus input so that anything that is written or drawn is rendered and saved as a digital (image or vector) file. Some digital notepads integrate OCR while others must be used in conjunction with an OCR app that supports handwriting recognition (e.g. Inqscribe®). With handwriting OCR, handwritten notes can be transformed into computer-readable text for further editing and multimodal access. Handwriting OCR is an emerging feature that is also becoming more prevalent, usable, and accurate in a number of mainstream note-taking apps including Nebo® and GoodNotes®. If using a touchscreen tablet is already part of an individual's workflow, installing a note-taking app with handwriting OCR on the tablet can replace the need for purchasing and carrying a separate device that is limited to writing and drawing.

Digital Pens/Pencils

For individuals who want to replicate the handwriting and drawing experience on a touchscreen tablet using a note-taking or drawing app instead of a dedicated device, a digital tool such as the Apple Pencil®, Logitech® Crayon, or Wacom® EMR pen is a required writing implement. While other options are becoming available at lower costs, at the time of writing, these three are the most popular options. Digitizing pens and pencils use palm rejection technology in which the user rests his or her hand on the screen (as he or she would when writing on paper) but the touchscreen will only activate with input from the digital pen or pencil. Depending on the app used in conjunction with the digital pen or pencil, the input can be saved as an image, handwriting can be converted into digital readable text, or the content can often be shared via e-mail, text message, or saved in the cloud. Digital pens and pencils typically connect to a tablet wirelessly via Bluetooth and must be charged prior to use.

Different tips can be used as needed for bolder or finer lines, while erasing capabilities vary depending on the app.

Stylus

Similar to a digital pen or pencil, a stylus allows an individual to engage with content on a touchscreen device. However, a stylus performs more like a finger while allowing for more precise input on a touchscreen. This feature can be useful when activating small buttons on an app or in situations that require the user to draw with more precision. A variety of styluses are readily available online from several vendors. Prices currently range upwards to $50, with the more expensive options having a heavier feel and sturdier construction. Some standard ballpoint pens might even have a stylus nub for dual functionality. It is important to remember that unlike a digital pen or pencil, styluses have no palm rejection technology, therefore the user must be sure to keep the palm elevated above the touchscreen. For this reason, a stylus should be reserved for activating buttons and drawing rough sketches, but not for more involved handwriting tasks on a touchscreen. Styluses conveniently do not require any charging, power, or wireless connection to use.

TACTILE AUTHORING TOOLS

- **Low Tech**
  - Slate and Stylus
  - Tactile Markers, Braille Labels, Braille Labelers
  - Braillewriters

- **High Tech**
  - Electronic Braillewriters
  - Electronic Notetakers
  - Alternative Braille Keyboards

Writers with stronger tactile skills will choose tactile authoring tools because they are the most efficient or preferred way for them to write. As indicated in **Chapter 2,** individuals with strong or developing tactile skills will also use braille for reading back the written word. A multimodal approach might involve using auditory methods to read back what is written but switching to braille for detailed editing and revision.

Low Tech

Low-tech braille-writing devices are sometimes referred to as manual or mechanical writing tools because the user physically embosses braille dots onto paper. By using either a manual handheld tool or their fingers to press levers on a mechanical device and directly emboss the dots of a braille cell, individuals can produce written work in hard copy braille. These tools offer portability, durability, dependability, and are much less expensive than high tech counterparts.

Slate and Stylus

One of the simplest tools for short braille writing tasks is the slate and stylus. It is a braille writer's equivalent to pencil and paper—it is portable and always works! The ease with which the slate and stylus can be used to label items and for jotting down brief notes makes it an essential tool to learn and master.

A slate is made from a flat piece of metal or plastic that is hinged on one side to allow paper to be placed in between its two halves. The bottom half of the slate has rows and columns of empty braille cells impressed into the metal. The top half of the slate has holes corresponding to the empty braille cells on the bottom half of the slate. The writer uses a stylus, a short, knobbed knobbed device with a pointed tip, to press or emboss the dots onto the paper through these holes in the slate to write braille directly onto the paper held in place within the slate. Because the holes are pressed away from the writer, and the dots are embossed in a reverse and backward orientation; the writer must have the spatial capabilities to produce comprehendible braille.

Slates are available in a wide variety of sizes ranging from one-line slates

Figure 4.1:
Slate and Stylus

A slate and stylus is best suited for simple writing tasks such as creating labels or taking notes. The writer creates braille by pressing the stylus's pointed tip through the slate, which holds a sheet of paper in place.

(best for making short labels), to multi-line slates and even full page slates. Each size offers different advantages depending on the nature and size of the writing task to be accomplished. For longer writing tasks, the slate and stylus is likely inefficient.

Tactile Markers, Braille Labels, Braille Labelers

Many items within one's environment contain no distinguishing tactile characteristics that allow for nonvisual identification. Tactile markers or a braille label can solve these accessibility gaps and can be customized to individual needs. For example, a laundry machine may have a rotating knob with only printed indicators but no tactile markings. Although a blind individual could use a visual interpreter app to help identify the indicators, this strategy might only be used initially so that an individual can place his or her own tactile markers or labels on the machine for ongoing accessibility. Depending on individual preference, braille might be preferred on a label while at other times a single dot (known as a "bump dot") will suffice to mark a button on a microwave or smartphone screen A simple Internet search for "tactile markers visually impaired" will yield numerous results like those found on APH's Vision-Aware site: https://www.visionaware. org/info/everyday-living/home-modifica tion-/labeling-and-marking/123.

Adhesive plastic sheets can be used to make labels of any size. Brailleables (from APH), Con-Tact® laminating paper, shelf liner, or adhesive labels are easily marked with a slate and stylus or braille writer and applied to items in the environment such as tactile map, spice containers, an appliance, or a classroom cubby or sign. Pre-made print-braille labels (available from APH) and a handheld braille labeling device such as the Reizen™ Braille Labeler can make it easier for a non-braille reader to assist with labeling tasks. The 6dot™ Braille Label Maker™ is an alternative braille labeling device for blind users who want a label machine experience with a six-key braille keyboard. Priced at almost $800, this is considered a luxury item more than a necessity because similar labels could be produced using a slate and stylus. In general, the tactile marker or braille labeling tool chosen depends on whether an individual is labeling for him- or herself or whether a sighted person is creating the label.

Braille writers

For longer writing activities on paper, braille users might prefer to use a manual braille writer, also known as a Perkins brailler. Similar to a manual typewriter, a brailler has a roller that feeds one sheet of paper at a time into the machine. Instead of a QWERTY keyboard, there are six keys from left to right that correspond to the six dots of a braille cell. The keys are separated in the middle by a space bar key, with a paper advance (line down) key on the left of the row and a backspace key to the right. As the user presses combinations of the six keys, dots are embossed on the paper to create one braille cell at a time. An *embossing head* (the actual piece of metal that embosses the dots) moves over the paper and works against the rubber roller as each braille cell is produced. A *carriage* allows the user to manually reposition the embossing head over the paper as needed. Using a brailler can be faster than using the slate and stylus, similar to how typing on a keyboard can be faster than hand-writing (recall that a slate and stylus is equivalent to pencil and paper, while a braille writer is equivalent to a manual typewriter).

Content Vocabulary Braille Writer

A braille writer is a typewriter with six keys that each correspond with one dot of a braille cell and a roll-up carriage for paper. The original Braille writer was invented by Frank H. Hall in 1892.

Figure 4.2:
Perkins Brailler (labeled)

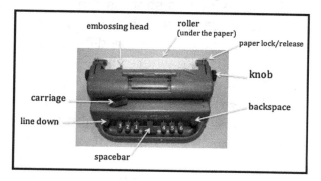

Note that a manual brailler requires enough finger strength and dexterity to press the keys with enough force to emboss dots clearly on thick paper. Finger isolation and directionality skills must also be sufficiently developed. For individuals who have difficulty pressing

the keys hard enough, straight or angled extension keys can be affixed to the braille writer. Straight extension keys are similar to the typical keys on a braille writer, but are longer and extend several inches toward the user. This extra length provides more lever-age and thus reduces the finger strength needed to emboss the braille and make an imprint on the paper. Extension keys are helpful for some users while they are developing greater finger strength, such as young children and individuals with motor disabilities. Angled or bent extension keys that bring the keys closer together toward the space bar are also available for individuals who have trouble pressing more than one key at a time.

Figure 4.3:
Braille Cell

A braille cell consists two columns of three dots numbered from one to six. Using a single dot or a combination of them, a braille cell can represent a number, let-ter, punctuation mark, or entire word.

Some braille users may have functional use of only one hand. These individuals can take advantage of the unimanual braillewriter, which allows the user to input braille with just one hand. After the keys on the left side of the device—representing dots 1-2-3—are pressed, these keys remained depressed while the user presses the desired keys on the right side of the device. When the user releases the keys representing dots 4-5-6 or the space bar, all keys are released and the braille character is embossed.

Braille readers who have decreased sensitivity in their fingertips have the option of using a braille writer that embosses braille in a larger format. This large-cell braille writer embosses the dots at approximately the same height as regular braille, but the space between the dots and between each cell or character is increased, making it easier for users to read what they have written. Extension keys can also be used with the large-cell and unimanual braille writers.

The greatest advantage to manual braille writers is the ability to create full-page braille (recall that RBDs offer only one line of braille for reading at a time). Beginning braille readers might even choose to double- or triple-space their writing to ease readability while authoring. Having the ability to format braille with paragraphs, lists, and vertical math problems can help an emerging braille reader develop an understanding of how information is organized in space.

Once these spatial references are developed, the braille reader can better understand how to format information in a virtual environment. Some readers might also prefer the softer feel of reading embossed paper braille rather than the harder metal or plastic tips that comprise braille dots on a RBD.

The main disadvantage of manual braille writers is that editing can be tedious. Because dots are embossed onto paper, corrections require dots to be flattened enough to be imperceptible to touch. A braille eraser can be a simple wooden or plastic device with a rounded point, or even the flat end of a pen or pencil. Many people simply resort to using a fingernail to depress an errant braille dot! Keep in mind that poorly erased braille can obscure readability of a new braille cell that is embossed on the same spot. Corrections are best carried out if errors are identified and revised as soon as the error is made. Because this is a purely mechanical process, it can be difficult to correct a mistake where there is insufficient space to enter additional characters. Because of the difficulty with correcting errors, the limitation to tactile access for review of the written work, and the ability to share the document only with another braille reader, high tech tools for tactile authoring methods should be introduced as soon as possible. At the same time, service providers must ensure that skills for using these low tech tools are well developed for proficiency with a varied toolbox.

High Tech

Braille is a primary and essential means of literacy for blind and some low vision individuals, but there are some inherent challenges when using a tactile literacy code. Low-tech tactile authoring tools, as described in the previous section, require a tactile authoring and revision process. This causes a "private" workflow limited to only the author and others who know braille. If needing to collaborate with a teacher or colleague who does not know braille, a system that offers an option for print output is essential. Tactile authoring tools that are compatible with a digital workflow offer prominent solutions; an individual can author in braille using a 6-key braille keyboard (or QWERTY keyboard if preferred) with a RBD, and the written work can be reviewed in a digital format that supports visual (digital text) and auditory (using text-to-speech including a screen reader) output in addition to tactile. These capabilities allow a totally blind student or employee to work seamlessly with sighted peers, instructors, and colleagues without any intervention from a service provider. Instruction in using high-tech tools should be introduced early alongside low-tech tools.

Tech Tip

See Paths to Technology post "Layla: 4 year old Learning VoiceOver and Braille."

https://www.perkinselearning.org/technology/posts/layla-4-year-old-learning-voiceover-and-braille-video

Electric Braille Writers

For individuals who have difficulty managing the force needed to emboss braille on a manual braille writer, electric braillers require less force and can be easier for embossing. Unfortunately, they are also prone to needing repairs. Although electric braillers have electronic components, the output is still embossed braille on paper with all the challenges associated with editing hard copy braille.

The Mountbatten. The Mountbatten is a variation of an electric braille writer that can help transition a student from a manual brailler to an electronic notetaker. It is compatible with varying weights of paper, is battery-operated, and offers text-to-braille or braille-to-text, which is especially helpful when a sighted teacher wants to support early literacy activities without knowing braille. As will be mentioned in **Chapter 5,** however, use of a braille translation feature does not replace the need for a qualified professional who can produce high quality and properly formatted braille for the student. The Mountbatten also has an option for erasing errors, which addresses the greatest disadvantage of manual braille writers. Because the Mountbatten is focused on supporting early literacy skills, it is designed toward younger students who benefit from the lighter key touch and auditory confirmation of letters as they are typed. The Mountbatten is available in a couple of models, which vary in features such as USB or wireless connectivity, printing, embossing and tactile graphics capabilities, and availability of a visual display. Because of the cost (approximately $1,000–$3,000 for used and new models as of the time of writing) and transitional nature of its use, some individuals will skip directly from a manual brailler to an electronic notetaker or RBD with a computing device rather than invest in this purchase. On the other hand, the multiple features for tactile, auditory, and visual engagement in the braille literacy journey can well justify the cost for some students.

Perkins Smart Brailler. The Perkins SMART Brailler® offers features similar to the Mountbatten but more resembles the Perkins Classic Brailler. The Smart Brailler allows users to choose from several voices for the audio output. A 4.3-inch screen displays large print letters and SimBraille (a braille font) of the text entered by the user thus allowing non-braille readers to see and read what is being written. Sighted instructors teaching braille reading and writing will find the visual display helpful in monitoring a student's progress. Those learning to write and read braille will find many of the features of the Perkins Smart Brailler very useful, especially the ability to receive immediate auditory and tactile feedback about the text entered. The full-page hard copy produced by the Perkins Smart Brailler and the Mountbatten Brailler provide the additional benefit to the writer of being able to better understand the physical layout and formatting of their written document, which can be very important

when completing math problems and scientific equations.

Electronic Notetakers

Electronic notetakers with braille keyboards and refreshable braille displays allow authors to use braille to create and compose a variety of digital text documents. Some users might prefer electronic notetakers because they weigh less than a laptop, have a longer battery life, and turn on immediately (rather than taking a few minutes for an operating system to boot up, as with computers). Their small size makes these devices particularly portable and easy to use in classes, meetings, or in transit. At the time of this writing, most notetakers do not have a visual display and are meant to support tactile or auditory engagement with information: however, video ports are available that allow connection to an external monitor for visual display. Individuals might prefer a familiar QWERTY or braille keyboard for input and synthesized speech or refreshable braille display for output. One variation, the QBraille XL (HIMS, Inc.), combines a braille keyboard with the function and navigation keys from a QWERTY keyboard. This facilitates authoring in coding programs that rely on the use of function keys. Output is available through synthesized speech or a built-in RBD. Most electronic notetakers contain word-processing software similar to that found on computers. While the features of these word processors are not as robust as those on computers, they are more than adequate for note taking with an option to complete longer writing tasks on a computer. Many of these devices can be connected directly to a printer or embosser to produce a written document in either print or braille. Recall that electronic notetakers can also be used as a RBD when connected to a computing device. This setup allows the user to take advantage of the best of many worlds: Braille or QWERTY input, use of a powerful word processing program, and braille and speech output to review and edit for a multimodal authoring workflow. In this type of digital workflow, written work can be embossed in braille on paper, displayed on a RBD, or printed in standard text.

It is important to remember that despite an individual's proficiency with an electronic notetaker, it remains important to develop efficient computer and keyboarding skills for competitive inclusion in educational and workplace environments.

Alternative Braille Keyboards

RBDs and electronic notetakers can be connected to any computer that supports Bluetooth or a compatible cable connection. This setup allows for braille input into a word processing app to create written documents. Another variant that is less powerful but significantly less expensive ($250 versus $1,000 and up at the time of writing) is the Power Chord Braille Keyboard from Touch Graphics, Inc. The Power Chord is a dedicated keyboard with six-key braille entry that connects via USB to a PC computer and allows the user to interact with a word processing program using braille

input. This can be a very valuable tool for people who are just learning braille, do not need the robust features of an electronic notetaker yet, or benefit from auditory feedback if used in conjunction with a screen reader. The Power Chord word processing program can also display a student's document in either print or braille with a single keystroke, making it easy for a teacher who may or may not know braille to check the student's work.

Some touchscreen devices also offer an onscreen keyboard. This type of keyboard relies on virtual keys for six-key braille input with no physical buttons. Usually, the user will rest the six fingers used for braille on the touchscreen, wait for the screen to calibrate the finger placement, then proceed to move all six fingers on the screen as if activating physical keys. At the time of writing, the onscreen keyboard is a feature found on the HumanWare™ BrailleNote Touch and Apple iOS (mobile) devices such as the iPod, iPhone, and iPad.

AURAL AUTHORING TOOLS

- **Low Tech**
- **High Tech**
  - Audio Recording
  - Speech Recognition (Speech-to-Text, Dictation)
  - Screenreaders

Low Tech

One low-tech authoring option that sacrifices one's independence for the sake of immediate access is the use of a human scribe. Some students might use a scribe when efficient keyboarding skills are not developed, if motor disabilities render handwriting and keyboarding inefficient, or if other writing tools are unavailable. When using a scribe as a testing accommodation, the individual must be trained in how to utilize a scribe. Punctuation conventions must be specified and individuals need to know how to direct a scribe in the review and editing process. Individuals beyond the school setting might use a scribe for practical purposes such as filling in a tip on a restaurant bill or completing a printed form when an accessible copy is unavailable. Sometimes it may simply be more efficient for the individual to use a scribe than another authoring tool.

High Tech
Audio recordings

Short recordings, more colloquially known as voice memos, can be very convenient for capturing a user's voice for auditory playback. Voice memos can be recorded to document a reminder, capture a sound experience (similar to taking a photograph), or to send an auditory message. Sometimes, an audio recording might be captured for later transcription into text by using a speech recognition program; this workflow is helpful for facilitating visual, auditory (via TTS), or tactile review of the resulting digital text document for further editing.

Speech recognition (speech-to-text, dictation)

Speech recognition refers to the process of converting spoken words into digital text. Also known as speech-to-text or dictation, speech recognition can be a go-to method for producing written work aurally and for students with multiple disabilities who are unable to write using traditional means. Dictation can be a powerful tool that enables students to write independently.

Tech Tip

See Paths to Technology post "Cody's O&M Adventures: iBook post."

https://www.perkinselearning.org /technology/posts/codys-om-adven tures-ibook"

Playback can be accomplished visually, tactilely using an RBD, or auditorily using TTS or a screen reader. The best use of dictation is for short messages for communication, especially messages among friends and not in a professional context in case of dictation fails. For longer writing tasks, many computers and word processors are now equipped with speech recognition features. While these features do not ensure complete accuracy, they are powerful tools for text entry and for controlling some electronic devices and appliances. When used for authoring, however, one significant challenge facing dictation users is editing the resulting text and making corrections when recognition errors occur. Positioning the text cursor, making the correction, and then proofreading the edit can be difficult for users who rely on voice commands alone. If an individual wants to edit the text with a screen reader or

RBD, the dictation and word processing apps must be fully accessible and compatible with the screen reader. If possible, using a manual input tool like a braille or QWERTY keyboard will be more accurate and allow more efficient editing.

Using speech recognition technology to manage electronic devices and appliances is becoming more advanced and prevalent. At the time of this writing, virtual assistants such as Amazon Alexa™, Apple Siri®, and Google Assistant™ use auditory commands for managing home systems including, but not limited to, security, heating and cooling, entertainment, and lighting. These tools can also be used to find information online and connect to any variety of apps for news, weather, and music. Finally, virtual assistants can be asked to take a note or send a message that the user dictates. Although this is certainly convenient, it is a healthy practice to be aware of privacy issues that can arise from devices that are always actively listening.

Screen Readers

When authoring, speech output allows the user to author in a word processing app and to hear the entire document spoken at the paragraph, sentence, word, or character level. Using this strategy, screen readers are more recommended than basic TSS tools that do not allow auditory navigation at the character and punctuation levels. It is recommended for an author to listen to the entire document to catch the most glaring errors before using a different

method (visual or tactile) for more precise editing. Take note that auditory review of written text alone is not a comprehensive editing method! Print or braille is necessary for catching dictation errors that result in homonym confusion, incorrect words, and poor or missing punctuation. Authors must also use print or braille to ensure a document is properly formatted.

NOTE-TAKING TOOLS

- **Annotating Written Texts and Notes**
- **Accessing a Copy of Notes**
  - Recorded Notes
  - Physical Notes
  - Digital Notes
- **Accessing "The Board"**
  - Screensharing
  - Video Magnifier

Although authoring as discussed thus far focuses primarily on producing written work for creating and sharing information with others, sometimes an individual must document information in a systematic way, such as when taking notes. When note-taking, an individual might choose different tools than would be used for authoring a complete written work. The nature of how information is documented might differ as well; for example, note-taking often uses personal shorthand and acronyms that are not used when authoring. Note-taking methods may also differ depending on whether notes are taken for oneself or for sharing with others. This final section will identify tools for the purpose of annotating written texts or accessing information that might be presented in lectures, discussions, and meetings. Each individual will have his or her own preferences for accessing such information, as well as note-taking methods. Most students and employees need to have some system of note-taking that allows them maximum efficiency and independence.

Annotating Written Texts and Notes

Note-taking is a multi-step activity that is achieved by combining several skills. An individual must access the information, write a note, and read back the note within context. A proficient note-taker will also have a system of outlining the content and organizing notes in notebooks or folders. **Sidebar 4.5, Note-taking Task Analysis,** shares one possible instructional sequence that can be used to develop one's note-taking skills. This section will emphasize tools for a digital note-taking system.

For nonvisual access, a note-taking system must be fully accessible for auditory (with a screen reader) and tactile (with an RBD) access. For low vision access, a user-friendly note-taking system will offer a simple interface with high contrast menu buttons, editing tools, and a full-screen mode. Handwriting OCR might be a valuable feature if the individual prefers to write by hand but has difficulty read-

ing his or her own handwriting or wants the option to review notes auditorily.

When taking notes on a text such as a book or article, it is helpful to use a reading app that offers the following usability features (in addition to any needed accessibility features):

- Allows import of various file formats for receiving a variety of texts such as ePub and PDF
- Insert in-text comments/notes
- Tag highlighted text with an accompanying note
- Export notes into a single file with tags to the text associated with the note
- Compatibility with an individual's computing device

To date, the most popular reading apps that include these note-taking features are VoiceDream Reader and Apple iBooks®.

Other times, an individual might want to take notes based on a lecture or workshop. While any of the aforementioned tools in this chapter could be used for that task, there are a few additional tools that are particularly useful and designed for note-taking. Based on the success of word processing apps and co-opted uses of these programs for note-taking, companies are now offering note-taking apps (for example, Microsoft® One-Note, Google Keep™, and Apple Notes). These tend to mirror the user experi-

NOTETAKING TASK ANALYSIS

Aside from the exceptional student, notetaking is a skill that requires systematic, thoughtful instruction. The learner needs to have prerequisite skills for reading and authoring to ensure success and minimal frustration in the notetaking process. Although each student will demonstrate individualized learning needs, the following task analysis describes one approach to notetaking that can be used to differentiate instruction:

- Locate an article that is familiar or of high interest to the reader
- Read the article using the student's preferred reading tool and access technology
- Identify one main section and related sub-sections of the article. Prompt the student to fill in details related to these sections.
- Encourage the student to identify the other main ideas and sub-sections of the article
- Using a notetaking app, have the student format a list of main ideas to form the beginning of an outline
- Review this list together—encourage the reader to add important facts and information under each main idea as it relates. Different access technologies might be used to read, insert, and revise the list.
- As the reader progresses, the instructor can provide less prompting to identify each main section and related subsections, while encouraging the reader to locate and insert more of the important information from the article.

It is important that a student's proficiency in using access tools (and changing which tools are used when) are reinforced throughout the notetaking activity.

ence of the parent word processing apps regarding accessibility and are intended to sync seamlessly with the associated cloud system. A number of other competitors also offer a variety of note-taking apps that are comparable if not more robust (See **Sidebar 4.6, A Selection of Popular Apps for Multimodal Note-taking**). These apps are distinguished by the intention to mimic writing in a notebook or notepad while using a touchscreen tablet with added functionality for attaching a file, saving or annotating an imported

Sidebar 4.6

A SELECTION OF POPULAR APPS FOR MULTIMODAL NOTETAKING

(Compiled September 2019)

- **Apple Notes**
- **Box Note**
- **Dropbox Paper**
- **Evernote**
- **GoodNotes**
- **Google Keep**
- **Microsoft OneNote**
- **MyScript Nebo**
- **Notability**
- **Notes**
- **Simplenote**
- **Zoho Notebook**

image, and recording audio. The apps support input via a keyboard, digital pen, or stylus; some apps also support input in math or scientific notation and handwriting OCR. Although the ultimate selection will be determined by individual preference, consider the following features when choosing which note-taking apps to introduce to a student or client:

- Compatibility with personal computing device
- Accessibility and usability with the student's access tools such as: screen reader, braille display (if student needs a screen reader and/ or braille display), reverse contrast, TTS
- Usability of app interface
  - Contrast of buttons and icons
  - Menu layouts
  - Ease of accessing accessibility features to adjust visual and auditory settings
- Ease of creating and organizing notes and notebooks, input options
- Ease of inserting, organizing, and finding information within a note
- Authoring and editing tools, including keyboard/stylus/digital pen input, handwriting OCR
- Multimedia support for adding audio recordings, pictures, files
- Compatibility to sync with a cloud storage platform
- Integrated OCR and TTS features
- Ability to annotate a worksheet or diagram
- Ability to sync across multiple note-taking devices
- Price

Accessing a Copy of Notes

At times, rather than taking one's own notes, the most efficient strategy is to ask a fellow student or co-worker to take notes on one's behalf. Although this method arguably sacrifices an individual's independence and personal analyses in documenting information, it is nonetheless an informed choice that any individual (blind or sighted) is entitled to make. For an individual who is blind or has low vision, notes taken by others must be formatted for nonvisual or low vision access. However, the needs of the note-taker must also be considered so that this service causes minimal disruption to his or her own workflow.

Recorded Notes

At times, an individual may want to request permission to record all or part of a lecture. When identified as an accommodation in an IEP or as part of a general accommodations plan, a student cannot be denied this request. If an individual prefers audio recording as his or her primary means of note-taking, he or she should choose a recorder with strategic external microphone placement as well as the ability to easily bookmark and locate specific sections within a recording. In addition, it is important to recognize how quickly large masses of recorded information build up. The user will benefit from an organized system of storage for efficient review of materials.

Physical Notes

The traditional means for sharing notes is making a paper copy. Copies can be made of notes using one of these strategies:

- Carbon paper. The notetaker places a layer of carbon paper between two sheets of regular paper to create a simultaneous copy. This method is becoming less common because carbon paper is less readily available and carbon copies can have poor

resolution, providing less than optimal readability for low vision access.

- Photocopier. A copy of the notes are made on a photocopier and physically shared. While photocopiers have the advantage of being able to enlarge notes, the disadvantage is the time necessary between taking the notes and sharing the photocopy.

Digital Notes

A digital copy of notes can be shared easily via a shared cloud location by sending a hyperlink to an online location or by attaching the notes as a file using an email or a messaging app. For nonvisual access, the notes must be in a readable digital text. Remember that digital images are not accessible unless they have an accompanying description (alt text), tactile graphic, or 3D model for full accessibility. A digital copy is often preferred for the following reasons:

- Since the notetaker is taking notes in a digital format, an electronic copy can be shared immediately.

- If using a collaborative work platform, the notes can be accessed at the moment of creation.

- The receiver is able to add annotations to a shared note.

- The receiver can use a preferred tool for accessing a digital note in a preferred visual, tactile, and/or auditory format.

Accessing "The Board"

Accessing information presented on a board can be a significant challenge for both service providers and blind or low vision individuals. Nowadays, chalkboards are less common, and information is instead presented under a document camera or on a projector screen, whiteboard, interactive whiteboard such as a SMART Board® or Promethean©, or on a large television. In many cases, individuals are encouraged to exercise an accommodation for preferential seating, which entitles the person to sit wherever he or she can best see the "board." Aside from exiling the individual to the front of the room in most instances, preferential seating can also be challenging due to glare from overhead lighting or windows, poor resolution on a projector screen or interactive whiteboard, and whenever information is presented on multiple boards around the room or from a single presentation stage, which make finding an ideal seat for viewing nearly impossible. When presenting information in this manner, the key is to facilitate *desktop access to information presented at a distance.* For nonvisual access, a digital copy of the notes in an accessible format makes this possible. For low vision access, a digital copy will also suffice, in addition to options that allow the content to be accessed on an individual's personal computing device for desktop viewing. Once an individual can access content on a personal computing device with a digital copy or a view-only format, then any number of tools can be used to accommodate the preferred format. Since nonvisual accessibility requires an accessible, digital copy of information presented on the board, the following two types of tools

provide additional options for low vision access.

Screen Sharing

Screen sharing is the process of mirroring the contents of a primary screen or projector on a secondary screen. Originally intended as a tool for computer technicians to view and control a user's computer remotely, screen sharing software is discussed here as another method for accessing information on the board. In most situations, the individual will be limited to viewing the teacher's or presenter's screen without controlling it. Note that screen sharing is not appropriate for nonvisual access because the projected materials cannot be manipulated for auditory or tactile access. The teacher or presenter's projector might be a computer, document camera, projector screen, or interactive whiteboard (for example SmartBoard© or Promethean©). The viewer's screen is usually a component of a personal computing device such as a mobile tablet, laptop, or monitor.

Screen sharing also allows an individual to share his or her screen to the larger presentation board during a group presentation. This method is excellent for individuals with multiple disabilities who want to use their computer's TTS system for an oral presentation while also navigating the presentation independently using access tools. Sometimes, it can be advantageous for an individual to reserve one device (such as a tablet) for screen sharing while taking notes on a different device (such as a laptop). Otherwise, if the same device is used for both screen sharing as note-taking, the screen can become crowded and requires frequent re-positioning as the user switches between apps. Once information is shared on a viewer's screen, visual access tools (for example, screen magnification, reverse contrast, color filters) can be used as needed, and information can be captured as a screenshot for later review and annotation as needed. Several screen sharing setups are possible.

- **A cable connecting the projecting device and the secondary screen or computing device.** This is most common with older document cameras or interactive whiteboards without wireless connectivity. Challenges include having a loose cable that can be a tripping hazard, and the fact that the individual remains "tethered" to the projecting device.

- **A Bluetooth connection between the presenter's computing device and the viewer's computing device,** where the presenter's device is displaying information on the board as an external monitor. This is a preferred setup when all the presentation materials originate from the presenter's computer.

- **A Bluetooth or Wi-Fi connection between the projecting device and the viewer's computing device.** This is the ideal setup but can be difficult to achieve if there are multiple sources of input for displaying information on the projecting

device (e.g., content from a computer and content from a document camera).

Screensharing applications are available for free or at a cost; some video conferencing programs also offer screensharing as a feature. (**See Sidebar 4.7, A Selection of Screensharing Apps.**) Considerations when selecting a screensharing app include the following:

- Compatibility with the teacher's or presenter's existing workflow
- Compatibility with a viewer's existing workflow
- Ease of connecting a viewer's screen to the primary screen
- Need for a one-time screenshare versus the ongoing need to share the same screen
- Cost

When an effective screensharing system is implemented, low vision individuals are no longer dependent on a preferential seating arrangement that might only provide inconsistent viewing quality.

Video Magnifier

The camera of a video magnification system can also be swiveled outward to gain desktop access to information presented at a distance. This is possible when the camera has a powerful enough optical zoom to maintain clarity and resolution while magnifying a target that is far away (similar to what a telescope would accomplish). The camera must also be connected to the video magnification system with an adjustable mount that allows for 360° positioning. This setup can be accomplished when a document camera or smartlens with wireless capability is used as part of a video magnification system. Although pointing a camera at a projection or display screen often results in poor resolution, this setup is ideal for instances in which there is information being presented on a stage (such as at a school assembly or conference presentation), and the camera can be set up in a location that is separate from where the low vision individual would like to sit. A monocular could also be used in this situation; however, viewing through a monocular can be challenging for some individuals depending on their visual impairment or additional disabilities. With a video magnification system that is setup for distance viewing, the information can be viewed easily with both eyes on the display of a personal computing device.

SUMMARY

Technology offers a wide variety of tools for nonvisual or low vision authoring and note-taking. Depending on the task and individual preferences, low- and high-tech tools can be used in many combinations to accomplish a range of tasks. No one tool can meet all the authoring needs of an individual, and needs might differ when authoring for oneself versus authoring for others. With a clear understanding of when each tool is most efficient and when it is not, service providers can introduce an initial selection of tools to a blind or low vision individual. Based on an individual's existing workflow and usability preferences, proficiency in using a range of low- and high-tech tools can contribute to building a valuable toolbox of technology that provides many access points. The knowledge of and flexibility in understanding the use of many different tools is required in order to successfully complete authoring and note-taking tasks as a student or employee.

CHAPTER 5
Technologies for Producing Materials in Alternate Formats

Ensuring that blind and low vision individuals have access to information requires orchestrating two important components: 1) assessing the individual's skills and personal choice in order that he or she can benefit from the available tools, and 2) having information available in accessible formats. Equipping individuals with the materials they need for school, work, and recreation, in a format they can access at the same time as sighted peers, is an ongoing priority for service providers. Advances in technology and increased advocacy for the rights of people with disabilities also lead to increased access to print, digital, and multimedia information.

In addition to best practices, a number of federal and state laws provide even greater protections for individuals with disabilities. Landmark federal statues such as the Americans with Disabilities Act (ADA), Section 504 of the Rehabilitation Act, and the Individuals with Disabilities Education Act require accessibility of information and communications from federal, state, or local government entities. Such information and communications are often disseminated as printed textbooks or public documents, from entities such as public schools, private non-religious universities, or community staples including banks, medical facilities, retail establishments, galleries, and museums. Dissemination of accessible information means that materials must be

made available in specialized formats including braille, large print, or accessible digital formats to ensure effective communication with all patrons, including those with disabilities.

Although some texts are available from commercial producers who specialize in alternate formats (for example, ePub, embossed braille, large print, or recorded audio), other educational materials and employment-related information—including worksheets, study guides, online courses, university policies and procedures, employer policies and guidelines, employee benefit forms, and other supplementary materials—may not be available. When unavailable, accessible versions must be produced to maintain an individual's access to needed information. Materials for K–12 students can be produced by a state department of education instructional materials center, a prison braille program, or any service provider who supports the educational access of a student. A service provider can be an employee of the local education agency (LEA) such as a TVI, certified braille transcriber, alternate media specialist, or any resource specialist or paraprofessional who supports students' instruction. Materials for higher education that are unavailable from a commercial producer can be produced by an alternate media specialist in a university or college disabled student services program. In either setting, alternate media production can also be contracted out to small-scale producers. Converting printed and electronic information needed to complete job requirements is sometimes left to the employee, although this is not a recommended practice. Reasonable workplace and school accommodations are mandated by federal law to ensure that a disabled student or employee is provided with the necessary equipment, appropriate training, and adequate time in his or her job duties to convert the materials into the accessible appropriate format. (See **Appendix A** for additional information about laws pertaining to materials in accessible formats and reasonable accommodations.)

Sidebar 5.1

NIMAS AND NIMAC

Goal Seven of the *National Agenda for Children and Youth with Visual Impairments* states that students using books in alternate formats should receive these books at the same time as their sighted peers receive regular print books. This seemingly simple concept became a multi-year national project involving a consortium of interested parties including educators, consumers, publishers, and accessible media producers (AMPs). This work culminated in the development of the National Instructional Materials Accessibility Standards (NIMAS). These are the standards that will be used by publishers to produce electronic files of textbooks. These files are being deposited and maintained at the National Instructional Materials Accessibility Center (NIMAC). These deposited files are not designed to be directly embossed by a student or used with an electronic notetaker.

So, what are NIMAS files and who can use them? NIMAS files are electronic files that contain the basic information found in a book. However, this is not a usable format for students and teachers. State education authorities (SEA) must agree to join in the program and coordinate with NIMAC by designating a small number of authorized users of the NIMAS files. These authorized users are usually the state Instructional Resource Centers, but other entities can be designated. The authorized user downloads the textbook files and then submits them to an Accessible Media Producer (AMP). The AMP works with the files and prepares them in the appropriate format to produce braille, large print, or some auditory format. The books are then provided to the student in the desired format. Technology provides the tools used by the AMPs to produce the books in the various formats. (For additional information on this topic see Renfranz, Taboada, and Weatherd, 2008.)

There are several excellent tools for producing materials in alternate formats for a blind or low vision individual. No matter which sensory channel the individual uses most effectively to complete specific tasks, or how information is best represented in an alternate format, any media can be converted into an alternate format for visual, tactile, auditory, or multimodal access. (Review **Chapter 2** for a discussion of technologies for accessing printed information, and **Chapter 3** for an overview of technologies for accessing digital information.)

The current chapter will focus on the specific tools and techniques needed to produce information in alternate formats for low or nonvisual accessibility. These tools and workflows will be of interest to any service provider who assumes the role of an alternate media specialist, and to blind and low vision individuals who prefer to create their own alternate media.

TECHNOLOGIES FOR PRODUCING MATERIALS FOR DIGITAL ACCESS

In most cases, alternate media in a high quality, accessible digital format allows for the most flexibility of access. Once provided with an accessible digital copy, a blind or low vision individual can access the content using any combination of visual, auditory, and tactile tools. Commercially, the ePub file format references clear standards for publishing accessible digital books. (See free iBook *Reach for the Stars* as the

gold standard for publishing an accessible digital book.) EPub files are most accessible when they are formatted with the appropriate markup semantics that define document elements such as the following:

- Headings which allow for the creation of an embedded table of contents to facilitate an overview and navigation of different sections
- Paragraph and list styles
- Table and form headings
- Alternate text for all images
- Self-described hyperlinks

More information about producing commercial accessible ePub files can be found on the International Digital Publishing Forum's website: http://idpf.org /a11y.

For in-house production, alternate media specialists and service providers can produce digital media such as handouts or lecture materials in a word processing or presentation program (e.g. Microsoft® PowerPoint, Google Slides™, Apple Keynote®). These formats require the same markup semantics as ePub files for comprehensive accessibility and an equitable user experience to those using printed media. In some cases, alternate media might need to be produced as PDFs, such as when using an annotation app to markup an image file, or if the document author simply prefers PDF format. Ensuring PDF accessibility can be challenging, but a comprehensive manual and ongoing trainings are available from Gaeir Dietrich, director of the High-Tech Center Training Unit (HTCTU) in the California Community College System. See **Chapter 3** for a more detailed presentation of digital file formats.

WebAIM offers standards and guidelines for formatting accessible digital media (www.webaim.org). These standards and guidelines introduce terms that can provide keywords to search for more specific online tutorials, and in the digital classroom, define how accessible instructional materials (AIM) need to be formatted. Equity is achieved when an individual is provided with an accessible version of materials (for example, digital, large print, or embossed braille formats) at the same time that sighted peers are provided a standard copy.

TECHNOLOGIES FOR PRODUCING MATERIALS FOR VISUAL ACCESS

- **Commercially Available Large Print**
- **In-House Production of Large Print**
  - Enlargements using a photocopier
  - Computer-based large print production

Acquiring large print materials can be done in several ways, including purchasing commercially produced large print texts or enlarging materials in-house. As with most of the technology options considered in this book,

production techniques may be particularly appropriate—or inappropriate—for certain individuals, depending on their needs. (See **Chapter 2** for additional information about accessing materials visually.)

Commercially Available Large Print

Large print books can be obtained from specialized vendors or from mainstream publishing houses that offer a large print collection. (For a listing of such publishers, see the U.S. Library of Congress's site on large print materials at https://www.loc.gov/nls/resources /general-resources-on-disabilities/large -print-materials/#_materials.) The American Printing House for the Blind (APH) has been a traditional provider of braille, large-print, and digital textbooks for students with visual impairments. When ordering through APH, these large-print textbooks are available at no cost to the local school system through the Federal Quota Fund system. (For more information, see **Sidebar 5.2: What Is the APH Federal Quota System?**) However, many students choose not to use them because they are larger than conventional textbooks and may require managing multiple volumes. Some publishers also offer their bestsellers as large print books and upon request, either PDF or ePub files. While non-educational titles are competitively priced with their standard print counterparts, commercially produced large print textbooks can be quite expensive. Although there remain fewer large print than standard-print books, the amount of large print titles continues to increase as publishers recognize a growing market among older readers. Large print books are commonly printed in a sans serif 14–16 point font on off-white paper that provides high contrast and reduced glare. However, while large print versions of popular titles are sized similarly to traditional books, they tend to be thicker and heavier. Non-textbook titles in large print are popular with some individuals, while others prefer to use optical devices in conjunction with standard print, still others may instead prefer a digital copy that allows multi-modal access.

In-House Production of Large Print

Another option for acquiring large print materials is producing them in-house. Keep in mind that it is preferable to produce digital formats rather than large print in house. Digital formats empower the individual to access information on-demand using any sensory modality, which allows for flexibility in access depending on the environment and task. Producing alternate media in large print should be reserved for select individuals situations.

- Young students or individuals who have not yet mastered tools for digital access or the proficient use of optical devices
- Individuals who are unable to manage tools for digital access or optical devices
- Individuals with an expressed preference for large print media
- For non-text materials that are not as easily accessed tactilely or auditorily in a digital format due to complex digital translations (e.g. math and scientific notations)
- When content is more efficiently completed by pen and paper (e.g., short quizzes, quizzes with diagrams that require annotation or include math and scientific notations). As always, the individual's preference must factor heavily into the decision of when to use pen and paper versus using a stylus on a touchscreen.

Remember that providing large print is best if an individual also has other tools and strategies for accessing print; limiting a low vision user reader to only visual access can decrease reading speed and cause visual fatigue, which can lead to poor ergonomics and migraine headaches.

Enlargements Using a Photocopier

The simplest method for producing large print is on a photocopier; it is readily available technology and the cost per page is relatively low. However, this method should be considered only as a backup method when computer production is not possible. Enlargements produced with a photocopier often have reduced resolution and cannot clearly capture the smaller details of text such as super- or sub-scripts. Most photocopiers can enlarge text or images from 100 percent to approximately 200 percent of the original. Enlargements typically require larger paper to reproduce the same layout as the original; as an alternative, portions of the original can be enlarged in segments and then reproduced onto the same size paper as the original before taping them together. Unfortunately, either option can be unwieldy.

Results are only as consistent as the source media. In order to determine what enlargement setting is needed on photocopier, you must first understand the individual's preferred print size. Once you know the target print size, different percentage settings can be experimented with to obtain the desired result. Dr. Amanda Lueck's *Decision-Making Guide for Print Size Selection* offers an easy formula to help determine the most appropriate print size. Recall that a comprehensive LMA supports media recommendations for different tasks, but these LMA recommendations and those based on calculations using a formula simply to provide an initial print size using a formula simply to provide a starting point. The reader will ultimately choose the print size that works best for a given task with a certain reading tool/strategy.

When using a photocopier to produce enlarged materials, be sure to do the following:

- Use a clean, clearly printed source document. A document that has been annotated or is a second-generation copy will result in a finished product that is difficult to read which will greatly reduce visual access.

- Fit the complete enlarged image on a single photocopy in order to avoid having to divide a single image among several pages attached together. Using tabloid-size paper can help keep enlargements on a single page.

Although using a photocopier to produce large print is usually the most readily available method, it should be reserved as a temporary solution until a better strategy for producing large print materials is determined. For example, for a band director who must quickly add a new piece of music at a concert, a photocopier is likely the best solution to enlarge a part for a low vision student. However, as convenient as it is to make large print copies using a photocopier in a pinch, do not continue to generate large print copies in this way if this is not the student's preferred method of reading, or is not the most efficient way for the student to access the material at hand. Degraded resolution, the difficultly of managing larger format paper, and being restricted to using only one sense for reading means that large print produced by a photocopier is likely not the best option for a low vision reader.

Computer-Based Large-Print Production

When materials are in an electronic format (such as a digital copy from the publisher, re-created digitally, or scanned and converted from a print copy), they can be easily reproduced as large print using a word processor. The materials can also be printed in the user's preferred font and point size with ideal line, word, and character spacing. In addition to text, graphics can be enlarged on-screen and then printed in a format that maintains clarity and proportion.

If the materials are unavailable electronically, the paper document must be scanned and treated with optical character recognition (OCR) before editing. When scanning a paper original to convert it to a digital file for large print production, the resulting document often requires reformatting to correct OCR errors or adjust layouts (especially if there are blank lines provided for students to write answers to questions, as might be found on a worksheet.) **Sidebar 5.3: Using a Scanner, OCR, and Word Processor to Produce Large-Print Materials** provides two examples that explain this process in more detail.

This method of producing large-print materials using a scanner, OCR, and word processor has many advantages over using a photocopier to enlarge a document.

Advantages

- Equipment needed for scanning and word processing is readily available; many scanning and OCR apps are available for mobile touchscreen devices and smartphones, with easy integration to cloud storage locations for easy retrieval from any computing device

USING A SCANNER, OCR, AND WORD PROCESSOR TO PRODUCE LARGE-PRINT MATERIALS

As the following examples illustrate, print materials can be produced with relative care in a large-print format and tailored to a student's preferences for font size/style and line/word/character spacing, using a system comprising a scanner (device or app), optical character recognition software (OCR), and a word processing program. This workflow is an alternative to having the material available digitally, which can then be easily adjusted by the individual according to his/her visual preferences and viewed on a tablet or other computing device.

Example 1

Ms. Mendez, a third-grade teacher, wants to conduct part of her science lesson outside in the park. She is going to have her students take with them a four-page packet of materials stapled together and clipped to a clipboard. The pages contain text, graphics, and questions with blank lines on which to write the answers. Ms. Mendez knows that she has two students in her class who have low vision but who access their materials visually. Rachel uses a video magnifier for reading, while Dimitri prefers to use a mobile touchscreen tablet.

Ms. Mendez knows that with proximity to a pond and impending fog, the students' devices would fare better if left indoors. The students would also prefer to use the same clipboard and journaling strategies as their peers. According to their learning media assessment and recommendations from the Teacher of the Visually Impaired (TVI), Ms. Mendez knows that Rachel prefers print materials in single-spaced Verdana bold 24-point font and Dimitri prefers double-spaced 16-point Arial font. How can she meet the needs of these two students and conduct her outdoor lesson?

Ms. Mendez contacts Mr. Polonsky, the students' TVI, several days before the lesson to explain what materials she needs to have adapted. Together they will decide to make the necessary adaptations for the two students and who will do it. In this case, Mr. Polonsky has trained Alecia, a clerical staff person in the school's media center to assist in the production of large print materials.

First, Alecia checks with Ms. Mendez to see if her materials packet is available as an electronic file. Many teachers at the school use a computer word-processing program to create classroom materials. Usually Ms. Mendez does have such a file, which saves time. (If she has the electronic file, Alecia can skip to Step 4 below.) In this case, however, she does not, so Alecia needs to scan the document as described in steps 1, 2, and 3 of the following procedure:

▫ Obtain a good, clean copy of the document and have a pre-determined workflow comprised of a scanner (hardware or app), OCR software, word-processing software, and a color printer.

▫ Scan the document, upload it to the cloud, and retrieve the document on a computer that has OCR software and a word processing program to transform it into text.

▫ In the word processing program: Execute spell-check and proofread the document to locate and correct any scanning/OCR errors.

▫ Execute the "select all" command to highlight all the text, then choose Verdana bold 24-point font to change the text to Rachel's preferred font and point size.

▫ Select the graphics in the document and use the program's drawing tools to enlarge the images. (Alicia will need to read a few paragraphs before and after the image to determine the level of detail that the student will need to view and understand the information presented. This may only require a small degree of enlargement of the image or it may require that the image be enlarged to the size of a full-page.)

▫ Check the blanks where the answers should be written, as they may not have scanned correctly, and insert additional space for answers if necessary, keeping in mind that the writer may need additional space for their answer depending on how large they prefer to write.

▫ Check to see if any reformatting needs to be done and make the appropriate adjustments, especially if there are multiple columns of text. If there are numbered items using a "hanging indent" the setting for the indent will need to be adjusted.

▫ Insert a line of dashes and page numbers to indicate where the original print page breaks.

▫ Save the file and print it on the color printer.

▫ Execute the "select all" command again, adjust the line spacing to double-space, and choose Arial 16-point font to prepare the same worksheet for Dimitri.

(Continued)

▫ Check to see if any reformatting needs to be done and make the appropriate adjustments. Most likely the blanks for the answers will need to be adjusted.

▫ Save the file under a different name and print it on the color printer.

▫ Staple the pages together and give them to Ms. Mendez.

Example 2

A student interning at an insurance company works with a colleague to prepare a three-page report for presentation at an upcoming meeting. The intern will need to read and refer to the information in the report during the meeting. He would prefer to have the information available in large print, rather than using his mobile touchscreen tablet (that might crash) or an optical device (since he is self-conscious about using this while presenting in front of a group). The paper copy will be dependable and he can turn down the corners of different pages that he might want to refer back to during the presentation. To produce a large-print copy of this report, the intern, or someone who works with him, might follow these steps:

▫ Check with the colleague to determine if the report is available as an electronic file. If it is, skip to Step 6. If not, continue to Step 2.

▫ Obtain a good, clean print copy of the document and have a system for scanning a paper document into a digital format using a scanner device or scanning app. take it to a computer system equipped with an optical scanner, OCR software, a word-processing program, and a printer.

▫ Once scanned, upload the document to a computing device with OCR software and a word processing program.

▫ After the document has been scanned and run through OCR, open the file in a word processing program.

▫ Execute spell-check and proofread the document to check for scanning recognition errors.

▫ Execute the "select all" command for the program and reformat the text into the desired font style, point size, and line spacing.

▫ Review the document to determine if any of the text needs to be reformatted and make any necessary adjustments.

- Insert a line of dashes and page numbers to indicate where the regular print pages break.

- Save the file and print it. The intern will now have a print copy of the report in his preferred visual settings.

- Relatively low cost per page
- Minimal staff training needed to produce customized large print
- Can be printed on letter-sized paper for improved discretion and easy storage in binders, notebooks, and folders
- Easily produced on-demand in any font, point size, or line spacing

Disadvantages

- Extra time is required to scan and then edit documents and texts.
- Images and graphical information sometimes need to be re-created digitally.
- Considerations when reproducing copyrighted work (see Sidebar 5.4, The Treaty of Marrakesh)–individuals must first purchase a copy of the materials for individual reproduction and use.

Users do not always want all materials in the same alternate format. For example, a student may want a standard-sized textbook with an optical device for math class, but then prefer to take the math test in large print. In addition, the same student might want to use a digital copy of a history textbook that provides either visual or auditory access. It might also be more efficient to read non-textbook materials, such as an information packet, in a 24-point or larger font, while keeping the worksheet with accompanying questions in a smaller point size. In that way, the student can easily refer to the reading material in the larger font size while filling out the worksheet without the inconvenience of needing to constantly flip back and forth between his materials. The ability to create materials tailored to an individual's specific needs enhances the efficiency and effectiveness of that reader's efforts. This flexibility in the use of fonts and point sizes can also greatly increase the efficiency with which adults complete both personal and employment-related tasks.

TECHNOLOGIES FOR PRODUCING MATERIALS FOR TACTILE ACCESS

- **Who Produces Braille?**
- **Braille Production Tools**
- **Braille Translation Software**
- **Embossers**
- **Tactile Media**
  - Tactile graphics
  - 3D models

THE MARRAKESH TREATY

According to the World Blind Union, less than 10 percent of materials published are in formats that are accessible to people who are blind or have low vision. The Marrakesh Treaty was developed to address this "book famine" for people with visual impairments.

The full name of the treaty is the Marrakesh Treaty to Facilitate Access to Published Works for Persons Who Are Blind, Visually Impaired, or Otherwise Print Disabled. Administered by the World Intellectual Property Organization (WIPO), the treaty was signed in Marrakesh, Morocco, in 2013, and became effective in 2016. The United States ratified the treaty in January 2019.

The Treaty of Marrakesh focuses on copyright laws as well as the exchange of works in accessible formats across international borders. Countries that ratify the treaty promise that their laws will allow people who are blind and the organizations that support them to make books in accessible formats without having to ask permission from a book's author or publisher first. The treaty's signers also agree that these books in accessible formats may be exchanged across national borders. This second provision allows people to access books that are otherwise only available abroad.

The full text of the treaty is available at https://www.wipo.int/meetings/en/doc_details.jsp?doc_id=241683.

Producing educational and employment-related materials for tactile access generally means providing the materials in braille, tactile graphics, and 3D formats, as appropriate. The goal is to provide the necessary information for students and employees in their preferred alternate format at the same time that sighted students or colleagues receive the same materials. Improvements in braille production technologies have enhanced the ability to produce high-quality braille and tactile graphics more efficiently in larger quantities and at decreasing costs. However, producing materials in tactile formats continues to be a time-consuming process because of the care required to format the materials correctly and to design the tactile media to adequately represent spatial information. The expense that accompanies the expertise and equipment required to deliver high-quality tactile media needs to be considered when budgeting resources to support a nonvisual learner or employee.

As noted earlier, the most recent reauthorization of the Individuals with Disabilities Education Act (IDEA, 2004) requests that textbook publishers provide files of their core student print curriculum materials in specialized file formats that ensure a high standard of production of alternate media in braille and digital formats (NIMAS, see **Sidebar 5.1** above). As standards and repositories for standardized and accessible digital file formats are implemented, the production of alternate media including braille, tactile graphics, and 3D models are poised to become more user-friendly and efficient. With the proliferation of digital media, tools and strategies for alternate media production are also evolving. Whereas alternate media used to focus exclusively on large print and embossed paper braille, alternate media now encompass accessible digital formats including digital multimedia (text, images, and video) in addition to print media. As mentioned in **Chapter 3,** modern technologies facilitate more efficient and independent access to braille than ever before. As a result, the formatting of digital media and multimedia is of major importance and can define an individual's experience when interacting with information. These concerns are of particular relevance when producing materials for tactile access, and will be further explored in the following section.

As described in previous chapters, braille and tactile media can be produced manually (such as with a slate and stylus), mechanically (such as a Perkins brailler), or electronically (computer-assisted). Which method is most efficient depends largely on the quantity of materials required, their durability, and the ability to replicate them in the future. Production methods will also differ according to whether an individual produces braille for him- or herself or if someone else creates it. Productions tools and methods will also differ according to task and the individual's needs. Shorter, consumable materials can often be produced with a manual device such as a slate and stylus or mechanical braillewriter. Braille documents of moderate length intended for a limited number of uses (such as a list of spelling words) or for reading whenever it is not possible to charge electronic devices can also be produced with a braillewriter. Lengthier documents such as reading packets, restaurant menus, or books can be more efficiently produced with computer-assisted braille translation applications or braille embossers that provide efficiency, speed, accuracy, and easy replication.

Who Produces Braille?

Braille books, particularly textbooks and other lengthy volumes, are most often produced by commercial braille vendors. The American Printing House for the Blind (APH) is among the largest braille textbook producers in the United States and has a long history of producing textbooks for the K–12 education market. However, during the last half of the twentieth century, as more braille readers entered mainstream public schools, the variety of titles that needed to be available in braille increased significantly. These factors also greatly affected the need for and production of braille books and materials for higher education. Most universities and colleges established services and on-campus centers for students with disabilities. Many have taken on the responsibility of providing materials in alternate formats and, in some cases, have put into place the necessary hardware, software, and staff to produce some materials in hard copy embossed braille and digital formats for access with an RBD. Due to the complexity of textbook design, many institutions of higher education rely on outside sources such as the Alternative Media Access Center (AMAC) or other commercial services to produce braille (www.amacusg.org).

Traditionally, braille volunteers—groups of individuals dedicated to producing materials in braille, often as a community service—have been one of the more widely used alternatives to commercial production. Volunteers become braille transcribers by completing training and becoming certified through the National Library Service for the Blind and Physically Handicapped (part of the U.S. Library of Congress) in Washington, D.C. These volunteers provide braille materials at little or no cost. Unfortunately, the pool of volunteer transcribers has been shrinking as retiring volunteers have not been replaced by new ones. Therefore, locating other sources of braille production has become necessary.

Since the 1970s, K–12 educators in the U.S., along with the assistance of several national organizations, have established instructional materials centers, or IMCs, (also known as instructional resource centers, or IRCs). The function of these centers is to share braille textbooks, create educational materials including tactile graphics, and to distribute these materials to students who need them. Most states have an IRC or IMC that acquires books (from APH, volunteer or paid transcribers, and other commercial producers) and makes them available on loan to students. Eventually, innovative thinkers began to tap into a labor force that had not been previously used: people serving long-term prison sentences. Many states have established prison programs in which inmates learn braille transcription and develop the expertise to train others (see **Sidebar 5.5, *Behind the Walls***). Joint efforts between state education and correction agencies have made these programs successful, while advances in technology have enabled better access to trainings and dissemination of resources. Some of these programs produce braille with volunteers and some use paid transcribers. The programs provide electronic braille files or hard-copy braille to IMCs. Most programs have proven to be cost-effective and beneficial to the prisoners as well as to the entities receiving the braille. The prisoners have an opportunity to participate in an activity that gives back to the community, is conducted in a comfortable environment, and allows them to feel good about

BEYOND THE WALLS

Adapted with permission from the CTEBVI website (California Transcribers and Educators for the Blind and Visually Impaired.)

Beyond the Walls is the brainchild of John Romeo. John is passionate about rehabilitation and wanted a way to leverage the knowledge base inside the prison programs for the greater good of the braille community. He envisioned a program where prison braille programs could create professional-quality, expert presentations for the CTEBVI conference.

John presented his idea at the APH prison braille forum and the response was overwhelming. In the end, *Michigan Braille Transcribing Fund (MBTF)*, the *Miami Accessible Media Project (MAPS)*, and the *Mountain View Braille Facility* were selected to be the first program partners. They have all put together first-rate presentations to support the professional development of braille transcribers.

something they are doing. Students benefit by having access to more braille materials. Cooperation between the corrections field and professionals serving people who are blind or visually impaired led APH to develop the National Prison Braille Network (NPBN). As of September 2019, the partnership has produced 43 programs in 28 states across the United States (https://sites.aph.org/pbf).

The increasing demand for braille materials has also led to the development of small-scale private production companies and a growing number of individual transcribers who produce a wide array of braille materials. These providers usually contract with school districts and state agencies, along with public and private businesses, to produce braille. They are a valuable resource in providing the materials necessary for students to receive a free and appropriate education.

Because of the increasing number of files that can be accessed with an RBD, publishers and digital talking book libraries such as Bookshare must also ensure their files are properly formatted to display correctly. Digital libraries that offer braille-ready files (those using the extension BRF) will benefit from having an in-house expert who ensures that files are formatted properly to provide braille readers an experience equal to that of sighted readers.

Other braille producers include personnel in the education and rehabilitation fields or any staff trained to support the design and delivery of braille formats. Professionals in the visual impairment and transcriber fields have been explicitly trained to produce accessible braille and tactile media. The scope of each professional's responsibilities will vary across different organizations. For example, while braille textbooks might be secured from commercial sources, personnel might also be tasked with producing less complicated components such as workbooks, worksheets, or handouts, or any other component not suited for I vendors may not take on. In some cases, a certified braille transcriber is hired to manage the braille production for a school district, county office of education, or organization. In other cases, each braille reader may be assigned a dedicated transcriber. Regardless of the job title, **all** personnel who prepare braille must receive sufficient training and be supervised by a knowledgeable braille transcriber in order to guarantee that braille materials will equal the quality of materials provided to sighted individuals.

New resources and technologies have led to significant strides in the timely provision and widespread availability of braille materials. To ensure that this continues to be the case, braille producers must be appropriately trained and have the necessary technologies. These methods are described in the following section.

Methods for Producing Braille
Manual, Mechanical, and Electronic Braille Production Tools

Low-tech devices for producing braille such as the slate and stylus and the manual braillewriter provide durable and relatively inexpensive options. These low-tech tools are analogous to using pen-and-paper—they are appropriate for short-run jobs that have an immediate use but are not efficient for large-scale production. The accuracy of format and spelling are dependent upon the person producing the braille. In contrast, higher tech electronic braillewriters provide some editing capabilities and the reduction of manual labor. While low-tech devices are generally portable and affordable, they lack the advanced editing features and embossing speeds needed for large-scale braille production, easy replication, and publishing. Larger production jobs require software, hardware, and high-speed embossers designed for heavy-duty use.

Braille Translation Software

The first electronic braille translator was developed in the 1960s through a partnership between IBM and APH. While this system was used in-house at APH, it was not available for general use until 1970 when the first braille translation software was written in a portable programming language (https://www.duxburysystems.com/duxhist.asp). While several braille translation programs have been developed, one has dominated the field for decades. The Duxbury Braille Translator, available for both Windows and Mac operating systems, can translate both literary text and mathematics into braille with support for 170 languages. Braille translation software is efficient and time-saving. Braille translators are similar to word processors, with some offering either a word processor or text editor as a basic component of their program. Text is entered directly from the keyboard, imported from scanned documents, or downloaded from the Internet or other sources. Text can be manipulated in several ways. For example, text scanned using OCR software often has formatting and recognition errors. The software can easily format text for braille, while recognition errors are corrected using commands for inserting and deleting. Although this kind of editing is important for producing braille quickly and efficiently, it is only the first step.

In addition, braille translation software allows the user to establish the formatting of the braille when it is embossed. To correctly convey the meaning of the printed information, it is essential that indentations, paragraphs, columns, tables, and other text styles follow the formatting rules and guidelines established by the Braille Authority of North America (BANA) (http://www.brailleauthority.org/publications-area.html). When braille is not properly formatted, it is difficult for readers to grasp the material's physical layout, which is fundamental to comprehension. Trained transcribers can use the numerous features of the braille translation software to ensure that headings, lists, outlines, poems, foreign language texts, reading order, and even mathematical and scientific notations are appropriately formatted.

Once the text is formatted, the program translates it into the appropriate braille code. The translated document can be displayed onscreen as SimBraille. SimBraille, short for "simulated braille," is a visual display of the braille dots arranged in patterns identical to how they will be embossed—something analogous to a braille "font." It can be viewed onscreen or printed by a standard printer. Transcribers and sighted service providers can use SimBraille to proofread the translation and text formatting before embossing it. When errors are located, the program's six-key braille editor mode allows the user to make corrections. This helpful feature allows the transcriber to use the computer's standard QWERTY keyboard to input braille. In this mode, the *f, d,* and *s* keys represent dots *1, 2,* and *3* of the braille cell; dots *4, 5,* and *6* are represented by the letters *j, k,* and *l* (See **Figure 5.1, 6-Key Braille Input on a QWERTY keyboard).** The transcriber can press one or several keys simultaneously to create braille letters as is done on a mechanical braillewriter. The six-key editor can manually produce complicated documents manually while also having the editing capabilities of a word processor.

The production of math and science content in braille has also benefited from new technologies. With implementation of the Unified English Braille (UEB) code in 2014, mathematics and science materials can now be transcribed using the same braille code as literary texts. However, because UEB implementation was left to each U.S. state's decision, a separate Nemeth Braille Code (1972) for math and

Figure 5.1:
Six-Key Braille Input on a QWERTY Keyboard

When editing SimBraille, braille transcribers can use the s, d, f, j, k, and l keys on a standard QWERTY keyboard to input braille.

science also exists. Having two codes creates interesting challenges and necessitates software that can easily translate between UEB and math codes depending on the braille reader's needs. There are several software programs that can produce math and science materials in either Nemeth Code or UEB. Although these tools are more complicated to use than those meant for literary texts, mastery of these programs can ensure braille readers' improved access to higher-level math and science materials. Regardless of users' braille preferences, braille translation software thankfully can accommodate both UEB and Nemeth.

The technologies discussed in this section—particularly braille translation software—make it easier and faster than ever before to produce braille. When discussing these technologies with administrators who may be unfamiliar with braille production and the needs of braille readers, it is extremely important to be clear that properly trained personnel are required to use them. Non-braille readers often believe that purchasing a translation program and embosser is all that is needed to meet the needs of a braille reader. They might also wrongly conclude that any clerical or support staff can produce braille without much training, by opening the desired material in the braille translation software, choosing the "translate" command, turning on an embosser, and then selecting the "emboss" command. Braille produced this way will likely have many errors that will make it difficult for someone learning to read braille to understand. Even though most text will end up in the translated document, the intent and meaning may not be clear because of improper formatting or other errors. Providing poor quality braille (with translation, spelling, and formatting errors), is the equivalent of giving print materials full of spelling errors and irregular line spacing and paragraph breaks to sighted readers. If it is unacceptable to provide sighted individuals a text full of errors, it is equally unacceptable to provide such text to braille readers.

Braille translation software is a wonderful tool that is becoming more convenient as it is further integrated into mainstream applications (for example, Desmos) and open source websites and apps (for example, Braille

Contraction Lookup Dictionary). However, it is not foolproof, and errors will be made. A user who lacks knowledge of braille will not be able to proofread the resulting braille documents to determine whether they are accurate. The expertise of a certified braille transcriber or a service provider who is knowledgeable about braille is needed to ensure that braille documents are accurate and formatted properly. **To repeat: Sighted students and employees would likely not tolerate error-filled print materials. These same high standards must also apply to braille materials for nonvisual readers.** Extensive training is needed for any staff member who is hired to produce braille (IDEA Sec. 602 (2)(D)).

Braille Embossers

Although braille translation software enables a transcriber to edit and format documents, it is hardware in the form of a braille embosser that produces the paper copy of a braille document (also known as "hard copy" braille). Some braille embossers use continuous tractor- or pin-feed paper in one long, continuous fan-folded stack, similar to those produced by dot matrix ink printers from the 1990s. After embossing, the pages need to be torn apart along their perforations. Other embossers use a more standard paper feed that allows a user to insert a small stack of individual sheets of paper and emboss one page at a time. Pages can be embossed single or double-sided (interpoint), and with or without accompanying print.

Thanks to formatting options in braille translation software and embossers that allow custom paper sizes, the production of braille on various sizes of paper is easily feasible. Transcribers can produce braille on 8.5×11-inch paper for braille readers who prefer letter-sized documents that can be stored in standard notebooks, folders, and envelopes. The same document can be produced just as easily on 11.5×11-inch paper for readers who prefer the fluidity of reading a longer line before needing to locate the beginning of the next line. In addition, embossers can be reformatted to produce braille on postcards and brochures that are printed on unique-sized paper. These technologies provide the braille transcriber and the braille reader with tools that assist in the efficient production and use of braille.

Braille embossers designed to perform light braille-production duties are known as personal braille embossers. These comparatively lightweight embossers are transportable and best suited for individual use. Their embossing speeds of 10–15 characters per second are adequate for short to medium-length documents. Documents of greater length will require the embosser to work continuously for long periods of time and can overtax the capabilities of these machines; using a personal embosser in this way will greatly increase the chance of needing repairs and significantly decrease its life. A single personal braille embosser is capable of meeting the needs of several beginning braille readers, or of one experienced braille reader for supplemental braille materials.

Embossers with greater speeds can operate at 25–60 characters per second and are able to emboss continuously for longer periods of time. Durability and speed are further enhanced by interpoint embossers that can emboss simultaneously on both sides of the paper. Interpoint braille saves a significant amount of paper and makes longer braille documents less bulky and easier for readers to carry and store. This type of braille embosser can meet the needs of several braille readers of varying experience levels and abilities in an educational or employment setting.

Commercial braille producers require embossers with even higher speeds and output. While embossers designed to operate at more than 100 characters per second for extended periods of time have greatly increased the number of commercial braille producers, these machines are also unfortunately prohibitively expensive for in-house production and for many smaller producers. Large-scale braille publishers might also use hardware and software to program and control presses and plates that are used to emboss multiple volumes of large texts. Both braille translation software and embossing hardware haver dramatically increased the production of braille.

At times, one still hears discussions about the "death" of braille. People outside the field of blindness frequently ask, "With all of the advances in technology and the increase of information provided in an audio format, isn't braille obsolete?" As discussed in **Chapter 3,** the answer is unequivocally "no." In fact, it is quite the opposite. Braille translation software and braille embossers ensure easier access to hard copy braille. An individual with the appropriate technology and training can produce braille documents on a wide variety of topics for educational, employment, and personal uses, thus providing greater access to braille than ever before. In addition, the use of RBDs facilitates even more immediate access to braille and information. Just as the prevalence of audiobooks has not replaced print for sighted readers, auditory access in general does not replace braille for nonvisual readers. Print and braille both remain relevant to ensure literacy and the ability to author written work.

Interlining

There are many situations in which it is useful to have the print translation or equivalent of braille available on the same page as the braille. For example, without these translations, general education classroom teachers, tutors, and family members might find it difficult to help a beginning braille reader decode a word or read a passage fluently. Also, sighted friends and colleagues might want to peruse a restaurant menu or presentation materials along with a blind or visually impaired person. Printing text either above or below the embossed braille on the same page is referred to as interlining. Braille can also be embossed on a clear overlay and bound with the print pages so that the printed text is visible while the braille is felt.

There are several methods for interlining braille. Embossers that are hybrids of a traditional braille embosser and an ink-jet printer can emboss braille and print text simultaneously. While hybrid devices are more expensive than a standard braille embosser, in situations in which collaboration or instruction between sighted and blind individuals is common, it can be worth the extra expense.

The SimBraille display option mentioned earlier, which is offered by most braille translation programs, allows print and braille readers to read the same information simultaneously without the need to print and emboss at the same time. The SimBraille document can be printed with ink on paper; selecting the "interline" option in the print dialog box prints a line of print text above each line of SimBraille. A sighted reader can see the print text translation for each line of braille while the braille reader reads a separate embossed braille version. Since it is possible to refer to specific lines or words in a line, it can facilitate communication between print and brille readers.

Braille Signage

A discussion of braille production is not complete without addressing the topic of braille signage. The Americans with Disability Act (ADA) codifies the requirement for braille signage throughout the public environment to identify elevators, restrooms, interior office numbers, and so on. While it can be difficult to determine the best location for a sign, once found, braille signs provide the necessary information to guide an individual in locating a particular room or office number. Even a brief Internet search reveals dozens of companies that provide braille signage. When installing braille signage, pay careful attention to the materials used to create the signs. Depending on how often some signs might be used, some materials may not be durable or long lasting. In addition, the quality of text might vary considerably among manufacturers. Unfortunately, it is not uncommon to find inaccurate braille in public places. Since many braille signs are produced on metal, it is necessary to investigate the texture of the actual dots; while some are easy to read, others may irritate or even cause minor lacerations on the reader's fingertips.

Tactile Media

When preparing materials for tactile access, braille is used to transcribe text—but what about images? Determining how to represent images for tactile access is important to ensure a comprehensive learning experience when producing alternate media. While some images are for visual interest only (sometimes known as "eye candy"), other images are imperative for conveying concepts that are not explained within the text. Although the meanings of most images can be communicated with a thoughtful verbal description, spatial information in the form of maps, charts, graphs, and diagrams are better produced via a 2D or 3D representation (See Figure 5.2, **Image Description Decision Tree from the DIAGRAM Center**). A good tactile graphic (2D) can convey scalar

Figure 5.2:
Image Description Decision Tree from the DIAGRAM Center

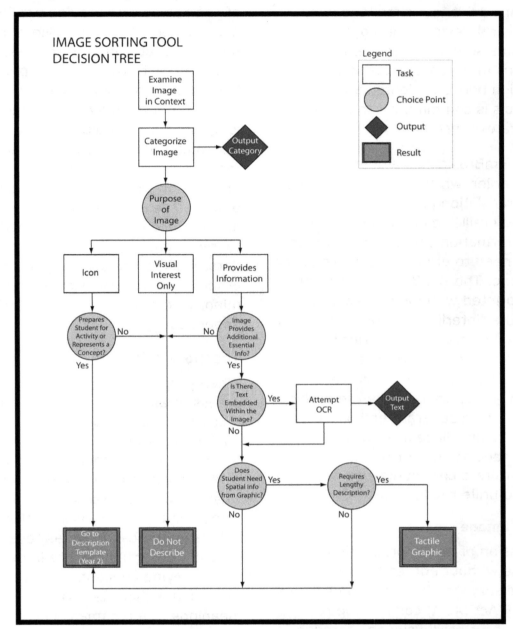

TECHNOLOGIES FOR PRODUCING MATERIALS IN ALTERNATE FORMATS

information while a 3D model enables exploration of a spatial concept. However, these tactile representations can look different from the original graphic—not every visual element is necessarily represented, but rather only elements that convey pertinent information.

A variety of techniques exist to produce images in a tactile format. Dependent on the learning objectives of the image, a decision tree can help determine whether a tactile graphic or a 3D model most accurately conveys the needed information. Generally, tactile graphics are preferred when an image cannot be adequately conveyed with a concise verbal description; 3D models are preferred for rendering objects that convey spatial concepts but are too difficult to explore in reality.

Both low-tech manual tools and high-tech electronic tools are used to create tactile graphics and 3D models. As was the case with braille production, durability, portability, available time, and the need for replication are key considerations when deciding which methods to use in a school or workplace. Tools for tactile graphics and 3D models may differ when a sighted individual is creating media for a blind or low vision person rather than when a blind or low vision person is creating accessible media for him- or herself. Common crafting supplies can be adequate to create one-off tactile graphics and models when more sophisticated methods are not available

or required. For example, it might be possible to find wooden balls of different sizes at a craft store instead of creating them with a 3D printer. Time is often the most important factor. For example, it may take only a few minutes to use a plastic stylus to create rudimentary raised lines on a plastic sheet that is positioned on a soft drawing mat. In contrast, creating a refined graphic with precise, crisp lines made by thermoform can take hours or even days. This section introduces some of the most common tools used in creating tactile media for the classroom or workplace.

Tactile Graphics

Commercially produced tactile graphics are becoming more widely available, and many volunteer braillists and transcribers also provide them for textbooks and other educational materials. However, the production of commercial quality tactile graphics is often time consuming and, if a commercial or other producer has not already created a needed graphic, adequate lead time is required for producers to create custom orders. Lead time varies depending on the availability of a commercial producer, but it is good practice to place a custom order at least one month in advance. Because of the advance notice required to request a custom tactile graphic from a vendor, service providers might instead choose to download a tactile graphic file from a repository and produce the tactile graphic locally. Repositories such as those listed at www.btactile.com aggregate files that have been designed for production as a tactile graphic or model and allow a user to access a pre-made design to produce materials methods that will be covered later in this section.

Sometimes there are occasions when individuals need tactile access to images that are not part of any standard curriculum and are unavailable commercially. In these cases, a tactile graphic or 3D model must be custom-designed and produced by a service provider or support staff member who fulfills the role of an alternate media specialist. An alternate (alt) media specialist is someone who is tasked with providing materials in an individual's preferred format: braille, large print, digital texts, audio, video, tactile graphics, or 3D models. The primary role of an alt media specialist is to maintain an organization's commitment to ensuring equal access for all individuals within the educational environment. Although an alt media specialist is a common job position in postsecondary education, it is rarely found in the K–12 setting. Instead, responsibilities for alt media often fall to the TVI or a paraprofessional who works under a TVI's guidance and specifications. It is possible that a braille transcriber whose employment sustainability is questionable because of a reduced workload can expand the scope of his or her responsibilities and be considered an alt media specialist with braille transcription certification. By training support staff to help with alt media, a TVI can better focus direct service hours to provide instruction to students.

The first step before producing a tactile graphic is to become familiar with the "Guidelines and Standards for Tactile Graphics" provided by the Braille Authority of North America (BANA), www.brailleauthority.org. See Figure 5.3 for Presley & D'Andrea's *Tactile Graphics Decision Tree*, which is another resource for guiding an alt media specialist when a tactile graphic is needed (this decision tree is a precursor to the aforementioned *Image Description Decision Tree*). Producing effective, high-quality tactile graphics requires both specialized tools and specialized training. It is not simply a matter of reproducing a print graphic with raised lines; in fact, in many cases a direct *reproduction* may be of very little value in communicating pertinent information to a tactile reader because much of the detail in an image is provided for aesthetic reasons only. Rather, a *representation* of the information, one that strategically conveys concepts with tactile distinctions and minimal tactile "clutter," will usually be more effective. Graphics that look good to the eye often have too much detail and will seem tactilely cluttered to the tactile reader. In other words,

Figure 5.3:
Tactile Graphics Decision Tree

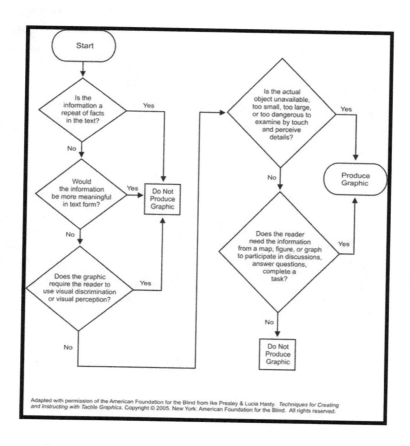

an effective tactile graphic often looks similar to but not the same as the original image. Thus, the person who creates tactile graphics needs to understand both the significance of the information intended to be conveyed by a print graphic and the most appropriate way to represent that information given a typical person's haptic perceptual abilities. With appropriate training and tools, and basic knowledge of research related to haptics and tactile exploration strategies, alternate media specialists and other service providers can learn to produce almost any tactile graphics. Keep in mind that tactile media production is time-consuming! When working with individuals who benefit from tactile access to images, remember the following:

- Budget sufficient time and resources for alt media production
- Involve individuals in their own tactile media production—teach them strategies to create their own points of access to ensure independence beyond the educational setting

Tactile graphics such as maps, charts, graphs, and diagrams for tests must be of high quality and created with replication in mind. In addition, these media often require high-tech tools that necessitate additional training. Other tactile media, such as for a class activity or curricular unit, might be adequately conveyed with lower quality but more quickly produced methods. (For ideas on creating quick, if less permanent, tactile graphics in the classroom, see **Tech Tip 5.1, Inexpensive Tactile Graphics on the Fly.**)

Tech Tip: Inexpensive Tactile Graphics on the Fly

Sometimes a subject or concept comes up unexpectedly that could be illustrated by a quick tactile diagram. There's no time to use one of the methods for producing high-quality, reusable tactile graphics described in this chapter. Luckily, there are several easy, low-cost, and rapid ways to create a tactile graphic that is meant to be ephemeral. These "on the fly" graphics are not necessarily intended to be saved or reused; they are meant to demonstrate a new concept quickly to a tactile reader in a "teachable moment."

- **Screen Board.** A particularly easy method of creating a quick tactile graphic is to use ordinary wire screen used in window screens to raise a texture on a regular piece of paper. A screen board can be made by cutting a piece of window screen and affixing it to a piece of sturdy cardboard, Masonite hardboard or thin plywood, and securing its edges with duct tape. (Metal screen works better than plastic/vinyl.) When a regular piece of paper is put on the board (not thick paper such as braille paper) a crayon can be used to make a drawing on the paper. The texture of the screen comes out on the paper where the crayon has been pressed into the screen and can be felt with the fingers. This is an extremely quick way to draw basic shapes and outlines. For example, if the kindergarten teacher has given all the students a worksheet with basic shapes on it for the children to color, it's easy to use a screen board to outline the shapes for the child with visual impairments to feel and participate in this activity. (Teaching Tip: One might also use a stencil of the shape clipped to the screen-board and have the youngster use a crayon to color inside the stencil. An additional activity might include placing a cardboard shape on the screen board and having the student trace around the edge of the shape with a a crayon.)

- **Swail Dot Inverter.** Another easy way to create simple graphics is with the Swail Dot Inverter (available from APH). This device is a metal stylus with a recessed tip. When paper is placed on the rubber sheet that comes with the set, the teacher or student can press the dot inverter into the paper, creating a tactile dot that is raised from the paper. The Swail Dot Inverter can also be used to outline a shape on a handout quickly.

- **Sewell Raised Line Drawing Kit** The Sewell Raised Line Drawing Kit comes with a rubberized clip

Tech Tip 5.1: (Continued)

board, a stack of thin plastic textured sheets, and a stylus. When the stylus presses down on the plastic pages on the board, a tactile line is created. This is a method for quickly making images that probably won't be reused, such as a geometry diagram the teacher draws on the board as an example of acute and obtuse angles.

- **Quick-Draw paper** The American Printing House for the Blind (APH) is the source for Quick-Draw paper, a thick one-time-use paper that creates quick graphics. When the teacher or student uses a water-based marker, the paper swells up to create a tactile line. In addition, APH sells a Textured Paper collection, which is a selection of brightly colored paper of varying textures that can be cut out and affixed to a background (paper, cardboard, etc.) to create textures, shapes, lines, and illustrations.

- **Wheatley Tactile Diagramming Kit.** APH also offers the reusable Wheatley Tactile Diagramming Kit (also referred to as the "Picture Maker"). The kit comes with a felt board to which shapes and thin lines backed with hook and loop fabric can be affixed to create a variety of pictures and diagrams.

- **Wikki Stix** are another reusable method for making quick diagrams. They are waxy, bendable, thin sticks that come in a multitude of colors. Wikki Stix stick to paper or to each other and can be used to make shapes, outlines, and other tactile

graphics. They peel off the paper and can be re-used as needed.

Some of the tools above can also be used by blind or low vision people to create graphical information for personal use or for sighted peers or teachers. There will always be a need to create high-quality tactile graphics using collage, tooling, and other methods. But for a quick "in the moment" diagram or outline, the tools described here can do the trick!

Due to the fact that many different types of graphics require a wide variety of different production methods and tools, this chapter focuses on the most common tools and methods. Maker communities are comprised of do-it-yourself innovations that involve tinkering with existing materials for renewed purposes. Along with engineering communities, these two sectors align naturally with accessibility initiatives and can provide inspiration for production tools and methods. For additional research related to tactile graphics and haptic perception, the reader can begin with Edman (1992), Lederman and Klatzky (2009), Rosenblum and Herzberg (2011), Zebehazy and Wiltong (2014), and Morash et. al. (2012, 2014).

Collage

Collage is a method by which materials of different textures represent the components of the print graphic, such as areas, lines, and point symbols. Some collage materials can be found at craft and hobby stores, while more specialized materials are available from vendors such as APH. Examples of such materials (limited only by one's imagination) include the following:

- *Area textures*: cardboard, textured paper (Feel 'n Peel Sheets), fine sandpaper, needlepoint backing, various fabrics

- *Line textures*: graphic art tape, string, wire, Wikki Stix®, puffy paint, hot glue, 3D pens (for example, 3Doodler®)

- *Point symbols*: cork, felt, paper circles created by a hole punch, balsa wood cutouts, foam shapes, basic cardboard shapes, small metal rings, brass fasteners

The textured materials are adhered to a base surface, then commonly labeled in braille to identify components of the graphic. Braille labels can be created on braille paper, self-adhesive labels or sheets, or laminating sheets (such as Con-Tact® paper) with either a Perkins Brailler or a braille labeler. The collage method can create a one-use tactile graphic or a master tactile graphic that can be repeatedly reproduced using a thermoform machine. [See **Sidebar 5.6, Thermoform for Creating High Quality Tactile Graphics.**,]

Tooling and tactile drawing boards

Tooling is a production method that uses special tools to press or imprint points, lines, and textures onto the backside of paper and other media to produce a raised image. Tooling is used on various materials including braille paper, transparency film, report covers, file folders, heavy-duty foil, and other thick paper, plastic, or aluminum sheets. Some of the tools needed for this production method are commonly found objects, while others are designed specifically for this purpose (for example, Tactile Graphics Kit from APH). Sewing tools such as crochet hooks, tracing wheels, large needles, leather tooling wheels, paper embossing and stenciling supplies, and craft sticks, are some of the items that are readily available at fabric, craft, or hobby stores. A rubber pad is important when using the tooling method because it provides a flexible backing that allows the tool to imprint or emboss the sheet without tearing it.

Tactile drawing boards are excellent low-tech production tools for creating instant tactile graphics. These are best used in the classroom when a teacher draws a diagram on the board that needs to be quickly re-created tactilely, or for an individual to create tactile drawings for recreational or work purposes. Note that because tactile graphics created with this method are hand drawn using a stylus or ballpoint pen, fine details and resolution are often sacrificed for the sake of speed. At the time of this writing, commercial options include the DRAFTSMAN Tactile Drawing Board, inTACT Sketchpad, Sensational BlackBoard, Reizen™ drawing board, and TactiPad. Homemade tactile drawing boards can be made with items from a hardware supply store; for example, a mesh screen that is

THERMOFORM FOR CREATING HIGH QUALITY TACTILE GRAPHICS

The thermoform machine can be thought of as a braille and tactile graphics copying machine. A thermoform machine reproduces tactile media with very crisp tactile resolution. The collage method is often used to create a master tactile graphic, which is then copied onto special plastic sheets such as Brailon using a vacuum form process. Multiple copies can be made using this process. Special thermoform "paper" made of thin sheets of plastic (e.g. Brailon) are needed so that when heated in the thermoform machine over the tactile graphic, the heat melts the plastic sheet and vacuum action sucks the paper down and around the tactile graphic. The sheet cools almost immediately and maintains the shape of the tactile graphic. Once the laborious process of creating the original collage is completed, the thermoforming process is very fast—the thermoform machine requires a few minutes to heat up, and after the heat setting is adjusted, each sheet takes mere seconds. A thermoformed tactile graphic replicates the textures and details from the original tactile graphic and withstands most tests of durability. Braille can be included in the original collage so that braille labels are thermoformed with the tactile graphic, however more sophisticated methods including laser cutting and silicone molds are often required to reproduce braille that is comfortable to the touch. Due to the large size of a thermoforming machine, costs associated with buying a machine and Braillon paper, machine maintenance, and limited students at one site that need the same tactile graphic, most thermoforming is done commercially by commercial vendors and test preparation companies. It is rare to see a thermoform machine at a school site.

---

fixed to a sturdy board can create excellent textured lines when used as a base with paper and waxed crayons.

Capsule paper and fuser machine

Capsule paper is a special paper coated with microcapsules that respond to irradiation (light energy) and heat.

Images are reproduced on the capsule paper by drawing with a carbon marker or pen, photocopying, or by using a computer printer. (Note that when using a new printer or photocopier, print a test page to ensure the paper will work well with the machine.) Next, the capsule paper is fed through a special machine called a *fuser* (for example, PIAF or Swell Form Machine) that uses light and heat to produce a raised line, surface, or texture wherever the ink appears on the page. Also known as swell graphics, puff pictures, and toaster graphics, this method is often used in schools because it is easy to produce and replicate with minimal supplies. This technique allows simple diagrams that do not require a great deal of labeling to be quickly prepared and then immediately provided to the student. Although differentiating among tactile details can be accomplished by varying line thickness and patterns, this production method generally does not enable the finer tactile resolution that can be obtained with other methods. However, this process is simple enough that students can use it to create their own graphics.

Tech Tip

For more information about this production method, see Paths to Technology post "Picture in a Flash: A Tactile Image is Worth a Thousand Words."

https://www.perkinselearning.org/technology/blog/picture-flash-tactile-image-worth-thousand-words

For a more portable alternative to a fuser, drawings made on capsule paper can also be raised using a Thermo or Swell pen. These pens apply heat rather than ink, and can be used to flatten a graphic in order to erase it on a plastic sheet when using a tactile drawing board, or, alternatively, can be used to raise ink on capsule paper.

3D Pens

3D pens comprise a developing group of fun tools for tactile media creation. The 3Doodler pen was the first of this kind of device, with more companies expanding the variety of options and features at the time of writing. These mainstream devices are handheld and work similarly to a glue gun; thin plastic sticks are fed into the barrel of the pen, then traditionally melted and extruded from a metal tip. The plastic sticks (usually ABA or PLA material, the same used by 3D printers) cool and harden within seconds, allowing the user to create sketches in 3D. These tools are typically designed for kids' crafting activities and can include various features such as: an on/off switch; adjustable temperature and extrusion speed settings; voice prompts; overheat alarm; auto shut-off; single or multiple filament extrusion; different pen weights; and LED display. Different pens also offer retractable or covered nozzle tips for added protection against heated elements. Newer variations of 3D pens are beginning to emerge that use non-heated elements and UV light instead of heating and cooling plastic elements.

When used for tactile media creation, 3D pens allow a blind or sighted user to quickly draw in 3D, create raised lines on a graphic, or construct a 3D object or replacement part. Considerations might include exposure of a heated nozzle while drawing (potential safety hazard), accessibility of the LED display if it replaces tactile buttons, and usability with managing the pen and coordinating fine motor skills during the drawing process. Given the portability and mainstream popularity of 3D pens, these are handy and portable tools for blind individuals to sketch on the go and create accessible art with sighted friends.

Computer-Assisted Tactile Graphics

Computer-assisted design uses a software application to create or edit an image digitally for production as a tactile graphic or 3D model. Using this method, tactile graphics can be produced using any of the aforementioned methods or exported to a braille embosser that supports graphics. More information about 3D printing will be presented in the next section.

As mentioned earlier, the most efficient way to produce tactile graphics is to locate an existing image or tactile media file and then copy or edit it as needed. APH's Tactile Graphic Image Library (TGIL) offers files for many images found in textbooks that are also available in braille and large print. BTactile.com is a free online meta-library that aggregates a growing number of tactile media libraries (including TGIL), and offers an additional feature for converting any image file into a braille file for embossing. Sometimes, a simple line-drawn image can be found using a Web search; these images can then be converted for embossing using BTactile's conversion tool, edited as

needed, or simply printed on capsule paper and raised using a fuser machine.

Several software options are also available for designing or editing an image. Some are mainstream word processing or drawing applications such as Apple Pages®, Microsoft Word, Google Docs, or Adobe® Photoshop®. An image can be easily imported or created within these programs and customized to deliver a tactile representation. Often an imported image will need to be simplified to minimize clutter in order to allow the reader to focus only on important details. A braille font can be downloaded and set to 29-point size to label a graphic within the program. This method generates standard-sized braille with the graphic rather than having to label the tactile graphic separately. This strategy is most suitable when using capsule paper and a fuser.

Other specialized programs are available such as TactileView or Firebird (more information at https://www .perkinselearning.org/technology/blog /creating-tactile-graphics-firebird -software). These programs offer more sophisticated design options specific to tactile details (for example, adjusting line or fill patterns). They also integrate a basic braille editor and translator to label the graphics (though it is still important to have some knowledge of braille to check translation accuracy), and are compatible with braille embossers for immediate tactile graphics output. Each program is compatible with different embossers; if an organization or individual already has a particular embosser, be sure that the tactile graphics software is compatible with it. Many braille embossers can produce tactile graphics using embossed dots. Some can emboss dots of variable height, while others offer variable spacing between dots. However, there are a limited number of textures available to create the tactile graphics. This may restrict the usefulness of this method for conveying more complicated graphical information such as 3D images and drawings with overlapping areas.

The capsule-and-fuser production method presents no compatibility issues with software—only a printed image is required. However, this production method is limited because the designer cannot vary the heights of the raised lines, surfaces, and points to differentiate among various graphical elements. While this limitation may not be significant when creating simple graphics, whenever more detail is needed to convey an image's information, the designer should choose an alternative production method.

3D Models

Similar to DIY options for tactile graphics, 3D models can sometimes be found in craft or hobby stores. More often, 3D models need to be created for a specific learning objective or to support tactile access to an image. One production method that is becoming more popular is 3D printing. While this technology is not new, it has traditionally been used in engineering and design environments. With its growing popularity in K–12 settings, makerspaces, and community libraries, 3D printing allows an individual to print a pre-made model or design and edit a 3D model to suit a unique need. Pre-made models are increasingly available from museums and public education organizations. Files for 3D printing a model locally are often posted for free. They offer users an opportunity to engage with rare or expensive artifacts that the public may not handle.

For nonvisual learners who benefit from tactile access, recall that 3D printing is only necessary when an image cannot be adequately described, requires the conveyance of spatial information beyond what a tactile graphic can illustrate, or when it is too difficult to acquire and explore an actual model (such as a museum artifact, a molecular or architectural structure, or a dangerous reptile). As with 2D tactile graphics, caution must be taken to ensure that the final product conveys the intended information clearly and accurately. For example, designers may use a 2D drawing of a fish to create a 3D model of it. However, the product is a compromise. It may offer some tactile features of the eye, fins, and gills, but it fails to offer a spatial representation of the roundedness of the eyes and body, or the shapes of a fin and gills. Due to the time and expertise needed to create a 3D print, this method is not generally recommended for producing tactile graphics or braille because methods such as embossing, slate and stylus, Perkins brailler, and swell, are much more efficient. When placed on a 3D model, braille can introduce too much tactile clutter, impeding exploration of the model. For this reason, 3D models are best labeled using auditory methods with support for RBDs (for example, the audio-tactile models by Touch Graphics, Inc.).

Just as it easier to create tactile graphics from a pre-existing source file, it can also be much easier to edit an existing 3D printing design rather than creating a new one. There are several repositories available for downloading files for 3D printing (STL file format).

- **Tinkercad™**
- **Thingiverse®**
- **YouMagine**
- **BTactile—2D and 3D files**
- **Imageshare (Benetech)—2D and 3D files**

These files can used as is or be customized using a computer-assisted drawing (CAD) program. Once a 3D printing file is ready for production, a 3D models can be printed locally, ordered commercially, or printed at a local library or makerspace. For individuals who are interested in printing locally, it is important to acknowledge that 3D printers require considerable maintenance and training. Other considerations when purchasing a 3D printer include the following:

- Availability of tech support
- Similar systems used by your colleagues (to help troubleshoot 3D printer issues)

- Compatibility with desired 3D filaments—different printers support different materials, and offer options for printing in single or multi-color.
- Size of printing bed, which determines how large of a model can be printed at one time
- Printing speed and resolution
- Whether the user interface is accessible for nonvisual operation
- Compatibility with design software and if accessible software if required
- Cost, which is chiefly determined by printer size and resolution

In many cases, it is more efficient to design a 3D model yourself and then outsource its printing to avoid having to store and maintain a 3D printer. Individuals who want to design or edit their own 3D models have several choices such as OpenSCAD, Tinkercad, or SketchUp®. As of the time of writing, only OpenSCAD uses a command-line interface that is accessible with a screenreader and allows a blind person to design for him- or herself. For service providers who have limited time for designing alt media, it is wise to contract with a provider for design and production services. At the time of this writing, community efforts such as the 3D Printed Educational Models Google group and See3D.com connect blind individuals' needs for 3D models with students and interested parties who are able to fulfill design and printing requests. Additional information and resources about 3D printing for education and accessibility can be found in NonScriptum's excellent blog post *3D Printed Teaching Models* (https://www.perkinselearning.org /technology/blog/3d-printed-teaching -models) and from the DIAGRAM Center (http://diagramcenter.org/3d -printing.html).

Remember that tactile media production can also be an interesting and enjoyable activity for individuals who are blind and visually impaired! Designers (including service providers, educators, and artists—even tech-savvy blind tactile media hobbyists) who are trained across the variety of production methods can help any individual develop an efficient and effective production workflow based on available resources. Since each method has strengths and weaknesses, ultimately, the concepts that an image is meant to convey should determine how the information is best represented. Designers and alt media specialists frequently use a combination of production methods to create the most effective tactile graphic or 3D model for conveying pertinent information. Having a wide array of production tools, trained and knowledgeable designers, and ample time to prepare tactile media are key to providing effective tactile access for people who are blind or visually impaired.

TECHNOLOGIES FOR PRODUCING MATERIALS FOR AUDITORY ACCESS

- **Audio Recording Equipment**
- **Editing Equipment**
- **Video description**

It is much easier today than ever before to find information available in an auditory format. Although the digital talking books and audiobooks presented in **Chapter 3** are auditory options, there are times when ready-made audio recordings are not available. In such cases, service providers, volunteers, and individuals with visual impairments can produce auditory materials using the methods and strategies described in this chapter. In addition, training materials can be created for learners to become more skilled and efficient in using auditory recordings and synthesized speech effectively. Youths and adults also need to learn effective strategies for recording information, such as classroom lectures, discussions, and important business meetings.

A variety of tools and technologies can be used to produce materials in an auditory format. Analog recordings have given way to digital recordings that can be easily produced with relatively inexpensive equipment and apps. Because **Chapter 3** has already addressed access to digital media, this chapter will instead focus its production.

The most common ways people access audio media are audio recordings or computer-based products using synthesized speech. Information can be spoken and digitally recorded, or saved in a digital format and read with a speech synthesizer. The technology and equipment used for recording, editing, and playback of auditory information has evolved rapidly for commercial and in-house production as well as individual recordings.

Audio Recording Equipment

Recording human speech requires a recording device and either an external or built-in microphone. Professional recordings are made in state-of-the-art recording studios using soundproof recording booths equipped with highly sensitive microphones, sound-absorbing walls, and top-quality digital recorders. Advances in general electronics and mainstream technology have reduced the cost of audiobooks and other sound recordings, making them available to a wider number of listeners. These improvements in affordable recording equipment and media have also made it possible for low-volume producers and individuals to make acceptable quality recordings outside a professional studio.

Audio recorders can either be stand-alone devices or apps installed on smartphones or computers. Although most recorders have a built-in microphone, an external microphone will make a significant difference in the quality of the recording. Omnidirectional microphones record sound from all directions; unidirectional microphones only record sound from one direction. This distinction is particularly important when recording in an environment with ambient noise; an individual might prefer a unidirectional microphone when recording a lecturer in a classroom, but prefer an omnidirectional microphone when recording sounds on a nature walk. High-quality external microphones range from inex-

pensive to studio-quality microphones with sound cancelling features that actively block ambient sounds, but can also significantly raise the cost. Sometimes, the internal microphone is adequate for making a personal note on the go. This method of recording is most popular when using a smartphone to send an audio message or take a note. Also called a voice memo, using an internal microphone to make a quick recording is similar to jotting down a note on a piece of paper. The quality does not need to be the best—only comprehendible when listening back. Sometimes audio recordings are made to capture a moment similar to how a camera is used to visually memorialize an instance.

Digital recorders save recordings as compressed (MP3) or uncompressed (WAV) file formats. Although uncompressed files have better sound quality because they capture all sounds waves, the resulting files are large and require more storage space. In contrast, compressed files have reduced audio fidelity but are smaller in size and easier to store. Individuals choose either compressed or uncompressed files depending on the required audio quality and available storage space. Although storage devices such as flash drives are still common, cloud-based storage affords far greater storage capacity. Once stored in the cloud, audio files can be accessed for playback on any number of devices by any number of users. As a standalone tool, digital recorders offer a bookmarking feature that allows the user to navigate to specific locations within a recording, a function that is harder to do with a computer-based playback app.

Most smartphones, touchscreen tablets, laptops, or desktop computers can also be used to create recordings. These devices generally come with built-in microphones or can be connected to an external microphone wirelessly or with a cable. Although most devices come with a pre-installed recording program, there are other free or commercial apps that provide improved sound quality. A recording app allows the user to record and edit any information needed for later review. For those who are already using a tablet or laptop in classes or meetings, a recording app is often preferred to a stand-alone device because it reduces the amount of equipment that needs to be carried. Most note-taking apps offer features for audio recording as well. Even though apps such as Evernote and OneNote are not marketed as recording apps, they do have a recording feature.

As mentioned in **Chapter 4,** smart-pens combine a recorder with a no-tetaker. For example, the Livescribe pen records audio as it writes, so anything missed in the written notes can be captured auditorily. Although a good idea in theory, as of the time of writing, smartpen technology unfortunately often captures excess ambient noise along with the speaker's voice.

Editing Audio Recordings

Once audio has been recorded, there are many editing tools that are compatible with a variety of file formats. As with any software, accessibility is a primary concern for individuals who are creating audio recordings for their own use. Editing a sound file might involve combining different segments from one or several recordings while deleting unneeded segments. Editing workflows are especially important for individuals who want to produce audio products for dissemination, such as a podcasts.

Playback Options

Audio recordings can be played using any number of methods. Recordings can be played in a music app or as a podcast; audio files can be played from within the cloud storage location. Recordings can also be shared via a hyperlink on social media or through a messaging app, a process similar to how others might share photos. Multimedia playback can provide some of the best user experiences; for example, Storyline Online is an award-winning children's literacy website that records actors reading children's books, and then plays back the audio while a video displays the book illustrations. Audio can also be recorded on switches for augmentative alternative communication or to facilitate simple cause and effect instruction (i.e., a student activates a switch to hear a playback of a brief segment of music).

At times, audio files are created for playback with synthesized speech instead of a human recorded voice. This playback option is used when a transcript needs to be generated or when a more standardized recording is desired. Some commercial video accessibility

TECHNOLOGIES FOR PRODUCING MATERIALS IN ALTERNATE FORMATS

vendors such as 3Play Media choose this method since it allows audio descriptions to be played back with both synthesized speech and a synced transcript for tactile access on an RBD.

Digital audio production has become so commonplace that anyone with a smartphone, tablet, or computer can produce materials for auditory access. These recordings can serve a variety of recreational, functional, educational, and employment purposes. While it is very easy to access digital audio, it is important that developing literacy by reading print or braille remains a core component of instruction. Auditory access should be provided only to supplement visual or tactile access, not to replace them. Finally, recall from **Chapters 2 and 3** the importance of auditory training for efficient use of auditory skills—individuals must be supported to shift from learning to listen, to listening to learn.

SUMMARY

Many tools are now available that improve the efficiency with which information and materials can be produced in alternate formats. Anyone can use a computer to produce printed text in a wide range of fonts and point sizes to meet the needs of readers with low vision. Braille translation software and braille embossers can be used by qualified braille transcribers and trained professionals to produce greater quantities of hard-copy braille faster than was possible with previous production methods. Tactile media including tactile graphics and 3D models are also more easily produced in-house while also being available from commercial sources. Finally, information can be made available in any number of multimedia and digital formats that allow visual, tactile, or auditory access using an assortment of tools. Remember that visually impaired students and employees are entitled to the provision of accessible materials, and should never be tasked with producing their own alternate media. Therefore, it is equally important that blind and low vision individuals are taught about the various production methods to create materials for their enjoyment and for the development of recreational and leisure activities. Strategies for implementing accessibility across all production methods is necessary to ensure that all individuals, blind or sighted, can create and share in the joy of information together. Technology has greatly increased access and production methods for and by people with visual impairments. All of these tools have made a dramatic improvement in the quantity and quality of information and materials that are available.

The flexibility inherent in using technology to produce materials in alternate formats allows service providers to dedicate more time teaching students instead of reducing instruction time to prepare materials. Specialized certifications are not required to produce alternate media, and therefore a greater variety of support staff can be trained to take on the role of an alternate media specialist. Braille transcribers who fear losing their jobs when a blind student graduates or who need to justify a full-time position can also be supported to re-envision their role as an alternate media specialist (Siu and Emerson, 2017). With the tools and strategies described in this chapter, the requirements of every individual with low vision or with nonvisual access needs can be met with appropriately formatted alternate media allowing for equitable engagement with information.

REFERENCES

AFB Directory of services for blind and visually impaired people in the United States and Canada. (2005). New York: AFB Press.

Edman, Polly K. (1992). Tactile Graphics. New York: AFB Press.

Hasty, L. (2008). Tactile Graphics website. www.tactilegraphics.org

Nemeth braille code for mathematics and science notation (rev. ed.). (1972). Louisville, KY: American Printing House for the Blind.

Renfranz, P. Taboada, S. & Weatherd, J. (2008). Progress and Stalemates: The Complexities of Creating a Textbooks-on-Time System for Blind Students. The Braille Monitor, 51(7).

CHAPTER 6
Strategies for Accessing Multimedia and Data

Since the first edition of this textbook in 2009, advancements in technology have drastically changed how we access information. In the modern classroom, most of these changes are driven by the inclusion of principles of universal design for learning (UDL) ("CAST: About Universal Design for Learning," 2015; Meyer, Rose, & Gordon, 2014). UDL details guidelines for teaching strategies that provide (Figure 6.1):

▫ Multiple means of engagement (Strategies that present information and content in different ways—how learners gather facts and categorize what is seen, heard, and read);

▫ Multiple means of representation (Strategies that differentiate the ways that students can express what they know—how learners plan and perform learning tasks, organize and express ideas);

Figure 6.1:
The Universal Design for Learning Guidelines

CAST (2018). Universal design for learning guidelines version 2.2 [graphic organizer]. Wakefield, MA: Author.

□ Multiple means of action and expression (Strategies that stimulate interest and motivation for learning—how learners get engaged and stay motivated).

In practice, this means that classrooms are flooded with a variety of multimedia, with everything from curriculum to assessment delivered on a technology platform. As a result, students with visual impairments need tools and strategies to access various forms of multimedia. Examples of these media include text, images, videos, infographics, and data visualizations.

Outside of the classroom, principles of UDL are applied to information design and conceived as user experiences. These experiences are evident anywhere an individual might encounter information—kiosks, websites, and even data presented as infographics on the Web for marketing or social media consumption. In a crossover space between classroom and community engagement, museums are a case study in using multimedia to present information, as patrons seek ways to read and interact with information given through text, still or moving images, and tactile artifacts displayed for visual access.

This chapter presents an overview of strategies that can aid an individual who is blind or visually impaired to access enhanced multimedia information independently and efficiently. Although the inclusion of accessible non-textual or dynamic media might seem like a daunting effort, current and emerging technologies can be employed by practically anyone to ensure access to multimedia information. These include a range of tools that are accessible to all, blind or sighted, to author and design information, as well as the tools needed to access information in all forms.

The discussion here is a counterpoint to the previous chapter, which focused on the **production** of alternate media. While individuals should also be familiar with those production tools for their value in accessing media in alternative formats, this chapter addresses strategies to **access** high tech multimedia. As you read through this chapter, imagine how the tools and technologies might fit into the following situations:

□ Classrooms that integrate technology for instruction and engagement

□ Flipped instructional models that expect students to interact with information outside of the classroom

□ Computer-based assessments

□ Public service announcements for transit information, health and safety awareness, and emergency warning systems

□ Public spaces such as museums, art galleries, libraries, and makerspaces

□ Hands-on learning environments such as science, engineering, and computing labs

□ Data-rich environments, either online or in physical workspaces

□ Travel for daily commutes, running errands, or for leisure and recreation

◦ Navigation in digital environments for daily work tasks, research, banking, management of personal files, or entertainment

From this list, it quickly becomes apparent that multimodal access to multimedia is critical for engagement in work, study, and leisure activities. Although the ideas are high-tech, consider how this chapter aligns with the overarching principles as discussed throughout the book:

◦ The importance of blind or low vision individuals' development and maintenance of literacy and skills needed for reading, numeracy, and critical thinking;

◦ The need to sustain proficient use of a variety of low- and high-tech tools that can be flexibly employed as needed under the command of the user; and

◦ The need for the information environment itself to be designed with an accessible architecture. This final piece ultimately depends on continued efforts to engage, align with, and collaborate with designers or engineers from the beginning of every new technology.

CONSIDERATIONS FOR ACCESSING DIGITAL IMAGES AND INTERACTIVE GRAPHICS

Previous chapters in this book have presented an overview of the tools needed for visual, tactile, and auditory access. This chapter diverges some-

what because of the nature of digital multimedia and the possibilities afforded by modern and emerging technologies. By discussing tools in terms of dynamic multimodal access, we focus on how information can be represented for every individual's interaction with data access, analysis, and synthesis.

The main advantage of multimedia content (See Figure 6.1: The Universal Design for Learning Guidelines) is that information can be represented and engaged within multiple ways. Accessibility of multimedia content must therefore deliver these same advantages to every user regardless of visual impairment.

As you read through this chapter, consider that to attain full community inclusion of blind and low vision individuals, the tools used to create and deliver multimodal access to multimedia information must also be accessible. Over the long term, students with visual impairments must be part of makerspaces, coding camps, engineering and computer science classes, and design conversations to ensure equal representation and opportunities in all communities where media and information are created.

The tools in this chapter are organized according to the different ways multimedia can be represented rather than by the sensory learning channel through which multimedia is accessed. This helps define the different types of available technology since multimedia can be accessed with visual, tactile, or

Figure 6.2.
Tactile Graphics Decision Tree. Image credit: AFB,
2005.

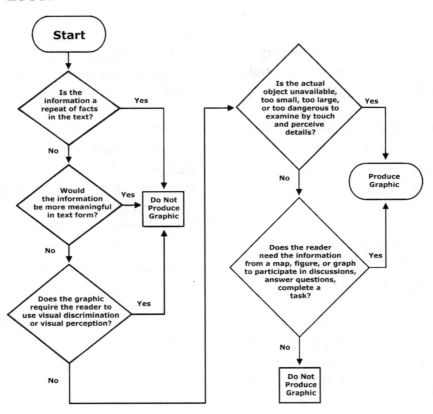

auditory strategies at the will of the consumer.

Because there are several methods designers can employ to represent multimedia information, a decision tree can help them decide which tools and methods will best represent different types of information. In this way, any designer, with or without specific training in visual impairment, can create and disseminate accessible digital multimedia.

The Braille Authority of North America (BANA) recommends the following decision tree, initially developed by Lucia Hasty and Ike Presley for the American Foundation for the Blind (2005), for deciding when an image necessitates a tactile graphic.

In 2014, the DIAGRAM Center updated the decision tree to address more specifically the multitude of images in accessible, digital talking books. Referred to as the Image Sorting Tool (Morash et al., 2015), this modified decision tree now recognizes the role of description in providing access to the majority of images in typical textbooks. A lesser number of

Figure 6.3.:
Image Sorting Tool

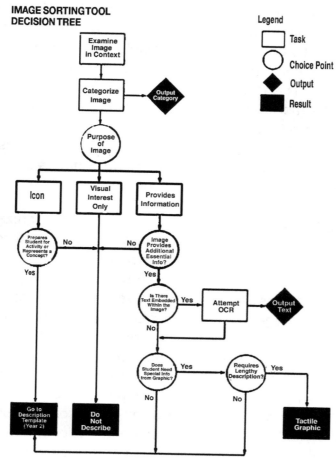

Credit: DIAGRAM Center

images require a tactile graphic, while even fewer images are best represented by a 3D model. The following sections discuss the thinking behind and tools for using description to access multimedia information, and how description can be integrated with other sensory experiences for multimodal access. The chapter will then discuss tactile access options in the same terms, and conclude with how these methods can aid in developing data literacy.

MULTIMODAL ACCESS TO DESCRIPTIVE CONTENT IN MULTIMEDIA: THE ART AND SCIENCE OF DESCRIPTION

(Contributing author: Joshua Miele, PhD; Associate Director of Technology Research and Development, Smith-Kettlewell Eye Research Institute)

In discussing how to provide access to digital multimedia, description is often mentioned only in passing; it often takes a back seat to more prominent topics such as screen readers, document accessibility, 3D models, wayfinding, and the like. This may be due to its general complexity, requiring a combination of topic knowledge, verbal skills, and editorial instincts from the describer. On the other hand, description's short shrift may simply result from the fact that it is so deeply ingrained in the process of making information accessible that we rarely recognize its central role in accessibility practices, extending well beyond images and video to document layout, screen reader design, and even lifestyle. (Recall Sidebar 2.3, Comparison of Visual Interpreter Apps)

While this section emphasizes classic description, such as for image and video accessibility, it is important to recognize that description is pervasive and indispensable in almost all accessibility practices. When making an accessible digital document, adding markup and structure (heading styles) allows easier navigation, but it also allows a screen reader to announce verbally details such as headings, sidebars, and lists (Refer to **Chapter 3** for more information). Although we do not usually think of it as such, document markup and structure is a form of description, as is a screen reader's announcement of buttons, menus, and other elements of an application or web page. Similarly, most wayfinding tools that use GPS or other location-based technologies are essentially providing environmental description about which features, businesses, or services are nearby, and where they are relative to

the user. Multimodal graphics and models that allow tactile exploration with audio annotation are also forms of description. Description is, in fact, a fundamental information accessibility principle, applicable in almost any context, and not just for images and video. Recognizing this fact helps us think about our own use of description, whether as providers or consumers, and clarifies how description makes images and video more accessible.

In its most recognizable form, description is the transformation of visual information into language and is most often used in making images, videos, and live performances and events accessible for blind viewers. For video, description takes the form of an additional voice-over track that announces visual elements of the content that are not apparent from the soundtrack (for example, on-screen text, gestures, facial expressions, actions, settings, etc.). For static images, descriptions are often included as captions or embedded as an attribute of the image itself (for example, alt text in an eBook or Web page). There are a number of excellent resources offering guidance on describing both static images such as charts and graphs, and dynamic visuals such as videos and plays

Each image type, whether static or dynamic, includes its own set of considerations, making the creation of exhaustive guidelines almost impossible. The guidelines for describing a simple bar chart might be relatively

IMAGE DESCRIPTION TEMPLATES AND GUIDELINES

By prescribing a template for how to describe different image types (for example, an infographic versus a line graph), a describer can more easily add information to create descriptions that follow a predictable format. With a standardized order in which information is presented, a reader can more quickly navigate through a description and work as efficiently as possible. Use of a template also guides describers who are not necessarily content experts to identify key elements of an image. This is helpful when alt text (image descriptions) are created by alternate media specialists who understand the accessibility needs but perhaps not the subject matter content. In order to help standardize and guide descriptions for charts and graphs related to science, technology, engineering, and math (STEM), The National Center for Accessible Materials (NCAM) developed a set of image description guidelines for general use. These guidelines were incorporated into templates that serve as a framework for complex descriptions that can be further edited as needed ((Morash, Siu, Miele, Hasty, & Landau, 2014).

The NCAM guidelines for STEM image descriptions are disseminated alongside overall guidelines for image description by the DIAGRAM Center (http://diagramcenter.org/making-images-accessible.html). The information addresses general principles of description in addition to reference points describing different types of images such as art, illustrated diagrams, relational diagrams, graphs, maps, and tables.

In cases where students might require more description and/or customized vocabulary to meet learning needs, the description guidelines can help a describer adopt a language style that provides enough context, is concise and objective, and ultimately effective in conveying the visual information to a low vision or nonvisual consumer.

straightforward, but when a bar chart includes multiple layers, colors, error bars, and so on, the guidelines can become lengthy and complicated. Thus, when considering all the possibilities for static images from bar charts to abstract art, as well as the unlimited diversity of dynamic images from documentary video to modern dance performance, guidelines for each specific case may not be as useful as a set of guiding principles for the creation and consumption of description for accessibility in general.

Principles of Creating Descriptions for Multimedia Content

Generally speaking, accessibility is an effort to provide an experience for a person with a disability that is essentially similar or equivalent to the experience of a non-disabled person. Whether this principle is applied to the design of a building, a curriculum, or a Web page, it means that the person with a disability should be able to enjoy and make use of the product or service in essentially the same way that a person without a disability does. In the practice of description for accessibility, this means that the image or video description should provide a similar experience for the blind viewer as the undescribed content does for a sighted viewer. This may sound like a tall order with the oft-quoted aphorism that a picture equals a thousand words, but, unless the sighted viewer is intended to dwell on a given image for the time it would take to read a 1,000-word description, the equivalence certainly does not hold. An accessible graphic (or video) experience should not require the blind viewer to spend much more time on the image than the sighted viewer does.

Whenever possible, descriptions should match the tone and intent of the original image or video. For example, images included in a web page purely as visual decoration do not require extensive description. In fact, including descriptions of "eye candy" may actually be a distraction from the intended experience of the web page, running counter to the definition of accessibility.

Similarly, including too many details in a video description may cause the experience of the blind viewer to diverge significantly from that of a sighted viewer.

Context and Editorial Capacity

Describing for accessibility presents a much more complex challenge than is required by a simple braille translation or captioning task. Description requires active editorial decision-making. In addition to considering the vast array of visual images that may need to be described, it is essential to take into account the context in which the description will be used, as well as the description's intended audience. How the description will be used, and by whom, influences how something should be described—or whether it should be described at all.

The act of description is highly subjective and requires clear editorial thinking on the part of the describer. For example, a description provided by a sighted person watching a movie with a blind friend is likely to be quite different from that provided by a professional describer. This is not simply due to a difference in skill, but includes the fact that the informal describer knows the blind viewer well and can therefore focus on aspects known to be of interest. The sighted friend is describing for a known audience of one, while the professional is describing for a generic audience with unknown tastes or sensibilities. In contrast, the friend may use shared vocabulary, social references, and the ability to pause the movie long enough to provide extended description. Without making any judgement about the relative quality of the two descriptions, we recognize the differences resulting from the editorial decisions made by the two describers based on their knowledge of the audience and the context: The sighted friend knows exactly who is listening to the description, as well as how the description is being used, while the professional describer must base editorial decisions on general knowledge of that particular movie's target audience.

One reason for the describer to exercise editorial power is to keep descriptions concise. Ideally, descriptions should provide the maximum information with a minimum of distraction from the original material. In other words, long descriptions are rarely better than concise ones because, as mentioned earlier, they may disrupt the context of the original image or the flow of the video.

Brevity, Relevance, and Tone

To keep descriptions brief, it is essential to be highly selective about what to describe. Describers must consider carefully what the graphic or video is trying to communicate, and then include only descriptive details relevant to that purpose. For example, a chart that displays a stock's price over time should include details about the time duration and the price range, but probably not the color of the axes or the size of the font used. When describing a video, visual details should be mentioned only if they are relevant to the

content, and should never be mentioned if they can readily be inferred from the existing audio track.

It is also important to recognize that different contexts require different types of description—educational, commercial, and social description each has its own considerations and requirements. Images and videos used in education need to use age-appropriate language, and should use terminology specifically drawn from the associated material or curriculum. Educational description, such as for images in textbooks or testing materials, must also strike an appropriate balance between clarity and not "giving the answer away." This means that the image describer may need to be well acquainted with the related content as well as the specific intent of the image within the context of the material.

Description produced for commercial purposes, such as for movies or television, generally is designed to be appreciated by as wide an audience as possible. The best examples take into consideration the probable audience for the movie or TV show, and then use vocabulary and references most likely to be readily understood by the intended viewers. Commercial describers also make it a point to steer clear of interpretation or use of informal language, often priding themselves on their objectivity and impartiality. While this aesthetic has acknowledged advantages, it can sometimes lead to a significant disconnect in tone between description and content—it can definitely detract from the mood of a love scene to have it narrated by a journalistically dispassionate reporter.

In contrast, image and video description created for use in social contexts thrives on informality. Images of weddings, summer vacation activities, birthday parties, or family reunions posted on social media are generally enhanced by interpretation and informal language. The viewers of these images and videos are likely to be familiar with the people and places in the images, and that intimacy should, to create an equivalent experience, extend to the description. When viewing a friend's wedding pictures, a description such as "a young woman in a white dress stands beside a man in a dark suit" leaves us cold. On

Sidebar 6.2

TOOLS FOR IMAGE AND VIDEO DESCRIPTION

As awareness about description's role in digital accessibility grows, some social media and content creation outlets have responded by including options for describing posted images and video. There are several approaches that various platforms utilize to do this:

- **Artificial intelligence.** Some organizations (such as Facebook) have incorporated early applications of artificial intelligence to recognize elements of an image. However, machine recognition often lacks the subjective interpretation that is essential to delivering a description that matches the relevance, context, and tone the image is meant to convey. For example, a photo of a group of friends sharing a picnic in a park might be interpreted as "this image may contain sky and a tree."

- **Authoring tools.** To date, the most effective description tools allow an individual to author description of images or videos as they are posted. Some platforms (such as Twitter, Microsoft Word, Moodle) prompt the content creator to add alt text at the time the image is uploaded/posted (Figure 1). Although in this case the responsibility for disseminating accessible content rests with the content creator, it facilitates the most relevant descriptions because the content creator understands the meaning and intention of the image.

- **Remediation tools.** Other platforms allow any individual to edit or add descriptions for content that has been created and disseminated by someone else. Although YouTube integrates features for anyone to edit captions that are auto-generated, the platform does not offer a comparable feature for video description. Developed by a third party, YouDescribe (Smith-Kettlewell Eye Research Institute) is a free web- and app-based tool that allows any individual to record audio de-

Sidebar 6.2

Screenshot of image description prompt in Twitter app.

scriptions to any YouTube video. By uploading and saving the descriptions for playback as the video plays, YouDescribe successfully bridges video accessibility shortcomings and user needs with a tool that allows for customized descriptions without infringing on protected content rights. 3Play Media is one example of a commercial vendor that offers services for customizing and embedding audio descriptions into any video; their workflow is unique from other vendors due to compatibility of text-based descriptions with a refreshable braille display.

the other hand, a description like, "Sally and Bill, still in their wedding outfits, looking completely exhausted," is entirely appropriate because those details are what Bill and Sally's sighted friends will take from the picture. Given the rise of social media and reliance on images to convey information, a growing number of tools have been developed to incorporate alt text, or description, in social media posts.

Description is a balancing act in which less is almost always more. The cleverness and creativity of the describer are indispensable, but should never be apparent. The best descriptions are written so clearly and match the tone so well that the viewer should never realize how much effort went into creating them. And, of course, there is no such thing as the perfect description. Because of the inevitable choices of what details to describe and which words to use to describe them, there are always possible improvements: ways in which to make your description slightly more clear, slightly more concise, and slightly less clunky. It is a craft that can continually be honed and improved, with each new image or video offering a new challenge for the dedicated describer.

Use of Description for Multimodal Access

Thus far, the discussion about description for access to information has centered on how to author descriptions to append to images and video. For the consumer, these descriptions can be accessed using various sensory channels.

Auditory access to described images and video.

When images are described, or have alternative text (alt text), the image itself does not appear any different to the visual user. However, for someone using a screen reader for auditory access, the alt text will be read by the screen reader and the consumer will hear the description read aloud. Auditory access to described images is typically only available when using a screen reader, although sighted readers can access alt text by hovering a mouse pointer over an image and reading the visual label that appears. When accessing audio descriptions for video, auditory access will depend on the tool used to author the descriptions. If a dedicated player such as YouDescribe was used to author descriptions on a separate audio track that plays alongside the video, the viewer will have the option to turn the description off or on while the original video plays. Every viewer (whether blind or sighted) can watch the same video and decide to turn up or down the description track volume without needing any additional assistive technology. This is similar to how individuals with and without hearing impairments can turn open captions on or off. However, if audio descriptions are embedded in a video (recorded onto the original audio track of the video), the descriptions are then played back as part of the video—similar to how closed captions always appear on the video screen.

Tactile access to described images and video.

Although discussions of description might imply auditory access, individuals who use braille can also access descriptions. Recall that when information is read aloud by a screen reader, it is also accessible with a RBD (See **Chapter 3** for detailed information on braille displays). This creates a seamless experience for those who are reading digital text with embedded images that have alt text. The text and image descriptions will appear on the RBD as the cursor moves through the text and images in the digital content. If an image does not contain alt text, the consumer will (sadly) get no information about the image when the cursor encounters it. For described videos, a commensurate experience is becoming more readily available for tactile access as technologies continue to advance. Traditional audio descriptions that record a human voice for simultaneous video playback is a purely audio format. For individuals who cannot access the audio track and need tactile access (such as consumers who are deafblind), transcripts of both captions *and* audio description tracks need to be provided as a text document that can be read by a screen reader and displayed on an RBD. At the time of this publication, commercial audio description vendors are now offering options for creating audio descriptions using synthesized speech; the use of synthesized speech instead of a human recorded voice allows users to edit the descriptions with text-based access that enables compatibility with screenreaders and RBDs.

Translation considerations for Subjects Related to Science, Technology, Engineering, Arts, and Math (STEAM)

Just as there are several file conventions to be aware of when accessing digital text (See **Chapter 3**), there are various file conventions used in disseminating and accessing digital scientific or math notation found in STEAM content. Sometimes, particularly in digital versions of print textbooks, equations appear as images, not as written text. In these cases, an image description that represents the equation as text may be sufficient for simple equations. Complex equations involving fractions, exponents, and other advanced mathematical notation need more intervention in order to be readable with text-to-speech or a braille display.

Equations and mathematical notation can be read by screen reading technologies if they are encoded properly. The technology used to make digital math accessible is changing quickly, but the means of encoding equations and mathematical notation is quite stable and will continue to represent good digital accessibility practice for years to come. The encoding schemes most widely used for math are similar to HTML (used for building Web content) or other markup languages in that they specify what each part of the equation or expression is, rather than worrying about how it should be laid out on the screen. When "marked up" by its parts (for example, when coding a fraction, its numerator and denominator must be identified), a mathematical expression can be read visually by the browser, in braille on a refreshable display, or with specialized text-to-speech navigation. The important thing to remember is that by properly encoding mathematical expressions you enable them to be rendered properly in whatever form the user needs.

The two most widespread mathematical markup schemes are LaTeX and MathML. Both are used extensively in mainstream applications for encoding math digitally and have been embraced by the digital accessibility community. Although details about LaTeX and MathML are beyond the scope of this chapter, there are a wealth of tutorials and resources for both online.

MULTIMODAL ACCESS TO TACTILE CONTENT IN MULTIMEDIA

Recall from our decision trees that there are several ways to ensure that digital images are handled appropriately for blind and low vision individuals.

- **Do not describe (the image is "eye candy" and conveys no pertinent information)**
- **Describe (most images are adequately accessible with a good description)**
- **Render a tactile graphic (a raised line drawing)**
- **Render a 3D model**

The previous section discussed best practices in description; this section will continue a parallel conversation in how to choose which format best represents an image when description is inadequate. Although different factors might inform the decision to choose a tactile graphic versus 3D model, both formats require similar considerations to ensure that information from an image is adequately represented for equitable nonvisual experiences.

Principles of Creating Tactile Content in Multimedia

The greatest advantage of the decision trees is that they guide a designer to consider how an image needs to be represented to a visually impaired consumer, even if the designer lacks extensive training in serving all the needs of this population. In other words, meaningful representation of visual information for nonvisual access is possible and can be done well by anyone who understands a few basic principles.

Meaningful representation of information

When translating images into a nonvisual format, the first step is to determine whether a description can adequately convey the necessary information. If a description is inadequate, then a tactile means must be considered. But how does one decide to represent an image as a tactile graphic or 3D model?

When working with tactile graphics, it is tempting to replicate the visual image simply by raising or embossing the lines of the image and creating a "tactile" graphic version of it. This can work well enough for certain images that represent truly 2D pictures. For example, simple line drawings of basic shapes (triangle, circle, square) can easily be rendered as tactile graphics by raising the outlines of the shapes so they can be felt by a reader.

In contrast, now consider a more complicated picture such as that of a motorcycle or the planet Saturn. If a designer simply raised the lines of a drawing of the motorcycle, it would feel like an oddly outlined shape of abstract lines. There would be no way for a reader to feel the relationships of the engine, wheels, seat, and handlebars to each other on a flat surface with raised lines. Similarly, raising the lines of a photo of Saturn would result in a tactile graphic that feels like a flat circle with a curved line bisecting it. Both of these image types would be more appropriately represented as a 3D model, which would be able to convey the shapes of features on a motorcycle and the flattened rings encircling the round planet of Saturn.

At this point, designers have a choice of how to provide the 3D models. Basing a rendering on an actual examination of a real item such as an actual motorcycle is almost always preferred to basing a 3D rendering on a photograph or illustration of the object (to be discussed below), but the rise of 3D printers now offers new options for printing objects as needed. While this technology has an easy appeal, not everything is ripe for 3D printing! When

3D modeling is available, it is best suited for printing objects that are otherwise too small (a chemical molecule), too large (the Eiffel Tower), too dangerous (a crocodile), or too fragile (a museum artifact) for an individual to hold and explore (Hasty, L. and Miele, J. A., n.d.). Without careful considerations for what subjects are appropriate to render through 3D print, it is easy to become enamored by this technology and contribute to longstanding misunderstandings of how to represent information effectively for nonvisual accessibility. Building good practices relates to a thoughtful understanding of how individuals with visual impairments actually interact with the world and synthesize information differently that people with typical vision.

Sidebar 6.3

RESOURCES FOR 3D PRINTING FOR ACCESSIBLE EDUCATIONAL MATERIALS (AEM)

What Is 3D Printing?

3D printing is a technology that has been around for many years, but has only reached more mainstream use in recent years. In the past, 3D printers were purchased by companies for manufacturing large quantities of materials or by individuals with specialized design expertise, but nowadays 3D printers are purchased and enjoyed by any person with an interest in making, such as those in maker and design spaces, libraries, schools, families, and even kid groups. 3D printers are great for tinkering with design software, engineering concepts, and experimentation with creating 3D models and replicas of common or unique objects.

A 3D printer is akin to a traditional printer in that a user sends a digital file to the printer and a physical print is output. Instead of an inkjet or laser printing head, a 3D printer has a heated metal nozzle, also known as an extruder. Instead of an ink or toner cartridge, a spool of plastic cord is connected to the extruder, which melts the plastic and forces the material through the extruder that moves back and forth on a flat printing bed. Imagine a traditional hot glue gun, only instead of glue, hot melted plastic is ejected and then hardens into shape as it cools. The extruder movement is determined by the digital file that is sent to the printer (typically .stl format) and moves along xyz-axis that are connected to the frame of the 3D printer. As the extruder moves back and forth, the plastic builds in layers and the object is created from the bottom up. Most 3D printed objects have ridges that can be felt or seen upon examination; these ridges show how the plastic layers build during the printing process and are commonly referred to as the "resolution" of 3D printed objects. Resolution typically improves (the object has less noticeable ridges) with higher quality 3D printers and can affect the amount of time it takes to print an object.

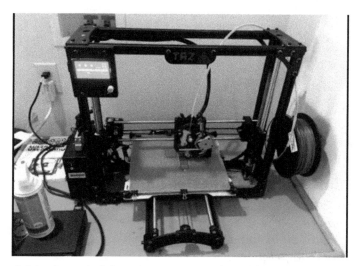

A black metal frame creates a box-like structure around a flat printing bed. A spool of blue plastic hangs from one side of the frame and the extruder is mounted on rods that suspend the nozzle above the printing bed. Credit: Neal McKenzie, AT Specialist, Sonoma County Office of Education

How can 3D printing benefit individuals who are visually impaired?

Although many visually impaired individuals whose primary access mode is nonvisual (in other words, these individuals require auditory and tactile media), 3D printing is an emerging mainstream technology that must be used sparingly to represent 3D models. According to Lucia Hasty (tactile graphics expert) and Dr. Joshua Miele (blind scientist and inventor), use of 3D printing for nonvisual accessibility should be limited to printing objects that are too large, too small, too dangerous, or too rare for a visually impaired person to tactually experience with the real object. Examples of each type include:

(Continued)

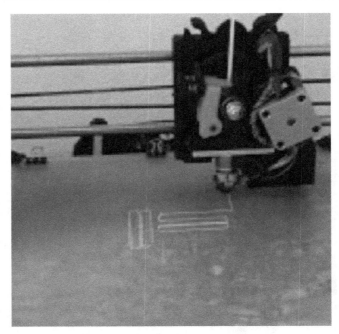

The beginning of a print shows the extruder mounted just above the print bed, and yellow outlines in the shape of rectangles are visible on the print bed.

The completed print shows 3 yellow rectangular box-shaped objects. Credit: Neal McKenzie, AT Specialist, Sonoma County Office of Education

- Too large = The Eiffel Tower, planet with rings such as Saturn, tectonic plates

- Too small = a ladybug, DNA molecule, chemistry element

- Too dangerous = A scorpion, horns on a bull, layers of an active volcano

- Too rare or fragile = A museum artifact such as dinosaur bone or fossil, seed head on a dandelion

Objects that are provided as tactile media should be provided as a real object rather than a 3D printed representation as much as possible. 3D printed objects can be difficult to comprehend when they don't necessarily embody the characteristics of the object or if the 3D printer has poor resolution (which results in thick ridged lines along the surface of the object). For example, it is better to give a child an actual teddy bear to explore rather than representing it as a hard, plastic, 3D printed model. Images that are adequately represented as a tactile graphic without having 3D spatial characteristics would also be better represented using any of the methods for tactile graphics production (see Chapter 5) rather than using a 3D printer. Lastly, 3D printing braille should only be used as a last resort when other methods of producing braille are not available (see Chapter 5).

In summary, it is important to refer back to the decision and image sorting trees in **Chapter 6** to determine if an image is best represented via a description, tactile graphic, or 3D model. If a 3D model is the best choice, then it is preferable to utilize a real object before resorting to 3D printing. The best uses of 3D printing are for printing replacement parts for items related to work tools or toy sets, for creating objects that meet an individual need, or for creating materials that need to be highly durable, resilient to liquids, and can be properly sanitized.

Considerations for choosing a 3D printer

3D printers can vary from a couple hundred dollars to several thousand dollars. The size of the printing bed determines the size of the objects one can print, and generally correlates to the price of a printer. Resolution (how fine the lines can be felt along the surface of the object) helps convey the quality of 3D printed objects and is also correlated to printer price. Other features a buyer might consider are print speed and whether the printing

(Continued)

bed is self-leveling (reduces maintenance needed to ensure the printing bed is level before and during printing). Usability of the control panel and interface are also considerations, and whether or not the printer uses open source or proprietary software. Most 3D printers are not accessible and cannot be utilized independently by an individual who is blind or visually impaired. This imposes a great limitation on blind individuals' ability to realize their own design capabilities. Inaccessible 3D printers might have a touch screen control panel or a visual display that does not speak the information. 3D models are designed using computer-aided drafting (CAD) software, which are also largely inaccessible except for OpenSCAD. This software is accessible for screen reader users because the interface is presented on a command line, which is readable by screen readers.

Despite all the above-named factors, the most practical consideration might be the availability of technical support for a specific printer. 3D printers require a fair amount of attention and comfort with technology to use CAD software and design files for 3D printing and to operate the printer itself. Patience, diligence, and bravery to troubleshoot issues is necessary to develop proficiency in using a 3D printer and maintain equipment health. Several file repositories exist in order to aid consumers who might own a 3D printer and can manage the equipment but have limited training in using CAD software. These repositories post design files (usually .stl) that individuals have created and posted for others to use and 3D print:

- **Thingiverse and Tinkercad**. Large communities of users who design and post files online for public consumption. The files are not vetted for quality or particular use by individuals who are visually impaired, so printing from Thingiverse or Tinkercad requires knowledge of best practices in representing information in a 3D format for nonvisual access. It is helpful to know which community members post files that are appropriate for use as accessible materials. Look for posts from "AT Neal.

- **American Printing House for the Blind (APH).** A federally-funded nonprofit organization that produces accessible educational materials for students who are visually impaired. In addition to a tactile graphics image library that hosts a repository for creating tactile graphics, APH also posts files for 3D printing replacement parts for the learning kits they distribute.

- **BTactile.** An online hub that allows a user to search multiple file repositories for 3D printing and tactile graphics. Variability depends on the quality and style of files across the various host organizations.

Where Can I Find More Information About 3D Printing Accessible Materials?

3D printing is a technology that attracts interest from a variety of fields such as design, architecture, STEM, makers, tinkerers, and education. Most people who are curious about this technology and are poised at the intersection of 3D printing and accessibility have either technical *or* pedagogical knowledge. A fewer number of people understand best practices in representing spatial information for nonvisual access while also possessing the technical acumen to carry out the 3D printing and design processes. For these reasons, communities that bridge the gaps in expertise are important to engage with in order to learn more about utilizing 3D printing for accessibility. Several organizations are worth noting due to their role in connecting groups of expertise that succeed co-dependently when implementing 3D printing for consumers who are visually impaired.

- **The DIAGRAM Center, a Benetech Initiative.** A nonprofit organization that specifically supports image accessibility, the DIAGRAM center is a hub that centralizes resources for 3D printing including guidelines for best practice, research papers, and tutorials including webinars and tools for decision-making.

- **Nonscriptum, LLC.** A for-profit company that provides training, manuals, and consulting in how to use 3D printing in educational and scientific communities. One of this company's most important initiatives is the development of a 3D Model Education Exchange, which is a free online group that allows non-technical stakeholders (such as teachers of the visually impaired, visually impaired individuals, parents) to request files for 3D printing objects they've identified to be useful for nonvisual learning. The requests are then fulfilled by engineering and design students who possess the technical skills to design a file but not necessarily the pedagogical knowledge to know what is needed for 3D printing. This group acts essentially as a matchmaking service between technical and pedagogical experts.

Teachers of students with visual impairments (TVIs) demonstrate competence in addressing all areas of pedagogical needs when they implement instruction throughout the Expanded Core Curriculum (ECC). Without the same training and preparation as TVIs, other service providers and designers can best develop an understanding of pedagogical needs only after committing adequate time and focus on collaborating directly with individuals who are visually impaired. Among these pedagogical needs, differentiated instruction is most important for students whose natural course of learning and development are affected by visual impairment. For example, a student who has never seen a cloud in the sky or watched steam escape from a kettle will benefit from additional direct instruction to understand those concepts before learning about the condensation and evaporation cycle. For adults or older youth who become visually impaired after the primary stages of learning and development, instruction in the ECC is less important and effective than linking new information to familiar schemas. These concepts are best applied before presenting new information to the student in a nonvisual manner; as with most teaching situations, it is always a good idea to check a student's conceptual knowledge before building towards new representations.

Editorial Capacity: Context and Clutter

Once a decision is made to create a tactile graphic or 3D model, further considerations must inform the design and presentation of the material. As with description, understanding the context and purpose of an image is essential to help a designer decide what which details to render and which ones to leave out. Too much clutter in a tactile graphic or 3D model will make it impossible to distinguish any details at all by touch, but, in contrast, too little detail does not provide enough information for the user. In other words, just as the case was with description principles, there is the need to be concise and selective in what to include in a tactile representation of an image.

Finally, the tactile content requires some form of labeling to provide information about what the user is touching. In traditional alternate media, this may be done in one of several ways: with another person who provides verbal description while the user examines the tactile graphic or model, by means of a tactile legend, or via braille labels. The first method provides the most customizable information to the consumer but is dependent on the availability of sighted assistance. The second method makes more demands on the user's ability to remember and synthesize tactile elements, but gives the user greater independence. The third method is the one that is most prone to confusing tactile media by introducing tactile clutter.

Two other methods have been experimented with on many occasions over the years with limited success: computer vision technologies and use of QR (Quick Response) codes. Computer vision approaches utilize a camera-based system to recognize where a finger is pointing and speaks the label. While this system synthesizes the role of sighted assistance to describe what the user is touching, practical uses are fraught with complications. Shadows and glare interfere with the camera's access, and because blind explorers usually touch with their finger pads rather than point with their finger tip, the camera's acuity in recognizing what specific item the user wants information about can be inaccurate. QR codes can be a very helpful alternative because of affordances for encoding in-depth information. Information about a graphic or model could then be read aloud or displayed on an RBD as soon as the QR code is scanned. Although promising in theory, QR codes can also be problematic for practical use—the QR codes are ink-printed and require tactile markings for a blind or visually impaired person to find the code, thus re-introducing the challenge of reducing tactile clutter. Extensive user testing will be needed to explore whether either method is a viable option for supporting tactile content.

Use of Multisensory Strategies for Multimodal Access to Tactile Content

This section will discuss how multimodal strategies can overcome several of the aforementioned limitations and considerations to provide independent access to information. Thus far, we have focused on the creation of tactile materials to represent images found in

media, and considered consumers using only tactile strategies to access the materials. We can now consider the possibilities for simultaneous, multisensory access to tactile materials.

Figure 6.4:
A Talking Tactile Map

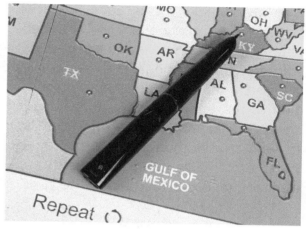

This tactile map uses a talking pen that provides information about different locations on the map. The reader can access several layers of information by using multiple pen taps on a particular location.

As discussed above, one of the greatest challenges in independent exploration of tactile materials relates to the need for labels to identify the parts of an image. Although labels are essential in visual images to name and explain features, the direct addition of braille labels on a tactile graphic or 3D model can alternatively add too much clutter and interfere with the tactile representation. We have already discussed the limitations associated with relying on a tactile legend or on sighted assistance for accessing labels; to these we should add that, beyond needing labels, most tactile materials also require some verbal introduction, context, or description to be effective. While this information can be provided in a digital text or brailled document, it may be difficult for an individual to digest the description while simultaneously examining the tactile graphic or model.

Now consider if the tactile material allows for a multisensory experience; that is, can the media be engaged via immersive, multimodal experiences that support a user's independent interaction with the information. Audio-tactile materials such as talking tactile graphics and talking models have the capacity to provide such experiences through auditory labels embedded in the tactile

graphic or model. Auditory labels leverage the strengths of each mode of representation while minimizing its limitations. The tactile format can provide the spatial representation that description cannot, and auditory descriptions can provide the labeling and narrated information that would otherwise cause clutter and cognitive load in a tactile format.

There are several types of technology available for creating and interacting with audio-tactile materials However, most tools were not developed for the purpose of accessibility and have instead been adopted as an accessibility "hack." Few tools are used widely among all practitioners who

Figure 6.5:
A Talking 3D Model

A talking 3D model—like this one of the National Mall in Washington, D.C—is an effective way to present information about a large area for a blind traveler to hold and explore. TouchGraphics, Inc.

AUDIO-TACTILE TOOLS AND MEDIA

Each of the technologies included in this sidebar are currently available for public consumption. The specific processes in producing some of these materials are unique to the developer, however the user experience remains similar across the various types of audio-tactile media. Each item below allows for tactile exploration while providing auditory supplementary information and labeling. For individuals who are deaf-blind and have hearing loss in addition to visual impairment, the auditory information must be further disseminated as computer-readable text captions for access with a refreshable braille display.

Talking tactile graphics

This media format provides immediate and direct auditory feedback to a consumer as a tactile graphic is explored. Tactile exploration is encouraged with both hands and multiple fingers (Morash, Connell Pensky, Tseng, & Miele, 2014) and auditory labels can be activated with a single touch.

Talking Tactile Tablet (TTT, Touch Graphics, Inc.)

The Talking Tactile Tablet (TTT) is one of few contenders for talking tactile graphics for classroom use. Tactile graphics and braille curricula are thermoformed or embossed before placing on a touchscreen tablet that is pressure sensitive. When various parts of the tactile media are touched, the corresponding audio label and auditory feedback are played back. Information can be recorded in layers so that each repeated touch activates another layer of information for the same point of interest on the graphic. This allows a great amount of information that can be provided auditorily in real time as the individual explores the graphic. Some of the programs for the TTT include a National Geographic Talking Atlas and the SAL2 Mangold Braille Reading Program.

In addition to the programs available for purchase, an Authoring Tool is also available and sold with a bundle of blank template sheets for the TTT. Any designer, blind or sighted, can create a tactile graphic or worksheet and tag each part of the media with audio feedback that the designer records.

(Continued)

Tactile overlays for touchscreen tablets

Touchscreen tablet devices such as Android tablets and Apple iPads can also be utilized with tactile overlays to provide similar experiences as the TTT. This approach requires digital media that are displayed on the tablet with descriptions embedded in the digital file, plus a tactile overlay that is attached to the screen. The overlays can be made with various plastic materials or other material that will conduct the finger touch to the screen. Commercially-produced examples include:

- Reach for the Stars iBook (Developed by NASA and SAS Institute) with tactile overlays from National Braille Press
- Talking building/floor maps (Shedd Aquarium, public floor maps in Google's offices)

Talking Pen applications

Tactile graphics can also be explored with auditory labels using a smartpen such as the Livescribe smartpen. The tactile graphic is created on special paper or similar material that conveys information to be read aloud as the pen touches various points on the tactile graphic. Auditory information can also be recorded and played in layers with repeated pen touches. These approaches require the consumer to explore the tactile graphic with one hand while maneuvering the pen with the other. Although smartpen-compatible paper can be purchased and used with a homemade tactile overlay (similar to how an individual can create their own talking tactile graphics on a touchscreen tablet),
it is more likely to find commercially developed products such as:

- Interactive Map of the United States (American Printing House for the Blind)
- STEM Binder including a talking tactile periodic table of elements (Touch Graphics, Inc.)
- Museum guidebooks (Intrepid Museum, National Museum of African American History and Culture; Touch Graphics, Inc.)
- Transit maps (Bay Area Rapid Transit [BART]; Smith-Kettlewell Eye Research Institute)

Sidebar 6.4

Talking Models

3D models, whether 3D printed or constructed using other materials, can also be programmed to talk and explored with auditory labels. Some instances of partial 3D (or 2.5 D) media raises entire areas of a graphic rather than just raised lines (like that of a tactile graphic). Whether 2.5 or 3D, consumers can interact with these models using tactile exploration strategies while accessing explanatory information and labels auditorially. Conductive filament or paint is used to link a consumer's touch to the corresponding audio file. Examples of talking models include:

- Interactive 3D campus maps (Perkins School for the Blind, Carroll Center for the Blind)
- Interactive 3D museum models (San Diego Museum of Fine Art, Queens Hall of Science, Shedd Aquarium)

work with individuals with visual impairments, but implementation of audio-tactile materials is becoming more prevalent, especially in community spaces such as museums that use these materials in interactive exhibits.

Whether multimedia is presented as a digital book with descriptions and accessible graphics or as a talking tactile graphic or model, remember that information in either format is immediately and independently usable by almost every member of a community. Thoughtful design of audio-tactile materials can create highly interactive learning experiences that combine the best intentions of UDL with the highest hopes for independent access to information. When done well, multiple means of representing information can align with accessibility and usability of

information for all individuals with and without visual impairments (Siu, 2016).

Most individuals, blind and sighted, have individualized learning preferences; some might consider themselves to be "visual" learners while others might be "auditory" or "kinesthetic" learners. Accessible multimedia therefore supports the range of learner types regardless of whether or not someone has a diagnosed disability. Materials that support the inclusion of consumers with a variety of abilities at the time of their dissemination can also be considered "born accessible"—that is, no additional remediation is needed to create independent access points regardless of how a user chooses to access information. The next section will further discuss how accessible multimedia can be used not just for access to information, but also for higher levels of synthesis to include engagement with data and quantitative literacy.

MULTIMODAL ACCESS TO MULTIMEDIA INFORMATION: DEVELOPING DATA LITERACY

(Contributing Author: Ed Summers; Senior Manager of Accessibility and Applied Assistive Technology, SAS Institute)

Participation in the twenty-first century knowledge economy requires a variety of skills that simply did not exist a few decades ago. Chief among them is "digital literacy" as defined by Paul Gilster in his book of the same name. Essentially, digital literacy extends the concept of literacy to the new media of digital technologies, such as computers, networks, and the Internet. The differences between information printed on paper and information accessed through digital technologies are many and profound. Because a full discussion is beyond the scope of this chapter, the following section will focus specifically on quantitative information or data.

The collection and analysis of data has been the cornerstone of the scientific method and human progress since the Scientific Revolution. The digital technologies that drive the knowledge economy are the direct result of the repetitive application of the scientific method to an ever-widening number of domains. The businesses that compose the knowledge economy use those digital technologies to collect, analyze, and leverage data from all aspects of their operations.

The ability to derive insights from large amounts of data creates tremendous competitive advantage for students and organizations in the private, public, and non-profit sectors. Employees who focus exclusively on this task are called "data scientists"; the need for quantitative skills, however, is not limited to them. Decentralized management structures and the widespread adoption of data-driven decision processes requires every employee in the modern organization to be able to understand the metrics that are used to track progress towards the goals of the organization so they can make informed local decisions.

The benefits of quantitative skills extend beyond employment. For example, individuals are required to make effective personal financial decisions concerning salary, retirement, budgeting, etc., and to reason effectively about many health-related decisions such as the risks and rewards of various treatments. In summary, having quantitative skills can bring great advantages to many areas of life.

We generally use the term "quantitative literacy" (QL) to refer to the minimum set of quantitative skills required to thrive in the twenty-first century knowledge economy. The American Association of Colleges and Universities defines quantitative literacy as a "habit of mind," competency, and comfort in working with numerical data. Individuals with strong QL skills possess the ability to reason and solve quantitative problems from a wide array of contexts and everyday life situations. They understand and can create sophisticated arguments supported by quantitative evidence and they can clearly communicate those arguments in a variety of formats (using words, tables, graphs, mathematical equations, etc., as appropriate).

Challenges

People who are blind or visually impaired face many barriers to quantitative literacy. Chief among them is data visualization. Data visualization is the practice of representing data in a graphical format such as charts, graphs, or maps. Data visualization is widely used to discover insights within data and share those insights with others. For example, it is common to view a sequence of readings from a scientific instrument such as a thermometer represented as a line chart. It is easy to discover trends and patterns within even large time series data sets when they are presented visually.

People who are blind or visually impaired experience many specific challenges regarding data visualization. First and foremost, it is challenging for stu-

dents who are blind or visually impaired to learn quantitative literacy skills because instructional materials and standardized tests use data visualizations extensively, and it is simply not practical for students to receive a customized large print or tactile version of every data visualization they encounter. This challenge is compounded by the widespread use of online instructional materials and adaptive tests, i.e., tests that adapt in real time by presenting questions that vary in difficulty depending on the responses of each individual student.

Second, it is challenging for working blind or visually impaired professionals to access data visualizations that are shared within the workplace even if they were able to acquire excellent quantitative literacy skills while in school. Again, it is seldom practical for working blind or visually impaired professionals to acquire custom large print or tactile versions of data visualizations. This situation is compounded by several factors, including a lack of support in workplaces that is generally available in educational contexts; for example, a TVI, and the recent evolution towards digital data visualization technology that is highly interactive and which updates in real time.

Finally, it is difficult for both students and professionals who are blind or visually impaired to use data visualization independently to discover insights within data because mainstream software tools (such as spreadsheet programs and statistical analysis software) are, quite often, not fully compatible with screen magnifiers and screen readers.

Without dwelling on the difficulties, we must explore the deficiencies of existing technologies so that we can create twenty-first century technologies that enable equivalent access for people with blind or visually impaired.

CRITERIA FOR EQUIVALENT ACCESS

- **Cradle-to-Grave Digital**
- **Affordable Hardware**
- **Independence**
- **Collaboration**
- **Sufficient Perceptual Power**

Some accessibility thought leaders define equivalent access as the ability for blind or visually impaired people to independently realize the same benefits as sighted peers for the same cost within the same amount of time. This definition is often based on personal experiences as a former blind or visually impaired student or decades of experience as a blind or visually impaired professional. The definition is even more strongly supported by blind or visually impaired scientists who have devoted their careers to the information sciences. With leadership from one of the contributing authors of this chapter, Ed Summers, one statistical analysis software company has been developing new accessible data visualization technology. Their research and develop-

ment team follows these criteria to assess emerging technologies and guide the company's product roadmap.

Cradle-to-grave digital

Nicholas Negroponte was one of the first people to discuss the benefits of representing information as digital bits rather than physical atoms in his 1995 book *Being Digital.* Bits are superior to atoms in several ways that are particularly relevant to the accessibility of data visualizations.

First, bits cost less than atoms. The cost advantage considers physical materials such as paper, physical machinery such as a tactile graphics printer, and time.

Second, bits are easier to transmit over long distances. For example, consider the difference between sending a digital representation of a graph via e-mail versus sending a physical representation of the same graph on paper via postal mail.

Third, bits are easy to change. For example, it is much easier to change the foreground and background colors of a digital image than it is to change these colors in an image that has been printed on paper.

Fourth, bits support interactivity. For example, consider a digital map of North America that first allows users to click on the United States to reveal a map of all the states, and then click on an individual state to reveal a map of the counties it.

Fifth, bits easily support the ability to receive updates from data sources that are changing in real time. For example, consider live streams of data generated by scientific instruments that measure constantly-changing conditions such as temperature, air pressure, or water salinity.

The cradle-to-grave digital criterion requires a completely digital life cycle for data visualizations so blind or visually impaired people can enjoy the benefits of digital representation while avoiding the costs associated with converting data visualizations to physical atoms.

Affordable Hardware

Mainstream sighted users generally perceive digital representations of data visualizations on monitors. Of course, monitors have been made affordable to be integrated into personal computers, laptops, tablets, and other devices.

The affordable hardware criterion requires devices that can display data using non-visual methods, and requires that the cost of those devices be roughly equivalent to cost of computer screens. At this writing, the cost of a computer screen ranges from about one hundred dollars on the low end to a few thousand dollars for large high-quality displays.

Independence

The independence criterion requires that blind or visually impaired people are able to create and perceive data visualizations without human assistance. It refers to the ability to create data visualizations from raw data. It also refers to the ability to perceive data visualizations directly without interpretation or assistance from teachers, peers, co-workers, family members, or friends.

Independence is critical for a variety of reasons. In classrooms, it enables an educator to assess the knowledge of blind or visually impaired students. In the workplace, it enables blind or visually impaired people to work independently and contribute original work to a field. In a personal context, it enables blind or visually impaired people to maintain privacy, such as managing a budget for personal spending.

Collaboration

The collaboration criterion enables blind or visually impaired people to participate fully in both diverse teams and large communities. In practice, this criterion requires that a fully-sighted person can create a data visualization that can be shared with other people whether they are fully sighted or visually impaired. It also requires that a person with a visual impairment can do the same.

Sufficient Perceptual Power

The sufficient perceptual power criterion requires that blind or visually impaired people can perceive the same information within data visualizations as fully-sighted mainstream users in roughly the same amount of time. However, it is expected that blind or visually impaired people will use different senses and different strategies to perceive that information. One example of this type

EMERGING TOOLS FOR SONIFICATION AND REFRESHABLE TACTILE DISPLAY

Keeping in mind that the following technologies were recently released or prototyped at the time of this publication, the reader should consider these tools as proofs of concept for future tools that can support independent, nonvisual interactions with data.

Sonification: SAS Graphics Accelerator and the Desmos Calculculator "Audio Trace" Feature

From the lab of one of this chapter's contributing authors Ed Summers, the SAS Institute developed the SAS Graphics Accelerator extension for Google Chrome and Mozilla Firefox. This product is envisioned as a state-of-the art implementation of sonification, to be used by any member of the general public. The extension enables alternative presentations of graphs that include metadata for text descriptions, tabular data, and interactive sonification.

The free Eeb- and app- based graphing calculator Desmos also offers a sonification feature called "audio trace." Similar to the SAS Graphics Accelerator, the audio trace feature enables a user to gain an overview of a graph and explore points of intersection and data auditorily. Desmos was designed with accessibility in mind; it is therefore a fully inclusive tool that is compatible with screen readers (can be used without a mouse), braille displays, and braille embossers.

Refreshable Tactile Display

Full screen refreshable braille displays are historically cost-prohibitive and remain an emerging technology until production and purchase are more affordable. Two prototypes have broken this barrier: the Graphiti and the Canute. These refreshable tactile displays are meant to display is tactile graphics specifically (not braille), and can refresh on demand as images on a computer change. This product will change how nonvisual learners can take adaptive computer-based assessments that include graphics and require data analysis.

of information is the ability to get a quick summary of a data visualization such as the trend of a line chart. Another example is the ability to quickly estimate the X or Y value of an outlier in a scatterplot.

Emerging Technologies

There are two emerging technologies that have a clear potential to satisfy all the criteria for equivalent access as discussed above: sonification and refreshable tactile displays. Readers are encouraged to monitor these emerging technologies with the expectation that they will be widely used by blind or visually impaired people in the near future.

Sonification is the practice of representing data using sound. Effective implementations of sonification will map dimensions of data visualizations to the characteristics of sound and then continue to use those auditory mappings consistently throughout the implementation. For example, the y-axis of a Cartesian plane may be mapped to the frequency of sound waves so that data points that are lower on the y-axis will have a lower pitch than data points that are higher on the y-axis. Data points along the x-axis then may be represented by their position within the stereo field,, with data points that are lower on the x-axis panned more left in the speakers or headphones while data points that are high on the x-axis are panned farther right. With practice, the user can learn to "read" the data through the variations in perceived position and pitch.

Refreshable tactile displays can produce images that can be perceived by touch. However, unlike paper tactile graphics, a refreshable tactile display can change the image being displayed on demand similar to how a computer screen can refresh images. Technical advances promise the ability to display parts of images at different heights for more detailed relief, or the ability to zoom in on part of an image for more detail.

Content Vocabulary
Refreshable Tactile Display

A **refreshable tactile display** is a device that allows the user to feel a succession of images that can be explored through touch.

Other promising refreshable tactile displays have failed to graduate to marketable products because of the exorbitant development costs required for a product with a small market share. Earlier prototypes that employ physical pins that refresh in a fashion similar to RBDs are starting to give way to tablet-style displays that rely on haptics for screen interaction and tactile engagement instead. As haptic technologies develop, it will be critical that technology developers consult with educators who have sufficient pedagogical expertise in training students for tactile access. Since most of the initial attempts have not included input from educators, they do not address issues such as the need for tactile exploration with both hands and multiple fingers (Morash et. al, 2014). These crucial oversights combined with limited testing on a wide range of user experiences in the initial design process are often the downfall of a well-intentioned idea. With improved integration of understanding of how blind or visually impaired individuals access information efficiently, it is hoped that the flexibility of emerging technologies can slowly evolve tactile graphics from the realm of physical atoms into the realm of digital bits.

SUMMARY

As we conclude this chapter and **Part 1** of this textbook, our hope is for the reader to feel equal parts exhausted and exhilarated by the many possibilities and technologies for individuals with visual impairments. This last chapter aims to build stronger bridges between communities that work in UDL and accessibility; by doing so, we can strengthen the power of stakeholders to achieve greater access to information for every individual within a community. For accessibility facilitators, as well as for advocates such as practitioners, families, and blind or visually impaired individuals, knowledge of how technology can be used to access information can help present use cases to designers and technologists who are new to thinking about nonvisual accessibility. Additionally, the inclusion of design and engineering terms is intended to empower advocates to engage more in initial technology design rather than limiting their role to the remediation of poorly-conceived inaccessible technology. By doing so, accessibility "warriors" can build their own bridges to collaborate with the developers, engineers, and administrators who affect the design and adoption of classroom and workplace tools.

Independent access to information depends both on how digital environments are built and on the efficacy of tools that engage these environments. Therefore, advocacy must be carried out on several fronts. As mentioned, practitioners and end users alike can do their part in keeping their own skills and language current in order to productively engage with community partners. It is also critical that the designers and community partners who hold power in building digital environments and tools recognize the impact of their choices. Decisions regarding how materials and information are disseminated can have ripple effects in the educational journey of a student that ultimately affect successful employment and productive membership in the community. Developers and engineers—even administrators who make purchasing decisions—can be essential change agents in ensuring accessibility for all members of a community. Partnership building, professional development, and awareness of sound accessibility practices can begin early in one's postsecondary education and career. Investing in early training will help develop a basic understanding of accessibility that can sustain one's practices regardless of the field of practice. Because digital environments and technological tools evolve quickly, new opportunities will always arise to improve or sustain the accessibility of mainstream technology. As we move rapidly into an increasingly digital world, multimedia accessibility must become a foundational principle of every designer's education.

REFERENCES

CAST: About Universal Design for Learning. (2015). Retrieved September 2, 2019, from http://www.cast.org/our-work/about-udl .html#.Wa4_uIqQxE4

Meyer, A., Rose, D. H., & Gordon, D. T. (2014). Universal design for learning: Theory and practice. CAST Professional Publishing.

Morash, V.S., Connell Pensky, A., Tseng, S.T.W., & Miele, J. (2014). Effects of using multiple hands and fingers on haptic performance in individuals who are blind. Perception, 43, 569–588.

Morash, V., Siu, Y.-T., Miele, J.A., Hasty, L., & Landau, S. (2015). Guiding novice web workers in making image descriptions using templates. ACM Transactions on Accessible Computing, 7(4), 12:1–12:21.

Siu, Y. (2016). Designing for all Learners with Technology. Educational Designer, 3(9). Retrieved from http://www .educationaldesigner.org/ed/volume3/issue9 /article34/index.htm

Part 2

The Access Technology Assessment Process

Receiving a new piece of access technology can be exciting for both student and service provider alike. This excitement can encourage students to "buy into" the instructional program and its technologies.
Artwork credit: https://cassfrayerdesign.com/

CHAPTER 7
Considerations When Conducting a Technology Evaluation

As we move from **Part 1,** which focused on tools that are available for nonvisual or low vision accessibility, to **Part 2,** which will focus on elements related to evaluation and implementation, remember this:

Technology Is Everything, but Everything Is Not Technology

Recall from **Chapter 1** that technology is ubiquitous—it is pervasive in many aspects of daily living, education, and employment. Without conscientious planning, developments in the digital world can threaten as much as facilitate one's independent and timely access to information. The role of technology for access to information is even more critical for people who require nonvisual or low vision access to the physical and virtual worlds—understanding this, other related skills and tools for analyzing, interpreting, and synthesizing information are equally important.

As with all approaches for conducting a comprehensive evaluation, multiple tools and measures must be used to capture a holistic understanding of an individual's current levels of functioning and ongoing needs. Weighing the pros and cons of a particular type of technology is only one element of a much larger process. Many other factors must be taken into consideration as well, with enough data collected to support all recommendations at the end of an assessment process.

Chapter 1 detailed what aggregate data are needed from multiple sources: a clinical low vision examination, observations across a variety of contexts, and, additionally for students in educational settings, a functional vision assessment (FVA) and learning media assessment (LMA). These sources of information all contribute data regarding an individual's sensory learning channels, how information needs to be accessed for different tasks, and the ideal format in which information must be available for optimal accessibility with and without technology. In part one of this textbook, each chapter included considerations for user needs and media formats alongside an overview of currently available technologies and tools. Part one could be thought of as *descriptions* of the various tools that might fill an individual's technology toolbox. Having a general understanding of the types of tools and range of available options is necessary in order to coordinate this knowledge with information from the multiple areas of assessment. Together, these data can support recommendations for acquisition, implementation, and instruction.

Now we embark on part two of the textbook: designing the toolbox that will hold all of one's tools. The following chapters will address how a service provider, school or workplace teams, and a student can work together to define a workflow for receiving, engaging with, and constructing information in the most independent and timely manner possible. The term "student" will refer to the individual who is the focus of the assessment and future technology instruction, regardless of whether the individual is a K–12 student or an adult who is receiving services. Along with defining the infrastructure needed to ensure a student's engagement, the service provider must also make recommendations for the most appropriate tools that are based on individual sensory learning channels, needs for multimodal access to information, personal preferences, and what tasks need to be accomplished. This chapter will introduce the reader to a conceptual foundation for assessment that will inform the evaluation process. Next, **Chapter 8** will present recommendations for evaluation preparations, selection of evaluation tools and methodologies, and determining what needs to be assessed.

Chapter 9 will focus on the mechanics of conducting a technology evaluation and how to integrate those data within a comprehensive report that provides holistic information and recommendations for a comprehensive training or education program. Finally, **Chapter 10** will define how technology must be conceptualized in order to fully define, develop, and advocate for what digital literacy means for blind and low vision individuals.

CONCEPTUAL FRAMEWORKS

Although theoretical, conceptual frameworks provide a foundation that unifies collaborators when approaching evaluation and strategizing recommendations, having a shared approach also provides common ground for collaborators who may have varied areas of expertise. In the areas of access, assistive, and educational technology, two major frameworks are often cited when discussing how to build an end user's toolbox and how to integrate technology into the classroom. While focused for the classroom, these frameworks can be similarly applied to consider the needs of individuals beyond the classroom. The main objective is to implement systems that consider the user and environment while maintaining enough flexibility to adapt as needs change. From there, the appropriate tools can be selected and customized to meet these needs. Incorporating these frameworks into technology evaluations will help practitioners update their knowledge and customize recommendations that will weather changes in the types of tools available and emerging technology innovations.

SETT framework.

In 1995, Joy Zabala published a framework to help guide technology recommendations for the classroom (http://joyzabala.com/Home.php). Known as SETT, this framework considers the Student, Environments, Tasks, and Tools in making assistive technology decisions. At the time that SETT was developed, it was conceptualized for *when* technology might be adopted in the classroom. It recognized the existing workflow of pre-digital classrooms and offered guidance for how to implement technology if a teacher

A SELECTION OF ASSISTIVE TECHNOLOGY ASSESSMENT TOOLS

Zabala's SETT Framework (Zabala, 1995) identified four components for evaluation as part of an assistive technology assessment: Student, Environment, Task, and Tool. These components carry through to several other assessment tools that were published some time later.

The QIAT (Quality Indicators for Assistive Technology) is a key resource that can guide the provision of quality AT services. The QIAT community is comprised of professionals who disseminate and update information about QIAT. While their efforts are focused on school settings, their recommendations can be applicable to any team and agency who is involved with the provision of high quality assistive technology services. Look for their resource *Quality Indicators for Assistive Technology: A Comprehensive Guide to AT Services* (2015).

Here is a list of other assessment tools related to assistive technology evaluation (McCarron, 2014):

- **ALDI = Advancing Learning in Differentiation and Inclusion.** The ALDI describes a framework for AT decision-making and helps practitioners develop action plans related to Universal Design for Learning (UDL) and Response to Intervention (RTI).

- **ETP = Educational Tech Points.** The ETP describes a 6-step process from referral to implementation, and considerations in impact of different contexts that influence the environment.

- **HAAT = Human, Activity, Assistive Technology.** The HAAT considers the person, the activity to be completed, and aspects of the AT tool. The combination of all three elements are considered within the context in which these interactions take place.

- **WATI = Wisconsin Assistive Technology Initiative.** The WATI is a popular tool that helps an evaluator identify the student, tools, and tasks within an environment.

For those interested in further AT research, here are some suggested starting points:

- A Framework For Modelling The Selection Of Assistive Technology Devices (ATDs) (Scherer, Jutai, Fuhrer, Demers, & Deruyter, 2007)

(Continued)

Sidebar 7.1 (Continued)

- Four Models Of Assistive Technology Consideration: How Do They Compare To Recommended Educational Assessment Practices? (Watts, O'Brian, & Wojcik, 2003)

- Existing models and instruments for the selection of assistive technology in rehabilitation practice (Bernd, Van Der Pijl, & De Witte, 2009)

References

Bernd, T., Van Der Pijl, D., & De Witte, L. P. (2009). Existing models and instruments for the selection of assistive technology in rehabilitation practice. Scandinavian Journal of Occupational Therapy, 16(3), 146–158.

McCarron, M. (2014, May 7). Michelle's Blog: Assistive Technology Assessment Models. Retrieved September 26, 2019, from Michelle's Blog website: http://michellemccarron.blogspot.com/2014/05/assistive-technology-assessment-models.html

Quality Indicators for Assistive Technology: A Comprehensive Guide to AT Services. (2015). Wakefield, MA: CAST Professional Publishing.

Scherer, M., Jutai, J., Fuhrer, M., Demers, L., & Deruyter, F. (2007). A framework for modelling the selection of assistive technology devices (ATDs). Disability and Rehabilitation: Assistive Technology, 2(1), 1–8.

Watts, E. H., O'Brian, M., & Wojcik, B. W. (2003). Four models of assistive technology consideration: How do they compare to recommended educational assessment practices? Journal of Special Education Technology, 19(1), 43–56.

Zabala, J. (1995). The SETT framework: Critical areas to consider when making informed assistive technology decisions. Retrieved from http://eric.ed.gov/?id=ED381962

chose to do so. From the SETT framework, several other assistive technology tools and frameworks were published but collected more value in the research communities than practitioners.

Nowadays, in modern classrooms, places of employment and individual's lives, technology is ubiquitous—that is, technology is everywhere! No longer is technology used in silo from other educational materials or common mundane tasks. Assistive technology is often used in conjunction with mainstream and instructional technologies, and information takes the form of multimedia including text, images, and

CONSIDERATIONS WHEN CONDUCTING A TECHNOLOGY EVALUATION

video. In fact, curricular and workplace materials are often in digital format as well as, or more than, paper media. Even presentations and lectures are often solely disseminated in a digital form without a non-technology mediated format unless there are paper handouts. Service providers who work with individuals who are visually impaired are now challenged to have a comprehensive understanding of how assistive technology must integrate with general technology within complex information- and data-driven environments. This shift in the context of assistive technology use necessitates discussion of another framework that assumes the prevalence of technology and the flexibility needed to accommodate the range of information and media.

TPACK framework

In recognition of greater adoption of educational technology in schools throughout the United States, Mishra and Koehler (2006) introduced an updated framework that defines how teachers must understand technology for best integration in the classroom. This framework recognizes that most technologies used in the classroom are not designed for educational use; rather, they are co-opted for use with teaching. The TPACK rationale is of particularly relevant to TVIs, who are challenged not only to adapt non-education focused technology, but also must further modify educational technology and instructional materials for nonvisual or low vision access. By doing so, TVIs must have a deeper under-

standing of the complexities of multimedia, affordances, and the constraints of mainstream and specialized tools, and how to differentiate accessibility solutions dependent on the pedagogical needs of learners with visual impairments. TPACK is achieved at the convergence of three areas of knowledge:

▫ **Technological Knowledge.** Knowledge of specific types of tools, including the affordances and constraints of different types of technology. Understanding of how different types of technology can be deployed to carry out various tasks.

▫ **Pedagogical Knowledge.** Knowledge of how various individuals access information. Understanding how an end user might employ different sensory channels when learning,

**Figure 7.1:
TPACK Framework**

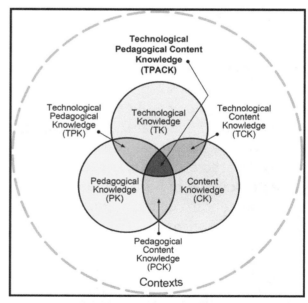

engaging with, and interacting with different types of information.

- **Content Knowledge.** Knowledge of the various forms information can take. Understanding how different tasks can be carried out to present and interact with information in different ways.

Although devised for students and technology implementation in the classroom, TPACK could be differentiated for practitioners who work with individuals beyond the classroom. For example, rather than defining content knowledge as instructional tasks and academic subjects, content knowledge in the workplace might address database management, manipulation of spreadsheets, digital filing systems, or crafting interoffice memos or public service announcements. Ultimately, applying a TPACK-like approach can help streamline an individual's needs for technology and prioritize recommendations for device selection and instruction.

For the purpose of this book, we will define TPACK as the primary knowledge types (Technological, Pedagogical, and Content Knowledge) and where they all overlap. The additional knowledge areas created by only two overlapping areas of knowledge are beyond the scope needed to illustrate how practitioners can approach a technology evaluation. Although it might be tempting to circumvent a theoretical framework and skip directly to the evaluation, giving even the briefest consideration to a framework can inform a more

efficient process in the long run. Without a knowledge base that considers a more holistic view of an individual's needs, recommendations will have critical failure points and limitations in team buy-in and practical implementation.

In practice, TPACK provides a framework for conducting a needs assessment (Kaufman, 1977) that captures necessary information from each body of knowledge for the purpose of supporting educational technology (Mishra & Koehler, 2006) (See **Appendix 8.5, Needs Assessment Template**). This idea of a needs assessment is not new (Hubert, 2003); as applied to assessing needs for a blind or low vision individual, the needs assessment must capture the following:

Pedagogical Knowledge (PK)

The service provider who is trained to facilitate nonvisual or low vision needs, along with the parents and the student, will best understand how nonvisual or low vision access requires differentiated information needs. PK can address *how* an individual accesses information based on the affordances and limitations of each sensory access method. In terms of the SETT framework, these needs help define the student, can allude to the learning or work environment, identify examples of tasks the individual can engage in, and provide inferences for appropriate tools. Identification of needs in this area will inform what *features* of technology would benefit the individual, depending on the task at hand. The following questions can help gather information that is needed to contribute to one's PK about a student:

- What tasks (if any) does the student rely on visual access to accomplish? What activities are difficult to carry out visually?

- What tasks (if any) does the student rely on auditory access to accomplish? What activities are difficult to carry out auditorily?

- What tasks (if any) does the student rely on tactile access to accomplish? What activities are difficult to carry out tactilely?

Information from this area of a needs assessment will guide the reader to specific sections of **Part 1.** The identified tasks will inform which chapter to begin with, while knowing the sensory access method will help the reader focus on the appropriate segment(s) within each chapter.

Content Knowledge (CK)

Personnel who work alongside the student are key collaborators who provide information that informs a service provider's content knowledge. CK identifies what the learning or work expectations are. In terms of the SETT framework, reported needs in this area help define the environment and tasks that an individual might encounter throughout typical daily activities, learning experiences, or in the employment space. The following questions will help an assessor gather information

that will help prioritize learning objectives and implementation strategies:

- During what activities is the individual currently dependent on sighted assistance (and could be more independent)?

- What activities are difficult for the individual to carry out in a timely manner with maximum independence as desired?

- What kinds of media are in the individual's education or work environment? What is the nature of the information the individual needs to access?

Construction of this CK will help contextualize areas for instruction and prioritize technology instruction.

Technological Knowledge (TK)

Technological knowledge is best developed via collaboration with information technology (IT) specialists, assistive technology specialists (including CATIS-certified professionals); tech-savvy colleagues, friends, or family members; and other individuals who use access technology regularly. It is of particular importance to engage with prolific and varied communities of practice (Wenger, 1998) in order to have sufficient resources available to a service provider. This area of a needs assessment prompts the evaluator to answer the following questions:

- What types of technology would enhance the independence and efficiency of the student's workflow (as related to how the individual accesses information)?

- What features of technology would enhance a student's independent and efficient access to information?

It is also extremely important that types and features of technology are identified using device- and brand-agnostic terms. When focused on determining needs for technology and advancing one's TK about a student, this open-minded approach will broaden and refine potential technology solutions. Often a service provider might identify a specific name brand for a student simply based on his or her own personal experience and familiarity with a particular device or application. This misstep results in limiting a student's options to only what is familiar to the service provider—and therefore limits creativity in determining holistic solutions that might better fit a student's needs and workflow. Identification of specific brand names are best reserved for the recommendations section of a purchasing request.

Ultimately, when conducting a technology evaluation, the evaluator must have a clear understanding of what a student's needs are, including how the individual is experiencing accessibility challenges. It is important to remember that capturing information for each area of TPACK is dependent on a collaborative, team-based approach. Different informants will contribute different pieces of information that, when taken together, can be utilized more effectively than information from a single

source. Taking this team-based approach also lessens the expectation for a single practitioner to achieve and maintain proficiency in every area of knowledge. While not a formal tool, a needs assessment can help organize the scope and breadth of information that an evaluator might encounter in the evaluation process. It is a conceptual starting point for stakeholders to construct their understanding about a student's needs and focus their discussions with the student before making final recommendations—this is important even if the student is school-age in order to maximize the student's willingness to use the technology. The following section will consider the possible stakeholders and roles each might adopt when a service provider coordinates a technology evaluation.

Members of a Technology Evaluation Team

All aspects of access technology, from evaluation to implementation, require collaborative efforts to ensure success (QIAT Consortium, 2005). Members of a technology evaluation team will vary depending on the student and the environment that will support technology and information access. For example, an educational team focused on meeting a child's needs in the classroom will differ from a rehabilitation or workplace team focused on meeting an adult's needs in the community or place of employment. Each context will have a unique workflow that requires definition in order for team members to fully understand how a blind or low vision individual must interact with information for optimal accessibility. Regardless of the context, each team member will contribute information based on his or her experiences with the student and perspectives of need.

Educational teams

Parents and guardians are often the best informants on how their child learns and accesses information. The student is another important informant and can contribute to his or her own needs assessment process. All of the above individuals can contribute very concrete information in pedagogical and content knowledge, and their expertise should not be overlooked when conducting a technology evaluation. A savvy parent, guardian, or student can contribute to TK as well! When parents are involved in the evaluation process, they can also be instrumental in students' implementation of technology (Kelly, 2009). Fully credentialed TVIs who are graduates of a comprehensive personnel preparation program should be equipped to evaluate and teach technology related to nonvisual or low vision access as part of instruction in the Expanded Core Curriculum (Hatlen, 1996; Holbrook, McCarthy, Kamei-Hannan, & Zebehazy, 2017; Huebner, Merk-Adam, Stryker, & Wolffe, 2004)—a well-trained TVI who continues to meet updated national teaching standards for TVI preparation (CEC Division on Visual Impairments and Deafblindness, 2019) should also demonstrate expertise that encompasses the competencies of a CATIS certification (and therefore not necessitate a CATIS-certified professional on the evaluation team). Because

of their understanding of PK, TVIs provide critical input to school teams that define which features of technology are needed to support various sensory learning channels. Data from an FVA and LMA can be used to provide this information. Collaboration with classroom teachers helps contribute information regarding content knowledge. Classroom teachers are knowledgeable about the educational technology they use in the classroom, the different activities in which they expect students to engage in, and how learning materials are presented. They define the learning environment that a student must access. For students with additional sensory and motor disabilities, related service providers in occupational and speech therapy can also provide information regarding what additional features or tools might be needed.

Finally, collaboration with a school's IT personnel, district technology administrator, and assistive technology specialist is essential to supplement a TVI's PK and TK, as well as brainstorm final recommendations for specific tools. All members of a school team must collaborate with these stakeholders in order to ensure seamless technology implementation within a student's education environment. When considering the expertise of these tech-related stakeholders, a CATIS-certified professional is a distinction among more generally trained technology specialists—for example, the typical assistive technology specialist generally knows the full range of technology to meet the diverse needs that stem from a spectrum of disabilities but has limited knowledge about the unique considerations and tools for meeting nonvisual and low vision needs. They are best equipped with global technological knowledge but must collaborate with a TVI to better understand technology needs as related to visual impairments. On the other hand, CATIS-certified assistive technology specialists *do* possess that added knowledge base about technology related to visual impairments and can contribute to the evaluation process without needing additional scaffolding to understand nonvisual and low vision accessibility.

TVIs who are well trained and have kept up with technology developments are capable of evaluating, recommending, and teaching students how to use technology that supports low- or nonvisual accessibility. These responsibilities are included within the scope of AT as described in the Expanded Core Curriculum, which TVIs are mandated to teach. However, when working with a visually impaired student with additional abilities, collaboration with an AT specialist is especially important to access the AT specialist's expertise regarding the breadth of technology beyond those options that meet low- or nonvisual needs. For these reasons, it is important to keep the language in needs assessments and recommendations as general as possible so that common threads can unite expertise from a variety of stakeholders. The deliberate use of device and software

agnostic terms leaves the greatest number of options for consideration. It is best to meet a student's needs by recommending specific features a technology must offer rather than recommending a specific product or brand name. If the expectation is based on features, it allows the educational team and the student it supports to easily swap equivalent tools into and out of the toolbox as needed while still complying with what was promised to the student. Ultimately, students need to understand their own accommodations and accessibility preferences well enough to identify the technology features they need in order to make and justify these decisions for themselves. Before a student exits the educational system and prepares for postsecondary education or employment, he or she needs to become the primary informant in each area of knowledge that TPACK encompasses.

Rehabilitation and workplace teams

Technology evaluations for community and workplace accessibility initiate from the end user, or consumer. Typically, consumers outside of the educational system seek assistance when there are specific tasks or activities that are difficult to accomplish independently and in a timely manner. The consumer must also share how he or she prefers to work, what kinds of tools have been successful in the past, and the goals he or she would like to achieve. In other words, an effective technology evaluation in the rehabilitation or workplace environment begins with the consumer, who can contribute most of the information regarding his or her own pedagogical and content knowledge.

Although a consumer might report what specific technologies he or she has used in the past, this individual might not always be aware of all the other types of technologies that have become available. With information received from the consumer, it becomes the responsibility of an assistive technology specialist to identify the available options and make recommendations for specific devices or programs to trial before purchase. Service providers who work with adult students can also demonstrate competency in evaluating and teaching access technology with a record of scholarship or via CATIS certification. Additional consult from peers and colleagues can further define needs related to tasks and activities the consumer must access and the environment in which the individual works and participates. This can be especially important in strategizing workplace accessibility and the accommodations that are needed for an individual to meet expectations for employment. Workplaces each have unique physical and digital environments that a blind or low vision employee must successfully navigate with compatible technology and accommodations. (See **Appendix A**.)

Personal Preferences and Role of the End User

In addition to the team members discussed previously, the role of the individual student in a technology evaluation cannot be undervalued.

Every technology evaluation should begin and end with the individual who is blind or visually impaired. The end user needs to be involved as much as possible in every step of researching, brainstorming, comparing and contrasting demo units, and identifying possible recommendations. Regardless of whether the individual is school-aged or an adult, he or she needs to be consulted before final decisions are made. There might be unknown personal preferences that require consideration, or particular usability aspects specific to the individual's dedicated use of the technology. Every blind or low vision individual must be empowered to make decisions that directly affect how he or she interacts with day-to-day information. Finally, personal involvement in the evaluation and device-testing phases of a technology evaluation can help ensure buy-in from children and adults alike. Without personal investments, willing adoption of new technology can be difficult; unfamiliar technology can be frustrating and requires a learning curve that takes time to overcome. Early experiences with technology and involvement in the evaluation process can facilitate self-determined behavior in blind and low vision students; as the end user of whatever technology is recommended, the student is and should always be an active participant and stakeholder in the process.

If the practitioner is sighted or not themselves an end user of the same technologies that are being discussed for his or her client, even more consideration should be given to a student's user experiences; in addition, it is wise in this case to consider input from a variety of other disabled individuals who use access technology, and resources from a community of practice. Maintaining consistent connections to—or at the very least exposure to—the larger community of blind or visually impaired individuals who use technology is critical in maintaining access to a varied base of technology users. As mentioned in **Chapter 1,** maintaining membership to one's own community of practice is essential to develop and sustain technology proficiency. These communities of practice should include individuals who are blind or visually impaired. By making these efforts, sighted practitioners can develop a deeper understanding of the pros and cons of various tools for nonvisual and low vision access to information. In other words, these communities of practice help build and then maintain a practitioner's technological, pedagogical, and content knowledge.

Infrastructure for Technology

Finally, the environment in which the end user must access information will affect recommendations of tools to improve efficiency and independent engagement. Infrastructure such as Wi-Fi and Internet connectivity, a district's or office's operating system, and administrative access to devices and networks are all logistics that will affect whether or not a tool is implemented or what additional workarounds are needed. Technical support for implementation, troubleshooting, and integration into existing workflows might

also affect which device is selected once the pool of options is narrowed. Finally, the computing ecosystem can also dictate which tools are considered and selected. For example, if a student can receive materials primarily through a cloud-based file sharing platform such as Google Drive, then accessibility features within Google-specific products (such as Google Docs) might be considered first. On the other hand, if a student must work across several devices at home and school, and the home devices primarily use iCloud (Apple's on-line file storage system) for materials such as iBooks, then the accessibility features within Apple products might be considered first.

Because infrastructure is such an important consideration in the final steps of a technology evaluation, before making recommendations, it is important to examine how an individual uses his or her current workflow to receive, interact with, and disseminate information. This can help identify other needs that can be addressed by optimizing the workflow so that it better supports integrated technology use and accessibility.

NEXT STEPS

By presenting these considerations, this chapter aims to give the practitioner a conceptual foundation for conducting a technology evaluation for individuals who are blind or visually impaired. Whether the practitioner is a TVI or another professional involved in the technology evaluation process, it remains important that any evaluation incorporates a

CONSIDERATIONS WHEN CONDUCTING A TECHNOLOGY EVALUATION

holistic needs assessment and team-based approach. The following chapters will detail the various aspects of a technology evaluation and provide guidance for each step of implementation.

REFERENCES

Hatlen, P. (1996). The core curriculum for blind and visually impaired students, including those with additional disabilities. RE:View, 28(1), 25–32.

Holbrook, M. C., McCarthy, T. S., Kamei-Hannan, C., & Zebehazy, K. T. (Eds.). (2017). Foundations of Education, Third Edition: Volume II: Instructional Strategies for Teaching Children and Youths with Visual Impairments (3rd ed., Vol. 2). New York, NY: AFB Press.

Hubert, M. (2003). The practice of needs assessment for the supply with technical aids in The Netherlands. Die Rehabilitation, 42(1), 52–59.

Huebner, K. M., Merk-Adam, B., Stryker, D., & Wolffe, K. (2004). The national agenda for the education of children and youths with visual impairments, including those with multiple disabilities. New York, NY: AFB Press.

Kelly, S. M. (2009). Use of assistive technology by students with visual impairments: Findings from a national survey. Journal of Visual Impairment & Blindness, 103, 470–480.

Mishra, P., & Koehler, M. (2006). Technological pedagogical content knowledge: A framework for teacher knowledge. The Teachers College Record, 108(6), 1017–1054.

QIAT Consortium. (2005). Quality indicators for assistive technology services.

Zabala, J. (1995). The SETT framework: Critical areas to consider when making informed assistive technology decisions.

CHAPTER 8
Evaluate the User Experience

Individuals who are blind or visually impaired are a heterogeneous group; their unique sensory access abilities, preferences, and information needs are as varied as those of sighted individual's. Although this book emphasizes one's independence in accessing independence and favors digital media and technology for affording privacy and timely access to information, the authors also recognize that not every individual will have the capability or preference for independence. The ultimate role of access technology is to facilitate an individual's **interdependence** as much as independence within a community (Bennett, Brady, & Branham, 2018). One of the goals of the assessment process is to identify strategies for maximizing the active participation of a disabled individual such that regardless of when or how assistance is desired, the individual is empowered to facilitate his or her own accessibility. In some cases, scaffolded strategies can gradually fade to independence. In other cases, the individual can become more proficient in directing assistance with the appropriate access technology (AT).

This chapter does not attempt to describe every tool, framework, or model for AT evaluation. With recognition for what these approaches contribute to the evaluation process (recall **Sidebar 7.1, A Selection of Assistive Technology Assessment Tools)**, this

chapter will instead present a process for defining a user experience in order to understand a student's present levels of performance. This understanding is a necessary first step before an evaluator can assess needs for technology. Once a baseline is established and a student's needs are defined, the most exciting part of the evaluation process can commence: "playing" with technology! **Chapter 9** will describe how the results of a needs assessment must dictate the latter steps of the evaluation. Based on an individual's needs, various types of technology can be evaluated for their appropriateness for the student, and an evaluator can determine how to optimize the current user experience.

In design fields that focus on user experience (UX), the two central concerns are an individual's needs and how to best meet them. UX designers follow a sequence of operations that then inform a holistic technology evaluation. The data collected in this evaluation is then used to improve UX design. Generally, any evaluation requires capturing an individual's current state of functioning, identifying areas of need based on that current state, proposing tools and strategies to maximize functioning, and finally communicating these data to a team for implementation. Altogether, this information can illustrate an individual's experience both with and without needed technology. The experience should convey how an individual uses his or her senses across various tasks, and how a particular tool might improve the independent, timely, and efficient access to information (Houde & Hill, 1997). Contextual factors such as social circumstances, time constraints, and environmental conditions also influence how an individual's experience should be considered. Also referred to as "experience prototyping" (Buchenau & Suri, 2000), this process entails three general activities that can inform a comprehensive evaluation.

- Understanding existing user experiences and context (*evaluation activities*)
- Exploring and evaluating design ideas for an improved user experience (*evaluation of possible tools, craft initial goals and recommendations*)
- Communicating ideas to a team (*evaluation report*)

With a focus on defining a user's experience, recommended tools can be considered starting points for exploration that will be further fine-tuned as an individual's workflow adapts to different tasks and environments. It is important to understand that technology implementation is an iterative process best conceptualized as attempting to *approach* an ideal—an ideal workflow for one situation may not be appropriate for another. Similarly, an ideal tool for one instance may not be ideal in another. Strategic iteration based on what educators refer to as *diagnostic teaching* is key to

maximizing the capabilities of an individual's toolbox of access technology.

Many people who are new to assessment often want a precise how-to, step-by-step guide to evaluation with a fill-in-the blank evaluation report template appropriate for all situations. This is very difficult—if not impossible! Although several tools and frameworks have been published to guide AT assessment, there is a visible gap between research and practice; there are ". . . no standardized, reliable, and valid instruments guiding the AT selection process . . . [nor] available data on the effectiveness of models to provide statistically relevant advantages of one AT selection process over another" (Bernd, Van Der Pijl, & De Witte, 2009, p.156). Further investigations are needed to validate the use of these tools for heterogeneous populations such as those found among individuals who are blind or have low vision. In addition, as the terminology shift from "assistive" to "access" technology implies, a technology evaluation for blind and low vision individuals must encompass far more than the specialized tools that have been designed for nonvisual or low vision accessibility; the pervasive nature of technology dictates a different understanding of how technology in general—including mainstream and specialized tools— impacts a student's access to information. Existing tools and processes specific to AT assessment simply do not cover the range of possibilities that a UX evaluation can.

For these reasons, the checklists and forms in this textbook are best used as graphic organizers for thinking, data organization, and information synthesis. Each step of the evaluation will highlight a companion form or checklist from the Appendix that can be used to guide the evaluator through that step. **However: Note that a single form or checklist would never be submitted as a comprehensive assessment** because federal regulations mandate the use of multiple tools for assessment (IDEA, 34 CFR §300.304(b)(1)). Consider TPACK as a theoretical framework that is relevant to technology adoption for nonvisual and low vision accessibility (See **Chapter 7**); **Chapters 8 and 9** offer one interpretation of a comprehensive evaluation process as it aligns with understanding an individual's needs based on an evaluation team's technological, pedagogical, and content knowledge specific to the individual who is being evaluated. With experience, this information will sufficiently guide the reader in customizing a path for assessment given unique evaluation contexts for different evaluation teams and individuals of interest.

Assessment is best approached with an open mind, as well as an open *will* to embrace unexpected findings. This process is also best embraced with persistence and fortitude—much like anything related to accessibility and technology! The checklists and forms in the **Appendix** can help alleviate uncertainties in the evaluation process by providing a general roadmap for collecting, organizing, and synthesizing assessment data. As his or her experience with technology evaluation develops, an evaluator might begin to customize his or her own evaluation process and fact-finding methods. No amount of book reading can replace the learning that develops from hands-on experience; trust the process and let each evaluation experience teach you what books cannot.

This chapter will present steps 1–5 of completing a technology evaluation, including how to capture a student's current user experience (also known as determining an individual's present levels of performance) and how to conduct a needs assessment. From this information, **Chapter 9** will present steps 5–8 of the evaluation, including how to specify which tools to trial, how to optimize UX, and how to present evaluation findings to the evaluation team as well as the individual. (Recall **Figures 1.1 and 1.2** for a more general overview processes in K–12 and Vocational/Rehabilitation services.)

A Comprehensive Technology Evaluation Process: Ten Steps

1. Identify the evaluation team
2. Conduct a file review
3. Collect data
4. Align data with areas of need
5. Understand the current UX and identify needs
6. Match student needs with appropriate technology options

7. Prototype improved UX

8. Define and recommend an optimal workflow

9. Draft an initial report

10. Finalize the report and invite opportunities for iteration

The time and effort required to complete an evaluation may seem demanding, but the importance of this process and its included activities are justified when all parties understand the impact that the appropriate technology and related infrastructure can have on the life of an individual. Performing a thorough evaluation and taking adequate time from the very beginning ensures that the evaluation is holistic and takes into account how tools will need to evolve along with a student's needs and skills. Focusing on the larger UX will support more sustainable recommendations to increase the chances that technology investments will accomplish the desired educational, employment, and personal objectives.

To ensure the provision of high quality (assistive) technology services, a set of Quality Indicators for Assistive Technology (QIAT) were developed as a guide for assessment and practice. (See **Sidebar 8.1, QIAT.**) Although the QIAT guidelines are geared toward supporting K–12 students, many of the ideas and concepts can also apply to adults in higher education and employment situations. Generally, technology evaluations in K–12 settings are more intricate than those in adult settings due to the number of involved stakeholders, skills that are yet to be developed, and the environmental variations an individual may experience within one school year and from one year to the next. However, the basic principles of technology assessment can be considered by any evaluation team and applied to a student of any age. Although the remaining chapters of this book will use the term "student," it is understood that this term refers to any individual who is the focus of any assessment, whether child or adult. Experienced CVRTs and others working with adults can modify each step of the evaluation to fit the needs and goals of evaluation within the rehabilitation or vocational setting.

Sidebar 8.1

QUALITY INDICATORS FOR ASSISTIVE TECHNOLOGY SERVICES

Considerations for Assistive Technology Needs: Quality Indicators

Consideration of the need for assistive technology devices and services is an integral part of the educational process identified by IDEA for referral, evaluation, and development of the Individualized Education

Program. Although assistive technology is considered at all stages of the process, the indicators outlined below are specific to the consideration of assistive technology in the development of the IEP as mandated by IDEA. In most instances, the indicators are also appropriate for the consideration of assistive technology for students who qualify for services under other legislation (e.g., Section 504 of the Rehabilitation Act of 1973 and the Americans with Disabilities Act). They specify critical guiding principles to be followed during assistive technology assessments.

1. Assistive technology devices and services are <u>considered for all students with disabilities</u> regardless of type or severity of disability.

Consideration of assistive technology need is required by IDEA and is based on the unique educational needs of the student. Students are not excluded from consideration of assistive technology for any reason. (e.g., type of disability, age, administrative concerns, etc.)

2. During the development of the Individualized Education Program, the IEP team consistently uses a <u>collaborative decision-making process</u> that supports systematic consideration of each student's possible need for assistive technology devices and services.

A collaborative process that ensures that all IEP teams effectively consider the assistive technology of students is defined, communicated, and consistently used throughout the agency. Processes may vary from agency to agency to most effectively address student needs under local conditions.

3. IEP team members have the <u>collective knowledge and skills</u> needed to make informed assistive technology decisions and seek assistance when needed.

IEP team members combine their knowledge and skills to determine if assistive technology devices and services are needed to remove barriers to student performance. When the assistive technology needs are beyond the knowledge and scope of the IEP team, additional resources and support are sought.

(Continued)

4. Decisions regarding the need for assistive technology devices and services are <u>based on the student's IEP goals and objectives, access to curricular and extracurricular activities, and progress in the general education curriculum.</u>

As the IEP team determines the tasks the student needs to complete and develops the goals and objectives, the team considers whether assistive technology is required to accomplish those tasks.

5. The IEP team <u>gathers and analyzes data</u> about the student, customary environments, educational goals, and tasks when considering a student's need for assistive technology devices and services.

The IEP team shares and discusses information about the student's present levels of achievement in relationship to the environments, and tasks to determine if the student requires assistive technology devices and services to participate actively, work on expected tasks, and make progress toward mastery of educational goals.

6. When assistive technology is needed, the IEP team <u>explores a range</u> of assistive technology devices, services, and other supports that address identified needs.

The IEP team considers various supports and services that address the educational needs of the student and may include no tech, low tech, mid-tech and/or high tech solutions and devices. IEP team members do not limit their thinking to only those devices and services currently available within the district.

7. The assistive technology consideration process and <u>results are documented in the IEP</u> and include a rationale for the decision and supporting evidence.

Even though IEP documentation may include a checkbox verifying that assistive technology has been considered, the reasons for the decisions and recommendations should be clearly stated. Supporting evidence may include the results of assistive technology assessments, data from device trials, differences in achievement with and without assistive technology, student preferences for competing devices, and teacher observations, among others.

Common Errors:

▫ Assistive technology is considered for students with severe disabilities only.

▫ No one on the IEP team is knowledgeable regarding assistive technology.

▫ The team does not use a consistent process based on data about the student, environment and tasks to make decisions.

▫ Consideration of assistive technology is limited to those items that are familiar to team members or are available in the district.

▫ Team members fail to consider access to the curriculum and IEP goals in determining if assistive technology is required in order for the student to receive free, appropriate public education.

▫ If assistive technology is not needed, team fails to document the basis of its decisions.

Source: Adapted from QIAT Consortium, "Quality Indicators for Assistive Technology Services" (revised 2007). Available: www.qiat.org.

STEP 1: IDENTIFY THE EVALUATION TEAM

At the beginning of the technology evaluation process, a coordinator must be identified. By adhering to the primary purpose of the evaluation (assessment of a UX and recommending tools and strategies to improve it), the evaluation coordinator can readily identify members of the evaluation team who can best contribute information and focus on which tasks and environments to assess. Any environments in which the student needs to interact with information (for example, a classroom, lab, meeting room, retail store, or entertainment venue) can be assessed. A comprehensive technology evaluation must capture the current UX first, and then identify strategies for improving the UX with recommended tools and strategies that can be optimized as an individual's needs evolve.

The evaluation team must comprise members who are collectively knowledgeable about the student's educational needs and abilities, functional implications of vision impairment and any additional disabilities, mainstream educational technology, and assistive technology related to improving the student's overall functioning. Every effort should be made to schedule meetings at times when everyone can attend. For larger evaluation teams, two separate meeting dates might be needed to accommodate scheduling conflicts. For students who are able to contribute information about their own needs and preferences (usually middle school level and higher, if not younger), it is important that they also attend each meeting. Younger or less mature students might be able to attend only one meeting; however, they should at least send a copy of notes, however brief, that can be shared at each meeting so that their contributions as a member of the evaluation team are always recognized.

Sidebar 8.2

A FIFTH GRADER'S NOTES FOR AN IEP MEETING

Frank's goals

- I want to get to 700 w.p.m. reading speed.

- I want screensharing to work so that teachers' notes can be broadcast to my laptop.

- I want special glasses for orchestra so I can read music notation and also see the teacher.

What's working well at school

- Homework, because I can do it on my computer

- Text to speech, in particular the reading speed using Voice Dream Reader

- Seeing what we do in the classroom—I can see the classwork and know what to do. I use my computer and I'm close to the whiteboard and the smart screen so I can see what I'm doing

What I want to improve

- Reading books on the computer—when I take notes and they're long, I want to be able to see all of my notes to study from.

- I don't get my magnifier out because I'm too embarrassed and there's not enough room on my desk.

- I should take vision breaks because my eyes get tired.

- Sometimes my eyes are too tired to read and see.

The evaluation coordinator determines what data are needed, carries out the assessment with contributing information from team members, and answers the following main questions in a comprehensive report:

- How does the student currently function in each environment that requires engagement with information? (*Determination of present levels*)

- What are the areas of need and which areas must be prioritized for instruction? (*Needs assessment*)

- How can the student's engagement with information (both accessing <u>and</u> producing) be improved for maximum independence and efficiency? (*Recommendations, goals and objectives*)

Each evaluation team member—especially the student—will contribute data to help the evaluation coordinator answer each of these questions.

Considerations for K–12 Assessment

In a K–12 educational setting, the ad-hoc evaluation coordinator is the person who best understands the student's needs and can best identify evaluation partners—most often the TVI. In some districts or counties, a different professional might coordinate the paperwork and meeting logistics while in other locations a TVI might coordinate everything. Most districts have pre-existing guidelines regarding how AT evaluations are to be conducted. The IEP team (inclusive of parents/guardians and the student) will comprise the evaluation team, including any professionals who are needed for additional input such as a district technology director; IT personnel; an assistive technology specialist if not already on the IEP team; a consultant from a state agency, technical assistance project, or school for the blind; or CATIS professional if the TVI lacks the technical expertise. In some cases, a private contractor might be hired; this contractor must be skilled in evaluating technology to meet low vision or nonvisual needs. In the case of a contracted general assistive technology specialist without experience specific to visual impairments, this professional must work in close partnership with the TVI. Parents are also entitled to invite additional people to the IEP team as desired. Note that according to federal mandates, the IEP team must convene within 60 days from when the assessment plan is signed.

Considerations for adult assessment

For college students and working age adults, the client's rehabilitation counselor is the evaluation coordinator. If the individual to be evaluated is an older adult, the evaluation instead will most likely be coordinated by a Certified Vision Rehabilitation Therapist (CVRT), a Clinical Low Vision Therapist (CLVT), or other professional service provider working with the individual. The rehabilitation counselor typically coordinates the evaluation team, which is inclusive of the individual, and invites professionals with specific areas of expertise as needed to assess the individual's needs and provide recommendations related to the individual's goals. These might include but are not limited to specialists in CVRT, AT, CATIS, employment, orientation and mobility (O&M), and rehabilitation teaching. The procedure for assembling an assistive technology evaluation team for an adult varies greatly from state to state. Some states have rehabilitation specialists or assistive technology teams who specialize in evaluations and can provide them. Because blindness and visual impairment are low-incidence disabilities, some state teams might lack a specialist in blindness technology and therefore assign the task to an independent contractor. In this case, specifying a CATIS professional can ensure that an appropriate evaluation is carried out. Evaluations of adults can be limited to an employment situation, services for independent living, or other specific need. The question becomes, what technologies are available that can assist the individual in accomplishing specific tasks required for a specific purpose?

> ### Content Vocabulary
> ### Low-Incidence Disability
>
> **Low-incidence disability** refers to diagnoses that occur rarely or in small numbers among a population.

Considerations for assessing individuals with visual impairments and additional disabilities

Individuals with additional disabilities often have complex and challenging needs; therefore, careful evaluation from knowledgeable specialists is imperative. A multidisciplinary team is vital for all those being assessed and is essential for those with visual and additional disabilities. Although **Chapters 2 through 5** focus primarily on various technologies for individuals with visual impairments, it is important to know that there also are many effective and innovative assistive technology tools available for individuals with limited motor control, communication difficulties, and cognitive disabilities (Copeland & Keefe, 2007; Downing, 2005). The sheer number and variety of these devices make it impossible to address all of them in this book. It takes trained, experienced team members to assess individuals with complex motor, speech, and cognitive needs, and each team member will need to provide essential information in order to give a holistic picture of the person and his or her needs.

STEP 2: CONDUCT A FILE REVIEW

In order to gain an initial understanding of a student, including approximate uses of vision and other sensory access channels, level of conceptual understanding, and extent of needs, the evaluation coordinator must review existing files to gather relevant background information. Information from the individual's records combined with functional data from formal and informal evaluations and observations are critical to the assistive technology evaluation process. Any information about the individual's use of AT in the past should be included as well as a list of questions and concerns compiled from everyone involved with the individual. **Appendix 8.1: Background Information for a Technology Evaluation** can be used to organize data from the file review.

In some cases, a file review does not offer sufficient information to begin the technology evaluation. If the necessary information is unavailable from available reports, the team will need to obtain this data themselves before continuing with the evaluation. For example, information about the individual's preferred literacy medium or learning media may not be available, so a formal learning media assessment (Koenig & Holbrook, 1995) will need to be completed before continuing with the technology evaluation. Information from the following assessments will be relevant to determining a starting point for assessment and considerations when making recommendations.

Medical eye reports from a medical provider (an ophthalmologist, not a nurse screening)

◦ **Visual acuities:** Acuity measures can inform a starting point for assessing functional print sizes, word or character spacing, and use of low vision or nonvisual strategies

◦ **Discrepancies between near and distance vision:** Challenges with accommodation (visual adaptation when focusing on information that is presented at a distance versus within a desktop) can justify strategies or tools for desktop access to information presented at a distance (for example, screen sharing, copies of class notes)

◦ **Discrepancies between left and right eyes:** Irregular binocularity or stereopsis can make reading a challenging task. Difficulties such as visual fatigue and tracking lines of text can be a reference point for nonvisual and low vision technologies such as TTS, screenreaders, text masking or highlighting, and adjusting word or character spacing

◦ **Visual field:** Understanding where and how a visual field is restricted can help determine how to present information during the evaluation and to support recommendations for preferential seating and how materials should be presented during instruction.

◦ **Eye health:** Irregularities such as dystrophy or missing parts of the eye anatomy (such as rod-cone dystrophy, aniridia), or interrupted physiology (for example, optic nerve hypoplasia) can help an evaluator infer needs for conditions such as, but not limited to, high contrast, light sensitivity (photophobia), color blindness, and visual fatigue or processing disorder.

- **Stability of the visual impairment**: An eye condition that is unstable or results in progressive vision loss requires a detailed evaluation of the manner in which the individual's vision fluctuates, and how this prognosis will impact how the individual will continue to access information as his or her needs change. It is important to note red flags that indicate when an individual's vision fluctuates and select technologies that meet a student's current needs that are also nimble enough to accommodate low vision and nonvisual access strategies.

Clinical Low Vision Evaluation

Optical devices, both near and distance, are one type of assistive technology that needs to be prescribed by a qualified low vision specialist. It is critical to know that the individual being assessed for technology is using the most effective optical system available while investigating additional options and tools. An appropriate eyeglasses or contact lens prescription can sometime improve an individual's visual functioning to a degree that technologies recommended before the examination are now no longer needed. (See *Foundations of Low Vision*, 2nd edition, APH Press, 2010, for additional information.)

Functional Vision Assessment (FVA) or Functional Low Vision Evaluation (FLVE)

Conducted by a TVI/CVRT or Certified Low Vision Therapist, an FVA provides information about how the student uses his or her vision for everyday tasks, both academic and nonacademic. Visual behaviors such as tracking, fixation, scanning, and visual perception skills can justify recommendations for features of technology that optimize an individual's visual access or use of alternate sensory strategies when vision is less functional. Data can also inform how materials must be presented for optimal viewing. (For information about conducting a functional low vision evaluation, see Anthony, 2000). (See *Foundations of Low Vision*, 2nd edition, APH Press, 2010, and *Foundations of Education*, 3rd edition for additional information.)

Learning media assessment (LMA)

The learning media assessment (LMA) assesses the efficiency of an individual's sensory access channels: tactile, visual, and auditory. Based on these data, identification of best formats for primary, secondary, and sometimes tertiary learning media are recommended. Although developed to assess school-age students, the LMA is strongly recommended when evaluating adults, especially when there is a question about which modality best meets their needs. The LMA provides critical information for all individuals regardless of age and should be a prerequisite assessment to a technology evaluation. LMA data are heavily referenced when exploring technologies for low vision or nonvisual access that may or may not differ depending on the task. When taken together with the FVA or FLVE, the LMA informs optimal font style, point size, lighting and contrast preferences, and impact of visual versus tactile versus auditory access on reading speed, fluency, and comprehension.

General or specialized medical, other related educational and psychological evaluations

Medical, psychological, and academic evaluations provide necessary information about an individual's motor, auditory, cognitive, behavioral, and academic functioning. Details contained in these reports can provide helpful clues to understand the student's ability to complete tasks and as well as his or her functional behaviors such as understanding of cause and effect, receptive language, memory, sequencing in tasks with multiple steps, and problem solving. It is important that any needed accommodations for these details are in place throughout a technology evaluation so that data are accurate and reflect the student's needs.

Formal and Informal Assessment and Observation Data, Most Current IEP or ITP if Available

Formal or informal assessments such as informal reading inventories, criterion referenced tests (such as end-of-chapter tests or tests based on grade-level standards), progress monitoring data from assessments required by the school or rehabilitation agency, and ongoing records completed during individual sessions with a student, can provide functional data within the context of various tasks and identify initial strengths, areas of need, and preferences. Summative information is usually reported in the IEP or ITP, which

also describes a present level of functioning at the time of the report. These data can function as a historical record for what has been tried, what has been effective, and what has not been effective. However, these data points should simply be noted and not necessarily limit what is explored in a technology evaluation.

Vocational or Rehabilitation Evaluation

Most state vocational rehabilitation agencies provide evaluations of adults under the age of 65. As with many other things related to vocational rehabilitation services, these evaluations may vary greatly throughout the U.S. and internationally. For instance, evaluations in one agency might be required to adhere to a standardized form or checklist while another agency might require a different template. An adult evaluation will identify abilities, interests, and skills in addition to addressing the student's needs and career goals. This type of information will assist the technology evaluator in selecting tools for exploration that might optimize a student's workflow for achieving individualized goals. See **Figure 1.2** for a more thorough description of the components of a vocational rehabilitation evaluation.

STEP 3: COLLECT DATA

Borrowing from frameworks for educational assessment and several AT models, a technology evaluation requires an ecological approach to gather data in all potential access environments. It also emphasizes individual supports when making recommendations and uses methods that construct an accurate representation of the learner. Data should also support valid and reliable decisions that are free from an evaluator's bias and emphasize a learner's strengths (Watts, O'Brian, & Wojcik, 2003).

The Georgia Project for Assistive Technology (GPAT, http://www.gpat.org /Georgia-Project-for-Assistive-Technology /Pages/Considering-Assistive-Technology -for-Students-with-Disabilities.aspx) offers an *AT Consideration Process Guide* (See **Appendix 9.1**) that can be used to collect initial data about the tasks, materials, and current strategies and tools that are in place for a student. This checklist can document information about and progress in essential areas like reading, writing, spelling, mathematics, oral communication, daily living skills, recreation and leisure, prevocational or vocational skills, and travel skills or mobility— slight modifications can be made when evaluating an adult student. For each task that the individual has difficulty performing unassisted, information is noted on whether the task is currently completed using accommodations, modifications, or with assistive technology. An accommodation describes how an individual can use differentiated tools or strategies to complete the same activity as nondisabled peers, while a modification replaces the activity with a different one that is easier for the individual to complete (Bolt & Thurlow, 2006). Tasks that are difficult for a

student to complete even with current modifications and accommodations may require additional solutions or technology that might or might not help with achieving optimal task performance; it is particularly important to note these tasks because they will become identified areas of need. Members of the evaluation team can contribute information on this form to help an evaluator gauge the student's present levels of performance. Data can be collected from several sources and environments using multiple methods such as observations, interviews with the individual and members of the evaluation team, and targeted assessment of an individual's skills.

Remember: Thinking in terms of capturing a student's user experience can facilitate regard for the evaluation as a holistic process that is focused on improving a student's access to information. Information from the evaluation team including the student is simply a starting point for understanding one user's experience. Given this information from the team, the evaluator must develop a plan for conducting additional assessment activities that will help triangulate the information and answer these questions (Rohrer, 2014).

- What do people report is happening (attitudinal data, gathered from interviews or a data collection form/ survey) versus what are people actually doing (behavioral data, gathered from multiple observations in multiple environments)?
- Why or how is the student completing a specific task at the moment

using the current strategy or tools (qualitative data, gathered from observations and interviews)?

▫ How much work can the student complete independently versus with assistance? How long does it take the student to complete a task (quantitative data, can be gathered from indirect reports from team members)?

Conduct a Thorough Environmental Assessment

Recall that the foundation of a strong assessment rests on a detailed understanding of the current UX. This entails using the methods noted above (interviews, observations, indirect reports, use of forms/checklists/surveys) to conduct a thorough assessment of the student's environment. There are many forms, checklists, and surveys available for collecting data about one's environment—and there will always be more as learning and work environments, as well as tools and devices change along with the nature of work and technology. See **Appendix Item B: AT Evaluation Checklist** for a thorough checklist that details the different types of technology for evaluation (organized according to how the tools are presented in **Part 1** of this book.) Note that this checklist must continue to be updated as tools and workflows change). What is important to remember is that each evaluator should follow a process that works for him or her, so long as it results in comprehensive data that describes each environment where a student might want to engage with information. Novice service providers will more likely benefit from using a form or checklist as an initial guide, while more experienced service providers might only reference a self-constructed, mental list of basic questions while writing notes.

Sidebar 8.3

A CONVERSATION FROM ONE ASSESSMENT VISIT WITH A LOW VISION STUDENT

The following transcript documents a conversation between an experienced TVI and her 7th grade student. Statements in parentheses indicate notes from the TVI.

Assessment Area: In-class instruction

TVI: Where do you like to sit in class?

Student: *Front close to TV (most rooms use Apple TV for presentation)*

TVI: On white board or projected instruction in class, what works best (what does not work well)?

Student: *It's fine. Maybe sometimes reflections and glare*

(Continued)

Sidebar 8.3 (Continued)

TVI: Is it better to have slides or a teacher presentation on an iPad or other device or view from your seat?

Student: *It's mostly fine; it's good to have the math teacher's slides. I get them from Google Drive and leave my iPad in math—math is the only class I use the iPad for and I don't take it home.*

TVI: What is the best way for you to get notes?

Student: *I just write or I get them from the teacher*

TVI: Can you usually read back your own notes?

Student: *Sometimes, but it's easier to fix mistakes on the computer.*

Assessment area: Classwork

TVI: How are you getting your handouts? What's the best?

Student: *(Shows a math handout enlarged on 11×17 paper, which seems barely large print with lots of blank space) This is fine. (We discuss digital options and organization) My organization is fine (good grades and eyes on binder support this claim).*

Student: *In math class we circle the problems to target to study for the test; I think I need the paper so it is easy to study those. But I might lose them (He makes an excellent point, if he is going to be comfortable with a digital workflow he needs a system that works. He likes stuff laid out. It's harder in middle school when they are being taught how to manage work and study. Later he will be expected to use his own system and the digital workflow won't be a "conflict" or be difficult to do within a class where 100% of kids are doing it on paper. It's hard to ask middle schoolers to do something different if they can "get by" with typical classroom materials. In late elementary and middle school the kids are just learning to organize and develop good study skills, versus in high school they need to organize and have good study skills to learn)*

TVI: What work is writing on paper and what is digital?

Student: *Lots of writing on paper. I like erasable pens. (observation of writing math problems shows he writes fast and sloppy and some digits are not readily legible—he had some hesitations reading back written work that was in his binder. Could be a "slow down" type of thing? He certainly can make more careful symbols and read it back).*

Sidebar 8.3

Assessment area: Writing/completing assignments

TVI: What are the pros and cons of writing on a device or handwriting?

Student: *I like writing but digital does allow for easier editing. I can type 30 WPM without looking.* (Yay! Feels like he is nearly at point that he does not think to keyboard; he appears more efficient keyboarding than handwriting and is also not bent over like when he writes on paper)

Assessment area: Reading

TVI: What are the best lighting conditions?

Student: *The normal room lighting is fine* (He does not use any task lighting)

TVI: How long do you read in one sitting?

Student: *We are supposed to read for 30 minutes—I usually read for 40*

TVI: Do your eyes feel tired after extended reading?

Student: *No, not really*

Assessment area: Self-determination

TVI: What are your goals for next year?

Student: *Maybe be more confident talking to teachers.*

Remember that the purpose of using a form or checklist is to ensure that data is collected in all areas that are relevant to the student and to the particular environment that is being assessed on that date. This is why it is challenging to recommend one singular form that can capture the nuances of every possible assessment condition. For example, if using the **AT Evaluation Checklist** with a functionally blind student, the sections related to screen magnification will only need a brief statement of "has no usable vision" to remind the team why this particular area will not be assessed. If many sections of this checklist are irrelevant to a particular student, this particular checklist should not limit what data are collected. When using any kind of form, let the form be determined by what information is relevant for each evaluation situation, adjust the form as needed, but do <u>not</u> let the form dictate what information is collected for a high-quality evaluation.

A thorough environmental assessment must include information that answers these three questions. (**Appendix 9.2 Environmental Assessment for Access Technology** offers a graphic organizer for organizing these data.)

What are the environments that this student needs to access?

Potential environments that require assessment include school (and ensuing classrooms, labs, recreation areas), workplace (and ensuing conference rooms, break rooms, offices), home, and various community spaces. Distilling what information is being disseminated or exchanged in each environment and identifying what systems currently exist for supporting these information exchanges are two key areas for understanding the infrastructure a student must engage with.

How is information being disseminated and exchanged?

Dissemination implies a one-way direction for simply accessing information; understanding how information is shared for consumption (for example,

print, digital, multimedia) can determine what group of tools to focus on in the later trial phases of the evaluation. For example, if office memos are exclusively sent to employees digitally through an online workspace, it would be a better use of the evaluation time to compare and contrast screen magnification tools rather than handheld video magnifiers. It is just as important to know how a student must author information for others. For example, if a different, totally blind student must create the weekly office memos for posting in the employee break room, it would be very important that he or she use a QWERTY or braille keyboard and an RBD to author the information to ensure professional quality writing. Dictation without an RBD would not be appropriate due to the difficulty in noticing typos or inserting formatting in a purely auditory format. Given the complexity of information that can be potentially exchanged in different environments, two additional questions can help focus data collection.

- **What has been working well for the student? What has been tried but was proven unsuccessful?** Prior to the technology evaluation, the student has developed a system for adapting to his or her current situation. As part of the evaluation, it is helpful to determine how a system is functioning and what is working well, and then to learn from what has not worked. These data will help refine a starting point when determining what workflows need optimization and which strategies or tools to introduce. This information can also help an evaluator prioritize which options to try first.

- **What is the workflow for each classroom or workspace?** Most students, both children and adults, want to fit in with their peers! Understanding how others in an environment engage with information sets a precedent for performance. Ideally, workflows that are universally designed accommodate *everyone's* independent and timely engagement with information, and therefore require minimal intervention when low- or nonvisual accessibility is needed. Some workflows need minimal updates to become universally accessible, whereas others may need complete revision.

What systems are supporting information exchanges in each environment?

An often-overlooked issue during a technology evaluation is the existing technology system. Every environment (school, workplace, home, or community) has an internal structure for organizing how information is exchanged. In the community, it might be as simple as a cork bulletin board for people to post solicitations. Some households might revolve around a whiteboard for organizing appointments. How will students who are blind or visually impaired access these systems and engage in the information that is exchanged? For example, has the school district adopted an inaccessible online curriculum or app? Does a 1:1 program implement a computing device with accessibility features that match a student's needs? It is impera-

tive that the evaluation team is attentive to these questions. A plan for how the student will participate in these and other activities is necessary to identify a task analysis for teaching the student the necessary skills to accomplish the tasks with the appropriate access technologies. Identifying the steps that comprise the task analysis is fundamental to writing IEP goals and objectives that provide sufficient time for the student to acquire the skills needed to successfully use access technology for hir or her education. These goals and objectives will ensure success in achieving participation and should align with findings from the technology evaluation and its recommendations. Many organizations including schools, non-profit agencies, and corporations are more high-tech and may use some form of an online management system. When hi-tech systems are in place for supporting digital workflows, Jessica McDowell's **Digital Workflow Planning Tool (Appendix 9.3)** can be a helpful form for collecting data that can more specially answer the following questions.

- **Has the school or workplace already adopted a technology plan? If so, what does it entail?** The technology plan could include a specific cloud computing platform, operating system, or online curricula or apps for learning and training.

- **What are the readily available technologies that typically sighted peers are using?** Answers related to this question will provide a sense of what kind of technical support is available for what types of technology. Certain technologies might also be more or less conducive to workflows that are specific to a particular operating system. When possible, aligning recommendations with existing systems or computing practices can facilitate easier implementation. It also allows for more readily available technical support from peers as well as technical personnel.

What are the tasks that are expected to happen in each of the student's environments?

Similar to understanding what typical workflows exist in an environment, an evaluator must also know what tasks people in each environment are expected to complete. Understanding tasks and expectations sets the performance standard for everyone, including the student who requires nonvisual or low access to information. In order for the student to earn membership and opportunities for leadership in each environment, he or she must be equipped to complete the tasks to the same or higher standard as typically sighted peers. Again, it is equally important that the student is successful accessing information as well as creating or authoring it. These tasks can include accessing or authoring printed or digital text, printed or digital images, and multimedia including videos, data visualizations, or 3D models. Use a variety of data collection methods to answer the following questions:

- In various information-rich environments, what are the expected tasks of everyone for accessing information?

- In various information-rich environments, what are the expected tasks of everyone for authoring information?

What are the student's (current) learning preferences?

Although it is listed last, it is not an indication that a student's learning preference is the least important factor to consider. In fact, learning preference is foundational information that an evaluator must learn about a student as it is a critical aspect of identifying how and what to optimize in the evaluation process. Initial insights can be gained from the file review; known traits or comorbidities associated with certain visual impairments can help an evaluator infer which sensory systems a student might prefer when accessing information. However, note that a student's preferences are not necessarily the most efficient methods he or she can use to engage with information! This discrepancy can occur when insufficient instruction has been given to develop a student's other sensory modalities, therefore limiting him or her to use the only sensory system to which they are accustomed. For example, a low vision student who is able to read print might have only been given preferential seating, a magnifier, and large print in his or her early school career. As a result, the student has not developed auditory skills for using TTS or a screen reader to read more efficiently, to complete larger volumes of work, or to reduce visual fatigue that results in migraine headaches. Using this example, during initial listening skills instruction, the student may still prefer visual access out of habit even though it provides limited efficiency. However, with ongoing practice and repeated positive experiences that optimize his or her UX with reading print, the student can develop proficiency in using auditory tools, and may begin to prefer auditory access for certain tasks. Developing greater proficiency in using a broader range of tools and strategies can help a student be more flexible in using different sensory systems for accessing different types of information or completing various tasks. Preferences and strengths can work in tandem so that tools and skills are adaptable to accessing information in different environments.

STEP 4: ALIGN DATA WITH AREAS OF NEED

Given all the collected data related to various environments, tasks, and sensory access preference, the next step is to identify and prioritize a student's areas of need. Although a student's input throughout the evaluation is critical, this portion of an evaluation can be difficult for students to self-report; this is especially true for students who are unaware that there is a more independent or efficient way to complete a task. This lack of awareness could be due to inconsistent instruction to develop sensory skills or technology proficiency, lack of tools and resources, or a combination thereof. Personnel who support a student's educational, vocational, or rehabilitation program can sometimes be unreliable informants in

this part of the evaluation—especially if they were the ones who unwittingly hindered a student's independence, thus enabling a perpetual state of dependency! For these reasons, it is important to weigh attitudinal data (what people report is happening) against behavioral data (what people are actually doing) (Rohrer, 2014). Interviews with the student, family, and personnel can provide the attitudinal data while discreet observations in multiple environments and across a range of tasks can provide the behavioral data.

Organize the collected data so that the following questions can be answered. (Additional data can be collected as needed in order to ensure detailed information for each area.)

- **When is the student dependent on sighted assistance?** This is a particularly important question to answer if a school-aged blind or low vision student has been assigned a personal aide or assistant, a role that will be referred to as a paraprofessional hereafter. (With adult students, a paraprofessional is a reasonable accommodation as dictated by the adult, rather than imposed as it might be in an education environment). Note that paraprofessionals who are assigned to a student due to medical concerns might be obligated to always remain nearby in case of a medical emergency. Otherwise, the roles and duties of a paraprofessional for a blind or low vision learner are to reinforce what is taught by the classroom teacher, TVI, or O&M specialist.

Other duties might include relaying information from the classroom, reporting problems, sharing news about upcoming events, adapting materials, and maintaining or troubleshooting technology as needed. Paraprofessionals might also act as a reader or scribe, with diminishing responsibilities as a student approaches graduation from the school system (Chamberlain, 2018; McKenzie & Lewis, 2008). Although the purpose of a paraprofessional is to "assist without doing for the student; be as invisible as possible; provide just the right amount of support—not too much and not too little; and to help the student reach his or her highest potential possible in the least invasive way possible" (Chamberlain, 2018), a student's perceived needs can sometimes differ from his or her actual needs. When this incongruence occurs, a paraprofessional can inadvertently hinder independence by over-assisting a student. These instances must be identified and then remediated as soon as possible while teaching the student needed skills to regain their independence. When a student is expected to be independent from a paraprofessional, the paraprofessional may be better directed to support alternate media production or any of the other previously described duties that do not involve direct instructional support. The technology evaluation can be a strategic process for a team who can benefit from knowing specific instances in which a student can be more independent overall, regardless of whether or not a paraprofessional is involved. The following

questions can further specify areas of need related to reduced independent access to information.

- **What is the student unable to access independently?** When alternate media is provided, the expectation is that the student develops proficiency with his or her tools to access educational materials independently. As mentioned earlier in the chapter, it can take time for a student to develop relevant sensory access skills while also learning how to use appropriate access technology. During these periods of learning, other strategies, such as asking for sighted assistance from a peer or paraprofessional, might be employed. Use of sighted assistance should not be the default method for engaging with information; it is best kept as a backup when other tools or strategies are unavailable. By conducting a thorough environmental assessment, it can be made clear whether a student is unable to access information because of a gap in skills or tools, or whether it is an accessibility issue.

- **When will personnel need to adapt materials into a unique format for the student?** Ideally, learning media and community information should be universally designed for *all* students' access. When universal design for learning (UDL) is achieved, meeting the needs of a blind or low vision student does not add significant time to the classroom teacher or support staff, and does not take instructional focus away from the whole class in order to accommodate one student's accessibility needs. In the evaluation, identifying those instances when personnel are adapting materials for a blind or low vision student can indicate an area that can be optimized in order to approach UDL. The need to adapt materials can also justify acquiring equipment required for alternate media production in cases when a specialized format *is* also the most appropriate learning media.

- **When is the student unable to access or produce work at the same time as sighted peers?** Accessible educational media should allow a student to access work at the same time as peers. There should also be a system in place for the student to deliver work to the teacher both independently and at the same time as sighted peers. When the environment is modified to support a student's access, a technology evaluation can then focus on assessing a student's skills and tools for efficiency. Identifying what to optimize is very important for anyone in a competitive school or work environment. Equally important is to identify what is currently working well so that the proper resources can be assured to support the current workflow. With an optimum workflow and skills, and appropriate access technology, a blind or low vision student can even surpass the efficiency of sighted peers' work completion. For example, nonvisual access tools can often facilitate a student to surpass the reading or typing speeds of sighted peers. In order to determine critical failure points that prevent a student from accessing or producing work at the same time as sighted peers, or to recognize what is working to ensure independent and timely engagement

with information, collect data so that the following questions can be answered.

- **Which tasks and workflows could be made more efficient?**
- **Which tasks or workflows are already optimized for a student's accessibility?**

Content Vocabulary
Alternate (Alternative) Media

Alternate (Alternative Media) refers to the mediums and formats used to provide information to individuals who cannot use standard texts.

The volume of data collected from an environmental assessment can seem daunting! However, once an evaluator has gathered enough data to understand the current user experience and describe a present level of performance, a needs assessment can help distill the collected data to identify the weak links in a student's current workflow.

A Needs Assessment Template (Appendix 9.4) can help organize all the data that are specific to a student's needs. This template aligns with the TPACK framework so that there is a broader conceptual relevance to each data point that allows alignment between the current UX and wherever weak links exist. This helps prioritize certain environments and tasks for immediate instruction (as supported by a learning goal and objectives) and emphasizes which sensory access strategies and tool proficiencies can be further developed. The template is provided as a basic form for an evaluator to identify the following, and then construct the related bodies of knowledge

- ▫ **Pedagogical Knowledge:** How does the individual use different sensory systems to access different types of information? (FVA, LMA)

- ▫ **Content Knowledge:** In what environments and for which tasks does the individual need to engage with information more independently?

- ▫ **Content Knowledge:** What kind of materials or media present information that the individual needs to engage with more independently?

- ▫ **Technological Knowledge:** Which technology features match the student's sensory access preferences, strengths, and needs?

- ▫ **Technological Knowledge:** Who and what are the available technology supports and constraints in each information-rich environment? What is the infrastructure for supporting technology for this individual? Sample data might include the following:

- Available Wi-Fi? Is it freely accessed, or password protected?

- Onsite or organizational level of IT support?

Like other forms included in the Appendix, the Needs Assessment Template is provided only as a sample form that the team can use; it should be understood that other forms can be found on the Internet and are available from other sources, such as state technical assistance projects, or developed by professionals to fit their own assessment styles and needs. Some school systems and state vocational rehabilitation agencies have their own required forms. In general, the evaluation team should use whichever form best captures the student's needs within an educational program, workplace, recreation and leisure activity, or community.

STEP 5: UNDERSTAND THE CURRENT AND FUTURE USER EXPERIENCES

In education settings, the evaluation needs to address all the areas within the learning environments that require a student to use technology to acquire needed information and complete required coursework. This can range from something as simple as the menus provided by campus food services (See Haben Girma's speech *The Courage to Fight for Chocolate Cake)*, to the more complex issues associated with accessing materials, online learning management systems, and school resources. In a work environment, the evaluation needs to address how the employee will access the various computing systems, databases, and training programs needed to accomplish his or her job duties, as well as the technology used by the employer to communicate information about events, meetings, for interactions with the human resources department, and to submit a help ticket to the IT department.

Following the steps for conducting a technology evaluation as described in this chapter will provide the evaluator with rich information to understand the current UX and describe present levels of performance. This information can identify what is working and what is not in each of the environments where an individual might need to access information. From understanding the current user experience and how performance expectations will evolve in the next school grade or as a result of a job promotion, the evaluator can begin to project how future UX needs to evolve to keep pace with a student's needs. Although an evaluation should focus on addressing current needs, ensuring sustainable technology adoption and strategic instruction is accomplished when the team can anticipate future workflows in the following year, in three years, and (if the student is a child) as an adult. Remember that although school-age students require a triennial comprehensive evaluation in order to reassess ongoing needs for services, every annual review can provide an additional platform for updating an IEP team's understanding of a student's present levels as well as update the needed technologies and supports for the following year. For adult students, updated evaluations can be requested whenever the individual's needs change. The next chapter will guide the reader through the remaining steps of a technology evaluation: How to match a student's needs with appropriate technology; consideration of relevant tools to help a student prototype improved experiences; crafting recommendations for optimal workflows; developing strategic goals and objectives; and drafting an initial report in an accessible format for the student and team to review.

REFERENCES

Anthony, T. (2000). *Performing a functional low vision assessment. In F. M. D'Andrea & C. Farrenkopf, Eds.,* Looking to Learn *(pp. 32–83). New York: AFB Press.*

Bennett, C. L., Brady, E., & Branham, S. M. (2018). *Interdependence as a frame for assistive technology research and design.* Proceedings of the 20th International ACM SIGACCESS Conference on Computers and Accessibility, *161–173. ACM.*

Bernd, T., Van Der Pijl, D., & De Witte, L. P. (2009). *Existing models and instruments for the selection of assistive technology in rehabilitation practice.* Scandinavian Journal of Occupational Therapy, 16*(3), 146–158.*

Bolt, S. E., & Thurlow, M. L. (2006). Item-level Effects of the Read-aloud Accommodation for Students with Reading Disabilities *(Synthesis Report 65). Minneapolis, MN: University of Minnesota, National Center on Educational Outcomes. Retrieved January 8, 2008, from the World Wide Web: http://education.umn.edu/NCEO /OnlinePubs/Synthesis65/*

Buchenau, M., & Suri, J. F. (2000). *Experience prototyping.* Proceedings of the 3rd Conference on Designing Interactive Systems: Processes, Practices, Methods, and Techniques, *424–433. ACM.*

Chamberlain, M.-N. (2018). *Helpful Hints for Paraprofessionals Working with Students Who Are Blind or Visually Impaired.* Future

Reflections, 37(3). Retrieved from https://www.nfb.org/sites/www.nfb.org/files/images/nfb/publications/fr/fr37/3/fr370302.htm

Copeland, S.R, & Keefe, E.B. (2007). Effective Literacy Instruction for Students with Moderate or Severe Disabilities. Baltimore: Paul Brookes

Downing, J.E. (2005). Teaching Literacy to Students with Significant Disabilities. Thousand Oaks, CA: SAGE Publications

Houde, S., & Hill, C. (1997). What do prototypes prototype? In Handbook of human-computer interaction (pp. 367–381). Elsevier.

Koenig, A.J. & Holbrook, M.C. (1995). Learning Media Assessment (2d ed.). Austin: Texas School for the Blind and Visually Impaired

Lewis, S., & McKenzie, A. R. (2010). The competencies, roles, supervision, and training needs of paraeducators working with students with visual impairments in local and residential schools. Journal of Visual Impairment & Blindness, 104(8), 464–477.

McKenzie, A. R., & Lewis, S. (2008). The role and training of paraprofessionals who work with students who are visually impaired. Journal of Visual Impairment & Blindness, 102(8), 459–471.

QIAT Consortium (2005). Quality indicators for assistive technology services. Downloaded Nov. 14, 2006 from http://www.qiat.org

Rohrer, C. (2014). When to use which user-experience research methods. Nielsen Norman Group.

Watts, E. H., O'Brian, M., & Wojcik, B. W. (2003). Four models of assistive technology consideration: How do they compare to recommended educational assessment practices? Journal of Special Education Technology, 19(1), 43–56.

CHAPTER 9
Optimize the User Experience

Every effective evaluation is based on a thorough needs assessment that helps the evaluator understand the current state of affairs—in other words, the current user experience (UX). Without this foundation, it is difficult if not impossible to derive enough information about a student to know what technologies to assess in an evaluation. Recall that Chapter 8 presents a number of methods and strategies for conducting a thorough assessment of each of a student's information-rich environments. Based on data from this comprehensive environmental assessment, subsequent steps are recommended for distilling these data into simple, organized lists that identify weak points in a student's workflow. The weak points actually become the strongest outcomes of the needs assessment! These instances define the context for when and how a workflow can be optimized—perhaps with the support of access technology. From developing a holistic understanding of a student's current UX and capturing present levels of performance in various environments, an evaluator will have developed sufficient technological, pedagogical, and content knowledge about a student's overall system for information access.

Remember that one of the key tenets of a technology evaluation is to focus on the *process* of determining how technology can improve or impede an individual's best access to information in a timely manner. Although this level of comprehensive assessment might only take place once every three years for a school-age student, or only when a critical need arises as with an adult-age student, ongoing assessment occurs naturally on the part of a service provider (known as "diagnostic teaching"), and on the part of the student as they become more proficient in using a broader variety of tools. The remaining steps of a technology evaluation as presented in this chapter will lead to the final product of a comprehensive report that integrates information from the FVA and LMA as it relates to technology recommendations. Connecting the technology recommendations with pedagogical knowledge about how a student can best leverage various sensory access modes will comprise an all-inclusive evaluation report (colloquially referred to as an FVLM(t)A[ECC] report).

> **Content Vocabulary**
> **Diagnostic Teaching**
>
> **Diagnostic teaching** is an educational approach that calls for teachers to assess a student's skill level while providing instruction and then tailor ongoing instruction to the results.

As listed below, **Chapter 9** will guide the reader through understanding steps 6–9 of a proposed technology evaluation process. These steps translate information about a student's current workflows to apply design thinking towards *optimizing* the UX and improving a student's independent, timely, and efficient access to multimedia (text, images, video) information.

1. Identify the evaluation team

2. Conduct a file review

3. Collect data

4. Align data with areas of need

5. Understand the current UX and identify needs

6. Match student needs with appropriate technology options

7. Prototype improved UX

8. Define and implement an optimal workflow

9. Draft initial report in an accessible format

10. Finalize the report and invite opportunities for iteration

Thus far, the evaluation process has referenced the following appendix items to help an evaluator collect and organize data.

- Background Information for a Technology Evaluation (See **Step 2, Conduct a File review, Appendix 8.1,** page 272)

- GPAT AT Consideration Process Guide (See **Step 3, Collect Data, Appendix 9.1,** page 299)

- Environmental Assessment for Access Technology (**Step 3, Collect**

More Data, Appendix 9.2,** page 302)

- Digital Workflow Planning Tool (**Step 3, Appendix 9.3,** page 303)

- Needs Assessment Template (**Step 4, Appendix 9.4,** page 305)

To problem solve how to optimize a UX, information from the Needs Assessment will be the most relevant for identifying workflows to experiment with, exploring different media formats and sensory access modes, and contrasting different tools before final recommendations are made. **Appendix B AT Evaluation Checklist** on page 381 will be useful in this chapter (**Step 7**) to ensure that a broad range of tools in each category of technology will be included for demonstration and trial. Knowing that suggested tools in this checklist will become outdated quickly as technology evolves, it is best to think of this checklist as a minimum selection of options for evaluation. Finally, an FVLM(t)A[ECC] report outline is presented in **Step 9,** with the understanding that the outline will be adapted to suit different evaluator's and student's needs, or not used at all in a setting where an evaluator must follow an organizationally-adopted report template.

Ready to start thinking about the latter half of an evaluation process now? Let's go!

STEP 6: MATCH STUDENT NEEDS WITH APPROPRIATE TECHNOLOGY OPTIONS

Remember that an LMA will contribute information to the Needs Assessment, which will help an evaluator identify types of technology that could be introduced for assessment in the evaluation. This part of the evaluation investigates the student's potential to use tools given his or her learning media preferences. The LMA and Needs Assessment data will also help identify relevant sections of the AT Evaluation Checklist that can be initially highlighted to focus on certain categories of technology. For example, if a student shows existing primary strengths with the visual mode, secondary strengths with her auditory mode, and few if no strengths for tactile mode, technologies for low vision and auditory access should be prioritized for further investigation. Technologies for nonvisual access might only be explored if tools for visual and auditory access are inadequate.

However, remember that a student's sensory access modes (primary, secondary, and sometimes even tertiary) can also be adaptable. For example, a student with decreasing vision might still use vision as her primary mode, supplement visual gaps with auditory access as her secondary mode, and only use her tactile mode for sorting coins to insert into a vending machine or for pressing an elevator button. However, if the student demonstrates potential for improving the tactile sensory mode (for example, if he or she demonstrates consistent progress in the *Braille Readiness Grid),* it would be prudent to explore technologies for visual, auditory, and tactile features even though her tactile mode is a tertiary strength. The additional inclusion of tools for tactile access is also justified by her progressive visual impairment; however without a clear prognosis (either medical or functional) of her vision loss, technologies that align with a tertiary mode should be selected only after careful consideration. When evaluating technologies related to any sensory mode, remember that there is a continuum of mastery—for example, this student with tactile mode as her tertiary strength is not likely ready to read and write proficiently using a braille display, but might be scaffolded towards that by using tactile markers and audio-tactile graphics with braille legends to aid development of her tactile proficiency as well as psychological buy-in about tactile efficiency. Similarly, a student whose secondary sensory mode is auditory might still rely on her vision when using TTS tools, but as her listening skills develop and her auditory listening speed increases, a screen reader will become a more efficient tool in the coming school year. Remember that initial selections and recommendations from a technology evaluation are just that—initial. A student's technology use is an ongoing evaluation process that can be updated at any time.

For these reasons and because every individual is entitled to the power of choice, enough options within each category of the **AT Evaluation Checklist** should be identified for sufficient points of comparison. Some sections of the Checklist offer many possible options—refer to the Needs Assessment data to narrow down these options and select the technologies that are compatible with each type of media that a student needs to access more independently.

After appropriate technology options are identified, select a few of them to prepare for an evaluation visit. An evaluator should have a bare minimum of two options per type of technology for initial comparison. Recall that **Part 1** of this book is organized according to workflows and tools; when selecting technology options for evaluation, it would be wise to review the relevant information in the related chapter ("Considerations") for each type of technology. This review will help the evaluator understand which aspects of what technologies to compare and contrast. For example, if a student could benefit from using a keyboard instead of writing by hand, bring a full-size QWERTY keyboard as well as a mobile one to get a sense of ergonomics, usability, and connectivity differences. Alternatively, bring two differently sized RBDs to get a sense of the usability between devices (for example, refresh rate, button placement, connectivity). If a student needs a video or screen magnification system, bring a sample of devices that demonstrate how different systems can be set up for integration in different environ-

ments. If an evaluator needs to evaluate certain tools that are not in their immediate possession (for example, a scanning app or RBD), free versions may be available that have enough functionality to allow a basic demonstration. Sometimes, free versions of program applications (whether a mobile app, browser-based program, or installed software program) are available for a limited time period, or there may be open source freeware options. Other apps might have a free version or come pre-installed on a given computer; they might lack more advanced premium features but as mentioned, offers enough functionality for a basic demo.

In addition to bringing a customized array of hardware and software to an evaluation, prepare several media formats that can be accessible with multiple modalities and tools, such as printed documents with basic black text on white paper, accessibly-formatted documents with alt text, bookmarked accessible websites, tactile graphics, and charts and graphs in printed and digital formats. In essence, bring a diverse variety of media that can be used for demonstrations with different tools for accessing printed and digital multimedia (for example, text, images, videos, data). Note that any materials that require reading should be at a level lower than the student's current reading level to ensure that the evaluation is truly assessing *access* and not reading skills. It can be helpful to ask the student to bring some of his or her own books, a notebook containing class notes, materials and handouts received in class, and the current technology being used. These familiar media will be a good starting point for demonstrating how different tools and strategies can support improved workflows for more efficient engagement with known sources of information.

A comprehensive technology evaluation will require access to, and knowledge of, all the different types of equipment that are identified for assessment. Dividing the evaluation among multiple evaluation dates can help avoid exhaustion or inattention, depending on the needs of the evaluator and the student. With experience, a deeper understanding of workflow components for various tasks will help an evaluator narrow down options to the most efficient combination of technologies for assessment. The evaluator must bring computing devices as needed to support each part of the evaluation. Knowledge of the basic functions of each device, and enough proficiency to use the variety of access technologies for accessing printed and digital multimedia, are also necessary to ensure successful demonstrations and fair trials of tools that are new to the student. If needed, it can be helpful for the evaluator to identify the workflows he or she might want to demo with a student and practice those specific workflows beforehand. Workflows for accessing printed and digital information, authoring, and literacy (including literary, numeracy, and data) must all be considered in a comprehensive evaluation.

Lack of access to certain technologies—particularly to high-tech devices—should not stop or delay the evaluation of workflows and related tools that can nonetheless be completed with available resources. Since a comprehensive evaluation may take several sessions, the process can begin by using readily available resources while the evaluator pursues options to obtain the equipment that is not currently available. Strategies for obtaining needed equipment can include the following:

▫ Using free versions of premium programs or apps

▫ Borrowing from colleagues, local blindness agencies, organizations with assistive technology services, other individuals who are blind or visually impaired

▫ Asking a vendor for a demonstration device for a trial period. This may be either the manufacturer or a third-party seller.

Once enough technologies are acquired, print and digital multimedia are prepared, and workflows are practiced as needed, an evaluator is ready to carry out the next step of the evaluation: exploring how to improve upon the workflows that were identified as weak points in the Needs Assessment.

STEP 7: PROTOTYPE IMPROVED USER EXPERIENCES

Environment is an important factor in a successful evaluation. A quiet room with adequate and adjustable lighting, comfortable and clean chairs and tables, and Wi-Fi access would be basic optimal conditions. A student must bring all AT he or she typically uses, including glasses, optical devices, computing devices, and mainstream and specialized technologies including a smartphone if relevant. Among the most important items to bring are snacks and water for sustenance throughout each evaluation session as well! As with any evaluation, note any medical and prescription history in the file review—be aware of if and when the student has taken medication, and any possible side effects that could influence the student's performance.

Remember that <u>prior</u> to this part of the evaluation, multiple observations of the student in his or her natural environments have already been completed; from these observations, tasks have been identified in which the student is currently dependent on sighted assistance or unable to access or produce work at the same time as peers **(Step 4).** This step of the evaluation will attempt to replicate these tasks as closely as possible and explore different tools for optimizing the student's current workflow to complete each task. In other words, the bulk of the evaluation time will focus on prototyping different strategies or tools for accomplishing a familiar task.

When selecting tools (based on the **AT Evaluation Checklist**) or knowledge from the evaluator, evaluation team including the family, or communities of practice, organize the tools according to which ones can optimize each workflow. If the same tool can support multiple workflows, bookmark that tool for evaluation across multiple tasks while acknowledging that the student might also prefer a single-function tool for some tasks (for example, a simple reading device versus a reading app on a multi-purpose computing device). Again, it is important to emphasize the power of choice here; typically-sighted peers typically have a multitude of choices for engaging with information and blind or low vision students are entitled to the same opportunities. An evaluator's own comfort level or biases with certain tools should not limit the choices that are offered to a student.

> **Content Vocabulary**
> **Communities of Practice**
>
> **Communities of practice** are groups of people who share a common interest and collaborate to reach both individual and group goals.

Before the evaluation or prototyping process begins, spend a few minutes discussing the student's current workflow and UX. Compare notes from the student's description of his or her independence and efficiency as well as what was observed by the evaluator (recall from Chapter 8 the value of comparing a student's attitudinal data with an evaluator's behavioral data). Discuss how a student is using his or her primary sensory mode and if he or she has experimented with using different sensory modes for the same task. It can also be informative to compare whether the student's understanding aligns with data from the LMA. Together, visualize what an ideal UX would feel like—get excited for what is possible! For some students, the evaluator might need to scaffold a student's imagination of how their current UX could improve. Next, the evaluator can demonstrate how alternate tools or strategies could be used to accomplish the same task. When appropriate, demonstrate two possible workflows so that the student can compare and contrast the benefits and disadvantages of each option. (To aid in the comparison and contrast process, the evaluator can reflect on the considerations that were discussed for each type of technology in **Part 1** of this book. These concepts should be reviewed prior to working with the student.)

Next, the student can choose which workflow he or she would like to review again, and the evaluator can demo the process again at a slower pace while describing each step out loud, focusing on how each sensory mode is being used with the tool. Remember to use clear, descriptive nonvisual language that avoids non-specific words such as *this, that,* or *there* so that concrete steps are com-municated to be understood by the student (Hudson, 2013). It is important that the evaluator has enough proficiency to carry out this demo. In addition, should technological challenges arise, troubleshooting can be used as a teachable moment for exploring unintended actions and practicing persistence and fortitude. With guided instruction, encourage the student to try to repeat the process he or she just observed. Note aspects of the process in which the student needs the most support. (Conceptual understanding of the virtual space? Orientation with a device? Fine motor coordination? Sensory efficiency?). After the student has had some time to demo the entire new workflow, or a few steps of it, prompt the student to brainstorm when he or she might use such a workflow, and for what purpose. How could this workflow improve his or her independence? Could it provide timeliness in accessing and completing work at the same time as peers? Finally, spend some time with the student to collaboratively discuss what skills he or she perceives are needed for proficiency when using this workflow. In order to identify areas of alignment, contrast the student's ideas with what the evaluator perceives are needed skills. This discussion sets the stage for Step 7 of the evaluation. This demo process can be repeated as many times as needed to trial different access technologies for the same or different workflows. Trials are concluded when the student and evaluator identify an optimal workflow for each task that is in need of improvement.

For each trial, **Appendix 9.5: Access Technology Trial Use Summary** on page 311 can be used to document information about how different tools work within an intended workflow. Throughout this demo process, the student's feedback and description of their experience are equally important to that of the evaluator's observations. Note that in addition to experimenting with different access technologies, media formats can also be explored to evaluate what would optimize a student's access to information. These experiments can be presented in many engaging ways and can introduce a student to new possibilities for engaging with information. Consider the following:

- **Experiment with alternate media.** Alternate media formats are best experimented with at this stage in the evaluation. Although aspects of experimentation with media could also be carried out as part of the LMA, assessing media as part of an AT evaluation will tie directly to technology recommendations. For example, the student with a progressive visual impairment mentioned earlier in this chapter could be presented with screen magnification or video magnification tools to analyze a digital or printed diagram. However, he or she should also be allowed to experiment in order to discover whether a tactile or audio-tactile graphic of the same diagram yields better access to details that were missed visually. This approach has the added benefit of developing other sensory modes for multimodal

access or for whenever a student anticipates the need to shift from low vision to nonvisual access as his or her eye condition changes.

- **Experiment with sensory efficiency.** Offering different formats for alternate media will naturally challenge the student to experiment with using different sensory modes as well—this can be very interesting for a student who has yet to explore different sensory strategies! For example, if a student with a neurologically-based visual impairment such as cerebral visual impairment (CVI) has difficulty parsing math symbols and scientific notations when they are presented in print or onscreen for visual access, offering math materials in an accessible, computer-readable version can allow the student to explore how he or she might engage with math auditorily using a TTS or screen reader tool.

- **Experiment with on-demand, multimodal access.** It is not unusual that the idea of on-demand multimodal access to information becomes an attractive entry point for a student to strengthen his or her sensory efficiency skills. Multimodal accessibility has several benefits. So long as the information is formatted for accessibility, it can be accessed visually, tactilely, or auditorily. These options empower the individual to select how he or she wants to access information at any given time, including tool selection, adjusting visual or auditory presentations as desired, and when to use low vision versus nonvisual strategies. All of these benefits allow a person to be independent from sighted assistance which can dictate access to information. For example, it is less important that an alternate media specialist is told what particular font size and style a student needs if the student is proficient with manipulating digital media. Instead, a student prepared to understand his or her functional vision and access technology, who is also provided with accessibly formatted media, can simply adjust a font size and style to suit their preferred viewing distance as needed, and switch from visual to auditory or tactile access as desired. If the student seems willing to switch among sensory modes, several considerations need to be made. Tools that support *on-demand* access will require more evaluation than tools for single-modal access, while alternate media formats that support *multi-modal* access must be identified for provision to the student. For example, a low vision student who could benefit from on-demand visual, auditory, and tactile access to reading will need all reading materials in an accessible, digital format that allows multi-modal access. The goal of these experiments is to inspire a student to re-imagine how he or she can engage with information. By demonstrating different methods for improving their workflows, students can become excited by the access technology that will transform their identity within a classroom or workplace. With an optimized workflow, the power dynamic in accessing information can shift back to the student. In short, the best tools allow every individual in a community to create, lead, and be a resource for others.

STEP 8: DEFINE AND RECOMMEND AN OPTIMAL WORKFLOW

Now that the bulk of the AT evaluation is complete, findings must be communicated for the evaluation team. Information from steps 8 and 9 will determine the following:

- What access technologies are purchased

- What alternate media are provided

- The infrastructure for supporting this student's information access (including implementation of accessible systems, curricula, learning management systems, and training programs; Information Technology (IT) for access to networks, printers, or embossers; administrative privileges for downloading needed apps; local, regional, state, or federal resources for technology support

- The need for personnel training

- What an instructional or training program must entail to prepare the student for immediate and future success (if a K–12 student), competitive employment, or achieving a desired lifestyle of independent or supported living.

In order to make these determinations, the evaluator must first define the optimal workflows that were agreed upon in collaboration with the student at the conclusion of **Step 6**.

When defining a workflow, remember to focus on the task that must be achieved. Also remember that an optimal workflow reduces a student's direct dependence on sighted assistance, and increases the efficiency of information access and production. It can be helpful for the evaluator to ask, "Could I produce a brief video that demonstrates this workflow?" If the answer is no, it could be an indication that the workflow is too complex and inefficient. For practical purposes, it might be helpful to create a demonstration to educate the evaluation team and provide an example of how the workflow actually looks. This can allow team members (including the family and student) to better strategize which supports or training are needed.

A workflow description must include the following components.

- The goal or task the student needs to achieve
- The needed access technology
- How media need to be formatted and provided to the student
- Workflow supports including personnel and IT

Each component of a workflow must also have a recommended backup to ensure that technology breakdowns do not lead to a complete accessibility failure. Every student must know how to troubleshoot problems and use backup tools as needed whenever a primary system fails. The best backup systems include a less optimal but

readily available tool, a low- or no-tech strategy, and a decision tree for asking for help. After an accessibility crisis passes, the student can focus on problem solving how the primary system failed and then advocate for improvements to the system needed to avoid a repeat failure. For school-aged students, additional instructional goals and objectives can help target the development of effective advocacy skills that will prepare them for the future. These self-advocacy skills may need several years to develop, so it is important to situate students for advocacy as early as possible. Adult students might benefit from connecting to peers and communities of practice to brainstorm ideas for advocacy on a case-by-case basis.

Select Tools that Support an Optimal Workflow

When deciding which tools are best for supporting a student's optimal workflows, two categories of considerations can help narrow down options: student-centered and logistical.

Student-centered considerations

The technology continuum. For a K–12 student, assume a three-year learning curve to shift from learning to use technology, to using technology for learning. (More information about technology implementation will be discussed in **Chapter 10.**) The sophistication of a student's tools can vary depending on the complexity of task. When selecting tools, it is helpful to project what tasks the student will need to accomplish in the next year and within the next three years.

Sometimes a tool might be selected as a stepping-stone, analogous to training wheels on a bicycle. This strategy can be appropriate when a student has yet to develop proficient sensory skills and can hone those skills by using a more basic device to complete simpler tasks. It can also be an option for a school district that support a larger population of blind and low vision students to maintain an inventory of access technology to re-allocate as needed. Other times, a tool might be selected that can grow along with a student's skills and meet both current and future needs. This strategy is be appropriate when a student is a quick learner and is adept at improvising with technology. This strategy may also be the more financially prudent option in a school district with fewer students and equipment, and which has less ability to re-allocate equipment as students' needs change.

For adult students, the process of learning might be significantly shorter due to more intensive self-study and motivation to achieve a concrete task for college, independent living, or employment. Depending on who is purchasing the technology for a student, there may or may not be a budget for updating technology as desired. Sometimes an agency (such as the Department of Rehabilitation) might purchase technology, sometimes an employer might, and other times adults might have to purchase it themselves. Budget considerations can determine whether technology is purchased with a continuum in mind including options to upgrade as a student develops proficiency

or if access needs change. Alternatively, if a student's visual impairment and access needs are stable, different tools might be selected for dependability and compatibility with free and open source applications that will sustain a longer period of use (Recall **Sidebar 3.6:** *Technology for Free*).

Student preferences and attitudes. Remember that students' preferences for using certain sensory modalities are usually consistent with which sensory system is the most efficient for the student at a given time. Recall from **Chapter 8** that students' sensory preferences *can* shift as their sensory efficiency skills evolve. Attitudes regarding how a student prefers to access information can also be emotionally-charged, particularly if the student has a progressive visual impairment. In these cases, it is important that selected tools can potentially leverage all sensory modalities so that different media can be accessed with different sensory skills on demand. In this way, students can shift sensory access modes as desired and the opportunity for experimentation is always present. For example, a low vision student who can no longer read print might not be willing to embrace braille as a replacement literacy method. In addition, that student also has not developed the prerequisite skills needed for fluent braille reading. In the meantime, it would be important to recommend tools for auditory access to printed and digital texts, which can serve as a bridge that maintains access to information while the student develops a mindset and skills for tactile proficiency. Note that although tools for auditory access to printed and digital texts might be recommended in order to take advantage of the student's strongest sensory mode for reading, other technologies might be recommended to support the development of the student's tactile skills for different tasks (for example, tactile graphics, audio-tactile graphics). This type of planning also aligns with a range of skills that will impact the technology continuum.

Student's current technology plan and experience with an operating system. If a student has existing tools in his or her toolbox, adopting new technologies that use the same operating system can ensure a shorter learning curve. In another situation, a student might already have a preferred personal computer, but needs to upgrade peripheral devices or install an additional app in order to optimize a workflow. In these cases, compatibility will likely be an initial determining factor before considering other options that would require the student to overhaul his or her toolbox completely.

Student's future expectations. Whether the student is in K–12 or a postsecondary, workplace, or independent living environment, understanding the student's ambitions can help anticipate expectations for technology proficiency and identify the mainstream or communication technologies with which the student might be expected to interact with in various environments. For

example, students who envision working in an office environment will need to have strong keyboarding skills in order to use a workplace computer to connect to an office network. To prepare for this environment, it might be more prudent to invest in a laptop with a braille display rather than a notetaker so that the student can exercise proficiency in the laptop-computing ecosystem while maintaining braille output as desired for authoring tasks. On the other hand, a student who does not expect to work in an office might accomplish everything he or she needs with a smartphone and braille display.

Students with additional disabilities. When evaluating a student with other disabilities in addition to a visual impairment, a multi-faceted evaluation team is essential. Different specialists evaluate different aspects of technology, and therefore recommend different tools depending on their area of expertise. Other team members might conduct evaluations regarding seating, positioning, ergonomics for computer access, mobility, communication, work site modifications, devices for daily living, modification of the home environment, and adaptation or modification of recreation and leisure activities. Collaboration throughout the evaluation is critical so that the vision specialist can recommend low- or nonvisual strategies as needed and relate an individual's visual functioning to evaluation behaviors. For students with developmental disabilities, selecting appropriate evaluation media will require additional consideration. Students' level of representation must be understood so that information is presented to the student in a meaningful way. In addition, a person more familiar to the student might be needed to elicit optimal assessment performance. It is important that device-mediated evaluation tasks are truly assessing what the evaluator intends to assess.

Logistical considerations

Although logistical considerations ideally should never determine a student's educational or training program, sometimes they inevitably do due to affordances such as the opportunity to troubleshoot with peers who use the same technology, the ability to be compatible with existing networks and operating systems, and the availability of existing trained personnel who are readily available as technical support. These logistics can be a factor in the school or workplace as well as the home environment. For students who live in communities and do not have reliable Internet connectivity, different technologies might also be selected that are less Internet-dependent.

Finally, the number of tools in a student's existing toolbox is another point of consideration. For students who work across multiple devices, the ability to sync work to a cloud-based account will allow them to start work on one device and finish it on another. This can help remediate environments that do not have consistent Internet connectivity; a student could work offline and then sync his or her work when he or she arrives in a location with Internet access. Particularly for students who already work across multiple devices, they might be hesitant to add yet another tool that they must transport. Instead, tools with multiple functions can be preferred over several single-function devices.

How to Draft Effective Goals and Objectives for Technology Implementation

Technology Goals for an Adult Student

For an adult student, goals are self-driven and documented upon contacting an agency for services. Goals for the technology evaluation might even align with goals post-evaluation because the adult is entering the evaluation process with a pre-determined set of needs as well as a list of specific tasks that he or she wants to achieve more independently. In other words, the Needs Assessment data from an adult student will likely resemble a general self-assessment and not the results from a comprehensive environmental assessment given to a K–12 student. Because of these reasons, a technology evaluation for an adult student will likely result in a list of recommended technologies rather than a less prescriptive set of goals for instruction. If instructional goals are listed, they might simply highlight the tasks for which the technologies are recommended, in order to facilitate the adult's achievement of over-arching goals. Instruction will be carried out in a more organic fashion rather than mediated on set progress periods like those set for K–12 students. For an adult student, the documentation of goals before and after a technology evaluation will likely vary depending on the requirements of each state and agency.

Technology Goals for a K–12 Student: How to Write Tech Goals for the IEP

Goals for K–12 students are federally mandated and prescribed within the IEP (Ott & Wakefield, 2016; Price-Ellingstad, Reynolds, Ringer, Ryder, & Sheridan, 2019). K–12 goals are intentionally more detailed because they *must* dictate how an IEP will be carried out over the course of a year until the next annual review. The federal regulations can actually be very effective in this case. With a creative mindset, strategically-written IEP goals and related objectives can define an annual lesson plan that includes a strategy for progress monitoring for the student. Goals that are federally-compliant follow a "S.M.A.R.T." (Lazarus, 2004) formula. Goals must be written such that each goal is:

- **S**pecific (details the skill and result you want the student to achieve)
- **M**easurable (how the student will demonstrate progress)
- **A**ttainable (can be achievable within a school year)
- **R**ealistic (aligns with the student's present level of performance)
- **T**ime-bound (target date for when the goal will be achieved)

In order to appropriately support the differentiated learning needs of students who are blind or visually impaired, writing strategic goals for technology implementation can likewise follow a differentiated recipe. If a number of workflows were evaluated for optimization, prioritize one or two that will have the broadest impact on the student's access to learning. For each workflow, use the following guidelines to craft a goal that will help ensure that the appropriate tools, media, and supports are provided to support this workflow. Each component of a comprehensive goal must identify the following:

- The setting, lesson, or activity for which the technology will be used)
  - Examples: During sustained reading time; In classes with paper handouts; In classes with notes on the board; or when non-text materials are displayed
- The recommended technology features the student needs to use; only use a brand name as an example
  - Examples: Touch screen mobile device with a comprehensive screen reader tool; mobile computing device with reverse contrast; an RBD with note-taking capabilities; a portable device with built-in camera for near and distance viewing
- The purpose of the technology
  - Examples: To complete written work; To read and annotate accessible digital talking books; To view and annotate digital worksheets
- The level of independence with which the student will perform

the task, identifying the type and number of prompts as appropriate

- Examples: Independently; with two or less verbal prompts; with hand-under-hand assistance

▫ How the student's progress will be measured

- Examples: For two out of three worksheets; for four out of five journal entries; for two out of three reading assignments

When complete, a comprehensive IEP goal for technology implementation might appear as follows:

When <u>assigned a novel in Language Arts</u> class, Sam will use a <u>mobile, personal computing device</u> with features for <u>text-to-speech, screen reader, and screen magnification</u> to <u>read and annotate accessible digital talking books</u> such as Bookshare books. He will do so independently for two out of three assigned books, for three out of four trials.

The underlined portions of this sample goal align with the recommended components from the goal recipe and accomplish the following:

▫ <u>Assigned a novel in Language Arts</u> = Identifies when the student will implement the technology and workflow

▫ <u>Mobile, personal computing device</u> = Identifies the type of computer the student needs in order to support this workflow and implies that the student must have this device at all times

▫ <u>Text-to-speech, screen reader, and screen magnification</u> = Identifies the types of tools the student needs in order to engage with information, and infers which sensory modes the student is expected to use in this workflow. When comparing different tools, these particular features will drive cost comparisons

▫ <u>Read and annotate</u> = Identifies the tasks that are included in this workflow. Understanding what the student needs to accomplish with technology also identifies what types of training the personnel must receive to support instruction in this area

▫ <u>Accessible digital talking books</u> = Identifies the format of alternate media needed for this workflow. The provision of alternate media is always the responsibility of the IEP team, and will be identified again as an item in the *Recommendations* section of the comprehensive report.

With an explicit goal that identifies all the tools and resources needed for a student to engage in his or her work, the student is entitled to receive all of these tools and resources as part of his or her IEP. Every piece of technology that is purchased for a student must have an IEP goal that supports its need. Because technology can break, be left at home, neglected to be charged, or improved with better options, it is of utmost importance to avoid identifying brand names and specific products in the goal so that any tool that meets the criteria can be used to fulfill the workflow. If a student can remain flexible regarding the tools that can support a workflow, it will help the student expand his or her toolkit, and help the IEP team remain nimble if changes in technology need to be made.

How to Write Objectives That Support an IEP Goal

While the IEP goal might describe the desired workflow, the related objectives (usually two to three per goal, depending on each school district's requirements) can function as a task analysis that breaks down how a student will be taught to use the appropriate sensory modes and develop needed technology skills. In summary, the IEP goal will describe the desired workflow and the objectives will describe the sensory skills and technology proficiency needed to engage in this workflow. It is easiest to write out a thorough task analysis first. The following is a sample task analysis for achieving the above goal and workflow.

- Activate an individual membership to an online library for accessible digital talking books
- Receive book assignments from teacher
- Turn on the computing device
- Open a reading app that allows for direct downloads from the online library for accessible digital talking books
- Search for and download the book to the app

- Adjust settings to read visually
- Adjust audio setting to read selected text segments with a text-to-speech tool
- Use a shortcut to activate and deactivate a screen reading tool to read continuously
- Use annotation tools to make a note on the text
- Access and review the notes using tools for visual or auditory access

After a task analysis is written, review the steps and select how many of them should be achieved in one progress period. That range of skills will be targeted for instruction and development in the first objective. Repeat the process until the entire task analysis has been distilled down to the number of steps equal to the objectives the district requires. In this example, if a school district has three marking periods, then three objectives for the goal will be written. Consider how many of the steps a student could learn in one marking period (in this case, in a four-month period of instruction for a fictional student named Sam):

- **Objective 1:** When assigned a novel, Sam will independently download the book and adjust the font size, line spacing, and color contrasts as needed. He will also use keyboard commands for adjusting the screen magnification tool. He will do so for two out of three assigned books, for three out of four trials.

- **Objective 2:** When reading an accessible digital talking book, Sam will use onscreen and keyboard commands with a text-to-speech and screen reader tool to listen to text at a minimum of 300 words per minute. He will do so with two or less verbal prompts for three out of four paragraphs for three out of four trials.

- **Objective 3:** When needing to answer questions or to prepare for a test about a book, Sam will use annotation tools to make notes on an accessible digital talking book and export the notes into a single file for study. He will do so with two or less verbal prompts to make at least three notes in one study session for three out of four trials.

By taking the time to outline a clear sequence of objectives that can be followed to achieve the goal, the TVI will naturally have a yearlong lesson plan to focus direct instruction for the student. By crafting the goal so that it is workflow-oriented, the purpose of the technology is always at the forefront of instruction. This mindset can facilitate more meaningful technology instruction that is more likely to be embraced by the student as immediate benefits are experienced. Understanding how the technology can support a workflow can also provide a more meaningful context for instruction; rather than pulling out a student from reading class to teach him or her how to activate and de-activate a tool, the student can start learning how to use technology in the natural environment for everyday tasks. As with most in-struction for blind and low vision students, TVIs must integrate instruction into the natural environment as much as possible; this helps students to understand how their skills affect seamless workflows that integrate successfully within a shared environment with typically-sighted peers. Instructional time in a separate location should be used judiciously to introduce an initial skill or tool, but integration back into the student's natural learning environment must occur as soon as possible. Older students who have had sufficient training and a strong baseline of skills can learn a technology outside of the classroom. Once they have had conversations with the TVI about what tasks the technology can support, older students can be trusted to apply the technology to optimize a workflow in the classroom (the TVI can schedule time for classroom observations or contact the classroom teachers to check that technology implementation is occurring as planned.) This generalization of skills more closely models what is expected with adult students and can be approximated as a K–12 student gain maturity and experience with technology proficiency.

Crafting Recommendations to Support Technology

As noted in the United Nations Convention on the Rights of Persons with Disabilities, "disability results from the interaction between persons with impairments and attitudinal and environmental barriers that hinder their full and effective participation in society on an equal basis with others" (The United

Nations, 2006). In other words, **the root of disabled access lies in how well a community ensures an inclusive environment that every individual can actively engage in.** Goals are written to ensure that a student develops proficiency in sensory efficiency and access technology. In contrast to goals, recommendations are written to outline how a workplace or education community can foster inclusive attitudes and universally-designed environments. The approach to crafting recommendations as described in this section is designed to be *pro*-active rather than *re*-active to what a student needs in order to access information as independently and efficiently as possible. If recommendations are developed to ensure information and technologies are made accessible in a student's environment, then a service provider's efforts can be focused on developing a student's skills rather than focusing on making materials and the environment accessible.

As is the case with the evaluation for blind and low vision individuals, recommendations must also be individualized to the heterogeneous needs of each adult and school-aged student. In addition, each report and set of recommendations will also be specific to the student *and* evaluation team. Goals are written to target students' skills, and recommendations are written to target how the environment and essential resources must be accessible to the student. A standalone access technology evaluation typically identifies the types and features of technology that a student needs, as well as recommends specific brand names of devices for purchase. This is most relevant in cases when an assistive technology specialist carries out a comprehensive AT evaluation or if an AT consultant is hired to complete an AT evaluation. In other cases, such as in the cases of many TVIs who are the accessibility facilitators (Siu & Emerson, 2017) and ad hoc technology specialists for a visually impaired students without additional disabilities, the outcomes of an AT evaluation need to be woven into a larger comprehensive report that comprises data from the FVA, LMA, and ECC assessment (FVLM(t)A[ECC]).

Recommendations for a standalone technology evaluation will therefore match the list of technologies that are identified for supporting an optimal workflow. (See this chapter's section **Select Tools that Support an Optimal Workflow.**) With each recommendation, it is equally important to identify the tasks for which the tool is best suited, and those for which it is not recommended. For each tool, including a rationale and justification for why it is being recommended can be helpful for the evaluation team's understanding. The rationale and justification for each recommended type of access technology can emphasize the following:

- Types of tasks it will allow the individual to complete
- Improved efficiency it will provide the individual in completing these tasks

- Possible cost savings of using one tool instead of several to complete multiple tasks and engage in multiple workflows

- Possible cost savings of not having to purchase or produce materials in alternate formats if digital multimedia is accessible

- Staff time saved with digital workflows that disseminate accessible media and reduce the amount of alternate media that must be produced

It is strongly recommended that each explanation emphasizes the features of the different types of technology, rather than recommending a specific brand of device or software. This maintains a current and future evaluation team's flexibility in meeting a student's access technology needs without being constricted to one particular brand. However, an appendix can be provided to the report that details recommendations for specific brand devices and resources, and where these can be procured. TVIs who address AT within a FVLM(t)A[ECC] are often asked to provide a similar type of appendix to help a administrators submit the purchase order. Otherwise, the recommendations that are included in the FVLM(t)A[ECC] are kept non-specific and are limited to the generic features and types of technology the student needs. If a TVI is not asked to provide an appendix with a list of items, it is strongly recommended that he or she explain the necessity of being contacted whenever purchasing decisions about specific models and types

of devices are made. A TVI's input is critical when finalizing a purchase order of access technology items to ensure that all considerations for nonvisual or low vision accessibility are adequately addressed.

Additional items for inclusion in a recommendations list for all reports (standalone and FVLM(t)A[ECC]) each need to identify supports and resources that will aid a student's workflows. Each student's success depends on recommendations that address the following:

- **Accessibility of information-rich environments**: Identify how information in physical and virtual environments can be designed for universal accessibility. Identify standards and guidelines as appropriate to inform an organization's technology procurement plans.

- **Media dissemination:** Identify how materials must be disseminated to the student in an accessible format.

- **IT support:** Identify how technical infrastructures must be maintained to support the student's workflow. For example, a student whose workflow is dependent on Wi-Fi must have his or her devices connected to an online network, or to a network through an item such as a personal hotspot (any device which converts cellular signals to Wi-Fi), even if sighted students are not given this privilege. For a student whose information access depends on connectivity, this is an entitlement rather than a privilege.

- **Access to technology:** Specify what tools and personal computing devices must be available to the student at all times. This assumption must be put into writing to ensure that the student can always use whatever tools are necessary for accessing information, even when others are not given that privilege. For a student whose information access is mediated by their access technology, this is an entitlement rather than a privilege.

Appendix 9.7: AT Recommendations Checklist on page 315 offers an initial list of items that can help an evaluator consider options for inclusion on a recommendations list; remember that the list will be different for each student, depending on the needs of his or her workflow. Recommendations can change as workflows evolve, and evaluators are encouraged to update and customize this checklist as needed.

Additional Considerations for a K–12 Student: Recommendations Within the IEP

Recall that the purpose of crafting technology-related recommendations in the IEP is to identify what supports are needed to ensure successful engagement in a student's workflows. Note that while IEP goals and objectives are *student-oriented,* the recommendations are *environment-* and *resources-* oriented. Remember that goals and objectives are focused on developing a student's skills, **not** assigning personnel obligations. The recommendations will identify those obligations and specify what learning environments, accessible educational media, tools and technologies, personnel support, IT, and professional devel-

opment must be in place to support the student. As aligned with IDEA, any tools and technologies a student needs for accessing his or her education must be available to him or her at all times. This federal mandate supersedes classroom and school rules that govern technology-usage and Internet privileges for typically sighted students as technology needed for access to information is an entitlement rather than a privilege for blind and low vision students.

Finally, as mandated in IDEA, recommendations for professional development can be included as appropriate so that professionals who need to support a student's technologies and workflows are adequately trained to do so. Because recommendations in the IEP also serve a function for identifying accommodations (Remember: accommodations are different from modifications), the **AT Recommendations Checklist or IEP Accommodations Tool, Appendix 9.8,** page 323, can be used to help crafting a recommendations list in an FVLM(t)A[ECC] report as well as to identify accommodations in the IEP for K–12 students.

> **Content Vocabulary**
> **Accommodations/Modifications**
>
> **Accommodations** are accessibility adjustments made for a student with a disability that still require the individual to meet general educational standards. **Modifications** result in changes in educational standards that lower the performance expectation as compared to non-disabled peers.

STEP 9: DRAFT INITIAL REPORT IN AN ACCESSIBLE FORMAT

The purpose of an evaluation report is to document how an individual was assessed, interpret the assessment data for the team, communicate the functional implications of the evaluation outcomes, and provide recommendations for instruction and ongoing facilitation of a student's access to information. Because the report will be reviewed by the student and evaluation team (including the family), it must be written using clear language with a functional definition that accompanies each technical term. When evaluating younger students who cannot fully read and comprehend the report independently, it remains a valuable experience to review the main takeaways together in a meaningful manner.

With the understanding that some evaluators will have a required report template to work with, any report that includes recommendations for nonvisual or low vision technology should include the following information:

▫ A summary of relevant information from the file review, including:

- Related FVA data: Presenting the functional implications of a student's vision will help explain how information is best accessed visually, or if or when nonvisual skills and media are warranted

- Related LMA data: Discussing which sensory modes are the most efficient for accessing different media formats will justify why certain types of technology were selected and alternate media formats recommended

▫ Present a couple of general categories of information accessibility that are broad enough to provide a context for implementing various workflows with technology. These categories can be inspired by the Needs Assessment and will therefore differ across students depending on which tasks hold the highest priorities for what each student wants to achieve. See **Part 1** of the book for ideas *such as*:

- Accessing printed and digital text

- Accessing printed and digital images

- Accessing math and scientific notations

- Writing and note-taking activities

- Accessing information presented at a distance

- Accessing desktop information

▫ For each category of information accessibility, present a concise summary of:

- The current UX (present levels of performance)

- What is and is not working well (data from **Steps 3 and 5**)

- Areas of need in which the student is dependent on sighted assistance or when the student is unable to access or produce work at the same time as peers (data from **Step 4**)

- What an improved workflow would entail, including what types of tools, alternate media, and sensory skills would be used in that workflow

- What benefits would be gained with the improved workflow

◦ Present one or two goals that are specific to technology implementation—each goal should relate to one of the categories of information accessibility that was identified earlier in the report. Remember that each goal should essentially describe an improved workflow that the student will learn over the course of the year (if a K–12 student) or in order to achieve a pre-set goal (if an adult student).

- Preface each goal with a baseline to describe how the student currently accomplishes the tasks as described in the goal
- Include objectives that follow a task analysis toward achieving the goal

◦ Provide a bulleted list of recommendations for the team. Remember that recommendations are environment- and resources-oriented, and should specify accommodations, alternate media, required infrastructure, modifications as needed, and testing accommodations, along with the training needs of personnel

◦ The evaluator's name, title, affiliation, and contact information

Either during drafting the report or upon completion, be sure to format the document for digital accessibility (see **Appendix 9.6: Accessibility Tip Sheet,** *page 313,* for resources on how to format a document for accessibility).

Adult students whose needs have just been evaluated for information access should receive a digital copy of the report that is likewise formatted for accessibility and usability. K–12 students can become practiced in receiving documentation in an accessible format, as well as any family members or professional colleagues who are on the evaluation team. For school-aged students who will transition to services provided an adult agency such as the Department of Rehabilitation, it is a basic professional courtesy to disseminate media in accessible formats should colleagues need low vision or nonvisual access to students' reports.

After the report is drafted, set up a time to review the report with the student. Review the main areas of need, the proposed goals, and discuss the skills the student and service provider will work on together. Review the recommendations list as a team so that the student understands how implementation of his or her accommodations will be a holistic effort to ensure his or her access to information. Ask the student if he or she has any questions or additional areas of concern or desires. If working with a young student, be sure to scaffold the explanations so that the information is meaningful to the student.

Repeat this process with the evaluation team, including the family in the case of a K–12 student. Each stakeholder might have different questions, concerns, or outcomes that could enrich the existing information in the report.

STEP 10: FINALIZE THE REPORT AND INVITE OPPORTUNITIES FOR ITERATION

With consideration for the student's and evaluation team's feedback, adjust the proposed workflows, goals, and recommendations as warranted. Keep in mind that the workflows and goals should be attainable within the year for a K–12 student. A plan for implementing the recommendations can also be discussed upon finalizing the report with the evaluation team, including the student whenever possible.

Although the report is in a final version at this stage of the evaluation, workflows, tools, and recommendations will remain dynamic. Needs for updated technologies and workflows will progress based on a two-pronged continuum: the tasks that the individual needs to achieve, and the skills and tools required to achieve those tasks. The recommendations in the final report of the evaluation can be viewed as a guide for a K–12 student's IEP team or an adult student's rehabilitation team. It can provide an understanding of how the recommendations fit into the individual's needs to access information-rich environments in the educational, employment, and independent living settings.

This report can also aid in the development of a larger informal technology and accessibility plan for all blind or low vision students in an organization by looking at a **technology continuum**

for skill progression. This approach can be enormously helpful in a school system or rehabilitation agency that will continue to address the access technology needs of students with low- or nonvisual access to information. Students at the beginning of the continuum might start learning with no- and low-tech tools while learning to experiment with high-tech tools. As proficiency develops, habits will shift to learning with high-tech tools, while no- and low-tech tools will be reduced to back up systems. As students keep optimizing their workflows, more powerful, complex, or multi-functional tools can streamline the number of tools in a student's toolbox. Particularly in a school system, where purchased technologies remain in the district after the student who first needed them graduates, students' evolving toolboxes mean that tools can often be reallocated. Larger school districts also mean that these students can create natural communities of practice amongst themselves to exchange additional troubleshooting support and iterate new technology solutions as needed.

Concluding the Technology Evaluation

Aside from respecting an individual's entitlement to information related to one's well-being, including the student in every aspect of the active evaluation facilitates the following:

- Recognition of his or her own strengths and preferences **(Step 3)**

- The development of natural trouble-shooting skills **(Step 4)**
- Strategic planning **(Step 5)**
- Thinking like an efficiency expert **(Step 6)**
- Confidence with experimentation and encouraging excitement for how a situation can always be improved **(Step 7)**
- Self-determined behavior by discussing how goals and recommendations will optimize their current situation **(Step 8)**
- Empowerment by being treated as a valued member of the evaluation and educational team
- Experiencing real access to information **(Step 10)**

Ultimately, the involvement of students of all ages throughout the technology evaluation captures their personal investment and "buy-in" to the instructional program and technologies that will be provided. If successful, students should leave the evaluation experience hopeful for and excited about what technology can offer. This excitement can be carried over to a future collaborative "unboxing" session where a student and service provider can experience together the opening, unpacking, and setting up of new devices and tools.

REFERENCES

Lazarus, A. (2004). Reality check: Is your behavior aligned with organizational goals? Physician Executive, 30, 50–52.

The United Nations. (2006). Convention on the Rights of Persons with Disabilities. Treaty Series, 2515, 3.

CHAPTER 10
Scaling Up Digital Literacy Skills

Following the conclusion of a comprehensive technology evaluation process, a student and his or her education or rehabilitation team has had a participatory experience in understanding the student's current workflows, what is and is not working, and which workflows need optimization. An evaluation report has also been disseminated to the student and team (including the family as applicable) that details what kinds of tools are needed to support tasks within each optimized workflow. From the proposed goals and list of recommendations in the evaluation report, the student and education or rehabilitation team should have a clear roadmap for what tools, workflows, and supports are needed to achieve equitable access to information. Although this roadmap details clear paths of performance for the student, the style of traveling down each path will differ for each student, teacher, and environment. The learning experience for all involved stakeholders will be most enjoyable—and successful—when it remains open to creativity and spontaneity, and when it is given sufficient time. This final chapter invites the reader on a journey to consider different strategies for scaling up a student's skills for success and will begin by reviewing the typical expectations of all students in an increasingly digital world.

In the tech-oriented world, information is inevitably and ultimately mediated by digital practices. These practices ascribe to an understanding of digital literacy that is often assumed when in actuality, this type of literacy is best developed with intentional instruction. For K–12 students, the International Society for Technology in Education (ISTE) defines seven standards that are "designed to empower student voice and ensure that learning is a student-driven process" (*ISTE Standards for Students*, 2016).

- **Empowered Learner** (Students leverage technology to take an active role in choosing, achieving and demonstrating competency in their learning goals, informed by the learning sciences)

- **Digital Citizen** (Students recognize the rights, responsibilities, and opportunities of living, learning and working in an interconnected digital world, and they act and model in ways that are safe, legal and ethical)

- **Knowledge Constructor** (Students critically curate a variety of resources using digital tools to construct knowledge, produce creative artifacts, and make meaningful learning experiences for themselves and others)

- **Innovative Designer** (Students use a variety of technologies within a design process to identify and solve problems by creating new, useful, or imaginative solutions)

- **Computational Thinker** (Students develop and employ strategies for understanding and solving problems in ways that leverage the power of technological methods to develop and test solutions)

- **Creative Communicator** (Students communicate clearly and express themselves creatively for a variety of purposes using the platforms, tools, styles, formats and digital media appropriate to their goals)

- **Global Collaborator** (Students use digital tools to broaden their perspectives and enrich their learning by collaborating with others and working effectively in teams locally and globally)

These standards define knowledge bases for engagement with technology and digital media similar to how common core state standards define expectations for engagement in math and language arts. For professionals who work with K–12 students, and especially those who are blind or visually impaired, understanding how differentiated instruction aligns with standards is necessary to provide comprehensive academic support while also addressing needs in the expanded core curriculum (ECC). Although the ISTE standards were developed for the K–12 context, there are relevant aspects for instructing adult students as well. For *any* professional who works with *any* age student, including younger and older adults, digital literacy as described by the ISTE standards cannot be assumed.

Individuals who have grown up with technology, known as "digital natives" do not necessarily generalize technology proficiency from personal or social uses to classroom contexts and work-related tasks (Marksbury & Bryant, 2019; Selwyn, 2009). Alternatively, students with well-developed study or work habits might not have learned how to leverage technology to optimize these habits for school or employment tasks. These standards can inspire mindful technology instruction so that a service provider can implement a holistic and all-encompassing program for any aged student.

> **Content Vocabulary**
> **Digital Native**
>
> A **digital native** is someone who grew up in the time when technologies such as computers, the Internet, and smartphones were already in widespread use. In contrast, a "digital immigrant" is someone who grew up before the digital age and has therefore had to adapt to digital technologies.

INSTRUCTIONAL OUTCOMES SPECIFIC TO STUDENTS WITH VISUAL IMPAIRMENTS

Traditionally, service providers who address literacy objectives for blind and low vision students focus on the "assistive" technologies and specialized formats needed for nonvisual or low vision reading and writing. Service providers who address scientific objectives focus on tools that develop numeric literacy. Data literacy as related to the common core target the development of students' global representations and data synthesis. For students who are visually impaired, digital literacy intertwines all of these literacies—literary, numeric, and data. Without it, these individuals cannot proficiently access all the opportunities the world might offer. So, what does digital literacy mean for blind and low vision students and how can they develop the skills to achieve it?

Digital literacy encompasses manipulation of all types of information for customized and equitable engagement with information. It requires a mindset in differentiating how information is organized in digital formats, and how to employ various tools to engage with media as strategically as possible. Too often, students who are visually impaired are trained only for access without developing the accompanying concepts needed for leadership regarding their participation. The shift from being a passive recipient of information to producer and disseminator requires students' understanding of how to manipulate their accessibility and shape information in physical and virtual environments.

For K–12 students, the individualized educational program (IEP) will follow the goals and objectives as written into the IEP document. These goals and objectives will also justify what technologies need to be purchased or made available to the student. The IEP is a contract that defines the legal obligations of the IEP team to support the student within a free and appropriate public education setting (Free and Appropriate Public Education, 34 CFR § 300.101). It is important that although the goals are written for annual progress and objectives define progress within smaller marking periods, these goals and objectives best reflect a greater continuum of skills that evolve from one year to the next. For this reason, understanding how each year's goals fit into the larger context of digital literacy can maintain consistent skill progression from year to year.

For adult students, goals are usually more self-directed, with a focus on learning how to use the most appropriate tools and technologies to achieve a desired lifestyle and to access reasonable accommodations in a workplace. The goals are also more specifically tied to a workplace or independent living environment and an identified set of needs. Depending on the needs of an adult student, the instructional goals might or might not support a greater continuum of skills within a broader scope of instruction.

Set Up the Student for Success

From the technology evaluation report or FVLM(t)A[ECC], an education or rehabilitation team can use the list of recommendations and accommodations as a reference for educating the community around a student about how to minimize inaccessible tools and practices that render a student disabled. A service provider can also use these recommendations as a platform for setting expectations about how services will be provided; it should be made both clear and firm that technology instruction *will* happen in the student's natural environments.

Because a student's success depends on the accessibility of the environment, it is important that the team aim for a short ramp-up period to implement any needed changes in the environment, set up a system for ensuring accessible media are properly formatted and disseminated, and purchase any needed tools and technologies as soon as possible (See **Appendix 10.1, Recommendations for Accessible Procurement Practices,** page 349). Depending on the expertise of the team, additional training for certain team members might also be warranted to ensure that service providers' skills can anticipate the needs of the student (IDEA, Sec. 602 (2)(F)). Considering that most low vision and nonvisual workflows require engagement in a digital workflow, the *Digital Workflow Planning Tool* (**Appendix 9.3:,** page 303, from **Step 3** of the evaluation process) can guide the team in setting up the initial supports for a student's workflow. Remember that a student's workflow is most efficient when it can work in tandem with other colleagues' or peers' workflows, and when the workflow is compatible with the organization's general technology plan. With these points in mind, implementing supports for a student's workflow should not require an inordinate amount of work.

The Instructional Environment for Teaching Technology

Technology instruction quickly becomes overwhelming when students are taught how to use these devices independently from an actual functional task. However, despite a service provider's best-laid plans, the needs of a student in certain situations really can seem overwhelming. Here are a few tips on how to prioritize instruction for manageability.

- **Take a triage approach and identify pragmatic technology use**
  - Focus on what tasks a student needs to accomplish with more indepen-dence
  - Focus on where a student needs more timely access to information
  - Focus on teaching technology features that align with the sensory mode a student uses most efficiently to perform different types of tasks and access information

- **Emphasize a student's independence in the technology learning process, and encourage him or her to discover various functions and troubleshooting strategies**
  - Focus on building a toolbox of no-, low-, and high-tech tools
  - Focus on developing backup strategies for when technology fails
  - Focus on connecting students to peers and mentors who are also visually impaired who can share their own strategies for success

- **Use a task analysis approach to break down the learning steps in how to use a specific technology for a specific task.**
  - Focus on the steps a student needs to learn first, and then build on small successes
  - Focus on teaching just the features a student needs to complete the task at hand. The other features of a tool can be taught later as needed.

Because instruction must be meaningful and dependent on naturally occurring workflows in the student's environment, the educational or rehabilitation team must understand that there must be a balance of instructional time within the student's natural environments as well as 1:1 in a separate location as needed.

Considerations for K–12 instruction

Because educational vision services for K–12 students must not interfere with regularly scheduled academic activities, TVIs must make accommodations for how their services are rendered. Push-in time (delivering instruction in the student's natural environment, such as a classroom) can be used to teach how to engage with learning content using technology. Pullout time (delivering instruction 1:1 in a separate location from a student's natural environment, usually in an empty classroom, library, or outside picnic table) is best used to focus on device operation and initial instruction to preview a new unit and differentiate concepts for nonvisual or low vision understanding. When the

presence of the TVI in a student's classroom is the exception and not the norm (what typically happens when parent volunteers stop going to teachers' classrooms), more pullout time is warranted, while reserving classroom time for the TVI to observe how or if a student is implementing his or her technology.

When and How to Introduce Technology

The technology learning curve will vary in length depending on a student's experiences related to his or her own sensory efficiency skills, as well as with general and access technologies. The technology learning curve follows a similar trajectory for learning any new skill, technical or not.

Figure 10.1:
The Technology Learning Curve

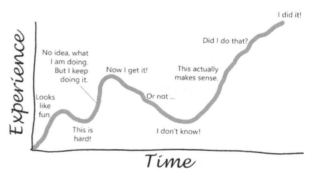

Credit: The Learning Curve, www.sascha-kasper.com

Other instructional goals, time, and resources might also be required if the student has related needs such as concept development, fine motor coordination, spatial perceptual comprehension (knowing where one is in relation to a physical or virtual environment), and sensory efficiency. These areas of instruction all contribute to the development of technology proficiency (Holbrook, Kamei-Hannan, & McCarthy, 2017). For students who only recently have been diagnosed with a visual impairment and are therefore learning nonvisual accessibility skills for the first time, more time needs to be invested in these ancillary areas of instruction versus simply learning new tools with a familiar sensory access mode.

The following technology instruction process is broken down for a student who is at the very beginning of an educational vision program and has yet to develop robust sensory efficiency and technology skills. For a student at this beginning stage, it is wise to budget for a 3-year learning curve to progress from learning technology to using technology for learning.

- **Year 1 = Introduce and experiment with technology, develop sensory efficiency and related ECC skills. Focus on how to use different senses to access information.**

- **Year 2 = Explore what technologies can do, experiment with what tasks can be completed with technology. Focus on how to manipulate devices, tools, applications, and media as desired.**

- **Year 3 = Use technology as a tool for engaging with learning media. Focus on the content and task, not the tool and technology.**

For students who are already technology proficient and simply adding a new tool to an existing toolbox, steps of the instructional process can be accelerated or skipped depending on each student's needs.

STEP 1: INTRODUCE TECHNOLOGY AS SOON AS POSSIBLE—BUT INCIDENTALLY AND ONLY FOR FUN

Even before a student acquires his or her own technology for the first time, incidental exposures to access technology provide important early learning experiences. For typically sighted students, their earliest knowledge about technology comes from watching how others interact with technology and access all forms of information. Young children see parents and siblings, even strangers, sending and receiving text messages, looking up information on a website or digital billboard or making a phone or video call on a smartphone, tablet, or computer. They also see others searching for a particular TV show online or making a digital to-do list. In addition, in a classroom, students see teachers managing all kinds of workflows and classroom technology well before they are taught how to do so themselves. Such tasks might include taking attendance on a chart, printing a document, searching for a specific page of a book, sending an e-mail, or writing a note on a Post-it® note or on the board. Typically-sighted students also have an established community of practice (CoP) with which to connect about technology (especially those who are digital natives). Friends, siblings, and relatives are partners in technology, and talk about various devices and apps well before students learn technology in a formal setting. Many early experiences with technology are mediated by these partners who often negotiate technology exploration time, such as when a student plays a game on a friend's smartphone, takes a photo or watches a video on someone's device, or receives the gift of an old device to experiment with.

Too often, blind and low vision students do not get these same opportunities for incidental learning. In order to facilitate these opportunities, service providers and family members must make additional efforts to enrich a child's environment with truly equitable learning experiences. For example, a future braille reader benefits from having a braille-rich environment. Similarly, any student who will use access technology in the future needs to observe and incidentally experience access technologies in naturally-occurring activities. Equitable incidental learning experiences might include hearing TTS or a screen reader while looking up information online or following a recipe; watching a movie with audio description; hearing someone use dictation to write an email, search for a video, or to make a note; or using a physical or onscreen magnification tool to enlarge details on a map or transit schedule. In the classroom, early exposure to classroom workflows and technology might include hearing a TVI use a screen reader on a computer to send a document to an

embosser, or seeing him or her invert screen contrast to read a story out loud, or using a stylus to take notes or fill in a form on a tablet. Every effort should be made to introduce a blind or low vision student to a community of his or her own. If other visually impaired students do not live locally, weekend and summer programs can be valuable–even for the whole family. Many schools for the blind offer short-course programs as well, which offer students a vibrant community of peers in addition to opportunities for learning. When negotiating exploration time with a blind or low vision student, set up the access tech he or she needs before-hand, and offer a platform for free exploration so that "don't touch" and "watch out" directives can be avoided. Devices and applications with options to limit a user's interactions can be very helpful (see APH's *Learn Keys*™ application, and the *Guided Access*® feature on iOS devices).

When students are finally given their own device, remember to make the unboxing process a collective, exciting event. ("It's new tech day!") If school district staff is required to do the initial unboxing in order to tag the item for inventory, be sure to request that all items are returned to the original packaging so that the student can enjoy this important event. Even the simple act of struggling to open the box can build a student's excitement towards receiving a new device! After tools are unboxed and set up, the student can also identify an appropriate place to store the device and discuss maintenance strategies such as how and when to charge devices as needed. From the moment the box is delivered to the student, the service provider should facilitate the student's sense of ownership and responsibility for it. The service provider must respect this nascent ownership and limit how often a teacher must "take over" a device from the student. In each subsequent step of technology instruction, it is strongly recommended that as much as possible, a service provider issues clear verbal descriptions (Hudson, 2013) when working with a student and his or her technology. A service provider's hands should only touch a student's device with expressed permission (preceded by a request such as "May I show you something?" or "May I try?") and only as needed (such as when a simple verbal description is ineffective and a hand-under-hand demonstration is needed, or for more complex troubleshooting or maintenance issues). This instructional habit helps the student maintain ownership of and responsibility for the technology, and is the beginning in developing a lifelong expectation for independent access to information.

> **Content Vocabulary**
> **Hand-Under-Hand**
>
> **Hand-under-hand** is an instructional technique in which a teacher shows a student how to perform an activity by having the student rest his or her hands on the teacher's hands, thus allowing the student to feel how the teacher is completing a task.

STEP #2: DEVELOP SENSORY LEARNING CHANNELS WHILE PLAYING WITH TECH

In addition to setting the stage for information access, early exposure to access technologies can develop a student's sensory efficiency skills

> **Tech Tip**
>
> See Paths to Technology post "Introducing Technology to Students with Visual Impairments: Toddler, Preschool and Kindergarten" for more information on introducing technology to our youngest students.
>
> https://www.perkinselearning.org/technology/blog/introducing-technology-students-visual-impairments-toddler-preschool-and

(See **Sidebar 10.1** for more information on introducing technology to our youngest students). Students who experience how information can be accessed using visual, tactile, and auditory means will naturally hone each sensory system according to what is most efficient for any given task. In order to support the multimodal development of a student's access technology skills, the service provider can refer to the tools that were recommended in **Step 8** of the technology evaluation process **(Chapter 8)**. Remember that recommended tools for instruction must include technology for the student's primary computing system *as well as* no- and low-tech options. In order to support a student's experimentation with different tools and sensory skills, the service provider should have enough understanding of each tool to understand how various no-, low- and high-tech options could be used to accomplish other tasks, as well as have a broader idea of the technology continuum for a student. No- and low-tech tools generally target one specific sensory mode for accessing information while high-tech tools and digital media can be used to experiment with multimodal access on-demand (the ability to switch to a different sensory mode at will within or between tasks). A graduated introduction of how each tool functions can allow the student to simply focus on experimenting with how he or she can use different senses to gain access to information in visual, tactile, or auditory formats. Remember that at this step, the student is not using the technology for any high stakes tasks yet—he or she is simply playing with the technology and exploring what a tool can do.

Keep in mind that a student's understanding of his or her own sensory efficiency skills occurs most organically when a sufficient number of incidental learning experiences are intentionally embedded into a student's natural environment. As is the case with typically-sighted students, it is impossible to quantify what a "sufficient" number of experiences is.

STEP 3: USE DIAGNOSTIC TEACHING TO DETERMINE INSTRUCTION IN RELATED SKILLS

Observing how a student engages with various tools during multiple explorations can be a valuable strategy for diagnostic teaching. Here are some examples.

- If given a QWERTY keyboard, can the student isolate one finger and activate one key at a time? Can he or she click and hold two keys at a time? (indicates fine motor coordination)

- If given a touchscreen device, how closely does the student bring the screen towards his eyes in order to click an app icon? (indicates how efficient vision is working to scan for information)

- If shown how to turn on TTS to read a webpage, does the student lean back in excitement to hear the information? Does he quickly remember how to activate TTS when needed again? (indicates strength and preference for auditory access)

A student's natural strengths are usually quickly apparent while simultaneously showing potential for how other skills can be developed. Depending on different personalities, some students might be more persistent in solving problems independently while others might seek more immediate assistance from others. It is important that before offering any guidance, a service provider

**Figure 10.2:
Drawing Is Fun!**

"Mario" is a first grader, has low vision, and draws for fun! Experimenting with a video magnifier allows him to use finer point markers and add finer details than he could without magnification. He immediately grasps the value of using a magnification device. Because he needs such a high level of magnification, his technology continuum includes auditory tools for reading and authoring and tactile skills for no-tech strategies with some daily living tasks

gives the student adequate time to experience a problem and learn what they can from it. If possible, guidance can be gently offered in the beginning of a task or before a student reaches frustration (for example, "Let me know if you want any help."). When offering guidance, limit feedback to clear, verbal directions as much as possible; taking the device away from a student in order to troubleshoot it or leaning over a student to handle the device yourself can be very disempowering to a stu-

dent's independent exploration. Basic troubleshooting skills can be introduced at this stage, such as turning devices off and on, and checking to see if devices are plugged in or sufficiently charged.

Remember to keep things fun and playful in this stage of exploration! These incidental learning opportunities should be brief but plentiful, with a focus on identifying areas of instruction as needed to support efficient work-flows in the future. Remember that for K–12 students, assistive technology instruction is only one of nine areas of the expanded core curriculum (ECC). Improving skills in some areas of the ECC can enhance technology proficiency, while technology proficiency can conversely enhance instruction in other areas of the ECC. Consider these examples of synergy between technology skills and the other eight areas of the ECC.

- **Career Education**
  - Professionalism (How do I build an attractive website? A resume?)
  - Employability (What technology skills are needed for different job responsibilities?)
- **Compensatory skills**
  - Computing concepts (What does it mean to save? Copy? Delete? Sync?)
  - Virtual environments (What is a folder? What is a desktop?)
  - Device actions (What does it mean to click? Double-click? Single-click? Bookmark?)

- Organization and executive functioning (How do I name a file and organize it in a folder? What does it mean to "run a search?")

- **Independent living skills**

  - Independence in completing daily tasks (How do I order food from a menu? Check my bank accounts? Browse a supermarket? Call a ride for my date?)

- **Orientation and mobility**

  - Virtual orientation (Where is the top of the page? Bottom of the screen? What does it mean to "scroll down?")

  - Virtual mobility (How do I go to the "next" page or screen? What does it mean to "go back" when looking at websites? What does it mean to move forward or backward through text?)

- **Recreation and leisure**

  - Equitable opportunities for engagement (What's on the scoreboard? What vehicle is that actor driving in the movie? How do I make that Tasty Vegan Pumpkin Pie recipe? How do I read a book series?)

  - Equitable opportunities for participation and leadership (How do I know what's in the museum? Where are the highest-rated coffee shops nearby?)

- **Self-determination**

  - Privacy in accessing and deliberating options (Do I have all the information I need to make an informed choice with as much privacy as a typically-sighted individual?)

  - Privacy in decision-making (Am I able to make choices with as much privacy as a typically sighted individual?)

  - Personal advocacy (Can I use the tools I need in order to complete different types of tasks? How can I remediate an inaccessible situation?)

- **Sensory efficiency skills**

  - Fine motor coordination (Can a student push two buttons at the same time?)

  - Listening skills (Does a student comprehend what is spoken out loud?)

  - Visual efficiency (What kinds of visual settings help?)

- **Social interaction skills**

  - "Reading the room" (What are other people wearing? How many people are here?)

  - Community engagement and networking (What does it mean to "follow" someone online? Who is in my social media network?)

These examples are just the beginning of how technology users can work with, and benefit from, instruction in other areas of the ECC. Remember that for each type of task and activity, a service provider must ensure fair introductions of no-, low-, and high-tech tools for each naturally occurring activity. Regular experimentation with a variety of tools for the same and different tasks will help a student gain proficiency in all of the various types of tools that will function as primary and backup systems.

STEP 4: INTRODUCE WORK-LIKE TASKS WITH FUN-FOCUSED CONTENT

Thus far, technology instruction has been comprised of strategically-placed incidental learning opportunities as mediated by play and exploration. Various tools have been explored in isolation with a focus on playing with different features and methods for accessing information. These experiences have focused on a student's development of sensory efficiency and related ECC skills, initial experimentations with no- and low-tech tools, and how various devices and apps operate. Now that adequate explorations with different technologies have provided a student with enough familiarity and a basic understanding of how to operate various tools, a workflow can be introduced to help the student **shift from learning the technology to using technology for learning.**

This transition can be nearly seamless, and with guided experimentation, can also happen organically. The ideal introductory workflow connects a few tools within a naturally-occurring activity. It is important that the tasks within a workflow are matter-of-fact and not a laborious hindrance to engagement in the workflow. In fact, each aspect of using a tool with which the student is already familiar with should optimize the workflow. The workflow should be low stakes, not anything that will be assigned a grade, and explored with enough flexibility to allow the student to interact with media that is interesting and highly motivating. By choosing a workflow that orchestrates a number of tools with which the student is already familiar, the service provider can help the student build fluency in using technology to accomplish a specific task.

Once a student demonstrates confidence with one particular workflow, he or she can be encouraged to independently explore how the same tools and devices can be applied to other workflows. This is a critical step in empowering the student to use technology for learning and to build a repertoire of positive experiences in using technology for accessing information. Once the student has gained sufficient proficiency in a workflow, then the workflow can be introduced to accomplish a high-stakes task such as completing a graded assignment with the highest possibility of success. While it is helpful for these initial experiences to be error-free and positive, remember that any guidance or scaffolding should remain hands-off and as light as possible to facilitate the student's active learning.

The following case study details how TVI Tina works with her student Mario to scale up his digital literacy skills. Consider how aspects of the instructional process align with the ISTE standards and consider how parallel experiences might be constructed for different students, technologies, tasks, and workflows in various environments.

LET'S TALK ABOUT TSUNAMIS!

Year One

In first grade, Tina introduced Mario to a variety of tools for magnifying print and digital media. Mario drew dinosaurs using markers, paper, and a video magnifier while practicing looking at an enlarged view on a screen. He also drew spaceships and action scenes on a touchscreen tablet using a digital pencil. In both cases, he experimented with on-screen magnification features to enlarge the viewing material. Tina also introduced Mario to a variety of tools for reading text. He experimented with typoscopes and a handheld magnifier. He was given large print materials and listened to teachers read out loud. He also clicked play and pause to activate TTS when presented with a book on a reading app and read online audio books narrated by a human voice while the pages were displayed on screen. Tina knew that these strategies would also fuel Mario's passion for reading books above his reading level. Eventually, Tina presented Mario with his own iPad®, a case with a Bluetooth® QWERTY keyboard, and his own digital pencil. Mario was very excited! He unboxed the items carefully, placed a few stickers on his iPad case, set his lock screen and wallpaper pictures, chose where to plug in the charger, and made a plan for charging his iPad and Pencil every weekend. With his new iPad safely housed in a case, Mario was then introduced to a few tools for authoring. He learned how to activate the dictation button on the onscreen keyboard and practiced making silly sentences appear on a digital notepad. He also practiced typing his name and using TTS to hear his name and the sentences he wrote read aloud. He faithfully brought his devices from home each day. Mario consistently checked the battery level on his device to ensure that it would always be ready to go. He even asked Tina for recommendations of books to read on his device in anticipation of a weeklong family car trip.

Year Two

In the first month of school, Tina used natural beginning-of-year activities such as writing about and drawing pictures related to summer vacation. She also accompanied Mario and his classmates on weekly library trips to review all the different ways Mario could use various tools for reading and writing.

One day, Mario's second grade class practiced how to look up information about a particular subject and discover interesting facts about it. Tina asked Mario to take out his iPad and asked if she could use it to prepare some something special for him to try. He assented to the request. Tina activated the device's Speak Screen feature. When asked what he is most interested in, Mario excitedly replied, "tsunamis!" Tina spelled the word one letter at a time by saying "T, left;" "S, left;" "U, right;" "N, right;" "A, left;" "M, right;" "I, right." (**Sidebar 10:1 _Tip for Pre-Keyboarding Instruction_** explains why she did this.) After Mario finished typing the word, Tina asked him to verify that it was spelled correctly. When she noticed that he leaned in very closely, Tina asked him if he remembered a way to make things bigger on the screen. He thought for a few seconds, then nodded excitedly and used the spread and zoom method on the screen. Tina reinforced the fact that when he made things on the screen larger, Mario could sit more comfortably and check the spelling on the screen.

Mario clicked the enter key to run the search, and was excited to see many results display about tsunamis! This time he remembered to enlarge the screen without Tina's prompting in order to view the images, and he then clicked on the most interesting one. He needed a few verbal reminders to click an image only once and to be patient while the image loaded. Mario's reading skills were still developing, so he relied mostly on sight words. However, Tina observed that he was highly motivated to read about tsunamis! (Is listening reading? (See **Appendix 10.2, Letter to a Concerned Parent,** page 350.)

Again, Tina asked if she could handle Mario's iPad to show him something. She used a verbal description to explain how she made a peace sign, placed her fingertips along the top edge of the screen, and swiped her fingers downward. Now that Tina had activated the TTS feature, Mario was delighted to hear his device read the article to him! Tina asked if he would like to try mak-

ing the iPad talk by himself. She used a whiteboard and asked Mario to pretend it was an iPad screen, and then practice how to apply the gesture to the whiteboard. When Mario demonstrated a smooth two-finger swipe from the top of the whiteboard, Tina encouraged Mario to click another link related to tsunamis and try the gesture on the iPad. Success! Mario independently activated TTS on this and subsequent webpages. At the end of the lesson, Tina and Mario brainstormed what else he could read with TTS on his iPad. She reminded him that TTS can work with most text he sees on a website, and even though it is not always perfect, he should still feel encouraged to try reading other materials online using TTS. She then downloaded Mario's current favorite chapter book into his iBooks library and quickly showed him how he could try reading that with TTS on his own.

A few weeks later, Tina worked with Mario during Writer's Workshop. The class was asked to identify facts about an animal for a writing activity to be turned in at the end of the week. Tina suggested that Mario try looking up an animal in the same way he researched tsunamis, and use TTS to listen to facts about his animal. She used this opportunity to assess whether Mario remembered how to enlarge the screen in order to check spelling and review images, as well as how to use the correct gesture to activate TTS. Tina knew that if Mario did not need to think about how to use each tool to accomplish a task within the workflow, he had successfully transitioned to using this technology for learning! If Mario still needed a reminder at a certain step, Tina could take a moment to review how to operate the tool. In cases in which Mario needs more than a moment to review a step, then Tina might need to provide more direct instruction related to the device's operation before re-introducing it to the workflow.

Year Three and Beyond

Because Mario is a learner in a high academic setting, Tina can predict that he will be expected to engage in high stakes computer-based testing starting in the third grade. Understanding that visual fatigue, visual acuity, and glare sensitivity are functional implications of his eye condition, Tina also knows that Mario needs to develop robust visual and auditory skills for multimodal access to multimedia information. She envisions a future where he will rely on auditory access for the most efficient way to read text, while also magnifying text with reverse contrast (polarity) when reading or editing visually. As a result, Tina conceptualizes a plan for Mario to use tools in his future that include text-to-speech (including a screen reader for continuous reading), screen magnification, font adjustments, and authoring materials in a digital format that could be easily rendered for visual and/or auditory access. Tina also predicts that if Mario uses auditory tools proficiently, he can reduce instances of visual fatigue and reserve his vision for more spatial tasks and content such as found in science and math classes. Across all environments,

Mario needs to have desktop access to information presented at a distance. As a result, Mario will need to understand how to use a variety of tools for engaging with distance information that are presented for desktop access (for example, screen sharing and screen magnification tools). Tina will update her instruction in each of these areas of need as they arise each year. By updating Mario's Needs Assessment (informally and mentally updated with each lesson as part of diagnostic teaching), Tina will be able to prioritize which tools to introduce for what tasks, in which environments, and for what purposes.

Mario's ability to access information efficiently and using multiple sensory learning channels will be dependent on accessible, digital multimedia. These formats will allow Mario to manipulate his learning media to his advantage and flex which tools he decides to use for each instructional task. Tina will need to be strategic when introducing a variety of different tools so that he understands how to make such decisions for himself. Mario will also need to explain what his low vision means in the classroom so that he can begin to advocate for how he prefers accessible educational media to be formatted and provided to support his learning.

Mario's case study describes how a student can begin to learn technology and how he shifts to using technology for learning. The following steps were taken to scale up his digital literacy skills.

TIP FOR PRE-KEYBOARDING INSTRUCTION

Mario's finger isolation skills are still developing and he is only able to isolate some of his fingers; he is not ready for full touch-type keyboarding instruction yet, and does not yet have the attention span to dedicate to a keyboarding program. Mario has a QWERTY keyboard that is attached to his iPad and like many of his classmates, is still getting oriented to matching letter sounds to the correct letter. However, Tina determines that because he understands left from right, he can start to familiarize himself with the keyboard by also orienting to the left and right sides of the keyboard. At this time, he is simply encouraged to type each letter with his left or right hand (using any finger), depending on the side of the keyboard each letter is on. Giving him a clue about which side of the keyboard to look for the letter also helps reduce visual fatigue and aids visual efficiency.

1. Playful low stakes activities were introduced with high interest content (drawing a dinosaur, learning about tsunamis)

2. Mario developed foundational sensory efficiency skills and knowledge of how to operate a number of no-, low-, and high-tech tools. He gained confidence by experimenting with different tools to accomplish similar tasks (drawing, reading, writing)

3. Tina selected naturally-occurring workflows that mimicked how a class task might be accomplished. Highly motivating, non-assigned content were selected to engage Mario. He successfully used technology to access information for learning.

4. Tina empowered the student for ongoing independent exploration ("See what else you can do when I'm not here!")

5. Tina introduced how to apply a familiar workflow to a high-stakes task. She used verbal, not physical prompts, to scaffold Mario's skills as needed to ensure success. Mario viewed himself as capable, or even more able than his peers in this classroom who were working on the same assignment.

STEP 5: BUILD A FOUNDATION FOR FUTURE SUCCESS

Ultimately, the most effective technology interventions are future-focused. Students must know how to use tools that will facilitate on-demand, multimodal access to multimedia information. Remember that addressing all areas of the ECC, including technology skills, is needed to prepare K–12 students for future success. For adult students who do not require instruction in the ECC, technology instruction should also prepare them for how to manage maintenance updates and provide more detail about accessible workflows for alternate media production. While K–12 students should also be introduced to workflows for alternate media production, it should be for the purpose of creative expression. This educational media should otherwise be provided in accessible formats so that materials accessibility does not impede classroom learning. When K–12 students graduate from secondary school, this preparation will give them the knowledge they need to advocate for appropriate alternate media in postsecondary settings and reasonable accommodations in the workplace.

College-bound students must be successful without the support of a TVI and related service providers after graduation. Adult students must also exercise proficiency in using access technology in order to maintain gainful employment. All students need to be knowledgeable about their eye condition, the functional implications of their visual impairment, and how to advocate for accessibility needs. In order to advocate for accessibility needs, students must develop fluency in explaining how they access information; what formats they require to access learning, work, or personal media; and why they need the specific tools they use.

Tech Tip

See Paths to Technology post "Student's Outline for eMail to New 8th Grade Teachers."

https://www.perkinselearning.org/technology/blog/students-outline-email-new-8th-grade-teachers

All individuals are entitled to appropriate and reasonable accommodations under education and employment laws, and it is important that they know exactly which ones they are entitled to.

Empowering a student to take charge of his or her own accessibility requirements can begin as early as possible, from preschool classrooms, to college lecture halls, to workplace and leisure environments. Students can develop the habits of speaking directly with the teacher, professor, or supervisor to explain their accessibility needs. By working directly with typically sighted peers in the community, students can also assure their teachers or employers that they will succeed when provided the appropriate accommodations.

The following strategies can help a student become the best advocate for their own needs.

- Role-play how to talk to a person of authority such as a manager or teacher about accessibility needs. Develop and practice an informal script for asking for accommodations so it becomes more natural to say.

- Develop accurate vocabulary to discuss accessibility issues, and advocate for device or software updates to improve the accessibility of a needed tool.

- Create social media posts, blogs, or video tutorials that teach others how to use various technologies to access information as would a nonvisual or low vision individual. Creating this content should naturally encourage the student to think about how and why he or she uses technology.

- K–12 students can create a short video to send to new teachers at the beginning of a school year. Film the student introducing him- or herself, explaining his or her visual impairment and accessibility needs. Include tips on how teachers can support the student's needed workflow.

- Introduce the student to blind mentors who can provide more nuanced information about troubleshooting and advocacy strategies in various contexts.

- Ensure that individuals are active participants in their own IEP or IPE meetings. Their voices should be heard in order to represent their own interests.

Finally, never underestimate the power of involving students in their own technology evaluation and instruction process. Students will naturally buy-in to recommended technologies when they are partners in identifying technologies to try, comparing different options, and setting instructional goals.

Tech Tip

See Paths to Technology post "Mastering Tech Skills: When and What?"

https://www.perkinselearning.org/technology/blog/mastering-tech-skills-when-and-what

Considerations When Preparing for Computer-Based Assessments

For K–12 students, most states have implemented online, computer-based assessments for high-stakes standardized testing beginning in the third grade. Prior to these testing situations, all students should be proficient enough in using the computer and accessibility tools and features so that the assessment truly assesses students' content knowledge and not technology skills.

TVIs are typically the person on an IEP team who needs to coordinate the technology instruction, ensures that proper accessibility settings for students are programmed for each, and makes sure that IT support is aware of the equipment a student needs on the day of practice tests and actual tests. Online test accommodations might differ across states depending on the vendor the state has contracted for providing the test. Assuming that the student has had adequate time to ramp up his or her technology skills for learning (and is no longer learning the technology), preparing a student to take a computer-based test by using accessibility tools can take several months.

Adequate preparation will determine whether a blind or low vision student can successfully take the test and be held accountable for his or her learning. **Appendix 10.3: Computer-Based Assessment Planning Checklist** on page 353 details a sample checklist for how to prepare a team for computer-based testing.

For adult students who need to take computer-based tests for training or employment purposes, collaboration with an organization's human resources and instructional technology departments is necessary to ensure the testing platform is compatible with the student's access technology. Assuming that work environments are accessible, an adult student can contact his or her rehabilitation counselor as needed if more or different access tools are needed to meet job responsibilities. Workplace accommodations must be provided to ensure that all work environments, both physical and virtual, are accessible. If challenges arise, a representative from the Department of Rehabilitation might be called upon to provide additional support and training to the employer. If further assistance is needed to ensure workplace accommodations are implemented, a disability rights lawyer can provide further consultation; the structured negotiation process is the best strategy for resolving issues amicably (Feingold, 2017).

Empower Students for Leadership

Any service provider working with a student of any age should consider the value of facilitating mountaintop moments (Rosenblum, 2018). Instead of saying to a student, "Let me help you up the mountain," the service provider should use instructional time to ensure a student has the skills he or she needs to *meet* the provider at the top of the mountain. This empowers students not only for access but also for leadership in their communities, to connect them with peer networks that can provide the inspiration and nuanced advice that sighted service providers simply cannot.

Technology is a great equalizer for engagement with information. Skills can be applied to support a student's achievement of a desired lifestyle, pursue any recreation and leisure interest, and if desired, to succeed in competitive learning and early work experiences. Keep in mind that work experiences and paid internships are important for students as soon as they reach the age where peers begin to pursue similar employment opportunities (Connors, Curtis, Emerson, & Dormitorio, 2014; McDonnall, 2010). For students who do not pursue competitive academic and employment endeavors, technology can ensure active participation in one's own life to the greatest extent possible. Finally, consider how technology can significantly change the power dynamic in any environment for any individual, blind and sighted. Those who have access to information are the ones who can lead or help others. In a network of peers, this exchange of information and expertise among community members maintains forward progress for everyone.

How Does Anyone Possibly Keep Up With Technology?!

This book has covered a sufficient breadth of access technologies for low vision and nonvisual access to information **as of September 2019.** As technologies, digital practices, and the nature of information advance quickly, service providers must keep up to date and remain savvy about what tools are available for supporting current workflows. Individuals employed in any profession, whether education- or rehabilitation-related or not, are responsible for updating their training and knowledge base as new tools and practices for working in a particular field evolve. In any profession, those who do not maintain their professional development simply cannot advance; worse, the lack of professional evolution can become a hindrance to the greater professional field. In the most non-ideal situations, clients and students bear the consequences of professionals who are ill-equipped to meet an individual's needs.

Given the seemingly infinite scope of technology, how does one possibly keep up with new developments, especially in a field where a student's success in life can depend on professional development? Fear not! Similar to how students can be encouraged to keep learning and progressing via their own communities of practice, so must professionals. Technology can also be leveraged with great success to connect with a multitude of communities of practice (CoPs) that function as ongoing, informal professional development. Those who connect with CoPs can take advantage of the collective resources, expertise, and professional practices that are necessary for maintaining and developing one's technology proficiency (Morash & Siu, 2016; Siu & Morash, 2014). Because a service provider's expertise develops naturally according to the teaching experiences they acquire with each new student, CoPs help identify the experts in various areas of technology and teaching. For example, one particular service provider might be known for her insights on RBDs and accessible apps because her students have been using many workflows that require those tools. Another service provider might be known for her expertise in using mainstream document cameras and tablets as video magnification systems. Yet another might become adept at 3D printing technologies and become the go-to person for support in that area. By engaging in vibrant CoPs where expertise in different areas is readily available, service providers should not feel that they must be experts in every type of technology. Rather, they must have sufficient knowledge to understand how to match the right *types* of technology to specific student needs, then have confidence in their ability to search for the information they need on demand. Options for how to engage with a CoP are abundant: in-person meetups; phone, video, or social media chats; online social media groups; blogs; website subscriptions; and listservs all offer various platforms for connecting. It is imperative that professionals determine which avenue fits best with their existing workflow and preferences, and then connect. Much can be learned from even passive engagement by reading the information that is exchanged among other members (colloquially known as being an online 'lurker,' or more academically referred to as a 'habitual spectator') (Siu, 2015).

Recommendations for personnel preparation

Determining how to prepare personnel to work with technology in any field can be very challenging. With regard to the fields of education and rehabilitation as related to visual impairments, the low incidence nature of the population that professionals serve can introduce additional complexities. Understanding that technology proficiency is best developed and expanded with direct experiences with students, knowledge about technologies that are learned in a personnel preparation program can expire quickly if a graduate does not immediately have any students who require a particular type of technology. However, as **Part 2** of the textbook reveals, broader understanding of how to conceptualize, evaluate, and analyze the fit of technology to a student's needs remains constant regardless of what technologies are currently in vogue. New teachers will benefit from training that introduces them to the breadth of available technologies as related to the features and functions each tool offers. More importantly, pre-service teachers must know how to evaluate various features of technology according to how they fit a student's needs. In order to do so, pre-service teachers must understand how technologies can optimize low vision and nonvisual workflows. It is recommended that at least one course of a personnel preparation program be dedicated to an introduction of specific high-tech tools, while holistic knowledge of how to flex no-, low-, and high-tech tools to accommodate different learning and accessibility needs are integrated throughout all other coursework within relevant workflows. Because technology is never used in isolation from a goal-oriented task, it likewise needs to be learned and understood within meaningful tasks and contexts. This is true for both students and future teachers alike.

Finally, recall the importance of engagement with a CoP for developing and maintaining technology proficiency! Personnel preparation programs are situated to help future teachers develop the habits for engagement that will sustain their professional development well after graduation from a training program. Course activities can be designed to facilitate students' connection to CoPs that offer information from more experienced practitioners, and seasoned practitioners can benefit from the cutting-edge knowledge that pre-service teachers gain in a comprehensive training program.

IN CONCLUSION

Ultimately, technology must deliver a sense of empowerment by optimizing one's workflow. Technology is often the ultimate mediator to ensure that everyone in a community, whether blind or sighted, has equitable access to information to the greatest extent possible. Remember that a holistic process of technology evaluation, instruction, and—most importantly—exploration is essential because for blind and low vision individuals.

Technology is everything, but everything is not technology

Even from the youngest ages, regardless of whether or not additional disabilities are present, every student, teacher, and rehabilitation team must set high goals for a student's lifestyle and potential achievements. As with instruction in other skill areas, outcomes of technology instruction must focus on building self-determined behavior as mediated by access to information, in order to reduce the need for a service provider.

As practitioners, our job is never finished regarding advocacy for equity. With the inclusion of information in physical as well as virtual environments, in both physical and digital formats, our work as accessibility facilitators is more critical than ever. We must be knowledgeable about practices that threaten our students' privacy and access to information, and how to leverage the appropriate tools and efforts to mediate those threats. Social media is a powerful tool for closer engagement with communities of practice than ever before, and with the power of a community, environmental and attitudinal barriers that disable members of a community can be deconstructed one by one. When we leverage this power of an entire field rather than as isolated individuals, our strength as a professional field has no bounds, and paves the way for future generations to have truly equitable access to information.

REFERENCES

Connors, E., Curtis, A., Emerson, R. W., & Dormitorio, B. (2014). Longitudinal analysis of factors associated with successful outcomes for transition-age youths with visual impairments. Journal of Visual Impairment & Blindness, 108(2), 95–106.

Free and Appropriate Public Education., 34 CFR §.

Holbrook, M. C., Kamei-Hannan, C., & McCarthy, T. (Eds.). (2017). Foundations of Education, 3rd Edition: Volume II: Instructional Strategies for Teaching Children and Youths with Visual Impairments (3rd ed., Vol. 2). New York, NY: American Foundation for the Blind Press.

Hudson, L. (2013). This, That and There. Retrieved September 30, 2019, from http://www.pathstoliteracy.org/blog/this-that-there

ISTE Standards for Students. (2016). Retrieved from https://www.iste.org/standards/for-students

Marksbury, N., & Bryant, E. A. (2019). Enter the twilight zone: The paradox of the digital native. Issues in Information Systems, 20(2).

McDonnall, M. C. (2010). Factors predicting post-high school employment for young adults with visual impairments. Rehabilitation Counseling Bulletin, 54(1), 36–45.

Morash, V. S., & Siu, Y. (2016). Social predictors of assistive technology proficiency among teachers of students with visual impairments. ACM Transactions on Accessible Computing (TACCESS), 9(2), 4.

Rosenblum, P. (2018). In conversation.

Selwyn, N. (2009). The digital native–myth and reality. Aslib Proceedings, 61, 364–379. Emerald Group Publishing Limited.

Siu, Y. (2015). A virtual water cooler: The ecology of an online community of practice to support teachers' informal learning (doctoral dissertation). Retrieved from doi: 10.13140/RG.2.1.1163.5605

Siu, Y., & Morash, V. (2014). Teachers of students with visual impairments and their use of assistive technology: Measuring teachers' proficiency and their identification with a community of practice. Journal of Visual Impairment & Blindness, 108, 384–398.

ACCESSIBILITY CONSIDERATIONS IN PROCUREMENT PRACTICES

Guest contributor: Lucy Greco, Web Accessibility Evangelist

One of the most important aspects of accessible technology is the environment a person has to work in. When a blind person needs to collaborate with his or her peers, he or she needs to use the same tools and not be disadvantaged by the accessibility of the tools. Because of this consideration, accessibility in every organization starts when you first acquire any technology.

Buying everything accessible is the ideal, but organizations are often pushed into not doing so. Here is a quick formula of how to deal with buying technology:

1. Have a process to vet the product. Vendors can fill out a standardized form so that the people buying the product understand how the vendor answers questions related to accessibility, and which are the critical items.

2. Ask the vendor to demonstrate how the product is used by people with disabilities. These demos should not be well-edited videos. We often find that vendors will create an edited video that makes things look good, but we want these videos to be real demonstrations so that it is clear that a person who needs assistive technology can actually use the product to accomplish what is needed.

3. Lastly—and this trumps everything—if something is not fully accessible, then have a plan and budget in place to make sure people with disabilities can still do their work. This means having real funding, and can include having money set aside to pay a human reader or scribe if the tool is broken.

When an organization is buying new tools, be sure that someone who knows how to use access technology is part of the buying team. Make sure that the organization *listens* when this person reports that something does not work.

Ultimately, I would hope that you don't buy inaccessible products but if you do, make sure you are not leaving your disabled users holding the bag.

See Section 508.gov, GSA Government-wide IT Accessibility Program for more information. (https://www.section508.gov/blog/Building-Accessibility-into-your -Procurement-Process)

LETTER TO A CONCERNED PARENT

A LETTER TO A PARENT WHO IS CONCERNED THAT LISTENING IS NOT READING

By Jessica McDowell, TVI/COMS

Dear Parent,

You had questions and I wanted to discuss them further. I proposed a goal for your son to listen to audio books. I heard your worry that listening was not really reading. This is a very common concern for parents and teachers. I would first suggest we zoom out to think about reading beyond the classroom and report cards. Also, we need to imagine your son in ten and twenty years. Because of his visual impairment, the ways your son experiences books will look a little different, but believe me, he will find magic and delight in reading.

I think the Digital Audiobook Player from the Library of Congress is a great tool that young readers can learn to use on their own. I think of this as a recreational goal. You may remember that recreation is an important area of the Expanded Core Curriculum for students with visual impairments. There are different ways to read and there are different purposes for reading. I would love for your son to have a way to listen to audio books independently and start to tell us the kinds of stories he finds fun and engaging.

Of course, students need to learn that symbols (print or braille) stand for speech sounds and make words. These printed letters or raised dots are how we share stories and information so someone at a different time and place can turn them back into language. Listening does not diminish the acquisition of print or braille reading. Reading is language processing. Decoding is just the part of reading where we take a symbol and turn it into language we can process. For many people, that means hearing the language in their head as they read.

So, it may be more accurate to ask, how do we balance language processing and decoding skills so your son develops strong literacy skills?

If you want to take a test on phonics and decoding skills, that must be done with eyes on print or with fingers on braille. If you want to discuss

(Continued)

a story and take a comprehension test, you could have read it in print, braille, or listened to a narrated audiobook or synthesized text-to-speech or heard it told with sign language. When we are presented with a page with a bunch of little lines or tactile dots, decoding is how we turn those symbols into language we can hear and process. For your son, of course we want to know how he is progressing with decoding large print text that is accessible. Learning to decode is the work of early elementary students but so is language processing and all that goes into experiencing a full literacy curriculum. Since reading visually can be fatiguing for your son, he can have breaks from the visual task and continue to develop his language processing skills using audio books. Eventually he will benefit from using text-to-speech for some reading.

Let's fast forward to high school and beyond—reading large print takes longer than reading regular size print. Large print on paper is rarely available, and it is heavy and awkward. Luckily, we have devices that make print accessible, and we can set the best size. My students often have conditions (like nystagmus) that result in visual fatigue or they have sensitivity to glare so they may not be comfortable reading off of a screen for extended periods of time. Listening is an important option. Of course, readers have choices. For a certain kind of book, a reader who is blind or has low vision may choose to listen to a book narrated brilliantly by an actor and love every minute of it. Prosody or the inflections and rhythm of speech may help comprehension in some instances, which is why young readers may benefit from narrated audiobooks. Other times, looking at print to study vocabulary usage or hearing text-to-speech to follow details and storyline may be preferred. For speed, which becomes vital for college and work with extensive reading loads, technology and text-to-speech helps level the playing field for people with visual impairments.

Our students have fond, warm memories of reading their favorite books just like we do, even if they read in a different way. We may associate memories of being curled up with dog-eared books with the rich imagery of characters, place, and storylines. It will be the same for your son but his book won't be the same one we held. We love the physical book that we read visually because we love the story and the experience. Your son won't read the small print book in dim lighting but he will have reading experiences that are just as rich.

With all that in mind, listening is a learned skill that follows a developmental progression. I work specifically on it with my students. My older students are excited to see their listening speed increase with practice and even surpass the visual reading speed of their peers. I personally read narrated audio books and also use text-to-speech extensively. When I discuss something I have read, whether I listened or read visually doesn't matter at all. Many students and adults may listen back to what they write during the editing process, which is valuable for students with visual impairments. So, developing listening skills for reading is an important tool in your son's tool box. He ultimately will be making decisions about how he reads; we need to make sure he can access all the options.

May I make a request? Please don't voice opinions or complaints about technology or alternative modes of reading in front of your son. We need him to be open and excited to try all routes to learning we can show him. You did not need to use text-to-speech to get through your high school literature class. You could see all the small print and using your vision did not lead to debilitating visual fatigue. When my kids hear their parents say, "I hate the computer voice," my students repeat that to me. What if your son heard you listen to a story read in a computer voice and then you said, "that was such a great story!" The message is that this is an acceptable and pleasant way to read.

Sincerely,
Jessica

APPENDIX A
It's the Law: Frequently Asked Questions About Assistive Technology Policies

Q. What will I find in this Appendix?

A. This appendix provides answers to some of the more frequently asked questions concerning how assistive technology is addressed by national and international law and policy. The answers provided below are not formal legal advice and are simply intended to offer the reader a baseline for understanding how law and policy at the national and international levels affect the availability and use of assistive technology generally. When it is particularly important to refer to a specific provision of law to answer a question appropriately, either the specific citation or the common name for that source is provided. For other questions, however, particularly when applying a number of different laws or regulations at the same time in a particular context, the answers below offer an interpretation and application of law and policy generally from an advocate's perspective, i.e., to support the opportunity and/or right of children, working-age adults and seniors with vision loss to fully benefit from assistive technology. While much of this appendix focuses on the delivery of assistive technology devices and services for students in the public special education system, a review of the following questions and answers should show the reader the breadth of policy contexts in which assistive technology is relevant.

Q. What are the various sources of law and policy that might deal with assistive technology?

A. Throughout this appendix, reference will be made to various sources of U.S. and international law. Remember that very rarely will there be a single "chapter and verse" in the law that addresses a specific situation once and for all. There are statutes which the U.S. Congress enacts and the President signs into law, there are federal regulations adopted by agencies of the federal government which implement acts of Congress, and there are a host of supporting materials, such as commentary written by federal agencies to accompany and explain their regulations, and formal policy guidance documents that agencies might issue offering further clarification in lay terms. It is the purview of the courts to interpret this extensive body of material and apply it to particular circumstances. Generally speaking, only statutes, regulations, and the decisions of the courts are considered authoritative sources of law, but the other materials can be very useful tools for advocates to turn to for technical assistance or clarification of what the law means or how a given agency may apply it. For example, if the U.S. Department of Justice settles a case before the court which results in the provision of assistive technology-related services to a college student with disabilities, the settlement agreement is only binding on the college in question, not per se on other colleges. However, other colleges will most certainly take note of the settlement agreement when deciding how they will deal with similar situations lest they too find themselves at odds with the Justice Department. And in the United States of course, there are bodies of law at the federal, state and local levels, each with their respective statutes, regulations, state court decisions, and accompanying materials which may have something to say about the rights of people with disabilities to appropriate services and technologies.

Q. Why is there so much focus in this appendix on assistive technology with regard to special education? What about assistive technology in other contexts, such as employment, public accommodations, health care, and other areas?

A. This appendix addresses assistive technology policy in a host of topical areas as it relates to children, working-age adults, and older adults with vision loss and who may have other disabilities. However, one of the reasons why so much attention is being paid in this appendix to special education has to do with money. While the special education system across the country is far from fully funded, tens of billions of federal and state dollars are devoted each year for children and youth with disabilities to receive a free appropriate public education. While there are other sources of federal- and state-level funding supporting the delivery of assistive technology devices and services in other areas, such as vocational rehabilitation or independent living, none of them is funded to an extent comparable to special education. Along with this sizeable national investment in special education come a lot of conditions that are placed on states and school districts by Congress for the purpose of ensuring proper use of federal dollars. Additionally, unlike many other national programs that provide various services to people with disabilities, special education services are rooted in the constitutional and civil rights of individuals with disabilities to equal educational opportunity. So, unlike other contexts, special education stands out because it is a system in which our country makes a substantial financial investment and that is also ultimately a national imperative to which children and youth with disabilities have a constitutional and civil right.

Q. How is assistive technology defined in America's special education law?

A. The Individuals with Disabilities Education Act (IDEA), the federal statute governing special education across the country, has a number of major components or "Parts." For children and youth ages 3 to 21, Part B of IDEA is that significant portion of the federal special education law that sets out the full array of services that states must provide if they are to receive federal financial assistance for offering special education and related services. IDEA Part B defines an assistive technology device as:

> . . . [A]ny item, piece of equipment, or product system, whether acquired commercially off the shelf, modified, or customized, that is used to increase, maintain, or improve functional capabilities of a child with a disability (20 U.S.C. § 1401(1)(A))).

Neither the IDEA statute nor the regulations define assistive technology in more detail. However, as explained above, very often, helpful clarification as to what the law means is provided by federal agencies in commentary that they publish along with the regulations they issue. While this commentary is not "the law" per se, it can describe things in greater detail than would be appropriate for statutes or regulations themselves. So with that, let us turn to that commentary to learn more about how assistive technology is defined. The U.S. Department of Education, the federal agency responsible for IDEA implementation, says that

> The definition of assistive technology device does not list specific devices, nor would it be practical or possible to include an exhaustive list of assistive technology devices. Whether an augmentative communi-

cation device, playback devices, or other devices could be considered an assistive technology device for a child depends on whether the device is used to increase, maintain, or improve the functional capabilities of a child with a disability, and whether the child's individualized education program (IEP) Team determines that the child needs the device in order to receive a free appropriate public education (FAPE) (71 Fed. Reg. 46547 (2006)).

This means that as new devices or other technologies are developed, they may be included as part of the IEP if they are determined by the IEP team to "increase, maintain, or improve" a child's abilities. The standard is whether the technology can or is likely to help the child access the curriculum.

Q. What are assistive technology services?

A. Assistive technology services are defined in the statute as

> Any service that directly assists a child with a disability in the selection, acquisition, or use of an assistive technology device (20 U.S.C. § 1401(2)).

The term includes

- evaluation
- acquiring a device for the child, either by purchase or lease
- customizing the devices to meet the child's needs

- maintaining, repairing, or replacing the device

- training or other assistance for the child, as well as the family, when appropriate

- training for the educators, rehabilitation specialists, and employers working with the child

- coordinating and using other therapies, interventions, or services with assistive technology devices, such as those associated with existing education and rehabilitation plans and programs

Inclusion of assistive technology services within IDEA means that a child is entitled not just to the provision of various devices. It is insufficient to receive a device without training and follow up as well. In discussing assistive technology services, the preamble to the regulations states that a

> service to support the use of Recordings for the Blind and Dyslexic [for example] [now known as Learning Ally] on playback devices could be considered an assistive technology service if it assists a child with a disability in the selection, acquisition, or use of the device. If so, and if the child's IEP Team determines it is needed for the child to receive FAPE, the service would be provided. The definition of assistive technology service does not list specific services (71 Fed. Reg. 46548 (2006)).

Q. What are the duties of an IEP team when considering assistive technology devices and services for children with vision loss?

A. IDEA requires that IEP Teams consider all of the "academic, developmental, and functional needs of the child" (20 U.S.C. § 1414(d)(3)(A)(iv)), as well as specifically "consider whether the child needs assistive technology devices and services" (20 U.S.C. § 1414(d)(3)(B)(v)). This means that every IEP Team must at least discuss whether or not assistive technology devices and services would help the child achieve a free, appropriate public education.

The Department of Education's *Educating Blind and Visually Impaired Students: Policy Guidance* (2000) discusses the importance of assistive technology for students with vision loss and places it in the context of the IEP Team's responsibility to address the student's ability to access information:

> Issues related to accessing information frequently arise in the education of blind and visually impaired students . . . . Therefore, it is especially important that IEP teams for blind and visually impaired students give appropriate consideration to these students' needs for assistive technology and the full range of assistive technology devices and services that are available for them, and this consideration needs to occur as early as possible. . . . [A] blind or visually impaired student's ability to become proficient in the use of appropriate assistive technology could have a positive effect on

the development of the student's overall self-confidence and self-esteem. Students taught the skills necessary to address their disability-specific needs are more capable of participating meaningfully in the general curriculum offered to non-disabled students (65 Fed. Reg. 36590 (2000)).

The duties of the IEP Team always boil down to providing access to information that results in a free, appropriate public education (FAPE). If assistive technology devices and services contribute to that goal, then the IEP Team should address them in the IEP.

Q. Are practitioners with special expertise about assistive technology devices and services part of a child's IEP team?

A. Given the legal requirements for the IEP team to consider assistive technology devices and services, a child with vision loss should receive an assistive technology evaluation as part of the development of the IEP. In many cases, the teacher of students with visual impairments will conduct this evaluation and will already be included on the IEP team. Other individuals can also be included on the IEP team, particularly if they have "knowledge or special expertise" about the child that can inform the discussion and development of the IEP (20 U.S.C. § 1414(d)(1)(B)(vi)).

Q. How do public agencies use assistive technology devices and services to ensure a free, appropriate public education?

A. The preamble to the regulations explains that each public agency is required to

> ensure that assistive technology devices (or assistive technology services, or both) are made available to a child with a disability if required as part of the child's special education, related services, or supplementary aids and services. This provision ties the definition to a child's educational needs, which public agencies must meet in order to ensure that a child with a disability receives a free appropriate public education (FAPE) (34 C.F.R. § 300.105(a)).

State and local education agencies ensure a free appropriate public education by evaluating a child's need for assistive technology on a case-by-case basis, including those devices and services in the child's IEP, and providing them at no cost to parents. A free appropriate public education is integrally tied to an individual child's ability to access information in the school environment.

Q. Who does the state education agency need to work with to provide students with assistive technology devices and services?

A. The State Education Agency is expected to work collaboratively with the state agency responsible for assistive technology programs (34 C.F.R. § 300.172(d)). This agency differs from state to state and is broadly interpreted as the agency funded by the Assistive

Technology Act of 1998 to provide assistive technology services to individuals with disabilities. Provision of assistive technology in a given situation can therefore be a shared role, and various state agencies should work together with the district to make sure assistive technology is provided as needed. However, the Assistive Technology Act programs across the states historically have not been funded very well by the U.S. Congress. Nevertheless, states are expected to pool the various funding streams available to meet the needs of students with disabilities. What is important to know, however, is that because special education is a civil right, inadequate federal or state budgets cannot be used by states and school districts as an excuse not to provide assistive technology devices and services.

Q: What responsibilities do Local Education Agencies (LEAs) and State Education Agencies (SEAs) have in providing training opportunities for teachers to learn technology recommended in the IEP?

A: Pre-service and in-service training and requirements for credentialing and for renewing teachers' credentials vary from state to state. There is nothing in IDEA that would obligate a district to pay to keep teachers up to speed on the latest technologies.

Q: When new technologies are recommended for a student, is the school system responsible to provide training for the TVI?

A: If instruction in a new technology is part of a student's IEP, then the school district is obligated to provide for that instruction. Their options could include training an existing employee to provide that instruction or to acquire services from someone who is prepared to provide that instruction to the student.

Furthermore, the term "assistive technology service" is defined in IDEA to include "training or technical assistance for professionals (including individuals providing education and rehabilitation services), employers, or other individuals who provide services to, employ, or are otherwise substantially involved in the major life functions of such child" (20 U.S.C. § 1401(2)). Since assistive technology and services must be considered in each student's IEP, then if the IEP spells out the provision of training/technical assistance for certain professionals as part of the assistive technology services for a student, then the state/district is obligated to provide that training/technical assistance to the teacher as specified in the IEP.

Q. There are lots of different programs, from Medicaid to vocational rehabilitation for example, that have some responsibilities for providing assistive technology. How should the school district or local education agency work with these other programs, and who pays for what?

A. The school district or local education agency (LEA) is ultimately responsible for providing assistive technology devices and services. But other federal or state laws may require a device or service to be purchased by non-education agencies. Such agencies cannot abrogate their responsibility even though the child is in school, and IDEA states that the financial responsibility of public non-education agencies, including Medicaid and other public insurers obligated under federal or state law or assigned responsibility under state policy, always takes precedence over the financial responsibility of the LEA (20 U.S.C. § 1412(a)(12)(A)(i)). On the other hand, the LEA cannot simply wait for another agency to provide a service, particularly if there is a delay that jeopardizes the receipt of services listed in the child's IEP, thus preventing the provision of a free appropriate public education. Although IDEA mandates that the chief executive officer of the state—such as the state superintendent of instruction or the commissioner of education—take responsibility for creating agreements among agencies to cover the costs of providing a free appropriate public education, it also states that the LEA must provide the service in the interim (20 U.S.C. § 1412(a)(12)(B)(i)).

Q. What funding sources can the state use to finance assistive technology devices and services?

A. States have considerable flexibility in funding. They are permitted to use funds "To support the use of technology, including technology with universal design principles and assistive technology devices, to maximize accessibility to the general education curriculum for children with disabilities" (34 C.F.R. § 300.704(b)(4)(v)). The Department of Education's *Educating Blind and Visually Impaired Students; Policy Guidance* also states that "In meeting the assistive technology needs of blind and visually impaired students, public agencies may use whatever State, local, Federal, and private sources of support available in the State to finance required services" (65 Fed. Reg. 36590 (2000)).

Q. When should assistive technology be considered for students with disabilities?

A. As early as possible, according to the policy guidance document *Educating Blind and Visually Impaired Students* (2000). Infancy is not too soon to consider assistive technology for students with vision loss.

Q. Are very young children, even infants and toddlers, entitled to assistive technology devices and services?

A. As with Part B (for children and youth ages 3 to 21), Part C of IDEA (describing early intervention services for infants and toddlers through age 2) includes assistive technology devices and services among the array of developmental, early intervention services that may be provided to meet the developmental needs of an infant or toddler. In accordance with Part C's focus on the infant or toddler's family, the definition of assistive technology service in the regulations for implementing Part C includes training or technical assistance for the child as well as—if appropriate—the child's family (34 CFR § 303.13).

For example, infants who are legally blind or who function at the definition of blindness (like their pre-school and school-aged counterparts) are eligible, through their states, to receive products from the American Printing House for the Blind. An early intervention provider or other authorized person can order and receive assistive technologies—such as light boxes and Sensory Learning Kits—and then bring these materials to the infant/toddler's home. The early intervention provider should provide orientation and instruction to both the child and his/her family members so that the assistive technologies can be used throughout the child's day in a natural learning environment (a home and/or day-care setting).

Q. Does IDEA cover assistive technology needed for use in settings other than the classroom?

A. According to *Educating Blind and Visually Impaired Students; Policy Guidance,* the regulations (34 C.F.R. § 300.105(b)) provide that such decisions are made by the child's IEP Team. The IEP Team can determine that a child needs access to a school-purchased device outside of the classroom in order to receive a free appropriate public education. If it is in the IEP, it must be provided at no cost to parents.

Q. What is the relationship between assistive technology and braille literacy?

A. Assistive technology devices and services are viewed as essential components of literacy for students who are blind as well as those with low vision. As the Department of Education's *Policy Guidance on Educating Blind and Visually Impaired Students* states:

> IEP teams must ensure that appropriate assistive technology is provided to facilitate necessary braille instruction. Likewise, for children with low vision, instruction in the appropriate utilization of functional vision and in the effective use of low vision aids requires regular and intensive intervention from knowledgeable and appropriately trained personnel (65 Fed. Reg. 36589 (2000)).

The *Policy Guidance* document also acknowledges that braille readers may need assistive technology devices for writing and composition (65 Fed. Reg. 36589 (2000)) and goes on to emphasize that decisions about assistive technology are individual determinations made by the IEP team, according to the needs of the child.

Q. What is the difference between an evaluation and an assessment, what about standardized testing, and how are evaluations and/or assessments conducted for students who are blind or visually impaired?

A. Sometimes the terms "evaluation" and "assessment" are used interchangeably, and because the two terms do have very similar meanings but particular uses, sometimes even educators and policy makers confuse the two. The term "evaluation" in the special education context should be used to refer to the specific activities and techniques that a professional, such as a teacher of students with visual impairments (TVI) undertakes to determine what kinds of specialized instruction, if any, a student should receive in order to obtain a free appropriate public education. For example, a Learning Media Assessment (LMA), in spite of its name, is an evaluation exercise administered by a TVI for the purpose of determining how a child with vision loss learns most effectively and through which medium or modality, such as braille, use of remaining vision, or both.

In contrast, the term "assessment" is best used to refer to examinations (such as high stakes or other standardized testing) administered to all students in school but which may need to be modified or otherwise administered in some specialized ways for those students who have disabilities. In general, students with vision loss receive the same assessments as students without disabilities, with the appropriate accommodations and modifications, which may include the use of assistive technology. Strictly speaking, while IDEA and another longstanding public education statute, the Elementary and Secondary Education Act, place certain obligations on states and schools to provide students with vision loss all the appropriate accommodations they may need to have equal access to school-, district-, or state-wide assessments administered to all students, it is landmark civil rights legislation, the Americans with Disabilities Act (ADA) and section 504 of the Rehabilitation Act, which enshrine the right of students with disabilities to the accommodations that states and schools must offer. Putting it another way, there is one set of federal law that establishes rights for people with disabilities, and there is another complementary set of federal laws that both direct and fund states, districts, and schools to do the right thing.

With regard to evaluations, the Department of Education's *Policy Guidance outlines the purpose and function of the kinds of assistive technology-relevant evaluations that students with vision loss are entitled to:*

> An assessment of a child's vision status generally would include the nature and extent of the child's visual impairment and its effect, for example, on the child's ability to learn to read, write, do mathematical calculations, and *use computers and other assistive technology*, as well as the child's ability to be involved in and progress in the general curriculum. For children with low vision, this type of assessment also generally should include an evaluation of the child's *ability to utilize low vision aids*, as well as a learning media assessment and a

functional vision assessment" (65 Fed. Reg. 36587 (2000); emphasis added).

Q. How do IEP teams decide which assistive technologies will benefit children who are blind and visually impaired?

A. IEP Teams consider multiple sources of information when composing an individual student's IEP, including

- the child's strengths
- the parents' concerns;
- the most recent evaluation results;
- the academic, developmental, and functional needs of the child; and
- consideration of special factors, such as braille and assistive technology (20 U.S.C. § 1414(d)(3)).

The team makes decisions about an individual child's IEP based on how the child will access the general education curriculum and ultimately how a free appropriate public education will be achieved. There is no magic formula. As already noted, the IEP team must consider the child's instructional needs in reading and writing and whether assistive technology can assist access to the curriculum.

Q. Would personal devices such as eyeglasses be considered assistive technology?

A. In the preamble to the IDEA regulations, the U.S. Department of Education explains that,

As a general matter, public agencies are not responsible for providing personal devices, such as eyeglasses or hearing aids that a child with a disability requires, regardless of whether the child is attending school. However, if it is not a surgically implanted device and a child's IEP team determines that the child requires a personal device (e.g., eyeglasses) in order to receive FAPE [free appropriate public education], the public agency must ensure that the device is provided at no cost to the child's parents (71 Fed. Reg. 46581 (2006)).

As a general rule, eyeglasses are considered personal devices because the child uses them out of school as well as during school hours. However, there may be cases where a student needs special eyeglasses, such as bifocals, or low vision devices (magnifiers or telescopes), without which he or she would not be able to see the chalkboard, read the computer screen, or complete mathematics exercises. In such cases, the eyeglasses or low vision device could be considered assistive technology and, therefore, provided at no cost to the student's parents, whether or not the item is also used outside the classroom. The key is how the child attains access to the classroom curriculum, not necessarily whether the child needs a particular device. The determination is made by the IEP team.

Further clarification of this issue is provided in the Department of Education's *Educating Blind and Visually*

Impaired Students; Policy Guidance (2000). This document informed local education agencies that decisions about assistive technology devices for students with vision loss should be made "on a case-by-case basis," and that

> consideration of the use of school-purchased assistive technology devices in a child's home or in other settings may be required. If the child's IEP team determines that the child needs to have access to a school-purchased device at home or in another setting in order to receive FAPE, a statement to this effect must be included in the child's IEP, the child's IEP must be implemented as written, and the device must be provided at no cost to the parents (65 Fed. Reg. 36590 (2000)).

Q. What is the National Instructional Materials Accessibility Standard (NIMAS)?

A. The National Instructional Materials Accessibility Standard (NIMAS) applies to print instructional materials published after August 18, 2006, and is defined as "the standard established by the Secretary [of Education] to be used in the preparation of electronic files suitable and used solely for efficient conversion into specialized formats" (20 U.S.C. § 1474(e)(3)(B)). NIMAS creates a standardized electronic file format that publishers will use to allow their print materials to be converted to a variety of specialized formats that are accessible to students with print disabilities.

Q. What are a state's responsibilities under NIMAS?

A. IDEA (20 U.S.C. § 1412(a)(23)) requires a state to

- submit a plan that assures the Department of Education that the state has policies and procedures in place to adopt NIMAS;
- to provide materials to students with vision loss and other print disabilities in a timely manner, whether or not it coordinates with the National Instructional Materials Access Center;
- to contract with publishers to prepare and submit the NIMAS file;
- to purchase materials from the publisher; and
- to "work collaboratively with the State agency responsible for assistive technology programs" (20 U.S.C. § 1412(a)(23)(d)).

Q. What is the National Instructional Materials Access Center and what are its duties?

A. IDEA (20 U.S.C. § 1474(e)(1)) established the National Instructional Materials Access Center (NIMAC) at the American Printing House for the Blind. NIMAC's responsibilities are to

- receive and maintain a catalog of materials created in NIMAS files;
- provide accessible print instructional materials at no cost to students with disabilities in elementary and secondary schools; and

- to "develop, adopt, and publish procedures to protect against copyright infringement" (20 U.S.C. § 1474(e)(2)).

Q. Why should I care about the NIMAS and NIMAC, and what do they have to do with assistive technology?

A. The NIMAS and NIMAC are the mechanisms that were put in place for the purpose of assisting states and school districts in providing students with vision loss or other so-called print disabilities access to printed textbooks and related materials in formats usable by them at the same time as their classmates without disabilities receive their standard print materials. These mechanisms have dramatically im-proved the timeliness of accessible materials and, particularly in tandem with the growing availability and afford-ability of refreshable braille displays, have helped to support braille literacy. Prior to NIMAS and NIMAC, states, school districts, and even individual teachers of students with visual impair-ments, had to navigate a labyrinth of obstacles to obtain an electronic ver-sion of a given textbook from a pub-lisher which would, inevitably, not possess the structure and other char-acteristics needed to be efficiently rendered into braille or other formats. The NIMAS and NIMAC help to stream-line the process of both obtaining con-vertible versions of texts from publishers and ensuring the quality of such versions. It is important to know, however, that the NIMAS and NIMAC pertain to the accessibility of printed instructional materials. Multimedia and other natively electronic instructional materials are outside the scope of NIMAS and NIMAC. Nevertheless, IDEA, as well as other disability civil rights laws as discussed below, place a clear obligation on states and schools to ensure equal educational opportunity and access, meaning that even though there is not a comparable structure in place to manage multimedia and other electronic materials as there is for printed texts, it is the responsibility of states and schools to either purchase accessible electronic materials or to adapt them for full and equal use by students with disabilities.

Q. If a student does not need or qualify for special education and related services, does that mean that schools have no obligation to provide assistive technology?

A. No. Just because a child may not be considered a special education student does not mean that the state or school district has no responsibility to provide the student with appropriate assistive technology. IDEA pertains to students who must receive specialized instruc-tion in order to participate in and pro-gress in the general education curriculum. However, even if it is deter-mined that a particular student does not require such specialized instruction and is therefore not per se eligible for special education and related services under IDEA, that student may never-theless be an individual with a disability protected by the Americans with

Disabilities Act (ADA) and section 504 of the Rehabilitation Act. Both Title II of the ADA and section 504 require that public schools provide reasonable accommodations to students with disabilities, accommodations which most assuredly can include the provision of specific assistive technology devices. School districts will frequently develop so-called 504 plans for those students who require an array of accommodations to participate fully in school, meaning that students and parents can, and should, work with school administrators to determine what kind of assistive technology may be needed. However, typically 504 plans are not the right vehicle for obtaining instruction in the use of assistive technology. Putting it another way, section 504 may get a particular device in the hands of a student, but if the student requires instruction in the use of the device, such instruction is provided and paid for under IDEA. Remember that the concept of assistive technology is a two-fold concept and should always be thought of as being inclusive of both devices and services. Since training in the use of assistive technology is critical, not just for a given piece of equipment but for the use of a variety of different tools, simply relying on a 504 plan to acquire a particular device may not meet all of a student's needs in the more complete way that IDEA is intended to achieve.

Q. What rights do post-secondary students have to assistive technology devices and services at the vocational and college levels?

A. While there is not a comparable system to IDEA at the post-secondary level, people with disabilities who enroll in vocational, technical, college/university, and professional degree programs have rights under the Americans with Disabilities Act (ADA) and section 504 of the Rehabilitation Act. As a technical legal matter, public post-secondary educational institutions will likely be covered by both Title II of the ADA (which pertains to the programs and activities of state and local government entities) and section 504 that covers recipients of federal financial assistance. While it is frequently the case that private colleges and universities receive federal financial assistance in some fashion that brings them under section 504, generally speaking, private post-secondary educational institutions are covered by Title III of the ADA (pertaining to public accommodations). Entities covered by ADA Title II have a slightly greater obligation to provide accommodations and make modification to their programs and activities for people with disabilities than do entities covered by ADA Title III. Public entities covered by ADA Title II must honor the person with a disability's preference for this or that particular accommodation, though ultimately the choice of which accommodation will be provided remains with the public entity. Private entities covered by ADA Title III are not under any kind of obligation to honor the preference of the person with a disability.

Post-secondary educational institutions must afford students with disabilities effective communication and the opportunity for full and equal participation in their educational programs. This means that, unless an institution can demonstrate that an undue burden would result from having to provide certain accommodations or from making modifications to their educational programs and services, such accommodations, and modifications must be provided. These accessibility obligations can potentially touch every aspect and function of an educational institution's operation, from the compliance of its online course delivery system with recognized web accessibility standards, to the production of class materials in specialized formats, to the need to work individually with a given student to address a student's unique combination of accessibility needs. Generally, post-secondary institutions, not unlike K-12 schools, are not expected to provide personal items like eyeglasses. However, if a student requires specific assistive technology devices in order to fully participate in the institution's educational programs, and providing such devices does not constitute an undue burden, then the devices must be provided.

Two brief case studies should illustrate the obligations of post-secondary educational institutions. The first case illustrates how claims of disability discrimination can be resolved to ensure that the assistive technology needs of students with disabilities are met. In 2016, Miami University in Ohio reached a settlement agreement with the U.S. Justice Department and a number of the university's students with disabilities, a settlement agreement that, as of this writing, is considered the gold standard in articulating the accessibility obligations of post-secondary educational institutions. (Read the full text of the settlement agreement at https://www.ada.gov/miami_university_cd.html). While the settlement agreement is only binding on Miami University per se and does not have the authority of a formal court decision, the agreement has put colleges and universities across the country on notice that accommodating students with disabilities requires a comprehensive, institution-wide approach for ensuring accessibility. Miami University not only agreed to ensure online accessibility and production of materials in accessible formats moving forward, but Miami also agreed to work individually with each student with a disability to assess each student's assistive technology needs.

The second case illustration should provide some clarity as to how significant the accessibility obligation is and how limited is the undue burden defense. In *Argenyi v. Creighton University*, 703 F. 3d. 441 (8th Cir. 2013), a medical school student with hearing loss requested extensive real-time captioning services for class lectures. The university refused claiming that the hundreds of hours of very expensive services requested would be unduly burdensome. However, the court rejected the undue burden claim noting that the question is not whether the cost of particular accommodations should be compared to the cost of a student's tuition or to any other measure; the question is whether it would be unduly burdensome for the institution to accommodate the student in light of the institution's overall capacity and resources.

So, what these two illustrations demonstrate is that the obligation to ensure full participation by students with disabilities extends to the need to account for students' assistive technology needs, and the costs for meeting those needs would have to be fairly extraordinary to rise to a level at which educational institutions can rightfully claim an undue burden. Of course, as always, everything depends on the unique circumstances of a given situation.

Q. What assistive technology resources are available to working-age adults who are unemployed and/or who are seeking employment?

A. The short answer here is that a working-aged individual with a disability who is not working and who is seeking employment can turn to the vocational rehabilitation (VR) system for assistance in acquiring both the necessary skills training and the assistive technologies that can prepare the VR client to join or reenter the workforce. The VR system also assists individuals who may be at risk of losing a job they may already have because of the onset of disability and the individual's unpreparedness to make necessary adjust-

ments to retain employment. The VR system is a federal and state partnership wherein the U.S. Congress makes approximately $3.5 billion annually available to states to provide a host of services, including assistive technology. About half of the states have a VR agency that is dedicated to serving clients who are blind or visually impaired; the balance of the states have a single VR agency that serves all clients within the state who have disabilities.

In the VR system, the key relationship that drives the provision of any and all services is the relationship between the VR client and that client's counselor. In very general terms, a counselor will work with the client to identify employment goals and formulate a plan for the client to pursue that involves the receipt of specific evaluation, instruction, and skills development. Title I of the Rehabilitation Act and its implementing regulations, administered by the U.S. Department of Education, are clear that assistive technology devices and services must be part of the critical conversations between the client and counselor. While clients have a right for their assistive technology needs to be met, those needs will vary from client to client. Whether this or that specific piece of equipment should be provided by the VR agency is a case-by-case determination. The candid assessment of many people with vision loss across the country is that some VR agencies, and certainly individual counselors, are more flexible and willing to be more experimental with various technologies than are other counselors and agencies. In many ways, while the counselor-client relationship should be one that is marked by cooperation and consensus, often the relationship is a negotiation that places a counselor who is trying to cope with the pressures of a bureaucracy with limited funding against a client who is eager to try the latest and greatest device. In the event that the counsel-client relationship breaks down, there are a number of next steps to consider, but the VR system has a built-in mechanism, the Client Assistance Program (CAP) to which clients can turn for help in resolving conflicts. On balance, however, counselors and agencies work hard to put appropriate assistive technologies into the hands of their clients.

Finally, private not-for-profit organizations may also be a source of support for training in the use of various assistive technologies and may even be able to help in whole or in part with the cost of devices. For nearly a century, Lions Clubs across the country have made the provision of eyeglasses and many other forms of assistance available to people with vision loss. Moreover, about half of the states in the country have at least one private community-based nonprofit agency that serves people who are blind or visually impaired; a few states have quite a number of such organizations. Indeed, many state VR agencies partner with their private nonprofit counterparts to provide assistive technology devices and services. While a private agency is generally speaking under no formal

legal obligation to make assistive technology devices and services available (they are charitable organizations), such agencies may have such obligations if they are formally partnered with a state VR agency. However, even if no public dollars support the private agency at all, the organization's mission to serve people with vision loss will nevertheless mean that services are often made available free of charge.

Q. What responsibilities do employers have to provide assistive technology devices and services to their employees with disabilities?

A. In general, employers must provide reasonable accommodations to their employees with disabilities. Title I of the landmark Americans with Disabilities Act (ADA) bars discrimination against people with disabilities by private employers with fifteen or more employees; a number of state laws go even farther and bar discrimination by private employers with merely one employee. It is important to know, however, that an employer cannot be held liable under the ADA for failing to provide an employee with a reasonable accommodation when the employer does not know that a reasonable accommodation is required or even that the employee has a disability for which such an accommodation is needed. Therefore, an employee's disability must be known to the employer, and the employer and employee need to communicate about the need for any reasonable accommodations. Employers are not required to provide those accommodations that would place an undue hardship, financial or otherwise, on the employer. An employer may not disqualify a candidate for a job because that candidate may need reasonable accommodations; the decision to hire the candidate must be made on the candidate's merits regardless of whether the candidate will or will not require reasonable accommodations.

There is no bright line test as to whether this or that particular accommodation will be reasonable for any employer to make. A transnational corporation with tens of thousands of employees would have a difficult time demonstrating that the purchase of several thousands of dollars' worth of equipment allowing an individual employee to perform a fulltime job would constitute an undue hardship. But given that most accommodations, including assistive technology-related accommodations, are decreasing in cost, even modestly sized employers would need to make an especially compelling case that this or that accommodation would be too difficult to provide. The cost of the accommodation is not compared to the employee's salary or to the budget for the specific department where the employee works, but is rather weighed against the overall capacity of the employer as a whole. Sometimes it is not necessarily the cost but the maintenance or ongoing complexity of assistive technology, or its interaction with a company's native information systems, that comes into question. But again, whether the accommodations involved are too costly or too difficult to manage

are assessed in light of an employer's overall staff and financial resources. Candidly, it is the experience of the vision loss community that it is not the need for potentially expensive technology that discourages employers from hiring people with vision loss; if discrimination happens, it is happening at the hiring stage and has much more to do with an employer's misunderstandings and negative attitudes about vision loss and disability generally.

Public employers, such as federal, state, or local government agencies also have nondiscrimination and reasonable accommodation obligations. Title II of the ADA, the Rehabilitation Act, and many state and local provisions of law require public employers to make reasonable accommodations for their employees, and the same kind of undue hardship analysis about such accommodations as described above applies here. Federal government employees also benefit from the provisions of section 508 of the Rehabilitation Act that requires federal agencies to buy, maintain, and use technologies that are accessible to people with disabilities. While the federal government has a mixed track record of compliance with section 508, in principle, a federal employee is not only entitled to reasonable accommodations in the form of assistive technology devices and services; employees should also be able to rely upon their federal agency employers to already have office equipment and other mainstream technology in place that is usable by employees with disabilities. A number of states have adopted state-level policies similar to those of section 508, meaning that many states honor the right of their public employees to expect accessible mainstream technology in the workplace.

Q. Do commercial businesses, such as banks, retailors, hotels and restaurants have any responsibilities for offering assistive technology devices and services?

A. The short answer is yes, but remember that the provision of assistive technology, like any other accommodation or modification provided under Title III of the ADA, must be reasonable and not result in an undue burden. Generally, public accommodations must ensure full and equal access to their goods, services, benefits, and other opportunities. Public accommodations must comply with recognized standards that ensure that their patrons who use assistive technology can access online content. Many retailers have been asked, and have agreed, to install point of sale machines with accessibility features that allow patrons to enter their personal identification numbers privately and independently. Museums are increasingly making their exhibits more accessible through digital audio guides. Pharmacies are increasingly providing their customers with both low and high tech means for identifying and reading prescription drug container labeling. These and many other examples illustrate how public accommodations can and should either make use of assistive technology to welcome their customers and patrons with disabilities or create environments that enable patrons to use their own personal assistive technology effectively.

One issue that has given advocates reason for concern has to do with public accommodations that operate exclusively online. It is crystal clear that the ADA requires places of public accommodation to make their facilities physically accessible to people with disabilities, and such public accommodations are also expected to make their websites accessible through compliance to recognized web accessibility standards. However, as of this writing, courts continue to be split over the question of whether online only commercial businesses are in fact places of public accommodation that are required to be accessible under the ADA. In National Association of the Deaf v. Netflix, 869 F. Supp. 2d 196 (D. Mass. 2012), the court concluded that an online only provider of digital video content must provide captioning and is otherwise subject to the accessibility obligations of ADA Title III. However, few other courts have come to similar conclusions, frequently deciding rather that the proprietor of a website alleged to be inaccessible must also operate a physical facility that is in some way related to that website if an ADA claim is to be sustained. However this issue is ultimately resolved, it is clear that the ADA broadly requires public accommodations to make websites accessible, which among other things means that their websites must be compatible with commonly used assistive technology.

Q. What about entertainment facilities, such as movie theaters, sports arenas, and on-stage live performance venues?

A. Yes, just like any other public accommodations, these kinds of facilities must be accessible to people with disabilities. In fact, the regulations implementing Title III of the ADA explicitly provide that movie theaters must offer patrons devices that can receive audio description for those movies that the theaters show that are described (the theaters are not required to provide description for movies that are not originally produced and distributed to theaters without description). Similarly, just as assistive listening devices should be provided to patrons of live theatre productions, so too should live performance venues offer audio description and the devices necessary to receive it. However, there are no unambiguous rules in place governing the provision of audio description during live performances, meaning that patrons interested in this accommodation should request it and advocate for it if it is not provided by the venue. In such instances, all of the reasonableness and undue burden analysis discussed earlier in this appendix applies.

Q. What assistive technology devices and services are made available to people with vision loss through public or private health care systems?

A. While the Medicare and Medicaid systems will provide an array of prosthetics and durable medical equipment to address a variety of medical and rehabilitative needs, neither system provides any appreciable coverage for the kinds of assistive technology suited to people with vision loss. Why? Arguments have been made over the years that devices such as low vision aids or other devices can help with the reading of prescription medication labeling and other activities related to personal health management. However, the regulations issued by the Centers for Medicare and Medicaid Services (CMS), the federal agency that oversees these programs, are very narrowly written to restrict coverage to equipment that does not merely provide convenience but which is inherently medical in nature. Thus, CMS allows for Medicare coverage for blood glucose meters that have accessibility features that are integral to the device (e.g., speech output built into the device itself). However, if a blood glucose meter must be physically or wirelessly connected to separately obtained assistive technology to provide speech output (technology that might very well also offer a wide variety of other benefits, such as an accessible smart phone with an app that wirelessly connects with the meter), Medicare will not generally cover that assistive technology.

Naturally, CMS tries to narrowly tailor all of their coverage rules where equipment is concerned because of the potentially enormous costs that broad coverage would incur. Nevertheless, the distinctions that CMS often makes can seem artificial and arbitrary, and the vision loss community has long been frustrated by the obvious inequity that exists between coverage for equipment meeting, for instance, orthopedic needs and coverage for equipment addressing blindness or visual impairment. It is precisely this inequity that has led vision loss advocacy groups to urge Congress to change the Medicare statute and drive CMS to modify its regulations to strike a better balance between virtually no coverage for devices meeting the needs of people who are blind or visually impaired and coverage for any conceivable piece of assistive technology regardless of how attenuated its connection might be to health care and medical necessity.

The Medicaid system is slightly different but is plagued by many of the same kinds of limitations as exist in Medicare. The Medicaid program relies heavily on the individual states to specify exactly which services and equipment each state will and will not cover. While there have been isolated reports of Medicaid coverage being extended for a few items of assistive technology, these are exceptions to the general rule and result from extensive challenges and appeals by individuals who are blind or visually impaired, their parents and advocates. Again, Medicaid does offer coverage for devices that are clearly medical in nature and that meet a wide range of health-related needs but not typically for vision loss-related needs. What makes the inequity in the Medicare and Medicaid systems particularly frustrating, beyond the denial of coverage of course, is that private

health insurers often take their lead from the public health insurers in terms of what they will and will not cover. Consequently, while the occasional exception to the rule is reported now and then, there are generally no private health insurance plans that provide coverage for the range of assistive technology devices and services that could be of tremendous benefit to policyholders with vision loss.

Q. How might the tax and Social Security systems support the provision of assistive technology?

A. Both the Internal Revenue Code and the Social Security Act acknowledge that assistive technology can be expensive. A competent tax advisor can help people with vision loss make use of available IRS rules allowing the costs incurred in purchasing assistive technology to reduce one's overall annual personal income tax obligation. Likewise, for Social Security Disability Insurance (SSDI) beneficiaries and Supplemental Security Income (SSI) recipients, myriad and sometimes complex rules allow the costs incurred in the purchase and maintenance of assistive technology to figure into the calculations that can ultimately keep cash and health care benefits coming even while beneficiaries/recipients earn income from work.

Particularly for individuals with disabilities who are, or want to be, self-employed and are receiving SSI or SSDI, the allowances for the purchase of assistive technology along with the other disability-related expenses recognized in the rules can really add up. In the Social Security system, benefits continue even if one has gone back to work when one can report certain incurred expenses that make that work activity possible. The frequently significant expense of assistive technology can therefore help to keep beneficiaries/recipients from exceeding allowable earnings limits and losing valuable cash and health care benefits.

Q. What assistive technology-related resources are available to older working-age adults and seniors with vision loss?

A. As noted earlier, America's public health systems do not typically provide coverage for the specific assistive technologies that would be of most benefit to people with vision loss. Given that both the Medicare and Medicaid programs are intended to serve retirees, and given that older people comprise the largest age group within the national population of people with vision loss, the failure of our national health care systems to address these unmet needs is a significant public health challenge.

The only national program that is specifically aimed at addressing the unique needs of older people with vision loss is the Independent Living Services for Older Individuals who are Blind (OIB) program. Established under Title VII, Chapter 2 of the Rehabilitation Act, the OIB program is a federal and state partnership that frequently works in tandem with private agencies for the blind to deliver services and supports to enable people 55 years of age and older with vision loss for whom employment is not likely or desired to remain self sufficient and independent at home and in community. The OIB program specifically provides:

- **independent living skills** using specialized adaptive devices and techniques for personal and household management.

- **communication skills** using large print, writing guides, and time-telling devices, and using braille for reading or labeling and making notes.

- **mobility skills** using specific orientation and mobility techniques, long canes, and other mobility tools for safe and independent travel.

- **low-vision therapy** using special low-vision optical and adaptive devices to make the most of remaining vision.

- **adjustment to vision loss** through connecting with and learning from others with vision loss to accept and effectively live with visual impairment.

The extent to which low vision devices and other types of assistive technology are made available to clients of the OIB program will of course vary from state to state and will depend upon the particular interests, needs and capabilities of each client. As noted earlier, state vocational rehabilitation (VR) agencies are also able to provide employment-related services to clients for whom an employment goal is appropriate. This means that someone who is 55 years of age or older who wants to enter or remain in the workforce should be served by the VR program. The very limited national resources of the OIB program should be used for those clients for whom employment is not the intended outcome. As of this writing, only about two percent of the eligible national population of individuals likely to benefit from the OIB program is currently receiving services. This is because congressional appropriations for this singular resource have never come close to meeting the overwhelming national need.

Q. What assistive technology resources are available to people with deafblindness?

A. As many, if not most, individuals with deafblindness have some residual vision or hearing, many persons with deafblindness can benefit from the same AT devices and services as those used by individuals with solely vision or solely hearing loss. There are, however, a few helpful resources, in the form of national programs, which can benefit individuals with deafblindness, specifically. One resource, iCanConnect, is a national program that provides qualified persons with both significant vision and hearing loss with free equipment and training. This program provides AT supports such as accessories, braille devices, computers, mobile devices, phones, signalers, and software to those who are deemed eligible after an initial evaluation. Information about eligibility and application details can be found at http://iCanConnect.org. Another resource, the National Center on Deaf-Blindness (NCDB), is a national technical assistance center funded by the federal Department of Education that works to improve the quality of life for children who are deaf-blind and their families. Their main website (https://nationaldb.org/) has a wealth of information related to supporting individuals with deafblindness. Further, after navigating away from their main page, the NCDB has an AT website (https://nationaldb.org/library/list/40) where they list: information related to specific AT initiatives in the field of deafblindness, websites that provide up-to-date information about newest advances in AT that support those with deafblindness, and recorded presentations and modules on the topic of AT for individuals with deafblindness.

Q. How are the rights of people with disabilities to accessible information and technology recognized internationally?

A. The United Nations Convention on the Rights of Persons with Disabilities (UNCRPD), which entered into force on May 3, 2008, was the first international human rights treaty of the 21st century. As of July, 2017, 174 countries - not including the United States - are parties to the treaty.

Important discussions of accessible and assistive technology appear in four articles of the UNCRPD, including in

Article 4: General Obligations, Article 9: Accessibility, Article 21: Freedom of Expression and Access to Information, and Article 29: Participation in Political and Public Life. The UNCRPD requires ratifying nations to:

- undertake and promote research and development surrounding the availability and use of new technologies, including information and communications technology (ICT) and systems suitable for persons with disabilities, as well as mobility aids, devices, and assistive technologies.

- give priority to affordable technologies and must provide information to persons with disabilities about the Internet, mobility aids, devices, and assistive technologies, including newly developed technologies.

- to provide public information through accessible formats and technologies, appropriate for different kinds of disabilities, at no additional cost. Countries must encourage providers of information via mass media and the Internet to make their services available to persons with disabilities.

- facilitate the use of assistive and new technologies to protect the right of persons with disabilities to vote by secret ballot and stand for elections.

Countries that are party to the treaty must submit regular reports on their implementation of these and other requirements of the UNCRPD. Learn more at https://www.un.org/development/desa/disabilities/

Although the UNCRPD has brought considerable attention to the rights of persons with disabilities at an international level, there remains much work to be done to raise awareness and to achieve access and equality around the globe. In the developing world, access to assistive technology often is a matter of income and social status. Notable organizations working to improve standards and increase access to assistive technology around the world include:

- Global Initiative for Inclusive ICTs (G3ict) (http://www.g3ict.org/)

- World Wide Web Consortium (W3C) (http://www.w3.org/)

- The World Blind Union's Technology Working Group (http://worldblindunion.org/)

- The World Health Organization's Global Cooperation on Assistive Technology (GATE) program (http://www.who.int/disabilities/technology/gate/)

APPENDIX B
Access Technology Evaluation Checklist For Blind and Low Vision Needs

Credit: (Siu, McDowell, Amandi, Wilton, 2019)

Student's name _____

Date of birth _____

Student's grade or workplace setting _____

Person completing checklist _____

Date(s) of evaluation _____

This AT checklist can help an evaluator document information that is collected throughout an assistive technology evaluation. Prior to completing this checklist, the evaluator is best prepared if the student's information from a comprehensive Functional Vision Evaluation (FVE)*, Learning Media Evaluation (LME), clinical low vision evaluation (if available), and relevant background medical information are available. Some of the background information can be used to fill out parts of the checklist. Based on prior assessment data, a student's technology needs will dictate which sections of the AT checklist to focus on; not every section of the checklist will be filled out for every student.

(Refer to the Needs Assessment to determine starting points for a technology evaluation)

Any prescribed eyeglasses or contact lenses should be worn as prescribed throughout all evaluation activities.

The AT Checklist covers the following categories of access technology:

- Technologies for Accessing Printed Text & Images (Chapter 2)
- Technologies for Accessing Digital Text (Chapter 3)
- Technologies for Authoring (Chapter 4)
- Strategies for Accessing Multimedia and Data (Chapter 6)

If an evaluator needs more information about how technology considerations support selection of specific devices, refer to the relevant chapter in *Access Technology for Blind and Low Vision Accessibility, 2nd Ed.* (Siu & Presley, 2020).

The following forms are recommended for use with this checklist:

- Background Information for Technology Evaluation
- Digital Workflow Planning Tool
- Needs Assessment Template
- Environmental Assessment

*The FVE must incorporate use of formal and informal tools and methods for data collection. A comprehensive FVE process for every student includes assessment considerations related to ocular and neurological visual impairments.

Tools for Visual Access to Printed Media

Does the student experience visual fatigue? _____ Yes _____ No

If yes:

- When does the student experience visual fatigue? (Examples: After 10 minutes of reading visually, when stressed or ill)

_____

_____

- ☐ Describe indications of visual fatigue for this student:

_____

_____

- How long can a student use his/her vision before experiencing visual fatigue?

_____

- What does the student do to recover and how long does it take the student to recover from visual fatigue? _____

_____

- Be sure to evaluate tools for auditory access for tasks that cause visual fatigue—dual media and multimodal access can reduce or eliminate visual fatigue.

Non-optical Tools

List any non-optical tools the student uses currently and note the condition of each tool (e.g., new, used - scratched):

_____

_____

_____

EVALUATE:

Large Print

- Preferred font style: _____
- Optimal print size in the preferred font style (lower case letter height in inches):

_____

- Reading speed at the preferred font style and print size _____
- When reading at this font style and print size, student experiences visual fatigue after _____ minute
- Student prefers increased . . .
  - ☐ Line spacing
    - ☐ Double-space
    - ☐ Other: _____

☐ Word spacing
☐ Character spacing (kerning)
☐ Margins

Reading and book stands, slant boards

- Does it need to be portable? _____ Yes _____ No
- Does the student need to use the stand to write?
  _____ Yes _____ No
- Does the paper media need to be held in place for the student?
  _____ Yes _____ No
- Does the student need an adjustable viewing angle?
  _____ Yes _____ No
- Size considerations for the student's desk? _____ Yes _____ No

Acetate Overlays, Typoscopes, Line Guides

- Does the student have glare sensitivity? _____ Yes _____ No
- Does masking help reduce visual clutter? _____ Yes _____ No
- Does the student require assistance to track lines of text?
  _____ Yes _____ No

Lighting and Contrast

- Does student need task lighting? _____ Yes _____ No
- Describe preferences: _____
- Does the student have reduced contrast sensitivity? _____ Yes _____ No
- Are there other lighting, glare, or contrast considerations to be aware of?
  _____

Optical Devices

Check any optical devices that have been prescribed to the student by a low vision clinic:

- Magnifiers. If checked, provide more information:
  ☐ Brand and model of magnifier:
  _____

  ☐ Magnification power (example: 2x, 5x, etc.):
  _____

  ☐ Built-in illumination? _____ Yes _____ No
  ☐ Is the magnifier: Handheld vs. on a stand vs. rests on the paper (circle one)
  ☐ Lighted or non-lighted? (circle one)
  ☐ When is the student recommended to use this magnifier?
  _____
  _____

  ☐ Other information:
  _____

- Telescopes or monoculars
  - ☐ Brand and model of telescope (monocular):

    _____

  - ☐ Magnification Power and Field (example: 4×12, etc.):

    _____

  - ☐ Focus with (circle one): One hand or both hands?
  - ☐ Spectacle-mounted? _____ Yes _____ No
  - ☐ When is the student recommended to use this telescope or monocular?

    _____

    _____

Video Magnification Systems

List any video magnification systems or CCTV the student uses currently:

_____

_____

_____

EVALUATE:

- What magnification power does the student need?
- Does the student need a display screen with high resolution? (Students who need higher levels of magnification need high resolution to maintain clarity as content is magnified)
  _____ Yes _____ No
- What screen size does the student prefer (See Chapter 3, screen size considerations)
  - ☐ 10-inch
  - ☐ 13-inch
  - ☐ 15-inch
  - ☐ Other: _____
- Will the display screen block the student's view of the board if direct access to the board is needed? _____ Yes _____ No
- What is the student's preferred print size for reading (lower case letter height in inches):

  _____

- Does the system need to be portable? _____ Yes _____ No
  - ☐ If Yes, does the system need to be handheld? _____ Yes _____ No
- Does the system need to be wireless? (not connected to a wall outlet)?
  _____ Yes _____ No
  - ☐ If Yes, what is the necessary battery duration? _____
- Needed features for the viewing application—check all that apply
  - ☐ Onscreen line reading guide
  - ☐ Text masking
  - ☐ Text highlighting
  - ☐ Text-to-speech
  - ☐ Continuous text, scrolling marquee, teleprompter mode
- Does the student have glare, contrast, or lighting considerations? (Refer to previous section "lighting and contrast" if needed) _____ Yes _____ No

If yes—does the student prefer:

☐ Reverse contrast (white font on black background)

☐ Enhanced contrast (of existing colors)

☐ Color filter (select preference)

    ☐ yellow font on blue background

    ☐ yellow font on black background

    ☐ red font on black background

    ☐ greyscale (no colors)

    ☐ other:

_____

- Does the student need magnification to access information at (check all that apply):

    ☐ Near (within arm's length)? _____ Yes _____ No

    ☐ Distance (beyond arm's length)? _____ Yes _____ No

- Identify tasks the video magnification system will be used for:

    ☐ Reading

    ☐ Writing and/or drawing

    ☐ Viewing small physical items (example: dice, soldering circuits)

    ☐ Viewing information on the board. If checked, be sure to evaluate tools for screensharing.

    ☐ Viewing presenters at the front of a room (such as at a conference or school assembly)

- Does the student need a standalone or peripheral video magnifier?

    ☐ Does student have an existing personal computing device, or will anticipate working with a personal computing device in the future?
    _____ Yes _____ No

    ☐ Can the student multitask (switch between different apps and tasks) on one device?
    _____ Yes _____ No

    ☐ How often does the student need video magnification in the classroom or workplace? (Remember: A video magnification system is only necessary to access printed media or for distance viewing when screensharing is unavailable—if a student has a digital copy or screensharing capability, a video magnifier is unnecessary)

    _____

    ☐ Does the student prefer a standalone video magnifier (CCTV) or a peripheral one that could be connected/disconnected from a personal computing device?
    (circle one)   standalone   peripheral

    ☐ Does the student desk space and position in-classroom need to be adjusted or considered based on the number of devices and plug-in requirements?
    If the student prefers a peripheral video magnifier:

☐ How quickly can the student connect the peripheral video magnifier to his or her computing device?

_____

☐ Accessibility and usability of viewing apps

    ☐ Can the student visually access the buttons/icons needed to operate a viewing app or video magnifier? _____ Yes _____ No

If no:

☐ Select a viewing app that is compatible with a screenreader

☐ Select a video magnifier with tactilely distinctive buttons/knobs (or modify/adapt existing buttons/icons)

- What types of tasks will the student use a video magnification system for?

  ☐ Spot reading and shorter visual tasks

  ☐ Longer reading tasks (if this is checked, be sure to evaluate needs for a scanning/OCR system and digital workflow)

Scanning and OCR Systems

- Scanning into a digital format for onscreen magnification and/or use with an annotation tool: Does the student need only visual access to print media?

  _____ Yes   _____ No

- Scanning into an editable digital format for onscreen magnification, adjustment of visual settings, and/or text-to-speech: Would the student benefit from visual and auditory access to print media?

  _____ Yes   _____ No

- Compatibility of scanning apps with the student's personal computing devices:

  ☐ Brand and operating system of mobile computing device (Smartphone, tablet): _____

  _____

  ☐ Brand and operating system of stationary computing device (laptop, desktop):_____

  _____

- Scanning + OCR capabilities: How much information does a student want to scan and access at one time?

  ☐ A whole document

  ☐ One page

  ☐ One paragraph

  ☐ A few sentences

  ☐ A few words

Tools for Tactile Access to Tactile Media

List any currently available . . .

- Devices/tools that the staff and/or student use for alternate media production of tactile media (braillewriters, braille embossers, stereo copiers (thermoform or fuser), 3D printers):

  _____
  _____
  _____

- Devices/tools the student uses currently for tactile access (embossed braille, braille displays, notetakers, tactile graphics, 3D manipulatives):

  _____
  _____
  _____

EVALUATE:
Braille

- Braille reading rate (i.e., words correct per minute):_____
- Braille codes needed (check all that apply):
  ☐ UEB
  ☐ Nemeth
- Student demonstrates fluency when reading braille:
  _____ Yes   _____ No
- Student demonstrates comprehension when reading braille:
  _____ Yes   _____ No
- Student requires tactile access only: Use a scan and OCR system to digitize text and emboss hard copy braille
- Student would benefit from multiple sensory inputs (i.e. tactile and auditory access)—Does the student need a scan and OCR system to digitize text for reading with a braille display and/or screenreader and/or visually?
  _____ Yes   _____ No

☐ Considerations for appropriately sized furniture for positioning and storage of braille materials and
_____

Tactile Graphics

- Does the student have any difficulties with tactile perception?
  _____ Yes   _____ No
- What tactile media experiences does the student have?
  ☐ Collage
  ☐ Embossed graphics
  ☐ Micro-capsule (made with a fuser or swell form graphics machine)
  ☐ Raised-line drawing tools
  ☐ Thermoform
  ☐ Other: _____
- How often does the student encounter images in the classroom that are not adequately represented by a verbal description and which they are unable to access visually?
  ☐ Daily
  ☐ Weekly
  ☐ Monthly
  ☐ Never
- Does the student have difficulties with using effective tactile strategies (e.g., tracking raised lines, locating tactile markers in a spatial array). ?
  _____ Yes   _____ No

Manipulatives and 3D Models

- Does the student encounter instructional or workplace media that are not adequately represented by tactile graphics? _____ Yes   _____ No
- Would the student benefit from learning with tactile manipulatives or 3D models?
  _____ Yes   _____ No

- Does the student have difficulties with motor coordination?

  _____ Yes   _____ No

- Does the student have difficulties with spatial perception?

  _____ Yes   _____ No

Tools for Auditory Access to Printed Media

List any tools for auditory access the student uses currently:

_____

_____

_____

EVALUATE:

- What is the student's current listening speed with adequate comprehension (words per minute (wpm)? _____

- Does the student have difficulties with auditory processing?

  _____ Yes   _____ No

Readers and Visual Interpretation Tools

- Does the student have a human reader listed as a test accommodation?

  _____ Yes   _____ No

  If yes: It is assumed that the student works with a reader regularly to complete non-test activities or interim assessments

- Does the student understand how to categorize information?

  _____ Yes   _____ No

- Determine if visual interpretation apps can be used with live interpreters without supervision. Take appropriate precautions if the student is a minor (under 18 years old) or is legally conserved. Is the student a minor or legally conserved? _____ Yes   _____ No

Scanning, OCR (text recognition), TTS, and Computer Vision Systems

- Would the student benefit from auditory access for (check all that apply):

  ☐ Spot reading or short tasks (on demand auditory access)

  ☐ Continuous reading or longer tasks

  ☐ Menu access

  ☐ Supporting access to information while transition from print to braille literacy

- Does the student require apps that are accessible with a screenreader? (Unable to visually access media controls)

  _____ Yes   _____ No

- What portable personal computing device that the student currently have? (Example: tablet, smartphone) _____

Talking Devices and Apps

- Does the student work in a lab or design environment and would benefit from talking lab or design equipment? _____ Yes   _____ No

- Does the student have any programming experience or interested in learning?

  _____ Yes   _____ No

  ☐ If yes, evaluate options for an electronic prototyping platform and support students to create accessible tools for specific tasks

TECHNOLOGIES FOR ACCESSING DIGITAL TEXT

List any personal computing devices the student uses currently (media player, smartphone, tablet, laptop, desktop, notetaker, etc.). Include: brand, model, device size, processor speed, RAM. What condition is each device in?

_____

_____

_____

_____

_____

_____

_____

EVALUATE:

Does the student benefit from multimodal access to information (visual+auditory, auditory+tactile, visual+tactile+auditory)? If yes, please refer to the Digital Workflow Planning Tool.

Considerations When Evaluating Needs for a Personal Computing Device

- Screen size (if relevant)
  - ○ What does the student prefer? _____
  - ○ How will the student carry a personal computing device?
    - ☐ Backpack (Maximum screen size should not exceed 16")
    - ☐ Rolling bag or cart
    - ☐ Wheelchair
  - ☐ Does the student require portability while working?
    - _____ Yes   _____ No
  - ☐ Resolution when magnifying content onscreen
- Physical set up and positioning of monitor/device
  - ☐ How large is the student's current desk? _____
  - ☐ Is there sufficient storage space for peripheral components and cords?
    - _____ Yes   _____ No
  - ☐ Is the student's desk (circle one):

    shared with others   personal
  - ☐ Will the display screen block the student's view of the board if direct access to the board is needed? _____ Yes   _____ No

- Accessibility of built-in apps, usability of built-in accessibility tools. Which accessibility features does the student need (evaluate each feature when comparing different devices to determine if a built-in feature will suffice or if an add-on tool is needed to deliver that feature that the student needs):
  - ☐ Apps that are accessible with a screenreader
  - ☐ Compatibility with accessible reading and notetaking apps
  - ☐ Screenreader
  - ☐ Text-to-speech (TTS) for Audio-Supported Reading; usability across multiple program applications
  - ☐ Screen magnification; usability when panning, compatibility with a screenreader if needed
  - ☐ Reverse contrast
  - ☐ Larger mouse pointer and cursor

□ Larger fonts

□ Adjustable screen brightness and color temperature

- Flexibility and robustness when switching between various access modes (tactile, auditory, visual)
- Other

    □ Battery life

    □ Time needed for full charge

    □ Availability of local technical support and troubleshooting

Considerations When Selecting A Reading App

- Accessibility with a screen reader and braille display (if student needs a screenreader and/or braille display)
- Usability of app interface

    □ Contrast of buttons and icons

    □ Menu layouts

    □ Ease of accessing accessibility features to adjust visual and auditory settings

- Compatibility with accessible digital talking books and related libraries such as Bookshare
- Compatibility with reading different file formats: DOCX, PDF, EPUB
- Compatibility with personal computing device
- Integrated OCR and TTS features
- Student would like to access narrated audio books from

    □ Learning Ally Including Voicetext (highlighted text + narration)

    □ National Library Service BARD: Braille and Audio Reading Download

    □ Commercial service such as Audible/Kindle with synchronized text and narration

    □ Other

Tools for Visual Access to Digital Text

List any tools for visual access to digital text that the student uses currently:

_____

_____

_____

<u>Evaluate student needs for:</u>

Visual Settings

□ Operating System Display Properties

□ Cursor Display Settings, Pointer Size

□ Font Styles and size

□ Contrast

□ Text highlighting and masking

□ Focus Enhancement

□ Page zoom

Screen Magnification

- Fine motor skill challenges? _____ Yes _____ No
- How does the student prefer to control the screen magnification tool?
  - ☐ Gestures
  - ☐ Keyboard commands
- Preferred font style: _____
- Optimal print size in the preferred font style: (lower case letter height in inches): _____
- Reading speed at the preferred font style and print size: _____
- When reading at this font style and print size, student experiences visual fatigue after _____ minutes. Explore tools for auditory and/or tactile access.
- Student prefers increased . . .
  - ☐ Line spacing
    - ☐ Double-space
    - ☐ Other: _____
  - ☐ Word spacing
  - ☐ Character spacing (kerning)
  - ☐ Margins
- Student prefers a (circle one): window zoom full screen zoom
- Student benefits from multimodal access while using a screen magnification tool—needs compatibility with a screen reader and/or braille display

Tools for Tactile Access to Digital Text

List any notetakers or braille displays the student uses currently:

_____
_____
_____
_____

EVALUATE:

This section will determine which types of braille displays would most benefit the student: Standalone braille notetaker (with built-in operating system), braille display for a personal computing device, braille display with note-taking capabilities ("smart" display)

- Display size
  - ☐ Does the student want a portable braille display?
    _____ Yes _____ No
  - ☐ For prolonged reading tasks, what size display does the student prefer? (How many cells?)
    _____
  - ☐ Are there instructional considerations for what size of a display is needed to support the student's current literacy level and/or displaying math problems?
    _____ Yes _____ No
    If yes, please provide more details: _____
    _____
    _____

- Refresh rate
  - ☐ Does the student want braille to auto advance as text is read?
    _____ Yes _____ No
  - ☐ What is the student's current braille reading speed? _____
- Orientation of navigation buttons; how does the student prefer to manually 'advance to the next line of text?
  - ☐ Using thumbs
  - ☐ Using fingers
- Tactile resolution; how does the student prefer their braille to feel?
  - ☐ Softer dots
  - ☐ Harder dots
- Pin noise; is the student sensitive to how the pins sound as they refresh?
  _____ Yes _____ No
- Compatibility with braille codes; which codes does the student use and encounter? (Check all that apply)
  - ☐ UEB
  - ☐ Nemeth
  - ☐ Computer
  - ☐ Foriegn Languages (identify which ones): _____
  - ☐ Music
- Compatibility with cloud computing platforms; identify which cloud computing platform(s) the student needs to access: (Check all that apply)
  - ☐ Google Drive
  - ☐ Google Classroom
  - ☐ Dropbox
  - ☐ Box
  - ☐ Other: _____
- Connectivity with personal computing devices; when connecting a notetaker or braille display to a personal computing device (i.e., laptop, tablet, smartphone), how does the student prefer to connect?
  - ☐ Wireless (circle one):   Bluetooth   Wifi
  - ☐ Wired (circle one):   USB   Mini-USB   Micro-USB
  - ☐ Other: _____

Tools for Auditory Access to Digital Text

List any text-to-speech (TTS) or screenreader tools the student uses currently:

_____
_____
_____

EVALUATE:
- What is the student's current listening speed with adequate comprehension (list in words per minute (wpm)? _____
- Does the student have any auditory neuropathy or processing considerations?
  _____ Yes _____ No

- Would the student benefit from auditory access for: (check all that apply)
  - ☐ Spot reading or short tasks (on demand auditory access)
  - ☐ Continuous reading or longer tasks
  - ☐ Supporting access to information while transition from print to braille literacy
- Does student need a standalone device/simple interface?
  _____ Yes _____ No
- Does the student prefer to multitask on one device? _____ Yes _____ No
- Can the student visually access the media controls for TTS?
  _____ Yes _____ No
  If no, then explore screenreader options

Considerations When Choosing a Screenreader With a Student

- Compatibility with the student's personal computing device
  - ☐ Windows [i.e. Narrator (built-in), JAWS and NVDA (add-on)]
  - ☐ Apple [i.e. VoiceOver (built-in)]
  - ☐ Browser-based [i.e. ChromeVox (built-in)]
  - ☐ Android [i.e. TalkBack (built-in)]
- Identify a freely available screenreader that can be downloaded to a flash drive for use with public or borrowed computers (backup screenreader): _____
- Can the student touch type fluently? _____ Yes _____ No
- Can the student hold down 2 or 3 keyboard keys at one time to perform a key command?
  _____ Yes _____ No
- Speech synthesizers
  - ☐ Which voice does the student prefer:

  _____

- Braille support
  - ☐ Who will pay for newer screenreader versions as an operating system updates? (Check 1):
    - ☐ School district/county
    - ☐ Workplace
    - ☐ Department of Rehabilitation
    - ☐ Student

TECHNOLOGIES FOR AUTHORING

List any authoring tools the student uses currently (paper, pens/pencils, digital pencils, braillewriters, slate and stylus, apps, speech-to-text etc.):

_____

_____

_____

EVALUATE:

- Does the student have any fine motor challenges?
- What is the student's reading level? _____
- What is the student's writing level? _____

Hardware

- Does the student need to touchtype? _____ Yes _____ No
  If yes: Avoid using an adapted keyboard unless there is a motor consideration
- How does the student prefer to write? (check all that apply, including more details for the types of tasks a student likes to complete with each tool):
  ☐ In braille
  ☐ With a 6-key braille keyboard and screenreader
  ☐ With a QWERTY keyboard and screenreader
  ☐ With a QWERTY keyboard and screen magnification
  ☐ Under a video magnifier
  ☐ Dictation
  ☐ Using a digital pencil and touchscreen device
  ☐ Using a bold line pen
  ☐ Using bold lined paper
  ☐ Other: _____
- How does the student prefer to copy information from the board?
  ☐ Receive a digital copy of notes
  ☐ Receive a paper copy of notes
  ☐ Use a video magnifier
  ☐ Take a picture of notes on the board
  ☐ Copy information from a whiteboard at the student's desk

Software

- Does the student need a keyboarding app that is accessible with a screenreader?
  _____ Yes _____ No
- Would the student prefer to use a screensharing program to access information on the board?
  _____ Yes _____ No
- Would the student benefit from a word prediction program?
  _____ Yes _____ No
  If yes: check for compatibility with a screenreader if needed
- Does the student need an accessible touch typing program?
  _____ Yes _____ No
  If yes: check for compatibility with a screenreader if needed
- Which word processing programs are compatible with the student's personal computing device?
  _____
  ☐ Choose a program that has features for creating and editing Heading Styles
- How can the student benefit from reviewing what has been written?
  ☐ Using a screenreader
  ☐ Using text-to-speech
- What is the online workspace of your student's school or workplace?
  _____

Considerations When Selecting a Notetaking App

- Compatibility with personal computing device
- Accessibility and usability with the student's access tools such as: screen reader, braille display (if student needs a screenreader and/or braille display), reverse contrast, TTS
- Usability of app interface
  - ☐ Contrast of buttons and icons
  - ☐ Menu layouts
  - ☐ Ease of accessing accessibility features to adjust visual and auditory settings
- Ease of creating and organizing notes and notebooks, input options
- Ease of inserting, organizing, and finding information within a note
- Authoring and editing tools, including keyboard/stylus/digital pen input, handwriting OCR
- Multimedia support for adding audio recordings, pictures, files
- Compatibility to sync with a cloud storage platform
- Integrated OCR and TTS features
- Ability to annotate a worksheet or diagram
- Ability to sync audio recordings with timing of written or typed input
- Ability to sync across multiple notetaking devices
- Cost
- Other: _____

Considerations When Selecting a Screensharing App

- Compatibility with a teacher's or presenter's existing workflow
- Compatibility with a viewer's existing workflow
- Ease of connecting a viewer's screen to the primary screen
- Need for a one-time screenshare versus the ongoing need to share the same screen
- Cost

Tools for Visual Authoring

- What is the student's preferred tool, pen or pencil? _____
- Does the student need yellow or gray paper for writing without glare?
  _____ Yes _____ No
- Does the student want to write or draw under a video magnifier?
  _____ Yes _____ No
- Does the student want to write or draw on a touchscreen device?
  _____ Yes _____ No
- Is the student able to read back her/his own writing without any difficulty?
  _____ Yes _____ No

Tools for Tactile Authoring

- Slate and stylus. When does the student use this tool? When could the student use this tool? _____
- Abacus. When does the student use this tool? When could the student use this tool?
  _____

- Braille writer. Which one does the student have? What is its current condition? _____

- Smart brailler. Student benefits from audio feedback when writing. What is its current condition? _____
- Braille display or notetaker. Which one does the student have? What is its current condition? _____
- Does the student have decreased tactile coordination or dexterity? _____ Yes _____ No

Tools for Auditory Authoring

- Does the student have intelligible speech that is recognized by dictation tools? _____ Yes _____ No
- Does the student have a scribe listed as a test accommodation? _____ Yes _____ No

  If yes: It is assumed that the student works with a scribe regularly to complete non-test activities
- Does the student prefer to listen and review what has been written? _____ Yes _____ No

TECHNOLOGIES FOR ACCESSING MULTIMEDIA AND DATA

List any tools and media formats the student uses currently to access multimedia and data:

_____
_____
_____

EVALUATE:
- How often does the student need to access videos to meet learning objectives?
  - ☐ Daily
  - ☐ Weekly
  - ☐ Monthly
  - ☐ Other: _____
- Does the student need audio description for videos? _____ Yes _____ No
  If yes (check all that apply):
  - ☐ The student needs video description for commercially-available videos
  - ☐ The student needs video description for YouTube videos
- List any online curricula or tools that the school district has adopted that is not accessible with the student's access technology: _____
- Does the student have sufficient background experience with manipulating data and hearing information to interact with sonification of data displays? _____ Yes _____ No
- Does the student need to interact with a Learning Management System (LMS) (examples: Moodle, Canvas, Google Classroom)? _____ Yes _____ No
- Is there staff support for producing alternate media? _____ Yes _____ No

APPENDIX C
Forms and Lists

APPENDIX 8.1 BACKGROUND INFORMATION FOR A TECHNOLOGY EVALUATION

Background Information for Assistive Technology Evaluation

Name: _____ Birthdate: _____ Grade: _____

School: _____

Referred by: _____ Reason for Referral: _____

Initial or Ongoing Evaluation: _____

Name of Technology Evaluator: _____

Additional Disabilities: None Describe: _____

Functional Implications of Diagnoses:

_____

_____

Current medication(s): _____

Reported/observed visual side effects: _____

_____

Eye Report Summary

Dr. _____ O.D.

Date(s) examined: _____

Eye condition and functional implications: _____

A. Distance visual acuity:

	Without Prescription	With Prescription	With Low Vision Device
OD	_____	_____	_____
OS	_____	_____	
OU	_____	_____	_____

B. Near visual acuity

	Without Prescription	With Prescription	With Low Vision Device
OD	_____	_____	_____
OS	_____	_____	
OU	_____	_____	_____

Information from Learning Media Assessment

Primary learning channel: _____ visua _____ tactile _____ auditory

Secondary learning channel: _____ visual _____ tactile _____ auditory

Tertiary learning channel (if applicable)I: _____ visual _____ tactile _____ auditory

Other: _____

Current recommendations:

Reading preferences (if reported)

Preferred visual format (specify): _____

       Point size: _____   Font: _____   Reading Distance: _____

       Approximate reading rate: _____ wpm

Preferred audio format (specify): _____

       Approximate reading rate: _____ wpm

Lighting preferences: _____

Braille approximate reading rate: _____ wpm oral _____ wpm silent

Experiences visual/physical fatigue after reading _____ minutes

Relevant visual information from clinical low vision examination: _____
_____
_____

Relevant visual information from Functional Vision Assessment: _____
_____
_____

Relevant visual information from medical, psychological, and academic evaluations: _____
_____
_____

Relevant visual information from teachers' observations and assessments: _____
_____
_____

Additional comments: _____
_____
_____

APPENDIX 9.1: GPAT AT CONSIDERATION PROCESS GUIDE

Georgia Project for Assistive Technology
Assistive Technology Consideration Process Guide

Student: _____ **School:** _____ **Date:** _____

The GPAT Assistive Technology Consideration Resource Guide is a companion document that will assist IEP teams in completing this form. Please refer to the Resource Guide for examples of instructional tasks and possible solutions to document within this Consideration Process Guide. Each column contains general examples for each area but is not considered all inclusive.

Directions for completing this Consideration Process Guide:

1. Using the student's present levels of performance, in which general area(s) does the student experience difficulty completing instructional tasks?

    ☐ Writing/Written Composition   ☐ Spelling   ☐ Reading   ☐ Math

    ☐ Study/Organizational Skills   ☐ Hearing/ Listening   ☐ Oral Communication/ Language   ☐ Seating / Positioning / Mobility

    ☐ Activities of Daily Living   ☐ Recreation and Leisure   ☐ Pre-vocational and Vocational   ☐ Other:_____

    ☐ No areas are identified. No further consideration is required.

2. **Column A:** List one area with one instructional task per row, such as Writing/Copying notes from board. Check the location(s) where the student needs to complete the task.

Complete columns B-E on each row until it is determined that the student completes the task independently, then stop.

3. **Column B:** List the standard classroom material currently used by the student to complete the task.

4. **Column C:** List the accommodations, modifications and/or strategies currently used by the student to complete the task.

5. **Column D:** List the assistive technology solution(s) currently used by the student to complete the task.

6. **Column E:** List other possible solutions the IEP team has identified (accommodations, modifications, strategies, AT devices and/or services).

A. Area and Instructional Task(s)	B. Standard Classroom Materials	C. Accommodations/ Modifications/ Strategies	D. Assistive Technology Solutions	E. Other Possible Solutions (Accommodations, Strategies, Assistive Technology Devices and/or Services)
☐ School ☐ Home/ Community	If not independent, continue to **C** →	If not independent, continue to **D** →	If not independent, continue to **E** →	
☐ School ☐ Home/ Community	If not independent, continue to **C** →	If not independent, continue to **D** →	If not independent, continue to **E** →	
☐ School ☐ Home/ Community	If not independent, continue to **C** →	If not independent, continue to **D** →	If not independent, continue to **E** →	
☐ School ☐ Home/ Community	If not independent, continue to **C** →	If not independent, continue to **D** →	If not independent, continue to **E** →	
☐ School ☐ Home/ Community	If not independent, continue to **C** →	If not independent, continue to **D** →	If not independent, continue to **E** →	
☐ School ☐ Home/ Community	If not independent, continue to **C** →	If not independent, continue to **D** →	If not independent, continue to **E** →	

Consideration Outcomes:

☐ No, assistive technology is not required. The student independently accomplishes instructional tasks in all general areas using:

    ☐ Classroom Materials

    ☐ Accommodations

    ☐ Modifications

☐ Yes, assistive technology (devices and/or services) is required.

    ☐ AT is required and the IEP team knows the nature and extent of the AT devices and services needed.

    ☐ IEP Team needs additional information (i.e., observation, trial use, consult with specialist, evaluation)

Completed by (include name and position):

Name	Position	Name	Position

APPENDIX 9.2: ENVIRONMENTAL ASSESSMENT FOR ACCESS TECHNOLOGY

What are the environments that this student needs to access? _____

_____

- How is information being disseminated and exchanged? _____

  _____

  - What has been working well for the student? What has been tried but proven unsuccessful?

    _____

    _____

  - What is the workflow for each classroom or workspace?_____

    _____

- What systems are supporting information exchanges in each environment? _____

  _____

  - Has the school or workplace already adopted a technology plan? If so, what does it entail?

    _____

    _____

  - What are the readily available technologies that typically sighted peers are using? _____

    _____

What are the tasks that are expected to happen in each of the student's environments?_____

_____

- In each environment, what are the expected tasks of everyone for accessing information?

  _____

- In each environment, what are the expected tasks of everyone for authoring information?

  _____

What are the student's current learning preferences? _____

_____

- What sensory access channels is a student currently relying on the most for accessing information?

  _____

  _____

APPENDIX 9.3: DIGITAL WORKFLOW PLANNING TOOL

Credit: (McDowell, 2019)

Planning Tool: Digital Workflow for Students who are Visually Impaired

Student Name:		
School:	Age:	Grade:
District:	Date Completed:	
Persons Completing Summary:		

Digital workflow refers to an efficient electronic system for accessing, processing, sharing and storing work. Digital workflow can reduce a student's reliance on others for accessible materials. Use of digital workflow is tied to assessment and goals and aims to increase a student's independence and self-advocacy. Digital workflow addresses needed skills for future access to work environments and higher learning. Considerations when planning for digital workflow:

- Developmentally appropriate practice and sequenced learning
- Environmental considerations and back up plans when using technology
- Teaching successful use of digital workflow does not happen in one session
- Allow for diversity of workflows
- Develop workflows collaboratively (students and teachers)

Information from Functional Vision Assessment (FVA) and Learning Media Assessment (LMA)
Student's primary and secondary learning media or student's use of dual-media or multi-media:

Considerations:

Information from Access Technology (AT) Assessment

Student uses:

- ☐ Large print
- ☐ Braille
- ☐ Digital Books (Daisy, Bookshare)
- ☐ Text-to-speech (TTS)
- ☐ Narrated audio books (Learning Ally, BARD/NLS, public library service)
- ☐ Computer w/screen reader and/or refreshable braille display (RBD)
- ☐ Specialized lighting

- ☐ Computer with magnification settings/software
- ☐ Dedicated braille notetaker
- ☐ Touchscreen tablet such as iPad
- ☐ Reading stand/slant board
- ☐ Enhanced visual presentation such as increased spacing, large font, reverse contrast (white font on black background)
- ☐ Video magnifier

- ☐ Hand-held magnifier or monocular
- ☐ Writing tools:
  - ☐ dictation
  - ☐ bold pen
  - ☐ 6-key braille keyboard
  - ☐ on screen writing with stylus
- ☐ Audio described videos
- ☐ Other:

Notes on current access technology and considerations:

Current digital workflow and classroom technologies:
Notes on general technology use. Does student use email, Google Chrome/Drive/Docs, Dropbox, other cloud note-taking or storage options? What devices, applications, and learning management systems (LMS) are used school-wide or in specific classes?

Implementing digital workflow, targeted areas:
What tasks and activities do we think technology could be an efficient tool for? What tasks and activities could student complete more independently? How are those tasks completed now and are there drawbacks to these methods? What academic, expanded core curriculum, and transition goals support use of digital workflow?

Roles of student, TVI, teacher, parents, paraprofessional:
When considering student's role, prioritize student's timely access to curriculum and delivery of accessible materials at the same time as classmates.

Training and/or support needed (student, staff, classroom teacher):

Future Considerations and Recommendations for future IEP planning:
How does use of digital workflow fit into long-term planning for student's needs?

Tool reflects considerations found in Wisconsin Assistive Technology Initiative. (June 2009). *Assessing Students' Needs for Assistive Technology (ASNAT)*. Retrieved September 2019 from www.wati.org.

APPENDIX 9.4: NEEDS ASSESSMENT TEMPLATE

Needs Assessment for Technology

Your Name

Student Info

Name (pseudonym):

Age at time of assessment:

Grade:

Classroom placement:

Background Information

Student Sensory Learning Channels

Primary learning channel

Tasks the student can do efficiently using this sense:

-

Tasks with limited success using this sense:

-

Secondary learning channel

Tasks the student can do efficiently using this sense:

-

Tasks with limited success using this sense:

-

Tertiary learning channel

Tasks the student can do efficiently using this sense:

-

Tasks with limited success using this sense:

-

Classroom, school, and community activities that the student currently requires assistance to engage in—and has the potential to be more independent.

Remember: you are not identifying present levels of performance

-

Types of (non-adapted) educational materials and instructional media that the student needs to access in various classes, labs, and electives

Language Arts

•

STEAM (Science, Technology, Engineering, Arts, Math)

•

Other

•

Technology Features That Would Benefit the Student

Remember: Use generic terms and avoid naming brands—each feature should match a sensory learning channel)

•

Potential constraints or challenges of implementing access technology in this student's environment

---

A Sample Completed Needs Assessment

Student: Summer Day

Background:

Summer Day is a 6th grade student with cerebral palsy, cognitive disability, speech impairment and a visual impairment due to optic nerve hypoplasia and nystagmus. Summer Day is able to walk independently in familiar environments when using a wall for trailing and physical support. Functional implications of his diagnosis include difficulty with balance, language delays, accessing print or pictures of less than 4", identifying colors, light sensitivity, ability to orient and navigate in unfamiliar environments independently, ability to identify objects, read and write. He attends a self-contained classroom for students with extensive support needs and is accessing curriculum at a 4 to 5-year-old level.

Sensory Learning Channels

Primary learning channel: Auditory

Tasks he can do well:

- Listens to simple directions from staff.
- Listens to audible books on tape.
- Identifies peers and staff by their voice.

- Alerts to the bell schedule.
- Socializes for leisure activity.
- Listens to music.
- Attends to calendar or simple small group activities.

Task with limited success:

- Listening to long stories or movies.
- Remembering and following multi-step instructions.
- Listening and comprehending abstract or complex instruction.
- Independently accessing curriculum on a variety of electronic devices.
- Playing with peers in a loud gym.
- Listening to instruction in large group settings.

Secondary learning channel: Vision

Task he can do well:

- Identify pedestrians in hallway and avoid them.
- Identify familiar people within 10 feet of him.
- Follow familiar routes within the school.
- Locates and folds towels.
- Locates food items in the refrigerator.
- Uses simple tools such as a vegetable peeler or a child's safety knife.
- Locates his desk and areas for instruction in the classroom.
- Locates everyday instructional tools and materials.
- Writes his name with 8 inch letters.
- Counts large images on a computer screen.

Task with limited success:
- Visually attending to movies.
- Attending to printed text or objects smaller than 4 inches.
- Visually tracking a ball or people moving quickly in the gym.
- Playing games on a computer or iPad.
- Reading picture menus.
- Locating small items that have been dropped or misplaced.
- Using a cursor to locate or move objects on a computer screen.
- Writing a sentence with a paper/pencil.
- Accessing computer based instruction due to small print.
- Attending to visual task lasting longer than 15 minutes.
- Looking at graphics in books.
- Gaining information from print based maps.
- Identifying street signs, traffic lights and walk/don't walk signs.
- Identifying and tracking moving vehicles.

- Detecting changes in walking surfaces.
- Visually identifying landmarks.

Tertiary learning channel: Tactile

Task he can do well:
- Hold a palm-sized object with one hand
- Grasp a handrail
- Use both hands to complete simple manual tasks such as folding towels, opening containers
- Cross midline when moving items across a table
- Clean up a workspace by putting objects in a container

Task with limited success:
- Placing paper clips on paper
- Using non-adapted standard scissors
- Sorting by texture
- Writing a sentence with a paper/pencil.

Classroom, school, and community activities that the student currently requires assistance to engage in—and has the potential to be more independent.

- Discriminating between ingredients in cooking activities (can of soup or fruit).
- Sorting, matching, or identifying objects by color.
- Identifying objects that are the same or different.
- Giving a written response to a question.
- Writing a story.
- Participating in computerized math and reading instruction.
- Reading a text and answering comprehension questions.
- Playing games during PE.
- Traveling independently using multiple routes in the school.
- Independently accessing his schedule and traveling to his related services classrooms.
- Following structured work schedules.
- Traveling in the grocery store, local restaurants, and local parks.
- Reading and selecting food items from a menu.
- Making a purchase at a store or restaurant.
- Planning and recommending activities to attend in the community.

Types of non-adapted educational materials and instructional media that the student needs to access in various classes, labs, and electives

Literacy
- Books—text and graphic novels
- Classroom calendar

- Worksheets
- Vocabulary sheets

Numeracy

- Worksheets
- Computer-based learning programs
- Flashcards

Other

- Menus
- Recipes cards
- Work schedules
- Cans of food
- Computer games
- Movies

Technology Features That Would Benefit the Student (list using generic terms):

- Text reader
- Voice to text
- Voice recognition software
- Computer/tablet with accessibility features
- Slant board
- Screen reader
- Computer based reading/ math software
- Magnification with screen reader
- Models of 2D and 3D geometric shapes
- Tactile-audio graphics
- GPS device
- Object identification device
- Color identification technology
- Sound localization tools
- Electronic organization
- Digital organizer for time management
- Low-tech organizers for materials
- Adaptive balls with audible beep for recreation and leisure
- Refer for additional assessment to explore adaptive mobility device for walking in unfamiliar environments

Potential constraints or challenges of implementing access technology in the student's environment

- 5 paraprofessionals work in the classroom with a weekly rotation for who supports which students

- The Wi-Fi network requires a guest login unless set up to connect otherwise

- Student devices are limited from downloading apps and extensions—need admin approval

- The classroom has very active students who tend to pick up items around the room and play

- Parents have smartphones but otherwise are not very tech savvy

- Classroom teacher is very overwhelmed with paperwork and has little patience to troubleshoot technology when issues arise

APPENDIX 9.5: ACCESS TECHNOLOGY TRIAL USE SUMMARY

Credit: (McDowell, 2019)

Access Technology Trial Use Summary
for Students who are Blind or Visually Impaired

Student Name:		
School:	Age:	Grade:
District:	Date Completed:	
Persons Completing Summary:		

Student's accommodations and use of low, medium and high-tech devices:

Information from Learning Media Assessment (LMA) and Functional Vision Assessment (FVA) including need for visual, tactile and auditory media, preferred print/symbol size, lighting or positioning needs, distance viewing information:

Type of technology to trial and environmental considerations. How would technology facilitate participation and access to classroom curriculum? What tasks and activities could be completed with increased independence and/or efficiency given use of technology?

Summary developed from Wisconsin Assistive Technology Initiative. (June 2009). *Assessing Students' Needs for Assistive Technology (ASNAT)*. Retrieved September 2019 from www.wati.org.

Task/s Being Addressed During Trial:

Criteria for Success:

Observation Notes:

Date	Tasks observed	Criteria met?	Comments (e.g. advantages, disadvantages, preferences, performance)

Future considerations. Does the use of this technology fit into long-term planning for student's needs? Use of specific device should be considered within larger access technology assessment. Are there other technology needs that should be considered?

Recommendations for IEP:

APPENDIX 9.6: ACCESSIBILITY TIP SHEET

Accessibility Tip Sheet
Compiled by Yue-Ting Siu, TVI/COMS, PhD., 2019

Classroom Best Practices

- Using Clear Descriptive Language, adapted from Classroom Collaboration, Laurie Hudson: http://www.pathstoliteracy.org/this-that-there
- How to Give an Accessible Presentation: https://youtu.be/9n9KacDbpzw
- BRCOE A11Y Hub
  - https://onlinelearning.berkeley.edu/courses/433559
- Introduction to Course Accessibility, 6 free online modules that cover aspects of accessible course design. Includes vignettes of user experiences from individuals with disabilities
  - https://bcourses.berkeley.edu/courses/1456326
- Designing for Accessibility with *POUR*, National Center on Accessible Educational Materials (AEM)
  - http://aem.cast.org/creating/designing-for-accessibility-pour.html

Documents Accessibility

- Creating Accessible MS Word Files
  - How to format headings in MS Word: https://youtu.be/vWoDq0S8Jsc
  - Written tutorial: http://webaim.org/techniques/word/
  - Checklist for MS Word Accessibility: http://www.hhs.gov/web/508/accessiblefiles/checklistword.html
  - How do I know if a document is accessible? https://youtu.be/lzLTs9Anw90
- Using Google Docs Headings: https://youtu.be/-DzoX21OExA
- How to Create a Self-Described Link (Turn Text into a Clickable Link): https://youtu.be/P4s3GZnE7tU
- Converting Documents to PDFs
  http://webaim.org/techniques/acrobat/converting
  - Checklist for PDF Accessibility
    http://www.hhs.gov/web/508/accessiblefiles/checklistpdf.html
- Creating Accessible MS Powerpoint Presentations http://webaim.org/techniques/powerpoint/
  - Checklist for MS Powerpoint Accessibility
    http://www.hhs.gov/web/508/accessiblefiles/checklistppt.html
- Checklist for MS Excel Spreadsheet Accessibility
  http://www.hhs.gov/web/508/accessiblefiles/checklistexcel.html
- Misc. resources: http://www.sjsu.edu/cfd/teaching-learning/accessibility/accessible-documents/

Multimedia Accessibility

Web Accessibility

- World Wide Web Consortium (W3C), Web Content Accessibility Guidelines: http://www.w3.org/TR/WCAG20
- WebAIM (Web Accessibility In Mind): http://webaim.org

Image Description

- Image Description Guidelines including STEM images: http://diagramcenter.org/table-of-contents-2.html
- Alternative Text on the Web: http://webaim.org/techniques/alttext
- Image Accessibility Considerations: http://webaim.org/techniques/images
- Image descriptions on Twitter
  - https://support.twitter.com/articles/20174660

Video Description

- Description tutorials: http://www.youtube.com/playlist?list=PLNJrbI_nyy9uzywoJfyDRoeKA1SaIEFJ7
- YouDescribe - A free service that allows anyone to describe a YouTube video. Videos can be played back with description by blind viewers and others who benefit from description (such as English Language Learners). http://www.youdescribe.org
  - Tutorial: http://youtu.be/c-GKbGCzeEc
- DisneyAnywhere app provides description for selected Pixar movies: https://www.disneymoviesanywhere.com/ - 14484

Performing Arts with Audio Description

- http://www.acb.org/adp/theatres.html - CA

3D Printing for Accessibility

- Introductory webinar: http://youtu.be/-0TSvNFf8Xw
- 3D Printed teaching models: https://www.perkinselearning.org/technology/blog/3d-printed-teaching-models
- 3D Printer Resources: https://www.perkinselearning.org/technology/posts/3d-printer-resources
- 3D Printed Educational Models Google group for requesting 3D model designs: https://groups.google.com/forum/#!forum/3dp_edu_models

Universal Design

- CAST (Center for Applied Special Technology)—National Center on Universal Design for Learning http://www.cast.org/udl
- ISTE (International Society for Technology in Education) https://www.iste.org

Miscellaneous

- Legal Updates Regarding Digital Accessibility: Lainey Feingold, www.lflegal.com
- Collection of TVI candidates' video demos of digital workflows and basic accessibility testing mainstream apps: SFSU VI Program Facebook page https://www.facebook.com/viprogramsfsu
- Apple Accessibility troubleshooting, questions, bug reports: AppleVis website
- Google Accessibility mailing list for troubleshooting, questions, bug reports: accessible@google-groups.com

APPENDIX 9.7: AT RECOMMENDATIONS CHECKLIST

Assistive Technology Recommendations Checklist

Name: _____

Date(s) of Evaluation: _____

Based on the results of the assistive technology evaluation, the following recommendations are made regarding assistive technology to support this individual's educational, employment and personal objectives.

Section I: Accessing Print Information

People with visual impairments will use a combination of tools and strategies to access printed information. Some will be appropriate for short reading passages and others will be necessary for longer assignments.

A. Accessing Print Information Visually

Check all that apply.

☐ Student/client should use regular print materials with optical devices.

    ☐ prescribed eyeglasses/contact lenses

    ☐ prescribed hand held magnifier

    Type: _____ _____ power ☐ illuminated

    ☐ prescribed stand magnifier

    Type: _____ _____ power ☐ illuminated

    ☐ prescribed hand held telescope

    Type: _____ _____ power

    ☐ prescribed spectacle mounted telescope

    Type: _____ _____ power

    ☐ other optical devices recommended in Clinical Low Vision Evaluation

    Specify: _____

☐ Student/client should use materials written with felt tip pen on regular blue lined notebook paper.

☐ Student/client should use materials written with felt tip pen on bold lined paper.

☐ Student/client should use materials written with felt tip pen on unlined paper.

☐ Student/client should use regular print materials enlarged on a photocopying machine.

    Specify: _____ times at _____ % enlargement.

☐ Student/client should use large print books.

☐ Student/client should use regular print materials scanned into a computer, edited, and printed in _____ point print in the _____ font.

☐ When possible, student/client should be provided with overhead lighting:

    ☐ from an incandescent bulb.

    ☐ from a fluorescent bulb.

    ☐ from a halogen bulb.

- ☐ from an LED bulb.
- ☐ adjusted with a dimmer switch.
- ☐ When possible, student/client should be provided with window lighting adjusted with:
  - ☐ blinds
  - ☐ shades
  - ☐ other. Specify: _____
- ☐ When possible, student/client should be provided with additional lighting from:
  - ☐ desk lamp
    - ☐ incandescent
    - ☐ fluorescent
    - ☐ halogen.
    - ☐ LED.
  - ☐ floor lamp
    - ☐ incandescent
    - ☐ fluorescent
    - ☐ halogen.
    - ☐ LED
- ☐ Student/client should use a book/reading stand:
  - ☐ braille bookstand
  - ☐ desktop model
  - ☐ portable model
  - ☐ floor model.
- ☐ Student/client should use regular print materials with a video magnifier.

  Specify type:
  - ☐ desktop model
  - ☐ flex arm camera model
  - ☐ portable model
  - ☐ video magnifier with (OCR) and (TTS) software
  - ☐ Specify essential features: _____

Comments: _____
_____
_____

B. Accessing Print Information Tactilely

Check all that apply.
- ☐ Student/client should use materials in braille.
- ☐ Student/client should use a bookstand to facilitate braille reading.
- ☐ Student/client should use an electronic/refreshable braille display to access printed and electronic information.
- ☐ Student/client should be provided opportunities to use tactile graphics created by various production techniques and in a variety of media including real objects, models, collage, tooling

and stenciling, thermoform, capsule paper and fuser, computer generated and commercially produced.

☐ Student/client should use tactile graphics to access maps, charts, diagrams, etc.

Comments: _____
_____
_____

C. Accessing Print Information Auditorily

Check all that apply.

☐ Student/client should use a live reader for accessing certain materials:
Specify: _____

☐ Student/client should use recorded materials for accessing some printed information.
Specify: _____

☐ Student/client should use eBooks for accessing some printed information.
Specify: _____

☐ Student/client should use a stand-alone scan & read system.

☐ Student/client should use a computer based scan & read system.

☐ Student/client should use a tablet based scan & read system.

☐ Student/client should use a smartphone based scan & read system.

Comments: _____
_____
_____

D. Accessing Information Displayed for Distance Viewing

Check all that apply.

☐ Student/client should be provided an accessible copy of information presented to groups on chalk/white boards, overhead projectors, computer projection systems, etc.

☐ Student/client should use a hand-held telescope for accessing chalk/white boards, overhead projectors, computer projection systems, etc.

☐ Student/client should use a video magnifier with distance viewing capabilities for accessing chalk/white boards, overhead projectors, computer projection systems, etc.

☐ Student/client should use a document camera with distance viewing capabilities for accessing chalk/white boards, overhead projectors, computer projection systems, etc.

☐ Student/client should use an electronic whiteboard connected to an accessible computer.

☐ Student/client should be provided audio described videos when available.

☐ Student/client should be provided a separate _____-inch monitor for viewing DVDs, movies, and other video presentations.

Comments: _____
_____
_____

Section II: Accessing Electronic Information

A. Computer Access—Output Devices

1. Visual

Check all that apply.

☐ Student/client should use a standard computer monitor
Optimal size: _____

☐ Student/client should use standard computer monitor w/ fully articulated monitor arm

☐ Student/client should use display properties settings in computer operating system (OS):
Specify _____

☐ Student/client should use accessibility options in computer (OS):

☐ Student/client should use OS screen magnification program
   ☐ Mac Zoom   ☐ Microsoft Magnifier   ☐ Chrome Zoom

☐ Student/client should use a dedicated screen magnification program.
Specify essential features: _____

Comments: _____
_____
_____

2. Tactile

☐ Student/client should use a refreshable braille display.
Specify essential features: _____

Comments: _____
_____
_____

3. Auditory

Check all that apply.

☐ Student/client should use OS screen reading program
   ☐ Mac VoiceOver   ☐ Microsoft Narrator   ☐ ChromeVox

☐ Student/client should use a dedicated screen reading program.
Specify essential features: _____

Comments: _____
_____
_____

B. Computer Access—Input Devices

1. Keyboard Use

Check all that apply.

☐ Student/client should use a standard keyboard.

☐ Student/client should use a standard keyboard with
   ☐ large print labels, light text on dark background.
   ☐ large print labels, dark text on light background.
   ☐ braille labels.

☐ Student/client should use a standard keyboard with locator dots to develop/improve keyboarding skills.

☐ Student/client should receive individual keyboarding instruction.

☐ Student/client should use a word processor and OS screen reading program for keyboarding instruction.

☐ Student/client should use a talking typing program for keyboarding practice and reinforcement of skills taught by instructor.

☐ Student/client should use a standard keyboard with accessibility options.

    ☐ StickyKeys

    ☐ FilterKeys

    ☐ ToggleKeys

    ☐ Other. Specify: _____

☐ Student/client should use a standard keyboard with hardware adaptations. Specify: _____

☐ Student/client should use an alternative keyboard. Specify: _____

Comments: _____
_____
_____
_____

2. Pointing Devices and Other Tools

Check all that apply.

☐ Student/client should use a standard pointing device like a mouse or trackball.

☐ Student/client should use an alternative pointing device. Specify: _____

☐ Student/client should have access to a copy holder that allows printed materials to be positioned at a comfortable viewing distance.

Comments: _____
_____
_____
_____

C. Accessing Other Electronic Information

1. Specialized Scanning Systems

☐ Student/client should have access to a scan & read system. Specify essential feature: _____

2. Electronic Notetaker

☐ Student/client should have access to an electronic notetaker with the following features:

    ☐ QWERTY keyboard

    ☐ braille keyboard

    ☐ synthesized speech output

    ☐ refreshable braille display

    Specify essential features: _____

3. Other Electronic Tools

- ☐ Student/client should use a _____ basic or _____ scientific large print calculator with numerals at _____-inches tall..
- ☐ Student/client should use a _____ basic or _____ scientific talking calculator.
- ☐ Student/client should use a computer-based calculator program/app with
  - ☐ screen magnification software,
  - ☐ screen reading software.
- ☐ Student/client should use a dictionary/thesaurus program/app on a computer with
  - ☐ screen magnification software,
  - ☐ screen reading software.
- ☐ Student/client should use a smart home device

Comments: _____

_____

_____

Section III: Communicating Through Writing

Producing Written Communication

People with visual impairments will use a combination of tools and strategies to produce written communication. Some will be appropriate for short writing assignments and others will be necessary for longer assignments.

Check all that apply.

- ☐ Student/client should use pen/pencil and paper
  - ☐ for short writing assignments.
  - ☐ for most writing assignments.
- ☐ Student/client should use felt tip pen or another bold marker.
- ☐ Student/client should use _____ bold line, _____ raised line, notebook paper.
- ☐ Student/client should use _____ bold line, _____ raised line, graph paper for math.
- ☐ Student/client should use crayons and a screen board for beginning handwriting and learning to write signature.
- ☐ Student/client should use a signature guide for signing name.
- ☐ Student/client should use a whiteboard with erasable markers.
- ☐ Student/client should use a computer with a math writing/editing program.
- ☐ Student/client should use a computer with a scanner and imaging software to complete forms.
- ☐ Student/client should use a laptop, or a tablet computer with an external keyboard, and word processing software for note taking.
- ☐ Student/client should use an electronic notetaker for note taking and other short writing tasks.
- ☐ Student/client should use a digital recorder or app as a back-up note taking tool.
- ☐ Student/client should use an accessible computer with word processing software.
- ☐ Student/client should use manual braille writer.

- ☐ Student/client should use manual braille writer with extension keys.
- ☐ Student/client should use a unimanual braille writer.
- ☐ Student/client should use unimanual braille writer with extension keys.
- ☐ Student/client should use slate & stylus.
- ☐ Student/client should use an electronic braille writer (Mountbatten Brailler, Perkins SMART Brailler). Specify features: _____

Comments: _____
_____
_____

Section IV: Additional Hardware and Software

Student/client should be provided with access to the following hardware & software;

☐ Macintosh computer system with

_____ GB memory   _____ GB hard drive   _____ USB ports   ☐ CD/DVD drive

☐ Windows compatible computer system with

_____ GB memory   _____ GB hard drive   _____ USB ports   ☐ CD/DVD drive

- ☐ Word processor
- ☐ Printer
- ☐ Internet access
- ☐ Flatbed Scanner

    Other: _____

Equipment needed to produce materials for student/client in appropriate format.

☐ Mac or Windows compatible computer system

_____ GB memory   _____ GB hard drive   _____ USB ports   ☐ CD/DVD drive

- ☐ Internet access
- ☐ Flatbed scanner   ☐ OCR software
- ☐ Word processing software   ☐ braille translating software
- ☐ Inkjet or laser printer   ☐ braille embosser/printer
- ☐ Tactile graphics production equipment. Specify: _____

Additional comments/recommendations: _____
_____
_____
_____

The recommendations made here may not all have to be implemented immediately. These suggestions are designed for a two- to three-year plan in which the student/client acquires certain skills and is then provided access to additional technologies that can facilitate his or her educational/employment program. During that time, new technologies are likely to become available that will enhance the individual's ability to accomplish tasks and maximize his or her potential. The specific devices recommended may no longer be available, but the access that they provide will continue to be a need for this individual and the appropriate tools will still need to be made available.

_____   _____
Assessment Completed by (*signature*)   Position

_____   _____
Assessment Completed by (*signature*)   Position

_____   _____
Assessment Completed by (*signature*)   Position

_____   _____
Assessment Completed by (*signature*)   Position

APPENDIX 9.8: IEP ACCOMMODATIONS TOOL

Credit: (McDowell, 2019)

Seis IEP Accommodations Tool for Students with Visual Impairments

Student: IEP Date:

This tool can be used to organize a student's IEP accommodations. Accommodations should be listed separately so that teachers receive a clear, user-friendly list. Goal is to be succinct yet thorough.

Due to outdated options and redundancies in pull-down options in Seis and need to write additional and more specific accommodations, drafting accommodation list before working in Seis can help streamline process.

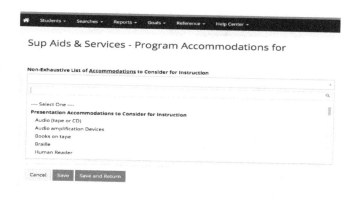

Page 1 lists the **pull-down menu options** in Seis.

Page 2 and 3 list common accommodations for VI students that can be added by selecting **Other** for write-in field.

*This is a work in progress and is by no means exhaustive, update to include your commonly-used accommodations, preferred wording, and district expectations.

Services—Offer of FAPE

Sup Aids and Services—Program Accommodations
Non-Exhaustive List of Accommodations to Consider for Instruction

1. Presentation Accommodations to Consider for Instruction
   - ☐ Other
   - ☐ Audio (tape or CD)
   - ☐ Audio amplification devices
   - ☐ Books on tape
   - ☐ Braille
   - ☐ Check for understanding by having student restate or paraphrase information
   - ☐ Human reader
   - ☐ Large print materials
   - ☐ Magnification devices
   - ☐ Notes outlines and instructions
   - ☐ Obtain student's attention before speaking
   - ☐ Provide directions in a variety of modalities
   - ☐ Recorded books
   - ☐ Repeat/rephrase responses of other students
   - ☐ Screen reader
   - ☐ Tactile graphics
   - ☐ Talking materials
   - ☐ Videotapes (or DVDs) and descriptive video tapes
   - ☐ Visual cues

2. Response Accommodations to Consider for Instruction
   - ☐ Other
   - ☐ Abacus
   - ☐ Assistive technology
   - ☐ Braille Writer
   - ☐ Calculation devices
   - ☐ Graphic organizer

- ☐ Monitor test response
- ☐ Note Takers
- ☐ Responding in test booklet
- ☐ Scribe
- ☐ Speech-to-Text
- ☐ Spelling and grammar devices
- ☐ Tape recorder
- ☐ Visual organizers

3. Setting Accommodations to Consider for Instruction
- ☐ Other
- ☐ Change location to increase physical access or to use special equipment

- ☐ Flexible seating to ensure auditory and visual access
- ☐ Reduce background noise
- ☐ Reduce distractions to other students
- ☐ Reduce distractions to the student

4. Timing and Scheduling Accommodations to Consider for Instruction
- ☐ Other
- ☐ Change schedule or order of activities
- ☐ Extended time
- ☐ Multiple or frequent breaks

Other write-in Presentation Accommodations

- ☐ Large print materials 18–24 point font (1/8 to 3/16 inch high lower case letters)
- ☐ Large print materials 24–36 point font (3/16 to 1/4 inch high lower case letters)
- ☐ Magnification devices, electronic (video magnifier) and handheld (dome magnifier)
- ☐ Uncluttered, well-spaced worksheets
- ☐ Slant board and/or reading stand
- ☐ Use bold black or dark blue markers for writing on the board or on paper/whiteboard at student desk
- ☐ When projecting on board, increase contrast and zoom in to make text large and clear and target visual focus
- ☐ Narrate what is being written on the board and use specific language (e.g., say "write your name upper left-hand corner" rather than "write your name here" combined with pointing)
- ☐ Assistive technology device with Text-to-Speech (TTS)
- ☐ Accessible tablet device
- ☐ Large screen computer (15" or larger)
- ☐ Digital books (electronic text) including membership with Bookshare.org, Learning Ally
- ☐ Digital textbooks in NIMAS (National Instructional Materials Accessibility Standard) format
- ☐ Multimodal presentation of highlighted text with audio (narration or TTS)
- ☐ Preview curricular materials, check for background knowledge
- ☐ Braille including presentation on Refreshable Braille Display (computer, tablet, braille notetaker)
- ☐ Mask extraneous information on page
- ☐ Materials use bold colors, avoid muted or pastel colors
- ☐ Provide concrete experiences, expand activities with manipulatives, real objects and tactile materials
- ☐ Described and captioned media including access to services such as Described and Captioned Media Program (DCMP) and YouDescribe.org
- ☐ Braille transcript of closed captioning text
- ☐ Graphic organizers, sequence of steps outlined, other supports for focus
- ☐ Mirror or pair devices to provide view on student's device of what is projected in class

Other write-in Response Accommodations

- ☐ Dictation using assistive technology
- ☐ Dark line writing tools
- ☐ Dark line paper
- ☐ Braille device with visual display
- ☐ Word prediction when using assistive technology
- ☐ Reduce visual/writing work output if knowledge of concepts shown
- ☐ Allow for needed processing time, wait until repeating directions or adding more supportive prompts

Other write-in Setting Accommodations

- ☐ Avoid sources of glare
- ☐ Preferential seating: define where (e.g., front and to the right of classroom, student sees with left visual field)
- ☐ use of slant boards, reading stands and well-fitted furniture for stable positioning and to promote visual access
- ☐ Maintain clear pathways in classroom
- ☐ Wear hat with visor to reduce glare.
- ☐ Provide orientation to new environments with ample time for student to explore
- ☐ Encourage others to identify themselves when they start an interaction with student and say hello/goodbye when coming/going
- ☐ Say your name when greeting student, identify adults and peers near student, if needed, narrate non-verbal communication
- ☐ Narrate social environment, describe what peers are doing on the playground and help student locate friends
- ☐ Use specific environmental cues (e.g., say "by the table" rather than "over there" combined with pointing)
- ☐ Reduce visual distractions, provide clear work space
- ☐ Peer notetaker or partner
- ☐ Shade options for outdoor activities

Other write-in Timing and Scheduling Accommodations

- ☐ Use accessible schedule and preview schedule changes
- ☐ Break down large projects to support meeting benchmarks before due date
- ☐ Alternative to pen and paper planner such as Google Calendar or other digital productivity app or tool
- ☐ If possible schedule PE early in day to minimize sun exposure

*   *   *

Other Lists (accommodations repeated from above)

Low Vision Academic Students

- ☐ Large print materials (define range of size)
- ☐ Magnification devices, electronic (video magnifier) and handheld (dome magnifier)

- ☐ Slant board and/or reading stand
- ☐ Use bold black or dark blue markers for writing on the board or on paper/whiteboard at her desk
- ☐ When projecting on board, increase contrast and zoom in to increase size and target visual focus
- ☐ Narrate what is being written on the board and use specific language (e.g., say "write your name in the upper left-hand corner" rather than "write your name here" combined with pointing)
- ☐ Dark line writing tools
- ☐ Dark line paper

O&M

- ☐ Monocular telescope
- ☐ Wear hat with visor to reduce glare.
- ☐ Provide orientation to new environments with ample time for student to explore
- ☐ Maintain clear pathways in classroom
- ☐ If possible schedule PE early in day to minimize sun exposure
- ☐ Shade options for outdoor activities
- ☐ Narrate social environment, describe what peers are doing on the playground and help student locate friends

CVI

- ☐ Uncluttered, well-spaced worksheets
- ☐ Reduce visual distractions, provide clear work space
- ☐ Provide concrete experiences, expand activities with manipulatives, real objects and tactile materials
- ☐ Allow for needed processing time, wait until repeating directions or adding more supportive prompts

Students with LD/ADHD/Autism

- ☐ Use accessible schedule and preview schedule changes
- ☐ Break down large projects to support meeting benchmarks before due date
- ☐ Alternative to pen and paper planner such as Google Calendar or other digital productivity app or tool
- ☐ Word prediction when using assistive technology
- ☐ Reduce visual/writing work output if knowledge of concepts shown

Orthopedically Impaired

- ☐ Maintain clear pathways in classroom
- ☐ Use of slant boards, reading stands and well-fitted furniture for stable positioning and to promote visual access

Deaf/Hard of Hearing

- ☐ Braille transcript of closed captioning text

APPENDIX 10.3: COMPUTER-BASED ASSESSMENT PLANNING CHECKLIST

Sample planning checklist for computer-based testing in California

(Jessica McDowell, TVI/COMS, Marin County Office of Education, CA)

CAASPP Planning Checklist for students with Visual Impairments (CAASPP = California Assessment of Student Performance and Progress)
*all information in this document subject to change

Student: District:

School: Statewide Student Identifier (SSID):

Review: **California School for the Blind's SMARTER BALANCED STATEWIDE ASSESSMENT SITE overview, instruction, documents and videos** http://www.csb-cde.ca.gov/csb_smarter _balanced.html

Know these resources:

The California Assessment of Student Performance and Progress website:
    http://www.caaspp.org

Smarter Balanced Assessment Consortium: Usability, Accessibility, and Accommodations Guidelines
    https://portal.smarterbalanced.org/library/en/usability-accessibility-and-accommodations -guidelines.pdf

California Department of Education Matrix One: Universal Tools, Designated Supports, and Accommodations for the California Assessment of Student Performance and Progress for 2016–17
    http://www.cde.ca.gov/ta/tg/ai/documents/caasppmatrix1.pdf

Long range planning . . .

☐ Research testing updates, find where most up to date info is

☐ For each student, the TVI must be the expert if there is no other technology specialist familiar with testing students with blindness or low vision. Don't expect general district special education tech support to know the nuances of testing for VI student.

☐ Student should be using all the technology and supports to access curricular tasks that you expect them to use during the test. Does student need updated technology assessment? Look at ways student will access on-line tests and new tools and technology expectations being implemented for classroom instruction and assessment.

The IEP before next test window . . .

☐ Review CAASPP Support and Accommodations for guidance and IEP planning

☐ Check to see what test/s student will be taking

☐ Decide the test location. If taken with the class, what computers will be used? Does student need an in-class alternative to a Chromebook (common class testing tool)? For instance, a desktop computer can be set up with the secure browser so student tests with class (need lead time to make sure that set up installed).

☐ Decide who will administer the test (if there is a reason why student needs an alternative setting, such as a braille student)

☐ Go to SEIS (or electronic IEP management site) Statewide Assessments page and update student's supports and accommodations

Early in school year . . .

☐ Contact CSMT (Clearinghouse for Specialized Materials and Technology) about test, will APH/CSMT provide performance task (PT) materials in accessible format? Or, check on-line for Classroom activities and have accessible materials created.

☐ Find out dates for testing
  ▪ Summative assessments *window* (if you are administering test, start testing at beginning of testing window)
  ▪ Summative assessment date
  ▪ Interim assessments
  ▪ Practice test
  ▪ Training test (shorter and does not include performance tasks)

☐ Look at digital library (instructional resources), you need a CAASPP login

☐ Look up keyboard commands for test (teach students)

You must find out who 3 key people are . . .

1. Who is District Test Coordinator/LEA CAASPP Coordinator? They put information in for CAL-PADS (California Longitudinal Pupil Achievement Data System)—student must be coded as VI. Who will upload accommodations and designated supports in the Test Operations Management System (TOMS)?

2. Who is School Test Coordinator/CAASPP Test site Coordinator? Work with this person early so questions and needs are addressed beforehand.

3. Who is test administrator (teacher, resource or you)? If you will be administering test, you will need a code from coordinator, they should know who you are and what you will need.

Do practice testing or training tests . . .

☐ You can go on as guest to the Student Interface Practice and Training Tests (no secure browser needed) via Practice and Training Tests link on CAASPP website

☐ Get username and password from Site Coordinator

☐ Load secure browser on practice machine (may need IT support)

☐ Contact district regarding trainings (you may need to attend to administer test)

Month before test . . .

☐ Have you handled becoming test administrator (form signed?)

☐ How do you or aide get read aloud training? (3–5th)?

☐ Do you have accessible materials for Classroom activity? Check http://californiatac.org/administration/instructions/assignments/ to find out which activities school is doing.

☐ If student is taking test with class, has an in-class alternative to a Chromebook been set up and loaded with secure browser?

☐ Does student need to run Zoom text or other accessibility software during test? Do they know how to set accessibility preferences in general accessibility settings? For either one of these, permissive mode must be set in TOMS.

☐ Some tech departments set up a special login screen (students do not see computer desktop, they login to computer with something like test/123 and secure browser immediately comes up—this could affect access general computer accessibility settings or could affect student's profile setting if they have login with preferences already set up). Permissive mode important—our students may need to use "regular" login rather than testing day login.

☐ For Print on Demand - Print on Demand is a Non-Embedded Accommodation and must be entered in TOMS (Must contact CalTAC for approval, at least 2 weeks before test).

☐ Decide how responses will be entered into the computer (by student or teacher). If you, then may need to sign CAASPP Test Security Affidavit ahead of time.

☐ Read Aloud Grades 3, 4, or 5 - District Test Coordinator must submit IAR (individualized aid request) for students who need the Read Aloud accommodation (see what info is needed below). This invalidates test scores but scores will be sent. Tell the person student grade, SSID, why IAR needed, which tests, and to check support for VI/blindness http://CAASPP.org/administration/forms/

Week before test . . .

☐ Confirm with Test Coordinator—if you are administering, how will you get passwords on test day?

☐ Confirm how to communicate with on-site tech person and on-site and district test coordinator on testing day (in case you run into problems)

Check IEP management system for:

Streamlined interface (embedded)—Presents test in an alternate, simplified format in which the items are displayed below the stimuli. Not tablet compatible. ***Have it marked for JAWS and braille users***. TA may be able to change it if accommodation is set in embedded accommodations. *Look at performance task also with student—PT may have more charts, diagrams and pictures to reference and having side-by-side beneficial (non-streamlined). Currently streamlined affects whole test so choose student's preference based on review of all tests.

Permissive Mode (embedded)—*enable* for students who need accessibility software (screen reader, magnifier). Without permissive mode you can't use accessibility software or the accessibility features built into computer. Default is disabled. Need to have it enabled for our students. Make sure no special computer login has been set by tech department that overrides access to accessibility settings.

Masking (embedded)—blocking out content that is not an immediate need.

Print size (embedded)—sets student's print size accommodation and is the print size the student should have when starting the test. It becomes default for all items. (default is 14 point). 1.5, 1.75, 2.5, 3 times.

Read aloud (non-embedded)
Grades 3, 4 or 5 - must submit IAR for individualized aide request

Print on demand
The district person HAS to get permission from CalTAC

CAASP coordinator (district needs to contact CalTAC and CDE and it must be approved by both before testing begins).

Magnification (non-embedded) The size of specific areas of the screen (e. g., text, tables, navigation buttons) may be adjusted by the student with an assistive technology device.
Other options:

Separate setting (non-embedded) accommodation

Scribe (non-embedded) student dictates responses (scribe must be trained)

Noise buffers (non-embedded)

Color contrast (embedded) Printed in contrast is non-embedded

Color overlays (non-embedded) over paper test.

Multiplication table (non-embedded)

Calculator (talking) is non-embedded

Abacus non-embedded

Reference Materials

Testing acronyms

CAASPP	California Assessment of Student Performance and Progress
CALPADS	California Longitudinal Pupil Achievement Data System
CalTAC	California Technical Assistance Center
CDE	California Department of Education
ELA	English language arts/literacy
ET	extended time
ISAAP	Individual Student Assessment Accessibility Profile
LEA	local educational agency
PT	performance task
RLA	reading/language arts
SC CAASPP	Test Site Coordinator
SSID	Statewide Student Identifier
TA	Test Administrator
TOMS	Test Operations Management System
UAAG	Smarter Balanced Usability, Accessibility, and Accommodations Guidelines

LEA CAASPP Coordinators, contact the California Technical Assistance Center (CalTAC) using one of the following methods:

Mail:	ETS Systron Business Center 2731 Systron Drive Concord, CA 94518
Phone:	800-955-2954
Fax:	800-541-8455
Hours	Monday–Friday 7 a.m.–5 p.m. PT
E-mail:	caltac@ets.org

Other useful documents:

Keyboard Commands For Students

Google CAASPP keyboard commands for students

INDEX

Credits

CPSIA information can be obtained
at www.ICGtesting.com
Printed in the USA
JSHW040758100721
16736JS00004B/25

9 781950 723034